NUMBER TWO HUNDRED AND THIRTY-TWO

THE OLD FARMER'S ALMANAC

CALCULATED ON A NEW AND IMPROVED PLAN FOR THE YEAR OF OUR LORD

Being Leap Year and (until July 4) 248th year of American Independence

FITTED FOR BOSTON AND THE NEW ENGLAND STATES, WITH SPECIAL CORRECTIONS AND CALCULATIONS TO ANSWER FOR ALL THE UNITED STATES.

Containing, besides the large number of Astronomical Calculations and the Farmer's Calendar for every month in the year, a variety of
NEW, USEFUL, & ENTERTAINING MATTER.

ESTABLISHED IN 1792
BY ROBERT B. THOMAS (1766–1846)

Rest not! Life is sweeping by,
Go and dare before you die;
Something mighty and sublime
Leave behind to conquer time.

–Johann Wolfgang von Goethe, German writer (1749–1832)

Copyright © 2023 by Yankee Publishing Incorporated, A 100% Employee-Owned Company

ISSN 0078-4516

Library of Congress Card No. 56-29681

Cover illustration by Steven Noble • Original wood engraving (above) by Randy Miller

The Old Farmer's Almanac • Almanac.com
P.O. Box 520, Dublin, NH 03444 • 603-563-8111

CONTENTS

2024 TRENDS
Facts to Ponder and Forecasts to Watch For   6

72

VERY *LUCKY* 13

Hello, friends! Since its start in 1792, this Almanac has had only 13 editors. This is about to change, as yours truly, number 13, steps aside after nearly 23 years.

Our founder and first editor, Robert B. Thomas (depicted on the cover), stated in his first edition that his mission (and hence that of every ensuing editor) was to be "useful, with a pleasant degree of humor." I will leave you to judge whether my contributions have been practical and amusing, but we all must acknowledge that this oldest continuously published North American periodical owes its longevity also to a considerable degree of luck—as do I.

One of my first assignments was to read every edition. In so doing, I saw how each of my predecessors had made his mark. I learned, for example, that in 1938—for reasons known only to himself—Roger Scaife, aka number 10, replaced the full weather forecasts with weather "averages." He needed no small amount of luck for the publication to survive his unintended impact, as sales of copies dropped precipitously.

I thought that I had a good idea in 2005, when I transposed the weather forecasts (usually in the back) with the Calendar Pages (always up front). For giving the predictions prominence, I expected a windfall of reader appreciation. Instead, I raised a windstorm of criticism, such as: "The Almanac is a calendar; weather should never supplant the calendar! Don't you know your job?!" Luckily, circulation held steady and I endured the tempest.

Another idea that could have sunk me was eliminating the tide times and heights in 2018. Your requests to reinstate the data showed me once again how much you care about this annual—and that again I had been pushing my luck.

Fortune has thus favored me even from the beginning. In the moments between being offered this job and accepting it, I was told that if I had any fear about being number 13, arrangements could be made for someone to sit in for a while so that I could start as number 14 without qualm or trepidation. Luckily for me—and, I hope, for you—I declined that proposition. Thank you for your abiding loyalty, trust, enthusiasm, and generosity. Join me in a cheer to the years!

–J. S., June 2023

However, it is by our works and not our words that we would be judged. These, we hope, will sustain us in the humble though proud station we have so long held in the name of

Your obedient servant,

4

2024 TRENDS

ON THE FARM

Increased demand for farmland in high-growth areas of the U.S. is pricing farmers and ranchers off the land. They are struggling to find comparable acreage to lease to maintain the viability of their operations.

–Gary Joiner, spokesperson, Texas Farm Bureau

FARMERS NEED WORKERS

■ Labor shortages on the farm have become the biggest challenge in the industry. Strategically becoming an employer of choice has become increasingly important for farmers hoping to attract, hire, and keep the best employees.

–Sara Mann, Ph.D., professor, University of Guelph

BUZZWORD
Grow-cers: grocery stores that sell produce from on-site indoor farms

CUSTOMER CONNECTIONS

■ Farmers' on-farm shops are inviting other local producers to sell their meat and produce.

■ Farmers are growing flowers and creating wedding arrangements, offering "you pick" options, or hosting you-pick-and-arrange events.

–Caitlyn Lamm, spokesperson, Iowa Farm Bureau Federation

FARMERS' CHALLENGES

■ Being an agricultural producer is particularly stressful these days, given the high input

FOLLOW US:

costs and interest rates, the diseases that affect animals or plants, unpredictable weather events, and ongoing labor shortages.

–Cameron Newbigging, spokesperson, Agriculture and Agri-Food Canada

STRENGTH IN NUMBERS

Farmers are teaming up to navigate challenges:

■ Egg farmers are forming co-ops.

■ Volunteers are being trained to provide social and emotional support to farmers they know.

TECH TAKEOVERS

The use of drones in agriculture is expanding rapidly.

–Ty Higgins, spokesperson, Ohio Farm Bureau

Farm drones . . .

■ plant cover crops

■ apply herbicides when soil is too wet for conventional machinery

■ drop cover crop seeds into corn and

Photo: johnnyscriv/Getty Images

BY THE NUMBERS

$485: average cost to rent a chicken coop and two egg-laying hens for 6 months

$35,000: annual labor cost per acre for California strawberry growers

5,500: tons of unsold grocery store food (e.g., bruised fruit, stale bread) used as chicken feed in the U.S., 2022

soybean fields prior to harvest (giving them more time to grow)

Farm robots . . .

■ use lasers to eliminate weeds without disturbing soil

■ pick ripe strawberries

■ apply fertilizer

FORWARD THINKERS . . .

■ use precision agriculture, with sensors and data analysis to optimize production and reduce costs

■ farm vertically in controlled indoor environments near urban centers for year-round crop production

■ raise fish, crustaceans, and mollusks in indoor aquaculture systems

–Daniel Levine, director, The Avant-Guide Institute

"FARMERS" EVERYWHERE

■ Farmers are demonstrating apple cidering, beekeeping, and maple sugaring to library patrons.

■ People are loaning their yards to students, who grow food there and then donate it to the community and/or to schools for use in cooking classes.

(continued)

IN THE GARDEN

Due to long wait lists, there is pressure on local governments to expand their community garden programs.

–Kathy Jentz, co-author, The Urban Garden *(Cool Springs Press, 2022)*

TOP GARDENING PROJECTS

1. creating vegetable gardens
2. planting flowering shrubs
3. growing new varieties of edibles
4. planting fruit trees
5. adding container gardens

–Axiom 2023 Gardening Outlook Survey

COMING TO OUR SENSES

■ Gardeners want a wider array of sensory experiences, with plants that invite the sniffing and scrunching of aromatic leaves or soft textures. Lilac, lavender, and anise hyssop are making a comeback.

–Cheney Creamer, chair, Canadian Horticultural Therapy Association

BUZZWORD
Yard-sharing: landowners allow growers to use their property in exchange for free or discounted produce

MORE NATIVE PLANTS

Renewing native ecosystems has become a big priority in both home gardens and public green spaces.

■ *At home:* We're planting blends of native wildflower seeds.

■ *In public areas:* Gardens are being planted with native plants that provide flowers, fruit, and seeds as food for pollinators.

–Cheney Creamer

(continued)

FOLLOW US:

'PONDEROSA' LEMON

INDOOR EXOTICS

Gardeners are growing fruiting, rare, and tropical plants indoors in containers for visual interest and as conversation starters. Top picks . . .

■ in hanging baskets, 'Cipo' sweet orange

■ fruit-bearing 'Ponderosa' lemon tree

■ 3-foot-tall, fruit-bearing 'Super Dwarf Cavendish' banana

■ flowering ginger plants
–Randy Schultz, founder, HomeGardenandHomestead .com

LEAFY STANDOUTS

■ Gardeners are planting with contrasting colors to make plants more visible in a sea of green.
–Chad Davis, director of Conservatories and Horticulture Design, Longwood Gardens

BEST CHOICES

■ 'Blue Chiffon' rose of Sharon, 'Ghost' fern, 'Nightrider' hybrid Asiatic lily, Ocean Sunset series 'Orange Glow' ice plant
–Jung Seed Company

GHOST FERN

■ ColorBloom series gerbera, 'Jupiter White' exacum, Hula series spreading begonia, AngelDance series angelonia, 'Big Blue' salvia, Solarscape series impatiens
–Ball Horticultural Company

BY THE NUMBERS

35% of gardeners have in-ground plots.

9% garden from balconies.

6% have indoor gardens.
–Axiom 2023 Gardening Outlook Survey

NEW VEGGIE VARIETIES

■ 'Amish Gold' slicer tomato, 'Dragonfly' hybrid pepper, 'Kai Kai' hybrid winter squash, 'Tricked You' hybrid jalapeño
–Jung Seed Company

■ 'Mochi' hybrid cherry tomato, 'Glow Stix Sunrise Mix' carrots, 'Bottle Rocket' cayenne pepper, Salanova series 'Red Tango' lettuce
–Johnny's Selected Seeds

'DRAGONFLY' PEPPER

EASY DOES IT

Robots are making garden chores easier by:

■ locating and eliminating broadleaf weeds

■ mowing the lawn

PEOPLE ARE TALKING ABOUT . . .

■ ornamental and edible plants in the same containers
–Kathy Jentz

(continued)

FOLLOW US:

Online & Locally at **Walmart** ☀

■ embracing a "live and let live" philosophy toward native insects
–C. L. Fornari, founder, Gardenlady.com

IN LIEU OF LAWNS

There is a move away from turf-grass lawns toward more sustainable landscape choices.

■ *in dry climates:* succulents

■ *in wet climates:* clover or moss
–Kathy Jentz

LANTANA

ZINNIA

HELPING NATURE

■ *To feed butterflies:* We're dedicating space in home gardens to grow monarchs' food sources.
–Andrew Bunting, V.P. of horticulture, Pennsylvania Horticultural Society

■ *On behalf of bees:* We're choosing bee-friendly blooms: coneflowers, pentas, salvias, and zinnias.
–Dave Forehand, V.P. of gardens, Dallas Arboretum and Botanical Garden

BUZZWORDS
Adaptogenic drinks: botanical-infused beverages to aid in relaxation without the use of alcohol

GOOD EATS

Food producers will find new ways to "upcycle"—using stale bread for croutons, brewing beer from surplus grains, and making vegetable broths from scraps.
–Sylvain Charlebois, Ph.D., Agri-Food Analytics Lab, Dalhousie University

WE'RE BUDGET-MINDED

■ Cost-conscious grocery shoppers are:
1. buying store brands
2. spending less on nonfood items
3. going to restaurants less frequently
4. avoiding costly items (meat, seafood, sweets)
5. comparison-shopping
–Gardner Food & Agricultural Policy Survey, 2022

EDIBLE ASSISTS

■ People are looking to up their home cooking game in easy ways. High-quality salts, oils, spices, meal starters, and condiments offer

(continued)

FOLLOW US:

assistance—with everything from cold-pressed almond oil to finishing salts.
–Jonathan Deutsch, Ph.D., director, Drexel Food Lab, Drexel University

"EASY DOES IT" INGREDIENTS

■ Consumers want to make meal prep easy but exciting.
–Denise Purcell, V.P., resource development, Specialty Food Association

We're using . . .

■ grain bowls as side dishes

■ dried pulled pork in entrées or soups

■ seafood boil ingredients (shrimp, crab legs, lobster, corn on the cob, sauce) sold frozen in a bag

■ flavor bases/seasonings for sauces, stews, and soups

FLAVORS WE'RE CRAVING . . .

■ globally inspired condiments, sauces, oils, and seasonings: Mexican salsa macha, West African shito sauce, Indian achaar

■ cocktails made with whey

■ chile peppers to flavor cheeses, beverages, and honey
–Denise Purcell

PEOPLE ARE TALKING ABOUT . . .

■ choosing animal-based meat over pricier plant-based alternatives

■ freeze-dried eggs and alternatives that are soy- or bean-based
–Katherine Basbaum, dietician, UVA Health

■ learning from butchers how to break down an entire side of pork or beef and/or how to make sausage

FOLLOW US:

BY THE NUMBERS

$16.19: average U.S. monthly fee for an interest-bearing checking account

$9,658: average U.S. balance required to avoid a monthly fee

54%: percentage of Americans who pay credit card bills in full each month

1.3%: percentage of Americans with a perfect 850 credit score

714: average credit score (scores range from 300 to 850)

$133: average cost of a shopping trip when parents shop solo

$179: average cost of a shopping trip when parents shop with kids

42%: percentage of workers who say that they're underpaid when they're actually being paid above market scale

MONEY MATTERS

After dramatic changes in interest rates, inflation, and market volatility, this year will be about balancing our budgets and mindful spending.

–Lisa Hannam, executive editor, MoneySense

WALLETS, WATCH OUT!

■ People who drank a complimentary cup of caffeinated coffee before shopping spent more and bought more items than those who had chosen decaf or water.

FINANCIAL RELATIONSHIPS

■ 43% of Americans in relationships say that their significant other doesn't know everything about their spending.
–Edelman Financial Engines

BUZZWORDS
Nesting renters: people who upgrade their living spaces despite not owning them

■ $29,878 is the minimum salary that makes someone "date-able."

■ 27% of people talked about salaries only after marriage.
–Western & Southern survey, 2022

(continued)

BY THE NUMBERS

79% of homeowners would rather renovate their current home than move to a different one.

16% of couples consider separating during home improvements.

$14,163: average amount spent on repairs or upgrades before putting a house on the market

$3,771: average value that a deep cleaning adds to a selling price

76% of people would buy a house that's ugly on the outside but perfect on the inside.

13% of Gen Zers consider home a physical space.

48% of Gen Zers describe home as a feeling that can be created wherever they go.

80% of young adults in the U.S. live less than 100 miles from where they grew up.

AROUND THE HOUSE

Folks will lean toward "editing" their homes to ensure that the items in them are things they love, have meaning, and serve a specific function.

–Jenny Marrs, host of HGTV's "Fixer to Fabulous"

R𝗑: RELAX
■ People are using plants and natural materials and adding spa bathrooms and retreat spaces for exercise and meditation.
–2023 Trends Outlook Report, American Society of Interior Designers

ARCHITECTURAL ROBOTICS
■ Beds will rise to reveal couches and tables underneath.

■ Walls with an entertainment center on one side and storage/shelving on the other will glide on a track, creating or concealing space.

WANTS AND NEEDS
■ car-charging stations

■ pantry space

■ outdoor kitchens
–Matt Tinder, director, The American Institute of Architects

WA-A-A-Y DOWNSIZING
■ Living small—in 1,200 square feet or less— is gaining ground.
–Fifi O'Neill, author, Small Homes, Big Appeal (CICO Books, 2023)

(continued)

FOLLOW US:

BUZZWORD
Funemployed: state of enjoying being unemployed, while looking for work

NICE TOUCHES
- skylights and periscopes
- compost bins set into kitchen counters
- furniture with space to grow seedlings

–Sheila Kennedy, FAIA, professor of architecture, Massachusetts Institute of Technology

SOLAR WITH STYLE
- solar roofing that looks like shingles, in black or terra-cotta
- solar shingles integrated within a roof (not on top of it)

FRESH IDEAS
- photo frames that charge phones
- gas fireplaces suspended from ceilings
- "scent styling": fragrances for rooms
- chairs with bookshelves and reading lights

–The Future of Home Interiors 2030, WGSN

CULTURE

People are infusing nature into every aspect of daily life.

–Mary Guzowski, professor, School of Architecture, University of Minnesota

PEOPLE ARE TALKING ABOUT . . .
- the Human Library, which offers people "on loan" to talk about specific topics, in the interest of civic engagement
- paper maps hung as artwork
- "sleep streamers" who video themselves while asleep and allow others to watch and/or trigger lights or sounds to wake them
- cars that play classical music when the driver is tense

WHAT WORKERS WANT
- knowledge of the range of salaries for all positions in a company (aka "pay transparency")
- cards, prepaid by the employer, for meals or groceries (to encourage healthier eating and workers eating together) or *(continued)*

Photos, from top: onurdongel/Getty Images; HomeCrux

FOLLOW US:

#1 PHARMACIST RECOMMENDED MEMORY SUPPORT BRAND

Prevagen® is America's best-selling brain support supplement‡ and has been clinically shown to help with mild memory loss associated with aging.*1

Prevagen®
Improves Memory®

REGULAR STRENGTH

SUPPORTS:
☑ Healthy Brain Function*
☑ Sharper Mind*
☑ Clearer Thinking*

ONE CAPSULE DAILY
Dietary Supplement

30 Capsules

Prevagen is available at stores nationwide.

Walgreens   **CVS/pharmacy**   🛡 RITE AID   **Walmart** ✳

1Based on a clinical study of subgroups of individuals who were cognitively normal or mildly impaired.

‡According to Nielsen data.

*These statements have not been evaluated by the Food and Drug Administration. This product is not intended to diagnose, treat, cure, or prevent any disease.

to use in ordering meals through an app (to support local restaurants)

- 4-day workweeks
- "financial wellness" programs to help with retirement planning, budgeting, debt management, and investment advice

ALL IN A DAY

- **3:00 P.M.:** time of day when most people feel the least energetic
- **4:** number of extra hours that Americans

say that they would need to finish their daily to-do list

- **5:** average number of things that people have on their to-do list on any given day

–survey by OnePoll on behalf of Dave's Killer Bread

BY THE NUMBERS

14% of U.S. toy sales are for people over 18 years of age.

91% of U.S. families report less stress after sharing a meal together.

10% of people expect an apology if a friend cancels plans.

ON THE ROAD

- 11.2 million U.S. households own an RV.
- 400,000 RV owners live in their RVs full-time.
- There are 1.6 million RV campsites in the U.S.

OUR ANIMAL FRIENDS

Tech is helping us to read the signals of our pets so that we can react quickly to protect their health and well-being.

–Christine Carrière, CEO, Pets Canada

BUZZWORD
Petflation: spending more money on your pets now than in previous years

PET COSTS

- Gen Zers, Millennials, and baby boomers are spending more than ever to keep their pet healthy, happy, and living longer.

–Phillip M. Cooper, president, Pet Industry Expert

(continued)

FOLLOW US:

FIREWOOD ALERT!

You have the power to protect forests and trees!

BUY IT WHERE YOU BURN IT.

Invasive pests like the emerald ash borer can hitchhike in your firewood. You can prevent the spread of these damaging insects and diseases by following these firewood tips:

▶ Buy locally harvested firewood at or near your destination.

▶ Buy certified heat-treated firewood, if available.

▶ Gather firewood on site where permitted.

What might be in your firewood?

SPONGY MOTH is a devastating pest of oaks and other trees. Moths lay tan patches of eggs on firewood, campers, vehicles, patio furniture — anything outside! When these items are moved to new areas, this pest gets a free ride.

SPOTTED LANTERNFLY sucks sap from dozens of tree and plant species. This pest loves tree-of-heaven but will feed on black walnut, white oak, sycamore, and grape. Like the spongy moth, this pest lays clusters of eggs on just about any dry surface, from landscaping stone to firewood!

ASIAN LONGHORNED BEETLE will tunnel through, and destroy, over 20 species of trees — especially maple trees. The larvae of this beetle bore into tree branches and trunks, making it an easy pest to accidentally transport in firewood.

EMERALD ASH BORER — the infamous killer of ash trees — is found in forests and city trees across much of the eastern and central United States. This insect is notoriously good at hitching rides in infested firewood, which is how most new infestations start — like the patch of trees now infested near Portland, Oregon. Don't give this tree-killing bug a ride to a new forest, or a new state.

DONT MOVE FIREWOOD.org

This graphic is for illustrative purposes only. Many of these pests will only infest certain types of trees, making it very unlikely for a single log to contain all species as shown.

Visit dontmovefirewood.org for more information.

- $1,320 is the amount projected to be spent annually, per U.S. pet, by 2025.
- 26% of Canadian pet owners will spend more on pet foods touting extra health benefits.
- $525, on average, is spent on veterinarian bills each year.

THE DATA ON DOGS
- *Fact:* Dogs can detect stress from their owner's scent.
- *Being studied:* Do dogs affect our health by changing our brain activity?

PEOPLE ARE TALKING ABOUT . . .
- robotic laser systems that ID poop to be scooped
- homeowners renting their yards by the hour for dogs that need space to run around

BY THE NUMBERS

60% of pet owners forgo gym memberships and exercise with their animals.

42% of pet owners won't stay in a hotel that doesn't allow pets.

$10,000 per year, on average, is paid by pet retailers to cats and dogs to try out new toys.

35% of Canadian pet owners allow pets to sleep in their beds.

15% of Americans own five or more pets.

- doggy doors that open remotely when owners aren't home

SERVICES WITH A SMILE
- Retailers are adding pet clinics.
- Drugstores are selling pet medications.
- Pet specialty stores are offering grooming, boarding, vet care, and dog training.
–Phillip M. Cooper

PET-FRIENDLY MUST-HAVES
- abstract art shelving for cats to climb
- dog-washing stations in mudrooms
- pullout drawers for food bowls
- dog caves under staircases

PETS ARE EATING . . .
- *fresh food* that's home-delivered already cooked or from refrigerators in pet aisles
- *insect- and plant-based proteins* to help heart, joint, dental, and digestive health or mental well-being
- *supplements:* probiotics for behavioral improvements; turmeric, pumpkin, and collagen for treats
–Phillip M. Cooper
- *freeze-dried food* "that's easy to use and will remain stable for long periods"
–Phillip M. Cooper

(continued on page 26)

FOLLOW US:

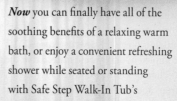
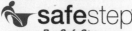

Choose Life
Grow Young with HGH

From the landmark book Grow Young with HGH comes the most powerful, over-the-counter health supplement in the history of man. Human growth hormone was first discovered in 1920 and has long been thought by the medical community to be necessary only to stimulate the body to full adult size and therefore unnecessary past the age of 20. Recent studies, however, have overturned this notion completely, discovering instead that the natural decline of Human Growth Hormone (HGH), from ages 21 to 61 (the average age at which there is only a trace left in the body) and is the main reason why the body ages and fails to regenerate itself to its 25 year-old biological age.

Like a picked flower cut from the source, we gradually wilt physically and mentally and become vulnerable to a host of degenerative diseases, that we simply weren't susceptible to in our early adult years.

Modern medical science now regards aging as a disease that is treatable and preventable and that "aging", the disease, is actually a compilation of various diseases and pathologies, from everything, like a rise in blood glucose and pressure to diabetes, skin wrinkling and so on. All of these aging symptoms can be stopped and rolled back by maintaining Growth Hormone levels in the blood at the same levels HGH existed in the blood when we were 25 years old.

There is a receptor site in almost every

cell in the human body for HGH, so its regenerative and healing effects are very comprehensive.

Growth Hormone, first synthesized in 1985 under the Reagan Orphan drug act, to treat dwarfism, was quickly recognized to stop aging in its tracks and reverse it to a remarkable degree. Since then, only the lucky and the rich have had access to it at the cost of $10,000 US per year.

The next big breakthrough was to come in 1997 when a group of doctors and scientists, developed an all-natural source product which would cause your own natural HGH to be released again and do all the remarkable things it did for you in your 20's. Now available to every adult for about the price of a coffee and donut a day.

GHR is now available in America, just in time for the aging Baby Boomers and everyone else from age 30 to 90 who doesn't want to age rapidly but would rather stay young, beautiful and healthy all of the time.

The new HGH releasers are winning converts from the synthetic HGH users as well, since GHR is just as effective, is oral instead of self-injectable and is very affordable.

GHR is a natural releaser, has no known side effects, unlike the synthetic version and has no known drug interactions. Progressive doctors admit that this is the direction medicine is seeking to go, to get the body to heal itself instead of employing drugs. GHR is truly a revolutionary paradigm shift in medicine and, like any modern leap frog advance, many others will be left in the dust holding their limited, or useless drugs and remedies.

It is now thought that HGH is so comprehensive in its healing and regenerative powers that it is today, where the computer industry was twenty years ago, that it will displace so many prescription and non-prescription drugs and health remedies that it is staggering to think of.

The president of BIE Health Products stated in a recent interview, "I've been waiting for these products since the 70's. We knew they would come, if only we could stay healthy and live long enough to see them! If you want to stay on top of your game, physically and mentally as you age, this product is a boon, especially for the highly skilled professionals who have made large investments in their education, and experience. Also with the failure of Congress to honor our seniors with pharmaceutical coverage policy, it's more important than ever to take pro-active steps to safeguard your health. Continued use of GHR will make a radical difference in your health, HGH is particularly helpful to the elderly who, given a choice, would rather stay independent in their own home, strong, healthy and alert enough to manage their own affairs, exercise and stay involved in their communities. Frank, age 85, walks two miles a day, plays golf, belongs to a dance club for seniors, had a girl friend again and doesn't need Viagra, passed his driver's test and is hardly ever home when we call - GHR delivers."

HGH is known to relieve symptoms of Asthma, Angina, Chronic Fatigue, Constipation, Lower back pain and Sciatica, Cataracts and Macular Degeneration, Menopause, Fibromyalgia, Regular and Diabetic Neuropathy, Hepatitis, helps Kidney Dialysis and Heart and Stroke recovery.

For more information or to order call
877-849-4777
www.biehealth.us

These statements have not been evaluated by the FDA. Copyright © 2000. Code OFA.

(continued from page 22)

YOUR HEALTH OUTLOOK

The mental health field is actively looking at video games to treat diseases in lieu of medication.

–Eric Alan Gantwerker, M.D., associate professor, Donald and Barbara Zucker School of Medicine at Hofstra/Northwell

SECRETS TO GOOD SLUMBER

- Schedule a "worry session" before going to sleep.

- "Savor": Review a good experience from the day in detail before drifting off.

BY THE NUMBERS

7.9 hours: mean sleep duration for Canadian adults

6:54 A.M.: wake-up time of the average Canadian

7:31 A.M.: wake-up time of the average American

29 pounds: average amount of weight Americans want to lose

R$_X$: A PLANT

Researchers have found that people . . .

- feel more peaceful after being near a tall plant for 15 minutes

- feel calmer and have sharper focus and better memory when near indoor plants

- react most positively to plants with dense foliage, bright green leaves, and rounded contours

COMING SOON

- wearables that track our exposure to sunlight

- carbon-absorbing paint made from demolished concrete

- apps that tell us where to get exposure to phytoncides (airborne chemicals given off by plants to protect themselves)

PEOPLE ARE TALKING ABOUT . . .

- "incidental" exercise—walking faster on the way to work, running up a flight of stairs, getting off the bus one stop early, squatting while waiting in line

(continued)

FOLLOW US:

FASHION

People are personalizing clothing with embroidery, patches, and yarn mending and by painting or dyeing fabric.

–Leslie H. Simpson, Ph.D., associate professor and coordinator, Fashion Design Program, Stevenson University

SWAP SHOPPERS

Thrifty fashion fanatics are swapping outfits . . .

- with each other
- at branded retail clothing stores
- at ticketed meetups held at parks, coffee shops, or wineries (for savings and to hear the stories behind the clothing)

BUZZWORDS
Two-mile clothing: comfortable clothes that are appropriate for work both at home and in the office
–WGSN

READY FOR ANYTHING

- Clothing will suit fluid lifestyles that include different workplaces (onsite or at-home), exercise preferences, and outdoor activities.

- Blazers will be waist-cinchable with bungee cords and toggles, for relaxed or fitted looks.

- Trousers will be cinched at the ankle.

- Tailored pants will have elasticized waistbands.

FOLLOW US:

■ Shirts will have removable sleeves and/or collars.
–Anika Kozlowski, fashion design assistant professor, Toronto Metropolitan University

THE LOOKS FOR WOMEN
■ suits and pants in dark denim

■ oversize trousers, jackets, and boyfriend shirts

■ wrap and slip dresses (layered with turtlenecks and slacks in cold weather)
–Lynn Boorady, professor and department head, Department of Design, Housing, and Merchandising, Oklahoma State University

THE LOOKS FOR MEN
■ *classics with a twist:* denim tuxedos; green loafers; chambray shirts paired with

track pants; khakis, loose-fitting and cropped

■ *minimalist:* blazers with no pockets, collars, or buttons

■ *casual:* business pants with drawstrings

FASHION CENTS
■ Consumers now think of the resale market value of items that they purchase.
–Lynn Boorady

PEOPLE ARE TALKING ABOUT . . .
■ *in summer:* jackets and vests, with fans

BY THE NUMBERS

25% of apparel and footwear shoppers are loyal to specific brands.

$2,086: what average U.S. consumers spend on apparel annually

$991: what average U.S. consumers spend on shoes per year

66% of clothing or shoe purchasers read up to 25 reviews before doing so.

$268: average value of never-worn outfits in closets

6% of adults have worn everything in their closet at least once.

76% of Canadians value feeling comfortable over looking stylish.

■ *in winter:* battery-powered, machine-washable, heated layers

■ stylish clothing for the wheelchair-bound (easy to get on/off while sitting)
–Leslie H. Simpson

■ lanyard-style, crossbody pouches to carry phones ■

BOUQUETS FROM BLOOMS AND BRANCHES

THE INGREDIENTS FOR YEAR-ROUND FLORAL ARRANGEMENTS MAY BE RIGHT AT YOUR FINGERTIPS.

BY LYNN COULTER

The next time that you desire an arrangement for your desk- or tabletop, browse your backyard, farmers' market, or vegetable plot. We've got a hunch that you can find plenty of natural materials to make beautiful, inexpensive arrangements within walking distance of your home—if you are willing to share cuttings and are prepared to ask permission. Here are some ideas.

FIND FLOWERS

Most bouquets start with flowers, of course, so aim to use the annuals, perennials, and bulbs already growing in your beds and borders. Nell Foster, an Arizona-based seasoned landscaper and environmental horticulturist who owns Joy Us Garden (Joyusgarden.com), likes to snip blossoms from alstroemerias, dahlias, hydrangeas, and zinnias because they last a long time after cutting. Foster also picks wildflowers such as bachelor buttons, black-eyed Susans, goldenrod, and wild yarrow. (Harvest only from your own property, unless you have clear consent from the property owner, and never take plants that are threatened or endangered.)

Be a little bit choosy. Some cut wildflowers, such as Queen Anne's lace, don't last long. "I've found that the thinner and more delicate the stem, like that of a California poppy or wild toadflax, the faster they wilt," reports Foster.

To prolong your flowers, recut the stems when you get home and put them into water right away. "Clear soda can be added for a bit of sugar, which flowers enjoy. I just usually change the water every few days to keep it fresh," Foster notes.

(continued)

DAHLIAS, COSMOS, AND HOPS COMBINE FOR A DISTINCTIVE SUMMER ARRANGEMENT.

31

AN AUTUMN DISPLAY
OF ARTICHOKES,
TOMATOES,
AND RASPBERRIES
BLENDED
WITH BORAGE,
CALENDULA, AND
ROSEMARY

MIX IN FRUIT AND VEGGIES

The farmers' market or even grocery store produce section can be a source for seasonal arrangements. Granny Smith apples, artichokes, brussels sprout stalks, purple eggplants, grape clusters, oranges, and pomegranates can add color and texture to arrangements.

"Stick fruit on wooden skewers, heavy-gauge wire, or wire saved from old silk flowers and have them coming up out of the bouquet," suggests Sara Jenkins-Sutton, who co-owns Topiarius Urban Garden and Floral Design (Topiarius .com) in Chicago. "Add asparagus stalks, leafy greens, herbs, and lettuce for beautiful, lush arrangements."

One mistake that beginners make, says Jenkins-Sutton, is not using enough materials, resulting in arrangements that look thin. "A few stems can be an elegant look. But it's more fun if you use a lot of one thing or maybe a couple of things. Go as full as you possibly can."

(continued)

CONTAIN YOURSELF

Store-bought or leftover florist vases will hold your home-made bouquets adequately, but try thinking beyond the glass. In autumn, Jenkins-Sutton gets creative with pumpkins from her vegetable patch: "Use a drill bit to make vase holes the size that you want and then insert your stems," she advises.

Other "patchwork" planter ideas can incorporate melons, pumpkins, or winter squashes that have been hollowed out. Set a glass jar inside to hold your cuttings and slip a plate or saucer under your veggie-vase to protect your tabletop. Good choices for harvesttime arrangements are chrysanthemums and trailing sweet autumn clematis.

For something completely different, Jenkins-Sutton puts lemons, limes, and pears into glass cylinders and then fills them with water and cut flowers. The fruit "act like a floral frog," she says, to hold the stems in place.

AN EARLY WINTER DISPLAY OF DAHLIAS, ZINNIAS, IVY, AND HYDRANGEAS IN A PUMPKIN VASE

(continued)

DAFFODILS AND PUSSY WILLOWS GUARANTEE A CHEERY SPRING BOUQUET.

BRANCH OUT

Different sizes of branches, stems, and twigs can anchor a display and make great backbones for informal arrangements, Foster observes.

Curly willow branches provide fascination in their natural brown and green state. Or, for a lively effect, spray paint them—try gold for the holidays. Similarly, fuzzy pussy willows add texture and a degree of fun.

In spring, cut branches from magnolias, spirea, viburnums, and witch hazels or flowering stems from apple, cherry, peach, and pear trees for your arrangement. Nicholas Staddon, a plantsman who has been working with breeders and plant explorers for more than 25 years, trims branches from forsythias, lilacs, and quince to force.

Autumn options abound. "Red- and yellow-twig dogwoods have stems that range from amber to red and drop-dead fall color," he notes. Also, look for dried hydrangea blooms to bring indoors, along with seedpods; stems studded with rose hips; or cuttings of bear grass, lily grass, and steel grass. "Many grasses produce magnificent plumes or flower heads," comments Staddon, who spritzes his flower heads with hair spray to help to keep the seeds from dropping. "Good choices are calamagrostis, sometimes called 'reed grass,' and miscanthus," he says.

To add sparkle in winter, coat branches, cones, and nuts with spray adhesive and sprinkle with glitter. At Christmastime, Staddon brings the hair spray back out to add shine to holly berries.

(continued)

DiTarando
Animal Art/Garden Elements

Roger's sculpture covers the gamut from fine art to whimsy, including functional garden elements, weathervanes, birdbaths, gates, fountains, and more. Given the sculptures' unique eclectic qualities, they work in sophisticated to comfortable environments.

www.ditarando.com • 860.614.2704

FORAGE FOR FUN

Use your imagination to identify other materials for your bouquets. Hot peppers add rainbows of color, while herbs such as dill and rosemary provide fragrance as well as texture. Foster drapes graceful vines of honeysuckle and wild sweet pea for a sense of movement. For trailing accents, cut cucumber vines or yellow-blossom squash vines. (Just remember: You're sacrificing some of your harvest when you cut from vegetable plants.)

Foliage that turns to a brilliant color in autumn is yet another option. Snip from maples, serviceberries, sumac, sweet gums, and other trees and shrubs.

If you can't find everything that you want in your own woods or yard, "walk around the neighborhood with your pruners and basket," Staddon suggests. "Knock on your neighbors' doors, ask if you can take cuttings, and give them your biggest, brightest smile." Share a bouquet of the cuttings later, and you may never have to ask again. ■

Lynn Coulter is an Atlanta-based freelance writer and the author of *Gardening with Heirloom Seeds* (UNC Press, 2006).

SUMMER FLOWERS AND HERBS MINGLE TO MAKE A FRAGRANT AND TEXTURAL BOUQUET.

Photo: Friedrich Strauss/GAP Photos

GO THE WITH GRAIN

WHETHER FOR BREADS OR BRAGGING RIGHTS, YOU'LL GET A RISE OUT OF GROWING GRAINS. **BY SARA PITZER**

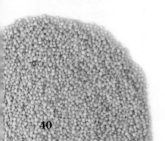

NEXT TO THOROUGH
PREPARATION OF
THE SOIL, THE MOST
IMPORTANT
THING IN SECURING
A GOOD CROP IS
THE PROPER SELECTION
AND PREPARATION
OF THE SEED.
–FACTS FOR FARMERS, 1870

AMARANTH

QUINOA

BARLEY

GRAINS TO GROW

AMARANTH AND QUINOA

Amaranth does best in warm climates; quinoa, in cool regions. Both are large, broadleaf, native American plants high in protein and other nutrients, easy to grow, and useful as grains or vegetables.

BARLEY

Barley is a fast-maturing grain that thrives in cool weather, does well in alkaline soil, and contains more soluble fiber than do oats.

BUCKWHEAT

Buckwheat improves soil as you grow it. The seeds grind into a strongly flavored flour.

(continued)

G rains are among the easiest plants to grow in home gardens, but before you drop that first seed into the ground, consider these questions:

- How much grain do you want or need to harvest: enough to make bread for a year, or are you experimenting with a new crop?
- Do you have the proper conditions: sun from dawn to dusk, an inch or so of rain or irrigation per week, and well-draining, moderately fertile soil?
- Can you buy equipment jointly with other growers or borrow or rent what you'll need (e.g., seed cleaners, seed hullers, winnowers, flour mills)?
- Will you have the time, energy, equipment, and muscle to harvest, thresh, winnow, and hull the grain?
- Do you have storage space that is dry and free of insects and rodents and where the temperature is consistent and no higher than 70°F?

HOW MUCH TO GROW

Start small. Growing grains is easy. Threshing, winnowing, and hulling them takes raw, brute energy. As a beginner, it's likely that you'll lose a lot of grain in these final steps. Consider a trial area in the first year so that you can learn how the grain behaves, what its cultivation problems are, how long it takes you to handle it, and how it is affected by varying climate conditions.

You'll get a decent yield and less grief from a modest plot of reasonable size—say, a 100-square-foot planting. A 10x10- or 20x5-foot bed fits nicely in a typical backyard and is manageable for planting and harvesting. Your

If your tired, achy legs and feet are preventing you from moving easily...

Now, a prickly herb has been discovered to....

BOOST BLOOD FLOW TO YOUR LEGS, FEET, AND HANDS WITH A 95% SUCCESS RATE VERIFIED BY CLINICAL STUDY

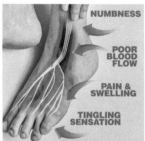

A re-discovery from the 1600s is causing a frenzy within the medical system. A weird herb has been shown in six clinical studies (and by thousands of users) to be very effective for leg and feet pain, burning and numbness – with no side effects – at low cost – and with no doctor visit or prescription needed.

This weird herb comes from a 12-foot tall tree that grows in Greece and other countries in Europe. In the old days, people noticed that when their horses who had leg and feet problems ate this herb – it was almost like magic how quickly their problems got much better. They called it the "horse herb". Then somehow with Europe's ongoing wars, this herbal secret got lost in time.

"It works for people who've tried many other treatments before with little or no success. Other doctors and I are shocked at how effective it is. It has created a lot of excitement" says Dr. Ryan Shelton, M.D.

Its active ingredient has been put into pill form and improved. It is being offered in the United States under the brand name Neuroflo.

WHY ALL THIS EXCITEMENT?

Researchers have found an herb originally from Greece that has been shown in six placebo-controlled medical studies (543 participants) to be effective and safe. This natural compound strengthens blood vessel walls and reduces swelling to stop the pain and suffering.

Poor blood flow in the legs and feet is one of the common problems

that develops as we age. Millions of Americans suffer from neuropathy and chronic venous insufficiency (CVI), edema, and other leg/feet problems – millions have these but are undiagnosed.

Today's treatments don't work for a high percentage of people – and they have side effects that make them hard to tolerate or that people do not want to risk. This includes prescription drugs, over the counter pain pills, surgery and compression.

HOW IT WORKS

Here's why you have pain now: Your arteries have weakened. Your arteries can't carry enough blood, nutrients and oxygen down to your legs and feet. This damages your nerves and causes your burning, tingling and numbness.

The herbs in the pill Neuroflo strengthen your arteries that carry blood, nutrients and oxygen to your feet and legs. It improves your circulation so oxygenated blood goes to the nerves and repairs them. This makes your nerves grow stronger so your pain fades away and your legs and feet feel much younger again.

Katerina King from Murrieta, California says, "I had hands and feet tingling and snapping and burning feeling. It made my life very uncomfortable. I had a hard time walking, my legs felt like they each weighed 50 pounds. Once I got in my car and my feet felt so heavy I couldn't even drive the car. With Neuroflo I have no more tingling, cold or burning painful legs and feet. It went away."

WHAT DOCTORS ARE SAYING

"Now I finally have a natural solution I can recommend to my patients who suffer from leg and feet problems and pain. I'm delighted because previous treatments were not effective, but Neuroflo has worked for every one of my patients with no side effects" says Dr. Eric Wood, N.D.

Dr. Ryan Shelton, M.D. says "This is new and different. It works for people who've tried many other things before. It is natural with no side effects. Don't give up hope for your leg and feet pain, burning, tingling and numbing. This pill is working for countless people after other treatments have failed them. I highly recommend it."

WORKS IN AMAZING WAY: A prickly plant was used in Europe in the 1600s to revitalize ailing legs. Lost over the centuries, it is now making a comeback as US doctors rediscover its impressive results – sending relief to thousands of users.

"Neuroflo is a terrific choice for people with leg and feet issues. The clinical trials in support of this herb show it is very effective for safe and fast relief," said Dr. Wood, a Harvard trained doctor who has appeared on award winning TV shows.

Now you can get a good night's sleep - peaceful, restful sleep – with no pain, tingling, zinging, itching or zapping. Improve your balance and coordination. No side effects – safe to take with other medications. Enjoy your favorite activities and hobbies again. Be more active, have more fun, enjoy life more. Don't risk irreversible damage to your feet and hands. Don't get worse and wind up in the hospital or a nursing home.

Neuroflo is GUARANTEED to work for you – or you will get full refund with a 90-day unconditional money-back guarantee. It is NOT sold in stores or online. No prescription or doctor visit is required.

50% OFF FOR THE NEXT 10 DAYS

This is the official release of NeuroFlo for readers of The Old Farmer's Almanac. Therefore, everyone who calls within the next 10 days will receive 50% OFF their first order. A toll-free hotline number has been set up for local readers to call for this 50% OFF savings. The number will be open starting at 7:00 am today and only for the next 10 days.

All you have to do is CALL TOLL FREE **1-877-304-7546** and provide the operator with the special 50% OFF discount approval code: **NEF158**.

Important: Due to NeuroFlo's popularity and recent media exposure on ABC, CBS, and FOX NEWS, phone lines are often busy. If you call and do not get through immediately, please be patient and call back. Those who miss the 10-day deadline for 50% OFF will have to pay more for NeuroFlo.

95% Reduction in LEG SWELLING, Verified in Clinical Study

... meaning, discomfort, water retention, leg swelling, tiredness and circulation **improved in 95% of test subjects**

Swollen legs are a warning sign. They mean blood and fluid is forced out of the blood vessels into the surrounding tissue. This causes non-stop pain. This is where Neuroflo's active ingredient is such a big help.

These statements have not been evaluated by the Food and Drug Administration. These products are not intended to diagnose, treat, cure, or prevent any disease. Results based upon averages. Models are used in all photos to protect privacy.

BUCKWHEAT

CORN

MILLET

CORN
The taste of home-grown cornmeal is delightful. To harvest corn as a grain, let a few ears go past their prime, then use your hand to twist the dried corn off the ears.

MILLET
Millet thrives in hot, dry climates. The seeds are encased in thin hulls; to remove them, rub a handful of grain between your palms.

OATS
Oats, a cool-climate crop, are easy to grow yet hard to hull. If you grow old-style oats to eat, find a method of hulling before you sow or else plant a hull-less oat strain. *(continued)*

first harvest of wheat may give you 4 pounds of grain, which will grind into 14 cups of flour—enough for three or four loaves of bread. As you gain experience, this same plot could yield as much as 26 pounds of grain or about 90 cups of flour—and enough bread for half a year.

However, even when you can't harvest what you plant, your efforts won't be wasted. Most small grains make a fine cover crop that not only cuts down on weeds and reduces erosion while it is growing but also produces a nutritious green manure that enriches the soil after you till the plants under.

PREPARING THE SOIL
It takes no more work to prepare the soil for grains than it does to get it ready for any other garden plant. Most grains thrive in loose, well-draining, moderately fertile soil in a spot that receives full sun all day. To ensure that your crops get a good start, test your soil.

SOWING STYLES
Grains are sown in narrow or wide rows or solid blocks. Because some grains are tall, run your rows north–south so that each plant in the row receives an equal amount of sun.

Narrow rows are the traditional planting pattern but not the most productive.

Wide rows are a great way for a first-time grain grower to start. With this method, you create 3- to

Train at home to

Work at Home

Be a Medical Coding & Billing Specialist

WORK AT HOME!

- ✓ Be home for your family
- ✓ Be your own boss
- ✓ Choose your own hours

SAVE MONEY!

- ✓ No day care, commute, or office wardrobe/lunches
- ✓ Possible tax breaks
- ✓ Tuition discount for eligible military and their spouses
- ✓ Military education benefits & MyCAA approved

Train at home in as little as 5 months to earn up to $46,660 a year!*

Now you can train in the comfort of your own home to work in a medical office, or from home as your experience and skills increase. Make great money…up to $46,660 a year with experience! It's no secret, healthcare providers need Medical Coding & Billing Specialists. In fact, the U.S. Department of Labor projects 7% growth by 2031, for specialists doing coding and billing.

10 Years	**7%**
5 Years	**Increase In Demand!***
Now	

No previous medical experience required. Compare the money you can make!

Coders earn great money because they make a lot of money for the people they work for. Entering the correct codes on medical claims can mean the difference in thousands of dollars in profits for doctors, hospitals and clinics. Since each and every medical procedure must be coded and billed, there's plenty of work available for well-trained Medical Coding & Billing Specialists.

Get FREE Facts. Contact Us Today!

 U.S. Career Institute®
2001 Lowe St., Dept. FMAB2A93
Fort Collins, CO 80525

1-800-388-8765
Dept. FMAB2A93
www.uscieducation.com/FMA93

SENT FREE!

YES! Rush me my free Medical Coding & Billing information package.

Name _____ Age _____

Address _____ Apt_____

City, State, Zip _____

E-mail_____ Phone _____

Accredited • Affordable • Approved
Celebrating over 40 years of education excellence!

★DEAC
DISTANCE EDUCATION
ACCREDITING COMMISSION

BBB.
ACCREDITED BUSINESS
A+ Rating

CB010

*W/experience, https://www.bls.gov/ooh/healthcare/medical-records-and-health-information-technicians.htm, 6/1/22

RICE

RYE

WHEAT

RICE
Rice requires wet soil and a long, hot growing season. It's perfect for those low spots in your yard that never dry. Rice can also be grown in pots.

RYE
Rye is almost immune to failure. In addition to being frost-hardy and growable in poor soil, it's also a good cover crop.

WHEAT
This cool-season crop is easy to grow, harvest, thresh, store, and grind in small amounts. In most regions, it is planted in fall and harvested the following spring.

4-foot-wide beds that are about 18 inches apart. The width depends on how far in you can reach to weed from both sides of the bed and the amount of space that the plants need while they grow.

When you plant in wide rows, you never have to walk on the bed to weed and the soil in the rows stays loose—perfect for root growth. You'll save money on amendments because you need to work only the soil in the planted rows. A wide row accommodates two or more rows of grain, depending on the spacing that the plants require.

Some crops, such as wheat and especially corn, can be grown in a solid block pattern. Essentially, this is a mini-field in which you broadcast the seeds evenly over the planting area.

Measure and mark out the rows with twine and stakes, then build up their height a few inches by scooping soil from the path onto the beds. Spread amendments over the rows and till them in. Finally, shape the rows so that the top is flat and level and the sides flare slightly at the bottom. Apply a thick layer of mulch on the path between beds or grow a cover crop such as clover to keep mud and weeds at bay and help to feed the soil for next year's garden.

Sow by digging trenches with your hoe, sprinkling in some seeds, and covering them. Alternatively, lightly scatter or broadcast seeds by hand across the rows. After the seeds are sown, work them into the soil with a rake. How deep to rake them in depends on the grain. Depths can range from ½ to 2½ inches. *(continued)*

SOW

GROW

HARVEST

SEED-STARTERS

- Locate garden seed companies that offer grains in small quantities or search online for "cover crop seeds" and "grain seeds." It will be easier to find unnamed varieties than named cultivars.

- Save seeds from each year's harvest to plant in the next year. (Check for any restrictions on saving your variety first.) Choose the plumpest seeds or those from the most productive plant (or earliest or most pest-free), and you'll one day be planting your own "improved" variety.

In order to get a good stand of plants, seeds and soil must be in contact. To ensure this, make a pass over the planting area with a lawn roller. No roller? Put down a plank and walk on it for the same result.

HARVESTING A SMALL PLOT

To harvest a small plot (up to 150 square feet), break the heads off the stems. Drop them into a bucket as you work, then spread them out to dry for several days before threshing. Alternatively, you could cut the grain with pruners, leaving a 12-inch stem; bundle a few stems; and hang the harvest to dry, as you would to dry herbs and flowers.

A sickle is a traditional tool that is well suited to small spaces and easy for a novice to use. Cutting with a sickle is a matter of grab-and-cut, grab-and-cut. For example, if you're right-handed, you would hold the stalks of grain in your left hand and swing the sickle with your right to cut at ground level. Kneel or crouch as you harvest so that you won't tire too quickly. Lay the cut grain in windrows (small piles along the row), with all of the heads pointed in the same direction. Let the grain dry for several days before threshing. For larger plots, try harvesting with a blade trimmer.

Although just basic guidelines, these are enough to get you started. And sow it goes! ∎

Excerpted and adapted from *Homegrown Whole Grains* (Storey Publishing, 2009) by Sara Pitzer and used with permission.

When it's built by *hand*, It's connected to the *Heart*.

For three generations, the builders, blacksmiths and craftsmen at Country Carpenters have put their hands and their hearts into designing and building the finest New England Style buildings available. Hand-selected materials, hand-forged hardware, all hand-built and hand-finished by real people. You can feel the difference in your heart.

NEW ENGLAND STYLE
Country Carpenters INC.
POST & BEAM BUILDINGS

COUNTRY BARNS, CARRIAGE HOUSES, POOL & GARDEN SHEDS, CABINS

Visit our models on display! We ship nationwide!

326 Gilead Street, Hebron, CT 06248 • 860.228.2276 • **countrycarpenters.com**

*Farmers across the continent
are keeping it local—economically
and environmentally.*

Farming Today

GOOD RAIN FARM
Camas, Washington

Stinging nettles, viewed as a noxious, invasive weed, are usually yanked out of yards or fields, but at Good Rain Farm, they're grown as a crop. "Stinging nettles are an Indigenous First Food, a staple of my people's diet for thousands of years," says farmer Michelle Week, who educates customers about her produce via recipes, blogs, and newsletters.

Week, who founded the farm in 2018, is of Sinixt (pronounced "sin-EYEKST") ancestry. Good Rain Farm (or *x̌ast sq̓it,* pronounced "hast SQUEE-ett," in the traditional language of the Sinixt, aka Arrow Lakes Peoples) is a 3-acre operation located on the rainy, foggy, west side of the Cascade Mountains.

The farm offers an internship program to train beginning farmers. "We grow over 100 varieties of plants that require a lot of hands-on care in a small space," reports Week, "and we could not do this detailed farm work without a lot of well-trained field workers."

Good Rain Farm has moved four times. "Finding farmland to rent is very difficult, and finding land to purchase for farming is nearly impossible, especially close to Portland, where our members mostly live," comments Week.

The farm serves 150 families through a seasonal community-supported agriculture (CSA) program. Customers receive Indigenous First Foods of the region such as rose hips, salmonberries (a cousin of black- and raspberries), wood sorrel, currants, camas root (a bulb), acorns, Oregon stonecrop (sedum), and wapato (a tuber). The farm also sells produce wholesale to local businesses, restaurants, and schools.

"I am really in the business of telling Indigenous Food stories," notes Week. "In this way, I am fighting the erasure and extinction of my people, of my language, and of my ancestral foods." Week proudly adds that about half of the CSA members receive low- or no-cost shares: "Poverty does not lessen people's desire and need for fresh, sustainably grown produce." ■ *(continued)*

for Tomorrow

BY KAREN DAVIDSON AND
STACEY KUSTERBECK

"I AM REALLY IN
THE BUSINESS OF
TELLING INDIGENOUS
FOOD STORIES."

51

"THERE ARE NO SHORTCUTS IN FARMING. IF YOU WANT TO DO IT WELL, THEN YOU NEED TO STRIVE FOR EXCELLENCE."

GOLDEN RETREAT VINEYARD
Summerland, British Columbia

If it's true that 10,000 hours of intensive practice are required to master complex skills, then David Kozuki would be a good example of this axiom. He was a medical researcher and a jazz pianist before becoming a wine-grape grower at age 36.

It was in his great-grandparents' apple orchard in Summerland that he found his true mission: growing grapes. With inherited responsibility for the property, he transformed it from an orchard into a 20-acre vineyard, which was incorporated as a business in 2007—but Kozuki's personal transformation was not yet complete. "I was a new farmer who had never driven a tractor," he recalls. "And since I had no farming experience, my crew wouldn't even allow me to do any handwork for several weeks."

Since this ominous start, Kozuki has proven adept at tending the vineyards by undertaking such chores as pruning dormant vines to maintain canopy architecture while thinning shoots to bring the vines into vegetative and fruiting balance.

His acumen proved critical in 2022, when unseasonable winter temperatures plummeted to –30°C (–22°F) and caused bud damage. "Prescriptive pruning decisions were assigned based on the degree of severity of the bud damage," he explains. "Selective thinning after bud break was a two-part decision: Identify whether the primary bud was viable, and if it were not, choose the most fruitful secondary buds."

This painstaking attention to detail was rewarded. A near-perfect growing season followed, with harvest yields off by only 10 percent from 5-year averages —a result known to be respected by his fellow growers in the Okanagan Valley. "I put into play that marriage of the structural rightness of science with the free-flowing swing of jazz," he concludes. "There are no shortcuts in farming. If you want to do it well, then you need to strive for excellence." ■ (continued)

GEMPERLE ORCHARDS
Turlock, California

Blooming cover crops of mustard and clover are planted between rows of almond trees on the 135 acres that make up Gemperle Orchards. "There are a million great reasons to do cover crops. But then, there is the other argument—that you are putting in more plants that will need more water," says grower Christine Gemperle, who manages the orchard with her brother, Erich.

Still, the cover crops allow water to penetrate the ground more deeply and their organic matter helps the soil to hold on to the water, so on balance, it's a net gain.

This is but one example of the complexities of the almond orchard, which produces over 300,000 pounds of almonds annually. "There are different tradeoffs with every decision," Gemperle points out—and many, if not most, of these involve water.

Gemperle grew up watching her father grow almonds and returned to the farm after earning a biology degree. The scientific expertise has value. "Farmers need to have some knowledge of engineering, biology, finance, business, chemistry—your hands are in so many pies at the same time," she says.

She and her brother host researchers on their property to study tree growth and water usage. In the summer of 2022, they measured water evaporation in the orchards; in time, this data will reveal exactly how much water is used. "To be on the edge of this emerging research, firsthand, is really important because these are all of the questions that growers need the answers to," reports Gemperle. The research will allow them to more precisely apply water and use less overall.

Scientists also study pollinators, another family interest. Her father was a beekeeper, with an understanding of the close connection between pollinators and almond-growing. Says Gemperle: "Almond growers have always had symbiotic relations with beekeepers. Our crops depend 100 percent on healthy bee populations." ■ *(continued)*

"TO BE ON THE EDGE OF THIS EMERGING RESEARCH, FIRSTHAND, IS REALLY IMPORTANT."

Photo: Gemperle Orchards

"WE WANT TO CREATE
A HIGH-FUNCTIONING
SOIL SO THAT
WE CAN WEATHER
DRY SPELLS."

UPLAND ORGANICS
Wood Mountain, Saskatchewan

Keep a living root in the soil as long as possible. This is one of the soil principles of married couple Allison Squires and Cody Straza, who are stewarding the 4,500 acres that make up their Upland Organics mixed cattle and organic grain farm. Since purchasing the land in 2010, they have been unearthing the secrets of soil microbial life. "It made us sad when we learned that the smell of freshly worked earth is actually organic matter oxidizing [releasing carbon]. Our aim is to keep carbon in the soil," says Squires.

This discovery led them to till-in their crops of lentils, flax, durum wheat, and Khorasan wheat only once a year. Disturbing the soil as little as possible also preserves moisture that can be as little as 1.25 inches per year. "We want to create a high-functioning soil so that we can weather dry spells," Squires reports.

To keep the soil in place, they plant cover crops such as oats, millet, yellow blossom clover, and nitrogen-fixing peas. "Cover crops can do anything, one thing at a time," notes Straza. "Once we identify the issue, such as nitrogen-building, weed suppression, grazing, or organic matter–building, we pick a few plants that will be keystone players."

To the surprise of these organic growers, livestock are the last building block. To utilize their burgeoning cover crops in 2018, they experimented with a neighbor's cows at a higher-than-normal number per acre. The cattle ended up grazing the top third of the cover crop and then trampling the rest before they could be rotated into the next block of forage. The resultant cow manure, however, paid off by returning organic matter to the soil. This convinced them to buy 300 cows of their own. They conclude: "Our method is a multilayer ecosystem that we now consider a whole-farm approach to sequestering carbon in the soil." ■ *(continued)*

JANIE'S FARM AND MILL
Ashkum, Illinois

About a decade ago, Harold Wilken watched as yet another semi-truck loaded with tons of organic wheat pulled away from his 3,300-acre farm bound for a feed mill in upstate New York. Suddenly, Wilken had an epiphany: "Why am I shipping my grain 700 miles away to feed chickens, when there are so many people nearby who eat bread?"

Finding a way to sell direct to these consumers called for major changes to Janie's Farm's operations—as well as collaborations with bakers, distributors, and even scientists. "A lot of things came together at the same time," Wilken recalls. He bought a nearby abandoned building, converted it into a large stone mill, and asked University of Illinois researchers for help in identifying the best grain to mill (the verdict: hard red winter wheat).

In the first production year, customers could choose from five high-quality, whole grain, organic flours. "People tried our flour, and word of mouth got out," Wilken reports.

Today, the mill offers 45 flours and grains, ships up to 100 orders direct-to-consumer daily, and sells about 450,000 pounds of flour annually. Wilken notes that most wholesale orders are delivered by him, as "it's important for me to develop these relationships, instead of just having a driver drop it off."

Recently, a visibly relieved bagel baker came out to meet the delivery truck, admitting that he'd been putting out a mediocre product after running out of high-protein bread flour from Janie's Mill. "Hearing that gives me real satisfaction in knowing that we're doing the right thing," Wilken observes.

The only downside of the close ties with customers is some weight gain, acknowledges Wilken: "All the bakers think the best way to thank the farmer is with a loaf of bread." ■ *(continued)*

"WHY AM I SHIPPING MY GRAIN 700 MILES AWAY TO FEED CHICKENS, WHEN THERE ARE SO MANY PEOPLE NEARBY WHO EAT BREAD?"

Photo: Janie's Farm and Mill

59

"WE DECIDED THAT THIS SYSTEM WOULD ALLOW THE COWS TO HAVE A GOOD LIFE."

CROVALLEY HOLSTEINS
Hastings, Ontario

Robots are keeping many Canadian dairy farms in the family. This is the case for Cynthia and John Crowley as well as the fifth generation of their family, sons Justin and Ryan. In 2016, the Crowleys decided to build a freestall barn that could house 110 Holstein cows and an automated milking system. The system's undercarriage has a robotic arm with suction cups that automatically detect where to attach to each udder's four teats. Each cow wears a neckband transponder with a unique electronic number, leaving her free to feed, rest, socialize, and be milked as desired. With these choices, she may decide to be milked up to five times per day—in which case, upon entering the milking crate, she is rewarded with sweetened haylage, the most tender early stage of the hay crop.

Swoosh—and the sensors record liters of milk produced per day, butterfat percentage, and more. All of these statistics can be viewed from the comfort of the office. In the past, dairy husbandry involved physical observation. Now it's more cerebral, requiring the review of daily data and patterns. For example, a cow's electronic collar tracks her behavior, such as distance walked per day. If a cow is restless, she's likely in heat and should be bred to produce next year's calf.

There's still hands-on care. For example, Cynthia feeds the calves. Newborns are closely monitored for two feedings of colostrum (immunity-boosting milk from the mother). There are other chores, but by adopting a robotic system, the family has released more time for analysis of overall herd production. "We decided that this system would not only allow the cows to have a good life but also enable us to have a more flexible, less labor-intensive one, too," says Cynthia, adding: "I don't milk cows anymore." ∎

Canadian profiles are by **Karen Davidson,** editor of *The Grower,* a leading Canadian horticultural magazine, and frequent contributor to the Almanac.
U.S. profiles are by **Stacey Kusterbeck,** a regular contributor to the Almanac.

Photo: Crovalley Holsteins

WE ALL FLIP FOR
PANCAKES!

BY SARAH PERREAULT

Flapjacks, griddle cakes, hotcakes, buckwheats, johnnycakes, flannel cakes. No matter what you call them, these are all generally the same thing—pancakes—and people have been loving them for centuries!

Although the 5th century B.C. Greek poets Cratinus and Magnes were the first to actually document "warm cakes" made from flour, honey, olive oil, and milk, there is evidence pointing to pancakes having been eaten much earlier. The 5,300-year-old remains of "Ötzi the Iceman," discovered perfectly preserved in a glacier on the Austrian-Italian border in 1991, revealed remnants in his stomach of an unleavened bread made of einkorn wheat. Tiny particles of charcoal attached to the sample indicated that the pancake-like food had been cooked next to a fire or on a hot rock.

Pope Gregory I (c. 540–604) inadvertently popularized pancakes among the masses. He decreed that Christians had to abstain from eating meat and animal products such as milk, butter, and eggs during Lent, the 40 days (not including Sundays) leading up to Easter on the Christian calendar that begin with Ash Wednesday. The faithful purged their households of the unwanted ingredients by making and consuming pancakes, doughnuts, and other pastries on Shrove Tuesday, the day before the fasting period.

The English have long celebrated the humble pancake. A pancake race in Olney, Buckingham-shire, dates from 1445. Legend has it originating with a woman who was cooking pancakes in advance of an

FUN FACTS

■ The pancake tortoise is named for the shape of its shell, which is flatter yet more flexible than that of a typical tortoise. This flexibility allows the agile tortoise to climb into small crevices to escape predators rather than retreat into its shell.

■ On February 8, 2016, in Rufford, England, James Haywood and Dave Nicholls set a record by stacking 213 pancakes to a height of 3 feet 4 inches.

■ Pancake ice can be found in both fresh and salt water. It sometimes forms when water that is beginning to freeze is disturbed by wind or waves. As each small piece of ice bumps into others, sharp angles around its edge are worn down to form a ridge or rim—giving it the appearance of a pancake.

WEARING AN APRON AND HEADSCARF, OLNEY RACERS FLIP A PANCAKE IN A SKILLET AT THE START AND FINISH OF A RACE.

imminent Shrove Tuesday church service. When she heard the church bells ring, she rushed out the door to attend the service—still wearing her headscarf and apron and with pancake-laden skillet in hand. (Headscarves were mandatory attire for women in church in those days.) In her honor and spirit, today's racers must wear an apron and headscarf and run with a skillet containing a pancake to be flipped at the start of the 415-yard race and then again at the finish line. The event has inspired runners from afar: In 1950, members of the Junior Chamber of Commerce in Liberal, Kansas, challenged Olney's residents to a friendly competition that has been going on ever since in their respective communities.

The Jewish holiday of Chanukah is also a time for partaking in pancakes. During this 8-day celebration, Jewish cultures eat latkes, or potato pancakes fried in oil. Oil plays a symbolic role in the festivities: After a revolt by Jews in the 2nd century B.C. that reclaimed the Temple of Jerusalem, it is said that the victors could find only a vessel with enough oil to keep the Temple menorah lit for just 1 day—yet miraculously it lasted for 8 days.

Hungry? Make some pancakes, even if it isn't Shrove Tuesday (Feb. 13 this year). Try out the following recipes or have fun by creating your own!

BLUEBERRY BUTTERMILK PANCAKES

1½ cups all-purpose flour
1¼ teaspoons baking soda
½ teaspoon salt
2 cups buttermilk

1 teaspoon vanilla extract
1 egg, separated
1 cup blueberries

In a bowl, combine flour, baking soda, and salt. Make a well in the center of the dry ingredients and into it put the buttermilk, vanilla, and egg yolk. Stir until barely combined.

In a separate chilled bowl, beat egg white until stiff, then fold into batter.

Using a ¼ cup measure, drop batter onto a hot, greased griddle or skillet. Sprinkle a few blueberries over each pancake and cook for 3 to 5 minutes, or until bubbles form. Flip pancakes and cook the other side for an additional 2 to 3 minutes. Serve warm. **Makes 4 servings.**

(continued)

LATKES

4 large russet potatoes,
  peeled and grated
1 onion, grated
1 egg, lightly beaten
2 tablespoons all-purpose flour
1 teaspoon kosher or sea salt,
  plus extra for seasoning
½ teaspoon baking powder
2 tablespoons vegetable oil,
  plus more as needed
freshly ground black pepper,
  to taste
sour cream, applesauce, or fresh
  dill, for topping

Place potatoes and onions in
a sieve or kitchen towel and
squeeze out any excess water.

In a bowl, combine grated
mixture, egg, flour, salt,
and baking powder.

Warm oil in a large, heavy
skillet over medium heat.
Drop batter into skillet one
heaping spoonful at a time
(don't crowd the pan).
Flatten gently; don't push
potatoes too hard into oil.
Fry in batches, adding more
oil, if necessary, for 4 minutes
per side, or until golden brown.
Drain on paper towels and
season well with salt and pepper.

Serve immediately with
preferred toppings on the side.
Makes 12 servings. ■

Sarah Perreault, food editor of
The Old Farmer's Almanac, prefers
pumpkin pancakes to all other
breakfast griddle goodies.

67

2023 RECIPE CONTEST WINNERS

We asked you for your best recipes using ginger,
and we received many delicious dishes. Sincere thanks
to all of you who took the time to submit recipes!

Styling and photography: Samantha Jones/Vaughan Communications

FIRST PRIZE: $300
**GINGER GREMOLATA
BAKED SALMON**
(recipe on page 200)

SECOND PRIZE: $200
**THAI GINGER
MEATBALL SALAD**
(recipe on page 200)

(continued)

FOOD

THIRD PRIZE: $100
**GINGER PEACH CRISP
WITH GINGER-INFUSED
WHIPPED CREAM**
(recipe on page 200)

ENTER THE 2024 RECIPE CONTEST: FAVORITE HOLIDAY DISH
Got a scary Halloween treat, super side dish for
Thanksgiving, festive New Year's punch, or other holiday favorite?
Send it in and it could win! See contest rules on page 251.

HONORABLE MENTION
GINGER SWIRL BUNS
(recipe on page 201)

(continued on page 200)

CURRENT EVENTS

Why the oceans hold a key to our future climate

Earth is a complex system in which a mosaic of parts—oceans, land, and atmosphere—interact to create and sustain life as we know it. Any changes to one part of this system can have cascading impacts on other parts. As the average global temperature steadily increases due to greenhouse gas emissions, ocean currents are shifting. The changes are so consequential that new observations, often with specialized equipment, make headlines. For example, one current, the Atlantic Meridional Overturning Circulation (AMOC), was first measured in the 1950s. In the '90s, observations suggested that it might have been weakening, or slowing. It is now the subject of intense focus because a weak AMOC could be dire for life on Earth.

WHAT IS AN OCEAN CURRENT?

Just as the trade winds and jet streams move air in our atmosphere, currents move the ocean waters. Ocean currents do not have banks like rivers do, but they are particularly strong around the edges of the ocean basins where the continents and seafloor topography direct (and redirect) their flow. The largest currents have names—for example, the Gulf Stream (the part of the AMOC that flows from the Gulf of Mexico northward along the east coast of North America) and the Humboldt

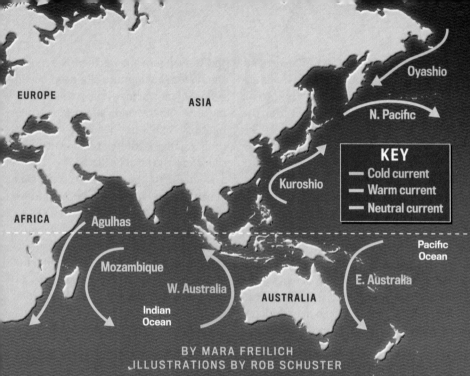

KEY
— Cold current
— Warm current
— Neutral current

EUROPE

ASIA

Oyashio

N. Pacific

Kuroshio

AFRICA

Agulhas

Mozambique

W. Australia

Indian Ocean

AUSTRALIA

E. Australia

Pacific Ocean

BY MARA FREILICH
ILLUSTRATIONS BY ROB SCHUSTER

Current (which flows northward along the west coast of South America)—which signify their importance to life on the continents.

Ocean currents transport enormous amounts of water. The Gulf Stream moves from 30 to 150 million cubic meters per second, depending on location. In contrast, all of Earth's rivers input 1.2 million cubic meters per second of freshwater flow into the oceans.

The AMOC carries heat—in the form of warm water—northward. The water releases heat that warms the atmosphere and affects atmospheric pressure and wind patterns. As the water cools, it becomes denser. Eventually, in the far north Atlantic, the dense, cold water sinks, forming subsurface currents that turn southward. In the deep ocean, this cold water spreads through all of the ocean basins.

But not all ocean currents flow predictably. Many move in swirling, chaotic patterns, variously merging and separating. Together, the currents connect all of the ocean basins in a global system known as the "ocean conveyer belt." The belt carries water both downward into the depths of the ocean interior and upward toward the sea surface. The deepest, densest cold waters in the Pacific Ocean may have last been in contact with the atmosphere hundreds of years ago!

HOW ARE CURRENTS FORMED?

Ocean currents are generated by multiple forces. One of these is wind, which pushes water, creating surface currents. However, ocean currents move more slowly than wind. The fastest ocean currents travel at speeds only slightly greater than 5 miles per hour. Below the surface, variations in the density of seawater also generate and drive currents.

One factor in seawater density is salinity. Salt water is denser than fresh water. When water evaporates from the ocean, the ocean becomes saltier. (The temperatures of both the ocean and the atmosphere affect how quickly water evaporates from the ocean.) Rain, rivers, and melting ice, like the thawing ice caps in Greenland, restore fresh water to the ocean—although these exchanges are not necessarily equal.

Another factor in ocean density is the water temperature. The oceans have absorbed 90 percent of the excess heat trapped on Earth by carbon emissions, dramatically reducing the amount that the atmosphere has warmed. Currently, the water flowing into the deep ocean is becoming warmer (due to the warming atmosphere) and fresher (due to ice melting) than it has been in a very long time, changing the water density and therefore the circulation.

Because of these two factors, this ocean conveyor belt—whose actions are complicated—is also known as the "thermohaline circulation" ("thermo" refers to temperature and "haline" to saltiness). Sometimes salinity and temperature have counteracting effects. In the cold North Atlantic, meltwater from the Arctic can make the northward-flowing water of the AMOC fresher

EDDIES AND CURRENTS

Ocean currents transport heat, making the east coast of North America warmer than the west coast at the same latitude. These currents have consistent patterns, but move in variable swirling paths called eddies and meanders. The Gulf Stream takes a meandering path as it transports warm water from south to north. Warm water is red and cold water is green and blue in the image below.

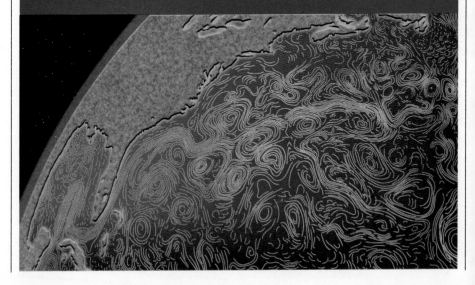

Graphic adapted from NASA

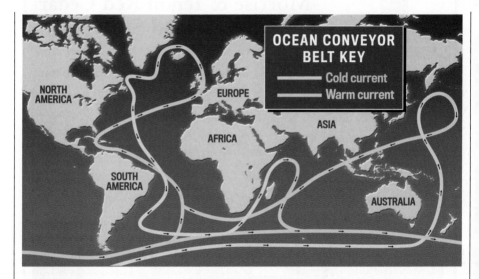

OCEAN CONVEYOR BELT KEY
— Cold current
— Warm current

and therefore lighter, thus preventing it from sinking to depth even though it is cold. Some scientists think that such an effect is one possible cause of a slowing AMOC.

WHY ARE OCEAN CURRENTS IMPORTANT?

Water has been found to be especially effective at redistributing and storing heat. Ocean water can absorb more heat than air in the atmosphere can without significantly increasing in temperature. The amount of energy required to warm a cubic foot of ocean by 1 degree C is nearly 5,000 times what is needed to warm a cubic foot of air by the same amount. During the summer, when the air is warmer than the ocean, the ocean absorbs heat. During the winter, when the air is cool, the ocean slowly releases heat back to the atmosphere. By doing so, the ocean has a moderating effect on the climate of nearby land. This is why, along the U.S. East Coast and

parts of Atlantic Canada in winter, the heat-radiating Atlantic Ocean can turn snowstorms into rainstorms.

Similarly, myriad ocean currents—from the southward-flowing Labrador Current in the Atlantic Ocean to the California and Alaska Currents off the West Coast in the Pacific—impact local and global weather by altering the temperature and moisture content of the atmosphere. As atmospheric winds travel over the ocean, they pick up—or lose—heat and moisture. The ocean has a moderating effect on temperatures over land when warm, moisture-laden (or cool, dry) ocean winds blow over it.

CATCHING THE WAVES

Scientists study the movement of ocean currents via arrays of moorings that contain instruments designed to measure seawater's speed, temperature, salinity, and other properties (e.g., nutrients and oxygen). This information, combined with satellite observations of the ocean

surface, has shown that ocean currents are variable, not steady. Some current patterns vary by tens of years ("decadal" variability is a common measure); the El Niño Southern Oscillation (ENSO) in the Pacific is one example of this. The Atlantic Multidecadal Oscillation (AMO), linked to the AMOC, is another. As our observational record gets longer, scientists can detect suggestions of variations in the strengths of the ocean currents and their properties. Such changes could have a significant impact on our climate and weather for a long time.

Far below the sea surface, ocean water is insulated from the rapidly changing atmosphere, and its temperature and salinity change very slowly. Nevertheless, conditions in the deep ocean are still often determined by conditions at the sea surface. Water whose temperature and salinity have changed during a storm in one time and place at the surface will re-emerge in a different location, carried there by the ocean currents. Polar melting or changes in storminess in one year affect global weather and climate years—even centuries—later because of ocean circulation.

Even small variations in the temperature, strength, and positions of ocean currents can have important impacts on weather. For example, if the Gulf Stream slowed its transport

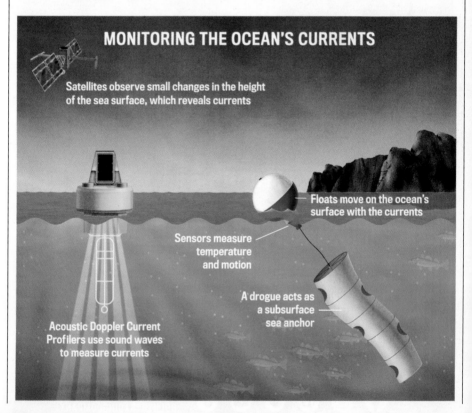

MONITORING THE OCEAN'S CURRENTS

Satellites observe small changes in the height of the sea surface, which reveals currents

Floats move on the ocean's surface with the currents

Sensors measure temperature and motion

A drogue acts as a subsurface sea anchor

Acoustic Doppler Current Profilers use sound waves to measure currents

Graphic adapted from NOAA

STRAIT DOWN

In the Denmark Strait between Greenland and Iceland, cold, dense ocean water (part of the down- and southward-flowing portion of the AMOC) sinks below warmer surface water onto a ridge that is 2,000 feet below the sea surface and then plunges to a depth of 11,500 feet. The Denmark Strait Cataract (waterfall) is more than three times the height of Angel Falls (aka Kerepakupai Merú) in Venezuela, which at 3,212 feet is the tallest waterfall on land.

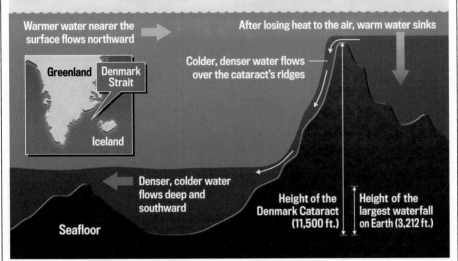

Warmer water nearer the surface flows northward

After losing heat to the air, warm water sinks

Greenland | Denmark Strait

Colder, denser water flows over the cataract's ridges

Iceland

Denser, colder water flows deep and southward

Height of the Denmark Cataract (11,500 ft.)

Height of the largest waterfall on Earth (3,212 ft.)

Seafloor

of heat from the AMOC, northern Europe would be somewhat cooler. (This possibility would not completely offset global warming. Currently, projections suggest that any cooling in Europe from ocean heat transport would only reduce, not eliminate, atmospheric warming from greenhouse gas emissions.)

Similarly, the position of an ocean current can determine where there is moisture in the atmosphere, how much of it there is, and where it goes. This can affect the strength of storms and the whole climate system. For example, in the U.S. Midwest, a warmer North Atlantic is linked to droughts, including the Dust Bowl of the 1930s, while in the African Sahel, the same configuration is connected to increased rainfall.

The ocean is a slow yet massive part of our climate system. While the paths of future ocean currents are not clear, what is certain is that changes in ocean circulation today may have dramatic impacts on weather even far from the coasts, as well as possibly lead to climate changes that affect weather—and lives—for hundreds of years. ■

Mara Freilich is an assistant professor of oceanography and applied mathematics at Brown University in Providence, Rhode Island. A hiker, backpacker, and bicyclist, she also enjoys ocean kayaking and snorkeling—despite her childhood fear of the sea.

SECRETS TO

STRAIGHT FROM "THE MAD FISHERMAN"

Boston's Charlie Moore—known to millions of TV fans as "The Mad Fisherman"—is famous for his passionate pursuit of fish and boundless enthusiasm for the sport of angling. We asked him how he got started and how anyone can learn to love fishing as much as he does.

When I was a kid in the late '70s, I was lighting up Boston Harbor on my 14-foot Boston Whaler. My first rod and reel were a Penn deep-sea fishing setup. I loved bringing flounder back to the dock, filleting them up, and having them for dinner.

Even at age 8, I felt like I was ahead of my time when it came to fishing. A lot of commercial boats were docked at Crystal Cove Marina in Winthrop, Massachusetts, where

> "EVEN AT AGE 8, I FELT LIKE I WAS AHEAD OF MY TIME WHEN IT CAME TO FISHING."

my father had ours. Captain Norman's boat really caught a lot of fish. Almost every day during the summer, he would walk down and ask my father if I could go out with them— which I did every time I could! I learned a lot about striped bass, cod, bluefish, flounder, and haddock and really grew up with a lot of different ways to catch fish.

Fast-forward to my late teens, when I started learning the art of freshwater fishing from my future father-in-law,

FUN FISHING

BY CHARLIE MOORE

PHOTOS BY P. T. SULLIVAN

fun when they fish, no matter who and where they are. There are many, many different methods, times, places, and lures for catching any fish—saltwater or freshwater—and they're all good! What's more, there's only one person who knows the "right" way for you to fish—*you!*

PRACTICE, PRACTICE, PRACTICE—OR NOT

Fishing is even more fun when you're *good* at it. The number one way to get better at anything is to make the most of your talents—and make no mistake about it, you already have what it takes.

Fishing is all about hand-eye coordination. Fish such as bass, bonefish, redfish, and snook require the cast to be precise, so anything that you can do to improve your overall strength and hand-eye coordination will help you over time. But we all do what we can with what we have, and any effort at all to hone your abilities is always great. Practice casting into a bucket in your backyard? Sounds good to me!

PUT IN THE TIME— ANY TIME, ANYTIME

The more time you put in at the water, the more adept you'll become. This doesn't have to mean going 10 miles out on a fancy boat—standing

Dick Latini. Going out with him to small ponds around the North Shore area of Beverly, Massachusetts, was really how I came to enjoy freshwater bass fishing.

Am I crazy for fishing? Or just crazy? Probably a lot of both, but somehow people took notice of my great enthusiasm for the sport, and the rest is history, as I have now made more than 400 fishing shows.

IT'S ALL GOOD

But this isn't about *my* story. It's about people having more

"THERE ARE MANY, MANY DIFFERENT METHODS, TIMES, PLACES, AND LURES FOR CATCHING ANY FISH, AND THEY'RE ALL GOOD!"

by a pond or stream counts just as much. As the saying goes, "You can't catch a fish without a line in the water." Invest some time in gaining experience, and you'll definitely be rewarded. But *fish!*

TIMING ISN'T EVERYTHING

As far as time of year goes, sure: Fish move. They react differently in different seasons, but this doesn't happen as much as you'd think. When bass fishing, I always make my first casts into no more than 10 feet of water because I believe that I can always find catchable shallow-water fish. Plus, it's a lot easier to catch fish alongside visible underwater structure than it is to find them around an underwater hump in 60 feet of water. Don't worry about the timing. Think about where you can most easily reach the most fish.

IT'S A CONFIDENCE GAME

People are always asking me how to catch largemouth and smallmouth bass all year long. What are the secrets? The magical patterns? The special techniques?

Well, the answers always come down to an old adage: "Keep it simple, stupid." If you love a ½-ounce spinnerbait like I do, then throw it all day long, every day, for 12 months a year. *The best lure in your tack-*

> "THE BEST LURE IN YOUR TACKLE BOX IS THE ONE THAT'S YOUR FAVORITE."

le box is the one that's your favorite. This bait is called your "confidence bait."

Put together your own special tackle box with your top five favorite lures, in different sizes and colors. When you're toting this to the dock or boat ramp or shoreline, there's no question about it—you'll be feeling confident and success will lie just ahead!

DON'T BELIEVE THE HYPE!

With regard to lures, don't believe the hype! Don't believe

in the latest and greatest lure or the latest and greatest color. *No, no, no.* Keep it *simple*. If your trusty Jitterbug lure worked in 1998, there's a good chance that the bass don't know what year it is now and will still bite it. Always stick with your "confidence" lures. You'll catch more fish.

WRITE YOU ARE

Keep a fishing journal, handwritten or on your phone or laptop, noting when and where you caught fish and what you

"IF YOUR TRUSTY JITTERBUG LURE WORKED IN 1998, THERE'S A GOOD CHANCE THAT THE BASS DON'T KNOW WHAT YEAR IT IS NOW AND WILL STILL BITE IT."

caught them on. After a while, you'll develop your own fishing patterns and styles, which will help you to catch more fish consistently during different times of year. As your success increases, so will your fun!

BE YOUR TRUE FISHING SELF

It's really funny. I tell people all the time that their personality will dictate their style of fishing. For example, I am high-energy and run at a million miles an hour. On the water, I am burning a ½-ounce Rat-L-Trap and a ½-ounce spinnerbait and then throwing them 400 times more than the average angler on any given day, which is upping my odds of catching more fish. But you can fish at any octane level you want—in whatever way is really *you*. If you're more slow-paced, no worries! Fish slow-paced. You'll still get good results if you make a lot of casts over time.

WHY WE'RE REALLY OUT THERE

Why is fishing so much fun for me? Well, it's the out-of-doors, the wildlife, the peacefulness, the excitement of rough water or bad weather, the ever-changing environment—you always need to be on your toes when fishing.

Unlike with almost any other sport, even when you have

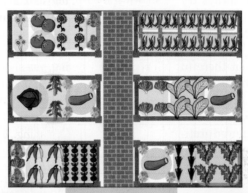

a bad day of fishing, it still offers up so much more. It's never a loss and always a big win, no matter what happens! For this reason, I always try to remember to be thankful for the opportunity to enjoy the natural world and the fun of fishing. We're out there to catch fish, sure, but we also should always appreciate that fishing is a total experience to be greeted with renewed gratitude every time we go out.

ONE MORE THING

Everybody has a different style. Everybody has a different technique. Everybody

> **"WHEN IT COMES TO FISHING AND EVERYTHING ELSE THAT I DO IN MY LIFE, JUST LIKE FRANK SINATRA SANG, I DO IT MY WAY."**

has an opinion: You should do this. You should do that. But in the end, I'm here to tell you that when it comes to fishing and everything else that I do in my life, just like Frank Sinatra sang, I do it my way— and to have the most fun fishing, *you* should, *too!*

And if you can take along an 8-year-old, please do! ■

A TV host since 1996, irrepressible angler **Charlie Moore**—"The Mad Fisherman"—can be seen in *Charlie Moore: No Offense* (worldwide syndication, Roku TV, Apple TV) and *Charlie Moore Outdoors* on the New England Sports Network (NESN). For more information, go to CharlieMoore.com.

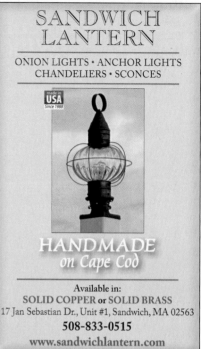

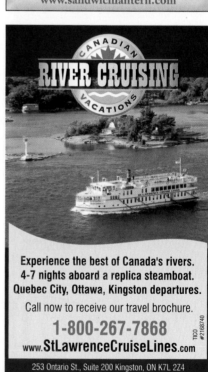

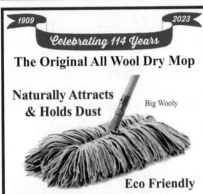

These weather maps correspond to the winter and summer predictions in the General Weather Forecast (opposite) and on the regional forecast pages, 206–223. To learn more about how we make our forecasts, turn to page 202.

THE GENERAL WEATHER REPORT AND FORECAST

FOR REGIONAL FORECASTS, SEE PAGES 206-223.

We are approaching the middle of Solar Cycle 25, which is increasing in intensity and already as strong as Solar Cycle 24, which possibly had the lowest solar activity in about 200 years. Such low activity has historically meant cooler average temperatures across Earth, but this connection has become weaker since the last century. We expect a neutral to perhaps weak El Niño later in the year, as well as a warm Atlantic Multidecadal Oscillation (AMO) and cool Pacific Decadal Oscillation (PDO). Also important are the equatorial stratospheric winds involved in the Quasi-Biennial Oscillation, or QBO. Under certain combinations of meteorological conditions, the polar vortex can be displaced from the North Pole, which could open the door for cold blasts to hit southern Canada and the central and eastern United States during this upcoming winter.

WINTER will be warmer than normal from New England and the Atlantic Corridor down to Florida, across the Gulf Coast and southern Texas, and in Alaska and near normal or colder elsewhere. Precipitation will be below normal in South Florida, the northern Intermountain and Pacific Northwest regions, and Alaska and near to above normal elsewhere. Snowfall will be above normal across most snow-prone areas, except for being below normal in the Pacific Northwest.

SPRING will be cooler than normal in the western Ohio Valley, from the upper Midwest to the northern High Plains, and in Oklahoma and western Hawaii and near normal or warmer elsewhere. Precipitation will be above normal from New England through the Appalachians into Florida, from the Deep South and Texas–Oklahoma across the southern High Plains to the Desert, and across Alaska and near to below normal elsewhere.

SUMMER will be hotter than normal from New England through the Atlantic Corridor; in Florida and the Deep South; in the eastern Lower Lakes; from the Upper Midwest to the Heartland; in Texas; across the High Plains, Intermountain region, and Desert Southwest to the Cali-fornia coast and north to the southern Pacific Northwest; and in Alaska and near normal or cooler elsewhere. Rainfall will be above normal in eastern Virginia and the Carolinas; in the Lower Lakes and western Ohio Valley, much of Texas and Oklahoma, the eastern Upper Midwest, the southern High Plains, and the northern Rockies; from southern Arizona and California up to the Pacific Northwest; and in northern Alaska. It will be near to below normal elsewhere.

Watch for **TROPICAL STORMS** along the Atlantic Corridor in late August, in the Deep South and Texas in mid-July, and in Texas again in late August and mid-September. **HURRICANES** may hit the Southeast and Florida in late August and the Deep South in early July and early September.

AUTUMN will be cooler than normal from the Atlantic Corridor and Appalachians down to Florida and from the Lower Lakes to the Ohio Valley and near normal or warmer elsewhere. Precipitation will be above normal from the Appalachians and Tennessee and Ohio Valleys into the eastern Lower Lakes and in Texas, California, and Alaska and near or below normal elsewhere.

WEATHER

TO GET A SUMMARY OF THE RESULTS OF OUR FORECAST FOR LAST WINTER, TURN TO PAGE 204.

THE OLD
FARMER'S ALMANAC

Established in 1792 and published every year thereafter
ROBERT B. THOMAS, *founder* (1766–1846)

YANKEE PUBLISHING INC.
EDITORIAL AND PUBLISHING OFFICES
P.O. Box 520, 1121 Main Street, Dublin, NH 03444
Phone: 603-563-8111 • Fax: 603-563-8252

EDITOR *(13th since 1792):* Janice Stillman
CREATIVE DIRECTOR: Colleen Quinnell
MANAGING EDITOR: Jack Burnett
SENIOR EDITORS: Sarah Perreault, Heidi Stonehill
ASSOCIATE EDITOR: Tim Goodwin
WEATHER GRAPHICS AND CONSULTATION:
AccuWeather, Inc.

V.P., NEW MEDIA AND PRODUCTION:
Paul Belliveau
PRODUCTION DIRECTOR: David Ziarnowski
PRODUCTION MANAGER: Brian Johnson
SENIOR PRODUCTION ARTISTS:
Jennifer Freeman, Rachel Kipka, Janet Selle

WEB SITE: ALMANAC.COM
SENIOR DIGITAL EDITOR: Catherine Boeckmann
ASSOCIATE DIGITAL EDITOR: Jennifer Keating
SENIOR WEB DESIGNER: Amy O'Brien
DIGITAL MARKETING SPECIALISTS:
Jessica Garcia, Holly Sanderson
E-MAIL MARKETING SPECIALIST: Eric Bailey
E-COMMERCE MARKETING DIRECTOR: Alan Henning
PROGRAMMING: Peter Rukavina

CONTACT US

We welcome your questions and comments about articles in and topics for this Almanac. Mail all editorial correspondence to Editor, The Old Farmer's Almanac, P.O. Box 520, Dublin, NH 03444-0520; fax us at 603-563-8252; or contact us through Almanac.com/Contact. *The Old Farmer's Almanac* can not accept responsibility for unsolicited manuscripts and will not acknowledge any hard-copy queries or manuscripts that do not include a stamped and addressed return envelope.

All printing inks used in this edition of *The Old Farmer's Almanac* are soy-based. This product is recyclable. Consult local recycling regulations for the right way to do it.

Thank you for buying this Almanac! We hope that you find it "useful, with a pleasant degree of humor." Thanks, too, to everyone who had a hand in it, including advertisers, distributors, printers, and sales and delivery people.

OUR CONTRIBUTORS

BOB BERMAN, our astronomy editor, leads annual tours to Chilean observatories as well as to view solar eclipses and the northern lights. He is the author of 12 books, including *Zoom* (Little Brown, 2015) and *Earth-Shattering: Violent Supernovas, Galactic Explosions, Biological Mayhem, Nuclear Meltdowns, and Other Hazards to Life in Our Universe* (Little Brown, 2019).

DAN CLARK writes the weather doggerel verse that runs down the center of the Right-Hand Calendar Pages. His late father, Tim Clark, wrote the weather doggerel for more than 40 years.

BETHANY E. COBB, our astronomer, is an Associate Professor of Honors and Physics at George Washington University. In addition to conducting research on gamma-ray bursts and teaching astronomy and physics courses to non–science majors, she enjoys rock climbing, figure skating, and reading science fiction.

CELESTE LONGACRE, our astrologer, often refers to astrology as "a study of timing, and timing is everything." A New Hampshire native, she has been a practicing astrologer for more than 40 years. Her book, *Celeste's Garden Delights* (2015), is available on her Web site, CelesteLongacre.com.

BOB SMERBECK and **BRIAN THOMPSON,** our meteorologists, bring more than 50 years of forecasting expertise to the task, as well as some unique early accomplishments: a portable, wood-and-PVC-pipe tornado machine built by Bob and prescient 5-day forecasts made by Brian—in fourth grade.

TED WILLIAMS, a Massachusetts-based nature writer, pens the Farmer's Calendar essays. He serves on the Circle of Chiefs of the Outdoor Writers Association of America and writes about fish and wildlife for national publications. He is the author of *Earth Almanac* (Storey Publishing, 2020).

Final Issue

Common Obverse

Now! Complete National Park Quarter Set Only $19.95!

Don't miss out! The final coin has been released and quantities are limited for these **Uncirculated Complete 56-Coin sets!** The first coin in this set was issued in 2010.

- **FREE** Shipping!

- **FREE** Gift: Uncirculated Lincoln Shield Cent

You'll also receive a handpicked trial selection of fascinating coins from our No-Obligation Coins-on-Approval Service, from which you may purchase any or none of the coins – return balance in 15 days – with option to cancel at any time.

Mail Coupon Now!
For Faster Service Visit:
www.LittletonCoin.com/Specials

Littleton
Coin Company®

Serving Collectors Since 1945

Offer Code: **25H420**

©2023 LCC, Inc.

THE OLD
FARMER'S ALMANAC

Established in 1792 and published every year thereafter
ROBERT B. THOMAS, *founder* (1766–1846)

YANKEE PUBLISHING INC.
P.O. Box 520, 1121 Main Street, Dublin, NH 03444
Phone: 603-563-8111 • Fax: 603-563-8252

PUBLISHER *(23rd since 1792):* Sherin Pierce
EDITOR IN CHIEF: Judson D. Hale Sr.

FOR DISPLAY ADVERTISING RATES
Go to Almanac.com/AdvertisingInfo or
call 800-895-9265, ext. 109

Stephanie Bernbach-Crowe • 914-827-0015
Steve Hall • 800-736-1100, ext. 320

FOR CLASSIFIED ADVERTISING
Cindy Levine, RJ Media • 212-986-0016

SENIOR AD PRODUCTION COORDINATOR:
Janet Selle • 800-895-9265, ext. 168

PUBLIC RELATIONS
Vaughan Communications • 360-620-9107
Ginger Vaughan • ginger@vaughancomm.com

CONSUMER ORDERS & INFO
Call 800-ALMANAC (800-256-2622), ext. 1
or go to Almanac.com/Shop

RETAIL SALES
Stacey Korpi • 800-895-9265, ext. 160
Janice Edson, ext. 126

DISTRIBUTORS
NATIONAL: Comag Marketing Group
Smyrna, GA
BOOKSTORE: HarperCollins Publishers
New York, NY
NEWSSTAND CONSULTANT: PSCS Consulting
Linda Ruth • 603-924-4407

Old Farmer's Almanac publications are available
for sales promotions or premiums. Contact Beacon
Promotions, info@beaconpromotions.com.

YANKEE PUBLISHING INCORPORATED
A 100% EMPLOYEE-OWNED COMPANY

Jamie Trowbridge, *President;*
Paul Belliveau, Ernesto Burden, Judson D. Hale Jr.,
Brook Holmberg, Jennie Meister, Sherin Pierce,
Vice Presidents.

Now available in the U.S. without a prescription!

Pill Used in Germany For 53 Years Relieves Joint Pain In 7 Days Without Side Effects

Approved by top doctors nationwide. Active ingredient numbs nerves that trigger pain. Relieves joint stiffness. Increases joint mobility and freedom.

By J.K. Roberts
Interactive News Media

INM — A pill that relieves joint pain and stiffness in 7 days without side effects has been used safely in Germany for 53 years. It is now available in the United States.

This pill contains an active ingredient that not only relieves pain quickly, but also works to rebuild damaged cartilage between bones for greater range of motion.

It can make your pain relief costs up to 82% less than using pain relief drugs and pain relief cream and heat products.

An improved version of this pill is now being offered in the United States under the brand name FlexJointPlus.

FlexJointPlus relieves joint pain, back pain, neck pain, carpal tunnel, sprains, strains, sports injuries, and more. With daily use, users can expect to feel 24-hour relief.

"Relief in pain and stiffness is felt in as few as 7 days," said Roger Lewis, Chief Researcher for FlexJointPlus.

"And with regular use, you can expect even more reduction in the following 30-60 days," added Lewis.

WHAT SCIENTISTS DISCOVERED

FlexJointPlus contains an amazing compound with a known ability to rebuild damaged cartilage and ligaments associated with joint pain.

This compound is not a drug. It is the active ingredient in FlexJointPlus.

Studies show it naturally reduces inflammation while repairing bone and cartilage in the joint.

Many joint pain sufferers see an increase in flexibility and mobility. Others are able to get back to doing the things they love.

With so much positive feedback, it's easy to see why sales for this newly approved joint pain pill continue to climb every day.

IMPRESSIVE BENEFITS FOR JOINT PAIN SUFFERERS

The 8 week clinical study was carried out by scientists across six different clinic sites in Germany. The results were published in the Journal of Arthritis in July 2014.

The study involved patients with a variety of joint pain conditions associated with osteoarthritis. They were not instructed to change their daily routines. They were only told to take FlexJointPlus' active ingredient every day.

The results were incredible.

Taking FlexJointPlus's active ingredient just once daily significantly reduced both joint pain and stiffness compared to placebo at 7, 30, and 60 days.

In fact, many patients experienced greater than 50% reduction in pain and stiffness at 60 days.

They also enjoyed an improvement in stiffness when first getting out of the bed in the morning, and an improvement in pain when doing light household chores.

The findings are impressive, no doubt, but results will vary.

But with results like these, it's easy to see why thousands of callers are jamming the phone lines trying to get their hands on FlexJointPlus.

HOW IT REBUILDS DAMAGED JOINTS

Scientists have discovered that after the age of 40, the body is no longer able to efficiently repair bone and cartilage in the joint. This results in deterioration and inflammation in the joint, leading to pain.

The natural compound found in FlexJointPlus contains the necessary ingredients needed for the body to rebuild damaged bone and cartilage.

This compound is known as NEM®.

"Essentially, it contains the same elements found in your joints, which are needed to repair and rebuild cartilage and ligaments," explains chief researcher, Roger Lewis.

There also have been no adverse side effects reported with the use of NEM®.

This seems to be another reason why FlexJointPlus's release has triggered such a frenzy of sales.

RECOMMENDED BY U.S. MEDICAL DOCTORS

"Based on my 20 years of experience treating people with osteoarthritis, FlexJointPlus receives my highest recommendation to any person suffering from joint pain and stiffness," said Dr. David Vallance, Rheumatologist from Ann Arbor, MI.

"I use FlexJointPlus every day for my stiff and aching joints. I also have my wife and daughter taking it regularly as well," said Dr. Oozer, G.P. from LaSalle, CA.

OLD FARMER'S ALMANAC READERS GET SPECIAL DISCOUNT SUPPLY

This is the official release of FlexJointPlus and so for a limited time, the company is offering a special discount supply to our readers. An Order Hotline has been set up for our readers to call, but don't wait. The special offer will not last forever. All you have to do is call TOLL FREE 1-800-540-7740. The company will do the rest.

IMPORTANT: Due to FlexJointPlus's recent media exposure, phone lines are often busy. If you call, and do not immediately get through, please be patient and call back. Current supplies of FlexJointPlus are limited, so customers that don't get through to the order hotline will have to wait until more inventory is available. Call **1-800-540-7740** today!

Approved by U.S. Doctors: U.S. medical doctors are now recommending the powerful new pill FlexJointPlus. Participants in clinical studies reported noticeable results in just days.

ECLIPSES

There will be four eclipses in 2024, two of the Sun and two of the Moon. Solar eclipses are visible only in certain areas and require eye protection to be viewed safely. Lunar eclipses are technically visible from the entire night side of Earth, but during a penumbral eclipse, the dimming of the Moon's illumination is slight. See the **Astronomical Glossary, page 110,** for explanations of the different types of eclipses.

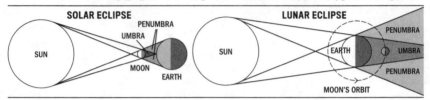

MARCH 24-25: PENUMBRAL ECLIPSE OF THE MOON. This eclipse is visible from North America. The Moon will enter the penumbra at 12:51 A.M. EDT on March 25 (9:51 P.M. PDT, March 24) and leave it at 5:35 A.M. EDT (2:35 A.M. PDT).

APRIL 8: TOTAL ECLIPSE OF THE SUN. This eclipse is visible from North America (except for Alaska). It will begin at 11:42 A.M. EDT and end at 4:52 P.M. EDT. The narrow path of totality in the U.S. extends northeast from Texas to Maine, crossing primarily through parts of Oklahoma, Arkansas, Missouri, Illinois, Kentucky, Indiana, Ohio, Pennsylvania, New York, Vermont, and New Hampshire. In Canada, it runs from southern Ontario to the island of Newfoundland, crossing through parts of southern Quebec, New Brunswick, and Prince Edward Island. For most other regions of North America, a partial eclipse will be visible. It is safe to look directly at the eclipse *only* during the brief period of totality. At all other times, you will need safety equipment such as "eclipse glasses" or a solar filter. (See "Behold Nature's Grandest Event!," page 158.)

SEPTEMBER 17-18: PARTIAL ECLIPSE OF THE MOON. Visible from most of North America, this is primarily a penumbral eclipse. On September 17, the Moon will enter the penumbra at 8:39 P.M. EDT (5:39 P.M. PDT) and umbra at 10:12 P.M. EDT (7:12 P.M. PDT). It will leave the umbra at 11:17 P.M. EDT (8:17 P.M. PDT) on September 17 and penumbra at 12:49 A.M. EDT on September 18 (9:49 P.M. PDT, September 17).

OCTOBER 2: ANNULAR ECLIPSE OF THE SUN. This eclipse is not visible from North America, although a partial eclipse will be visible from Hawaii. It will begin at 5:43 A.M. and end at 11:47 A.M. (HAT).

THE MOON'S PATH

The Moon's path across the sky changes with the seasons. Full Moons are very high in the sky (at midnight) between November and February and very low in the sky between May and July.

FULL-MOON DATES (ET)				
	2024	2025	2026	2027	2028
JAN.	25	13	3	22	11
FEB.	24	12	1	20	10
MAR.	25	14	3	22	10
APR.	23	12	1	20	9
MAY	23	12	1 & 31	20	8
JUNE	21	11	29	18	7
JULY	21	10	29	18	6
AUG.	19	9	28	17	5
SEPT.	17	7	26	15	3
OCT.	17	6	26	15	3
NOV.	15	5	24	13	2
DEC.	15	4	23	13	1 & 31

New Blood Flow Breakthrough Helps Men Enjoy Strong, Long-Lasting Intimacy – At Any Age

Men across America are raving about a newly enhanced potency supplement that helps achieve healthy blood flow on demand

After age 40, it's common knowledge that performance begins to decline in many men. However, a new, performance empowering pill is showing that any relatively healthy man can now enjoy long-lasting, and frequent intimacy – at any age.

This doctor-designed formula, created by leading anti-aging expert Dr. Al Sears, has already helped men overcome low and sinking libido -- and has recently undergone a potency-enhancing update – with remarkable new results.

When the first pill -- **Primal Max Black** -- was first released, it quickly became a top-selling men's performance helper, promoting intimacy across America.

It worked by supporting healthy testosterone levels. However, Dr. Sears soon realized that this isn't the only challenge men face with performance. That's when he turned his attention to blood flow.

And this became **Primal Max Red**.

THIS PROVEN SOLUTION IS MORE MECHANICAL THAN HORMONAL

Truth is, once blood flow slows down for men, no matter how exciting it is, it won't be enough without the necessary amount...

So enjoying intimacy without healthy blood flow becomes difficult for most men.

Luckily, a Nobel prize-winning scientist discovered the simple answer to help support

performance strength and confidence -- by boosting vital blood flow -- and enhancing this essential performance function.

Using this landmark Nobel Prize as its basis, **Primal Max Red** enhanced healthy blood flow for untold millions of men around the world with the use of strong nitric oxide boosters.

While **Primal Max Black** helped maintain optimal testosterone, **Primal Max Red** tackles a lesser-known challenge.

Director, Al Sears MD, who has authored over 500 scientific papers and has appeared on more than 50 media outlets including ABC News, CNN, ESPN, Discovery, Lifetime, and many more say, *"Less than optimal blood flow can be part of a huge problem that affects a lot of men. And it needed to be addressed once and for all, so men would not dwell on it. Then, once we optimized it and had a great deal of success, we set out to see if we could do even better."*

The former formula had excellent results. However, new research showed that for even faster, anytime, anywhere results, increasing the dose of a key compound was needed.

So, one of the three nitric oxide boosters in the new **Primal Max Red**, L-Citrulline, was clinically boosted to 9000 mg, and the results were astounding. Which is no surprise considering that 5000 mg is considered a "normal amount" -- giving the new version nearly doubled the blood flow boosting power.

Men who had previously been unsure about their

A new discovery that increases nitric oxide availability was recently proven to boost blood flow 275% - resulting in improved performance.

power and stamina were overjoyed to be back to their old selves and to get and maintain a healthy bloodflow when they needed it.

BETTER BLOOD FLOW, STRONGER RESULTS

The best way to promote healthy blood flow throughout the body is with the use of **Primal Max Red**. By using it, when exciting signals leave the brain, blood flows much faster like it used to.

This critical action is how men across the country are enjoying full and satisfying performance at any age. No need to bother with testosterone-boosting shots, blue pills, or shady capsules that have no effect.

Primal Max Red can effectively promote healthy blood flow that most men can use for maximum intimacy. This is leading to more greater capacity and satisfaction, coupled with long-lasting performance.

"There was a time when men had little control when it came to boosting their blood flow," Dr. Sears said. "But science has come a long way in recent years. And now, with the creation of nitric oxide-boosting

Primal Max Red, men can perform better than ever, and enjoy intimacy at any age."

Now for men across America, it's much easier to stay at their performance peak as they get older.

HOW TO GET PRIMAL MAX RED (AND FREE PRIMAL MAX BLACK):

To secure free bottles of **Primal Max Black** and get the hot, new **Primal Max Red** formula, buyers should contact the Sears Health Hotline at **1-800-906-4782** TODAY. "It's not available in retail stores yet," says Dr. Sears. "The Hotline allows us to ship directly to the customer." Dr. Sears feels so strongly about **Primal Max**, all orders are backed by a 100% money-back guarantee. "Just send me back the bottle and any unused product within 90 days from purchase date, and I'll send you all your money back."

Call NOW at **1-800-906-4782** to secure your supply of **Primal Max Red** and free bottles of **Primal Max Black**. Use Promo Code **OFAPMX0823** when you call. Lines are frequently busy, but all calls will be answered!

BRIGHT STARS

TRANSIT TIMES

This table shows the time (ET) and altitude of a star as it transits the meridian (i.e., reaches its highest elevation while passing over the horizon's south point) at Boston on the dates shown. The transit time on any other date differs from that of the nearest date listed by approximately 4 minutes per day. To find the time of a star's transit for your location, convert its time at Boston using Key Letter C (see Time Corrections, page 238).

STAR	CONSTELLATION	MAGNITUDE	TIME OF TRANSIT (ET) BOLD = P.M. LIGHT = A.M.						ALTITUDE (DEGREES)
			JAN. 1	MAR. 1	MAY 1	JULY 1	SEPT. 1	NOV. 1	
Altair	Aquila	0.8	**12:53**	8:57	5:57	1:57	**9:49**	**5:49**	56.3
Deneb	Cygnus	1.3	**1:43**	9:47	6:47	2:47	**10:40**	**6:40**	92.8
Fomalhaut	Psc. Aus.	1.2	**3:59**	**12:03**	9:03	5:04	1:00	**8:56**	17.8
Algol	Perseus	2.2	**8:09**	**4:13**	**1:13**	9:14	5:10	1:10	88.5
Aldebaran	Taurus	0.9	**9:37**	**5:41**	**2:41**	10:41	6:37	2:37	64.1
Rigel	Orion	0.1	**10:15**	**6:19**	**3:19**	11:19	7:15	3:16	39.4
Capella	Auriga	0.1	**10:18**	**6:22**	**3:22**	11:22	7:18	3:18	93.6
Bellatrix	Orion	1.6	**10:26**	**6:30**	**3:30**	11:30	7:26	3:26	54.0
Betelgeuse	Orion	var. 0.4	**10:56**	**7:00**	**4:00**	**12:00**	7:56	3:56	55.0
Sirius	Can. Maj.	-1.4	**11:45**	**7:49**	**4:49**	**12:50**	8:46	4:46	31.0
Procyon	Can. Min.	0.4	12:43	**8:43**	**5:44**	**1:44**	9:40	5:40	52.9
Pollux	Gemini	1.2	12:49	**8:50**	**5:50**	**1:50**	9:46	5:46	75.7
Regulus	Leo	1.4	3:12	**11:12**	**8:12**	**4:12**	**12:09**	8:09	59.7
Spica	Virgo	var. 1.0	6:28	2:32	**11:29**	**7:29**	**3:25**	11:25	36.6
Arcturus	Boötes	-0.1	7:18	3:22	12:23	**8:19**	**4:15**	**12:15**	66.9
Antares	Scorpius	var. 0.9	9:32	5:36	2:36	**10:33**	**6:29**	**2:29**	21.3
Vega	Lyra	0	11:39	7:43	4:43	12:43	**8:35**	**4:35**	86.4

RISE AND SET TIMES

To find the time of a star's rising at Boston on any date, subtract the interval shown at right from the star's transit time on that date; add the interval to find the star's setting time. To find the rising and setting times for your city, convert the Boston transit times above using the Key Letter shown at right before applying the interval (see Time Corrections, page 238). Deneb, Algol, Capella, and Vega are circumpolar stars—they never set but appear to circle the celestial north pole.

STAR	INTERVAL (H.M.)	RISING KEY	DIR.*	SETTING KEY	DIR.*
Altair	6 36	B	EbN	E	WbN
Fomalhaut	3 59	E	SE	D	SW
Aldebaran	7 06	B	ENE	D	WNW
Rigel	5 33	D	EbS	B	WbS
Bellatrix	6 27	B	EbN	D	WbN
Betelgeuse	6 31	B	EbN	D	WbN
Sirius	5 00	D	ESE	B	WSW
Procyon	6 23	B	EbN	D	WbN
Pollux	8 01	A	NE	E	NW
Regulus	6 49	B	EbN	D	WbN
Spica	5 23	D	EbS	B	WbS
Arcturus	7 19	A	ENE	E	WNW
Antares	4 17	E	SEbE	A	SWbW

*b = "by"

New Bladder Control Pill Sales May Surpass Adult Diapers By 2025

Drug-free discovery works, say doctors. Many adults ditching diapers and pads for clinical strength pill that triggers day and night bladder support.

By J.K. Roberts
Interactive News Media

INM — Over 150,000 doses have shipped to bladder sufferers so far, and sales continue to climb every day for the 'diaper replacing' new pill called BladderMax.

"We knew we had a great product, but it's even exceeded our expectations," said Keith Graham, Manager of Call Center Operations for BladderMax.

"People just keep placing orders, it's pretty amazing," he said.

But a closer look at this new bladder control sensation suggests that maybe the company shouldn't have been caught off guard by its success.

There are very good reasons for BladderMax's surging popularity.

To begin with, clinical studies show BladderMax not only reduces embarrassing bladder leakages quickly, but also works to strengthen and calm the bladder for lasting relief.

Plus, at just $2 per daily dose, it's very affordable.

This may be another reason why American diaper companies are starting to panic over its release.

WHAT SCIENTISTS DISCOVERED

BladderMax contains a proprietary compound with a known ability to reduce stress, urgency, and overflow leakages in seniors suffering from overactive bladder. This compound is not a drug. It is the active ingredient in BladderMax.

Studies show it naturally strengthens the bladder's muscle tone while relaxing the urination muscles, resulting in a decrease in sudden urgency.

Many sufferers enjoy a reduction in bathroom trips both day and night. Others are able to get back to doing the things they love without worrying about embarrassing leakages.

"I couldn't sit through a movie without having to go to the bathroom 3-4 times," says Theresa Johnson of Duluth, GA. "but since using BladderMax I can not only sit through a movie, but I can drive on the freeway to another city without having to immediately go to the bathroom."

With so much positive feedback, it's easy to see why sales for this newly approved bladder pill continue to climb every day.

SLASHES EMBARRASSING LEAKAGES BY 79%

The 6 week clinical study was carried out by scientists in Japan. The results were published in the Journal of Medicine and Pharmaceutical Science in 2001.

The study involved seniors who suffered from frequent and embarrassing bladder leakages. They were not instructed to change their daily routines. They were only told to take BladderMax's active ingredient every day.

The results were incredible.

Taking BladderMax's active ingredient significantly reduced both sudden urges to go and embarrassing urine leakages compared to the placebo.

In fact, many experienced a 79% reduction in embarrassing accidents when coughing, sneezing, laughing or physical activity at 6 weeks.

HOW IT WORKS IS INCREDIBLE

Studies show that as many as one in six adults over age 40 suffers from an overactive bladder and embarrassing leakages.

"Losing control of when and how we go to the bathroom is just an indication of a weakening of the pelvic muscles caused by age-related hormonal changes," says Lewis.

"It happens in both men and women, and it is actually quite common."

The natural compound found in BladderMax contains the necessary

As new pill gains popularity, products like these will become unnecessary.

ingredients needed to help strengthen bladder muscles to relieve urgency, while reducing frequency.

Plus, it helps relax bladder muscles, allowing for complete emptying of the bladder.

This proprietary compound is known as EFLA940®.

And with over 17 years of medical use, there have been no adverse side effects reported.

RECOMMENDED BY U.S. MEDICAL DOCTORS

"Many of my patients used to complain that coughing, sneezing or even getting up quickly from a chair results in wetting themselves and they fear becoming a social outcast," reports Dr. Clifford James M.D. "But BladderMax changes all that."

"BladderMax effectively treats urinary disorders, specifically overactive bladder," said Dr. Christie Wilkins, board certified doctor of natural medicine.

OLD FARMER'S ALMANAC READERS GET SPECIAL DISCOUNT SUPPLY

This is the official release of BladderMax and so for a limited time, the company is offering a special discount supply to our readers. An Order Hotline has been set up for our readers to call, but don't wait. The special offer will not last forever. All you have to do is call TOLL FREE **1-800-615-9302**. The company will do the rest.

THE TWILIGHT ZONE/METEOR SHOWERS

Twilight is the time when the sky is partially illuminated preceding sunrise and again following sunset. The ranges of twilight are defined according to the Sun's position below the horizon. **Civil twilight** occurs when the Sun's center is between the horizon and 6 degrees below the horizon (visually, the horizon is clearly defined). **Nautical twilight** occurs when the center is between 6 and 12 degrees below the horizon (the horizon is distinct). **Astronomical twilight** occurs when the center is between 12 and 18 degrees below the horizon (sky illumination is imperceptible). When the center is at 18 degrees (**dawn** or **dark**) or below, there is no illumination.

LENGTH OF ASTRONOMICAL TWILIGHT (HOURS AND MINUTES)

LATITUDE	JAN. 1–APR. 10	APR. 11–MAY 2	MAY 3–MAY 14	MAY 15–MAY 25	MAY 26–JULY 22	JULY 23–AUG. 3	AUG. 4–AUG. 14	AUG. 15–SEPT. 5	SEPT. 6–DEC. 31
25°N to 30°N	1 20	1 23	1 26	1 29	1 32	1 29	1 26	1 23	1 20
31°N to 36°N	1 26	1 28	1 34	1 38	1 43	1 38	1 34	1 28	1 26
37°N to 42°N	1 33	1 39	1 47	1 52	1 59	1 52	1 47	1 39	1 33
43°N to 47°N	1 42	1 51	2 02	2 13	2 27	2 13	2 02	1 51	1 42
48°N to 49°N	1 50	2 04	2 22	2 42	–	2 42	2 22	2 04	1 50

TO DETERMINE THE LENGTH OF TWILIGHT: The length of twilight changes with latitude and the time of year. See the **Time Corrections, page 238,** to find the latitude of your city or the city nearest you. Use that figure in the chart above with the appropriate date to calculate the length of twilight in your area.

TO DETERMINE ARRIVAL OF DAWN OR DARK: Calculate the sunrise/sunset times for your locality using the instructions in **How to Use This Almanac, page 116.**

Subtract the length of twilight from the time of sunrise to determine when dawn breaks. Add the length of twilight to the time of sunset to determine when dark descends.

EXAMPLE:
BOSTON, MASS. (LATITUDE 42°22')

Sunrise, August 1	5:37 A.M. ET
Length of twilight	– 1 52
Dawn breaks	3:45 A.M.
Sunset, August 1	8:03 P.M. ET
Length of twilight	+ 1 52
Dark descends	9:55 P.M.

PRINCIPAL METEOR SHOWERS

SHOWER	BEST VIEWING	POINT OF ORIGIN	DATE OF MAXIMUM*	NO. PER HOUR**	ASSOCIATED COMET
Quadrantid	**Predawn**	N	**Jan. 4**	25	–
Lyrid	Predawn	S	Apr. 22	10	Thatcher
Eta Aquarid	Predawn	SE	May 4	10	Halley
Delta Aquarid	Predawn	S	July 30	10	–
Perseid	**Predawn**	NE	**Aug. 11–13**	50	**Swift-Tuttle**
Draconid	Late evening	NW	Oct. 9	6	Giacobini-Zinner
Orionid	Predawn	S	Oct. 21–22	15	Halley
Northern Taurid	Late evening	S	Nov. 9	3	Encke
Leonid	Predawn	S	Nov. 17–18	10	Tempel-Tuttle
Andromedid	Late evening	S	Nov. 25–27	5	Biela
Geminid	**All night**	NE	**Dec. 13–14**	75	–
Ursid	Predawn	N	Dec. 22	5	Tuttle

*May vary by 1 or 2 days   **In a moonless, rural sky   **Bold** = most prominent

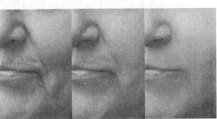

THE VISIBLE PLANETS

Listed here for Boston are viewing suggestions for and the rise and set times (ET) of Venus, Mars, Jupiter, and Saturn on specific days each month, as well as when it is best to view Mercury. Approximate rise and set times for other days can be found by interpolation. Use the Key Letters at the right of each listing to convert the times for other localities **(see pages 116 and 238).**

GET ALL PLANET RISE AND SET TIMES BY ZIP CODE VIA ALMANAC.COM/2024.

VENUS

Our nearest planetary neighbor starts 2024 as a morning star in the east just before dawn. On January 1, Venus shines at a dazzling magnitude –4.0, bright enough to cast shadows in rural areas when the Moon is absent. The splendor eventually fades as it falls closer to the sunrise while still a magnitude –3.9, which it maintains through mid-October. Its superior conjunction with the Sun happens on June 4, after which it can't be easily seen until late July, when the planet returns as an evening star moving upward in dusk's twilight. Look for a Venus–Moon conjunction on August 5. Autumn and then especially December bring a dramatic improvement, as Venus climbs to its maximum 47-degree separation from the Sun while brightening to a magnitude –4.4 at year's end.

Jan. 1	rise	4:17	E	Apr. 1	rise	5:57	C	July 1	**set**	**8:57**	E	Oct. 1	**set**	**7:38**	B
Jan. 11	rise	4:38	E	Apr. 11	rise	5:45	C	July 11	**set**	**9:01**	E	Oct. 11	**set**	**7:30**	B
Jan. 21	rise	4:57	E	Apr. 21	rise	5:33	C	July 21	**set**	**8:59**	E	Oct. 21	**set**	**7:27**	A
Feb. 1	rise	5:13	E	May 1	rise	5:23	B	Aug. 1	**set**	**8:52**	D	Nov. 1	**set**	**7:30**	A
Feb. 11	rise	5:21	E	May 11	rise	5:14	B	Aug. 11	**set**	**8:42**	D	Nov. 11	**set**	**6:39**	A
Feb. 21	rise	5:25	E	May 21	rise	5:09	B	Aug. 21	**set**	**8:30**	D	Nov. 21	**set**	**6:54**	A
Mar. 1	rise	5:23	E	June 1	rise	5:09	A	Sept. 1	**set**	**8:15**	C	Dec. 1	**set**	**7:13**	A
Mar. 11	rise	6:18	D	June 11	**set**	**8:30**	E	Sept. 11	**set**	**8:01**	C	Dec. 11	**set**	**7:34**	A
Mar. 21	rise	6:09	D	June 21	**set**	**8:46**	E	Sept. 21	**set**	**7:49**	B	Dec. 21	**set**	**7:55**	B
												Dec. 31	**set**	**8:15**	B

MARS

Earth and Mars meet every 26 months, so the Red Planet has alternating good and bad years for viewing—2024 being one of the latter. Mars starts off dim, distant, and tiny and remains that way during the entire first half of the year. It has neither a conjunction with the Sun nor an opposition to it in 2024, and it never brightens enough to outshine the stars. Attention will turn to Mars in the fall, though, as it reaches a very bright magnitude 0 in early November, in Cancer, and hovers just above the Moon on November 21. Mars's best moment will arrive on December 18, when it has an extremely close and beautiful conjunction with the Moon while shining at an eye-catching magnitude –0.89.

Jan. 1	rise	6:24	E	Apr. 1	rise	5:15	D	July 1	rise	1:58	B	Oct. 1	**rise**	**11:31**	A
Jan. 11	rise	6:17	E	Apr. 11	rise	4:54	D	July 11	rise	1:39	B	Oct. 11	**rise**	**11:15**	A
Jan. 21	rise	6:08	E	Apr. 21	rise	4:32	C	July 21	rise	1:20	B	Oct. 21	**rise**	**10:57**	A
Feb. 1	rise	5:57	E	May 1	rise	4:10	C	Aug. 1	rise	1:02	A	Nov. 1	**rise**	**10:35**	A
Feb. 11	rise	5:44	E	May 11	rise	3:47	C	Aug. 11	rise	12:46	A	Nov. 11	**rise**	**9:11**	A
Feb. 21	rise	5:29	E	May 21	rise	3:25	C	Aug. 21	rise	12:31	A	Nov. 21	**rise**	**8:42**	A
Mar. 1	rise	5:14	E	June 1	rise	3:01	B	Sept. 1	rise	12:15	A	Dec. 1	**rise**	**8:08**	A
Mar. 11	rise	5:57	D	June 11	rise	2:39	B	Sept. 11	rise	12:01	A	Dec. 11	**rise**	**7:27**	A
Mar. 21	rise	5:37	D	June 21	rise	2:18	B	Sept. 21	**rise**	**11:46**	A	Dec. 21	**rise**	**6:39**	A
												Dec. 31	**rise**	**5:44**	A

BOLD = P.M. LIGHT = A.M.

JUPITER

The largest planet starts the year as a conspicuous evening star, high in the southeast at nightfall. It then steadily falls lower toward the sunset until it's too low to observe in April. Jupiter passes behind the Sun on May 18 and reappears as a morning star, in Taurus, in June. The fascinating gas giant steadily approaches Mars from August 1 to 13 until they hover together in a close conjunction from August 13 to 16. Rising 2 hours earlier each month, Jupiter is in opposition on December 7, its biggest and brightest night of the year.

Jan. 1	set	2:06	D	Apr. 1	set	10:07	E	July 1	rise	3:06	A	Oct. 1	rise	9:49	A
Jan. 11	set	1:28	D	Apr. 11	set	9:39	E	July 11	rise	2:34	A	Oct. 11	rise	9:10	A
Jan. 21	set	12:52	D	Apr. 21	set	9:12	E	July 21	rise	2:02	A	Oct. 21	rise	8:30	A
Feb. 1	set	12:13	D	May 1	set	8:44	E	Aug. 1	rise	1:26	A	Nov. 1	rise	7:44	A
Feb. 11	set	11:37	D	May 11	set	8:17	E	Aug. 11	rise	12:53	A	Nov. 11	rise	6:01	A
Feb. 21	set	11:05	D	May 21	rise	5:16	B	Aug. 21	rise	12:20	A	Nov. 21	rise	5:17	A
Mar. 1	set	10:38	D	June 1	rise	4:41	A	Sept. 1	rise	11:39	A	Dec. 1	rise	4:33	A
Mar. 11	set	11:08	D	June 11	rise	4:09	A	Sept. 11	rise	11:03	A	Dec. 11	set	6:50	E
Mar. 21	set	10:39	D	June 21	rise	3:38	A	Sept. 21	rise	10:27	A	Dec. 21	set	6:05	E
												Dec. 31	set	5:20	E

SATURN

The universe's most beautiful planet begins 2024 as an evening star in Aquarius. After a decade-long occupation of the zodiac's most southerly constellations, Saturn finally moves up and away from that unfavorable position. Its rings—now almost edgewise to our view—can be seen through any telescope with more than 30× magnification. In mid-February, the Ringed Planet becomes too low to observe before gliding invisibly behind the Sun on February 28. It emerges as a morning star during the next few months, meeting Mars on April 10–11 low in the east 40 minutes before sunrise. Its opposition and closest approach occur on September 8, after which it remains high and glorious the rest of the year.

Jan. 1	set	8:42	B	Apr. 1	rise	5:32	D	July 1	rise	11:45	D	Oct. 1	set	4:41	B
Jan. 11	set	8:08	B	Apr. 11	rise	4:55	D	July 11	rise	11:05	D	Oct. 11	set	3:58	B
Jan. 21	set	7:34	B	Apr. 21	rise	4:18	D	July 21	rise	10:26	D	Oct. 21	set	3:16	B
Feb. 1	set	6:57	B	May 1	rise	3:41	D	Aug. 1	rise	9:41	D	Nov. 1	set	2:31	B
Feb. 11	set	6:24	B	May 11	rise	3:04	D	Aug. 11	rise	9:01	D	Nov. 11	set	12:51	B
Feb. 21	set	5:51	B	May 21	rise	2:26	D	Aug. 21	rise	8:20	D	Nov. 21	set	12:12	B
Mar. 1	rise	6:25	D	June 1	rise	1:44	D	Sept. 1	rise	7:35	D	Dec. 1	set	11:30	B
Mar. 11	rise	6:49	D	June 11	rise	1:06	D	Sept. 11	set	6:07	B	Dec. 11	set	10:53	B
Mar. 21	rise	6:12	D	June 21	rise	12:28	D	Sept. 21	set	5:23	B	Dec. 21	set	10:16	B
												Dec. 31	set	9:40	B

MERCURY

The speedy innermost planet zips from morning to evening twilight and back again several times a year. Mercury appears as a predawn morning star from January 1–27, with a strikingly close but very low conjunction with Mars on January 27. As an evening star in the west, Mercury is both bright and easy to view from March 14–25. Its best moment is probably on July 7, when it hangs just below the crescent Moon while shining at a brilliant magnitude –0.2. From September 1 to 16, Mercury is again visible as a predawn morning star.

DO NOT CONFUSE: *Saturn with Mars on March 29 in the morning. Mars is higher and orange.* • *Mars with Taurus's brightest star, Aldebaran, on July 30, next to the crescent Moon. Both are orange, but Mars is slightly brighter.* • *Mars with Jupiter when they meet in mid-August. Jupiter is much brighter and yellow-white.* • *Uranus with the Pleiades star cluster during November. The planet is just to the right of the stars, looks distinctly green (through binoculars), and doesn't twinkle.*

ASTRONOMICAL GLOSSARY

APHELION (APH.): The point in a planet's orbit that is farthest from the Sun.

APOGEE (APO.): The point in the Moon's orbit that is farthest from Earth.

CELESTIAL EQUATOR (EQ.): The imaginary circle around the celestial sphere that can be thought of as the plane of Earth's equator projected out onto the sphere.

CELESTIAL SPHERE: An imaginary sphere projected into space that represents the entire sky, with an observer on Earth at its center. All celestial bodies other than Earth are imagined as being on its inside surface.

CIRCUMPOLAR: Always visible above the horizon, such as a circumpolar star.

CONJUNCTION: The time at which two or more celestial bodies appear closest in the sky. **Inferior (Inf.):** Mercury or Venus is between the Sun and Earth. **Superior (Sup.):** The Sun is between a planet and Earth. Actual dates for conjunctions are given on the **Right-Hand Calendar Pages, 121–147;** the best times for viewing the closely aligned bodies are given in **Sky Watch** on the **Left-Hand Calendar Pages, 120–146.**

DECLINATION: The celestial latitude of an object in the sky, measured in degrees north or south of the celestial equator; comparable to latitude on Earth. This Almanac gives the Sun's declination at noon.

ECLIPSE, LUNAR: The full Moon enters the shadow of Earth, which cuts off all or part of the sunlight reflected off the Moon. **Total:** The Moon passes completely through the umbra (central dark part) of Earth's shadow. **Partial:** Only part of the Moon passes through the umbra. **Penumbral:** The Moon passes through only the penumbra (area of partial darkness surrounding the umbra). See **page 102** for more information about eclipses.

ECLIPSE, SOLAR: Earth enters the shadow of the new Moon, which cuts off all or part of the Sun's light. **Total:** Earth passes through the umbra (central dark part) of the Moon's shadow, resulting in totality for observers within a narrow band on Earth. **Annular:** The Moon appears silhouetted against the Sun, with a ring of sunlight showing around it. **Partial:** The Moon blocks only part of the Sun.

ECLIPTIC: The apparent annual path of the Sun around the celestial sphere. The plane of the ecliptic is tipped 23½° from the celestial equator.

ELONGATION: The difference in degrees between the celestial longitudes of a planet and the Sun. **Greatest Elongation (Gr. Elong.):** The greatest apparent distance of a planet from the Sun, as seen from Earth.

EPACT: A number from 1 to 30 that indicates the Moon's age on January 1 at Greenwich, England; used in determining the date of Easter.

EQUINOX: When the Sun crosses the celestial equator. This event occurs two times each year: **Vernal** is around March 20 and **Autumnal** is around September 22.

EVENING STAR: A planet that is above the western horizon at sunset and less than 180° east of the Sun in right ascension.

GOLDEN NUMBER: A number in the 19-year Metonic cycle of the Moon, used in determining the date of Easter. See **page 149** for this year's Golden Number.

MAGNITUDE: A measure of a celestial object's brightness. **Apparent magnitude** measures the brightness of an object as seen from Earth. Objects with an apparent magnitude of 6 or less are observable to the naked eye. The lower the magnitude, the greater the brightness; an object with a magnitude of –1, e.g., is brighter than one with a magnitude of +1.

(continued)

ASTRONOMICAL GLOSSARY

MIDNIGHT: Astronomically, the time when the Sun is opposite its highest point in the sky. Both 12 hours before and after noon (so, technically, both A.M. and P.M.), midnight in civil time is usually treated as the beginning of the day. It is displayed as 12:00 A.M. on 12-hour digital clocks. On a 24-hour cycle, 00:00, not 24:00, usually indicates midnight.

MOON ON EQUATOR: The Moon is on the celestial equator.

MOON RIDES HIGH/RUNS LOW: The Moon is highest above or farthest below the celestial equator.

MOONRISE/MOONSET: When the Moon rises above or sets below the horizon.

MOON'S PHASES: The changing appearance of the Moon, caused by the different angles at which it is illuminated by the Sun. **First Quarter:** Right half of the Moon is illuminated. **Full:** The Sun and the Moon are in opposition; the entire disk of the Moon is illuminated. **Last Quarter:** Left half of the Moon is illuminated. **New:** The Sun and the Moon are in conjunction; the Moon is darkened because it lines up between Earth and the Sun.

MOON'S PLACE, Astronomical: The position of the Moon within the constellations on the celestial sphere at midnight. **Astrological:** The position of the Moon within the tropical zodiac, whose twelve 30° segments (signs) along the ecliptic were named more than 2,000 years ago after constellations within each area. Because of precession and other factors, the zodiac signs no longer match actual constellation positions.

MORNING STAR: A planet that is above the eastern horizon at sunrise and less than 180° west of the Sun in right ascension.

NODE: Either of the two points where a celestial body's orbit intersects the ecliptic. **Ascending:** When the body is moving from south to north of the ecliptic. **Descending:** When the body is moving from north to south of the ecliptic.

OCCULTATION (OCCN.): When the Moon or a planet eclipses a star or planet.

OPPOSITION: The Moon or a planet appears on the opposite side of the sky from the Sun (elongation 180°).

PERIGEE (PERIG.): The point in the Moon's orbit that is closest to Earth.

PERIHELION (PERIH.): The point in a planet's orbit that is closest to the Sun.

PRECESSION: The slowly changing position of the stars and equinoxes in the sky caused by a slight wobble as Earth rotates around its axis.

RIGHT ASCENSION (R.A.): The celestial longitude of an object in the sky, measured eastward along the celestial equator in hours of time from the vernal equinox; comparable to longitude on Earth.

SOLSTICE, Summer: When the Sun reaches its greatest declination (23½°) north of the celestial equator, around June 21. **Winter:** When the Sun reaches its greatest declination (23½°) south of the celestial equator, around December 21.

STATIONARY (STAT.): The brief period of apparent halted movement of a planet against the background of the stars shortly before it appears to move backward/westward (retrograde motion) or forward/eastward (direct motion).

SUN FAST/SLOW: When a sundial is ahead of (fast) or behind (slow) clock time.

SUNRISE/SUNSET: The visible rising/setting of the upper edge of the Sun's disk across the unobstructed horizon of an observer whose eyes are 15 feet above ground level.

TWILIGHT: See **page 106**. ∎

Note: These definitions apply to the Northern Hemisphere; some do not hold true for locations in the Southern Hemisphere.

2023

JANUARY

S	M	T	W	T	F	S
1	2	3	4	5	6	7
8	9	10	11	12	13	14
15	16	17	18	19	20	21
22	23	24	25	26	27	28
29	30	31				

FEBRUARY

S	M	T	W	T	F	S
			1	2	3	4
5	6	7	8	9	10	11
12	13	14	15	16	17	18
19	20	21	22	23	24	25
26	27	28				

MARCH

S	M	T	W	T	F	S
			1	2	3	4
5	6	7	8	9	10	11
12	13	14	15	16	17	18
19	20	21	22	23	24	25
26	27	28	29	30	31	

APRIL

S	M	T	W	T	F	S
						1
2	3	4	5	6	7	8
9	10	11	12	13	14	15
16	17	18	19	20	21	22
23	24	25	26	27	28	29
30						

MAY

S	M	T	W	T	F	S
	1	2	3	4	5	6
7	8	9	10	11	12	13
14	15	16	17	18	19	20
21	22	23	24	25	26	27
28	29	30	31			

JUNE

S	M	T	W	T	F	S
				1	2	3
4	5	6	7	8	9	10
11	12	13	14	15	16	17
18	19	20	21	22	23	24
25	26	27	28	29	30	

JULY

S	M	T	W	T	F	S
						1
2	3	4	5	6	7	8
9	10	11	12	13	14	15
16	17	18	19	20	21	22
23	24	25	26	27	28	29
30	31					

AUGUST

S	M	T	W	T	F	S
		1	2	3	4	5
6	7	8	9	10	11	12
13	14	15	16	17	18	19
20	21	22	23	24	25	26
27	28	29	30	31		

SEPTEMBER

S	M	T	W	T	F	S
					1	2
3	4	5	6	7	8	9
10	11	12	13	14	15	16
17	18	19	20	21	22	23
24	25	26	27	28	29	30

OCTOBER

S	M	T	W	T	F	S
1	2	3	4	5	6	7
8	9	10	11	12	13	14
15	16	17	18	19	20	21
22	23	24	25	26	27	28
29	30	31				

NOVEMBER

S	M	T	W	T	F	S
			1	2	3	4
5	6	7	8	9	10	11
12	13	14	15	16	17	18
19	20	21	22	23	24	25
26	27	28	29	30		

DECEMBER

S	M	T	W	T	F	S
					1	2
3	4	5	6	7	8	9
10	11	12	13	14	15	16
17	18	19	20	21	22	23
24	25	26	27	28	29	30
31						

2024

JANUARY

S	M	T	W	T	F	S
	1	2	3	4	5	6
7	8	9	10	11	12	13
14	15	16	17	18	19	20
21	22	23	24	25	26	27
28	29	30	31			

FEBRUARY

S	M	T	W	T	F	S
				1	2	3
4	5	6	7	8	9	10
11	12	13	14	15	16	17
18	19	20	21	22	23	24
25	26	27	28	29		

MARCH

S	M	T	W	T	F	S
					1	2
3	4	5	6	7	8	9
10	11	12	13	14	15	16
17	18	19	20	21	22	23
24	25	26	27	28	29	30
31						

APRIL

S	M	T	W	T	F	S
	1	2	3	4	5	6
7	8	9	10	11	12	13
14	15	16	17	18	19	20
21	22	23	24	25	26	27
28	29	30				

MAY

S	M	T	W	T	F	S
			1	2	3	4
5	6	7	8	9	10	11
12	13	14	15	16	17	18
19	20	21	22	23	24	25
26	27	28	29	30	31	

JUNE

S	M	T	W	T	F	S
						1
2	3	4	5	6	7	8
9	10	11	12	13	14	15
16	17	18	19	20	21	22
23	24	25	26	27	28	29
30						

JULY

S	M	T	W	T	F	S
	1	2	3	4	5	6
7	8	9	10	11	12	13
14	15	16	17	18	19	20
21	22	23	24	25	26	27
28	29	30	31			

AUGUST

S	M	T	W	T	F	S
				1	2	3
4	5	6	7	8	9	10
11	12	13	14	15	16	17
18	19	20	21	22	23	24
25	26	27	28	29	30	31

SEPTEMBER

S	M	T	W	T	F	S
1	2	3	4	5	6	7
8	9	10	11	12	13	14
15	16	17	18	19	20	21
22	23	24	25	26	27	28
29	30					

OCTOBER

S	M	T	W	T	F	S
		1	2	3	4	5
6	7	8	9	10	11	12
13	14	15	16	17	18	19
20	21	22	23	24	25	26
27	28	29	30	31		

NOVEMBER

S	M	T	W	T	F	S
					1	2
3	4	5	6	7	8	9
10	11	12	13	14	15	16
17	18	19	20	21	22	23
24	25	26	27	28	29	30

DECEMBER

S	M	T	W	T	F	S
1	2	3	4	5	6	7
8	9	10	11	12	13	14
15	16	17	18	19	20	21
22	23	24	25	26	27	28
29	30	31				

2025

JANUARY

S	M	T	W	T	F	S
			1	2	3	4
5	6	7	8	9	10	11
12	13	14	15	16	17	18
19	20	21	22	23	24	25
26	27	28	29	30	31	

FEBRUARY

S	M	T	W	T	F	S
						1
2	3	4	5	6	7	8
9	10	11	12	13	14	15
16	17	18	19	20	21	22
23	24	25	26	27	28	

MARCH

S	M	T	W	T	F	S
						1
2	3	4	5	6	7	8
9	10	11	12	13	14	15
16	17	18	19	20	21	22
23	24	25	26	27	28	29
30	31					

APRIL

S	M	T	W	T	F	S
		1	2	3	4	5
6	7	8	9	10	11	12
13	14	15	16	17	18	19
20	21	22	23	24	25	26
27	28	29	30			

MAY

S	M	T	W	T	F	S
				1	2	3
4	5	6	7	8	9	10
11	12	13	14	15	16	17
18	19	20	21	22	23	24
25	26	27	28	29	30	31

JUNE

S	M	T	W	T	F	S
1	2	3	4	5	6	7
8	9	10	11	12	13	14
15	16	17	18	19	20	21
22	23	24	25	26	27	28
29	30					

JULY

S	M	T	W	T	F	S
		1	2	3	4	5
6	7	8	9	10	11	12
13	14	15	16	17	18	19
20	21	22	23	24	25	26
27	28	29	30	31		

AUGUST

S	M	T	W	T	F	S
					1	2
3	4	5	6	7	8	9
10	11	12	13	14	15	16
17	18	19	20	21	22	23
24	25	26	27	28	29	30
31						

SEPTEMBER

S	M	T	W	T	F	S
	1	2	3	4	5	6
7	8	9	10	11	12	13
14	15	16	17	18	19	20
21	22	23	24	25	26	27
28	29	30				

OCTOBER

S	M	T	W	T	F	S
			1	2	3	4
5	6	7	8	9	10	11
12	13	14	15	16	17	18
19	20	21	22	23	24	25
26	27	28	29	30	31	

NOVEMBER

S	M	T	W	T	F	S
						1
2	3	4	5	6	7	8
9	10	11	12	13	14	15
16	17	18	19	20	21	22
23	24	25	26	27	28	29
30						

DECEMBER

S	M	T	W	T	F	S
	1	2	3	4	5	6
7	8	9	10	11	12	13
14	15	16	17	18	19	20
21	22	23	24	25	26	27
28	29	30	31			

Love calendar lore? Find more via Almanac.com/2024.

A CALENDAR OF THE HEAVENS FOR 2024

–Beth Krommes

The Calendar Pages (120–147) are the heart of *The Old Farmer's Almanac*. They present sky sightings and astronomical data for the entire year and are what make this book a true almanac, a "calendar of the heavens." In essence, these pages are unchanged since 1792, when Robert B. Thomas published his first edition. The long columns of numbers and symbols reveal all of nature's precision, rhythm, and glory, providing an astronomical look at the year 2024.

HOW TO USE THE CALENDAR PAGES

The astronomical data on the **Calendar Pages (120–147)** are calculated for Boston (where Robert B. Thomas learned to calculate the data for his first Almanac). Guidance for calculating the times of these events for your locale appears on **pages 116–117.** Note that the results will be *approximate*. Find the *exact* time of any astronomical event at your locale via **Almanac.com/2024.** You can also go to **Almanac.com/SkyMap** to print each month's "Sky Map," which may be useful for viewing with "Sky Watch" in the Calendar Pages.

For a list of 2024 holidays and observances, see **pages 148–149.** Also check out the **Glossary of Almanac Oddities** on **pages 150–151,** which describes some of the more obscure entries traditionally found on the **Right-Hand Calendar Pages (121–147).**

ABOUT THE TIMES: All times are given in ET (Eastern Time), except where otherwise noted as AT (Atlantic Time, +1 hour), CT (Central Time, –1), MT (Mountain Time, –2), PT (Pacific Time, –3), AKT (Alaska Time, –4), or HAT (Hawaii-Aleutian Time, –5). Between 2:00 A.M., March 10, and 2:00 A.M., November 3, Daylight Saving Time is assumed in those locales where it is observed.

ABOUT THE TIDES: Tide times for Boston appear on **pages 120–146;** for Boston tide heights, see **pages 121–147.** Tide Corrections for East Coast locations appear on **pages 236–237.** Tide heights and times for locations across the United States and Canada are available via **Almanac.com/2024.**

The Left-Hand Calendar Pages, 120 to 146

On these pages are the year's astronomical predictions for Boston (42°22' N, 71°3' W). Learn how to calculate the times of these events for your locale here or via **Almanac.com/2024.**

A SAMPLE MONTH

SKY WATCH: The paragraph at the top of each Left-Hand Calendar Page describes the best times to view conjunctions, meteor showers, planets, and more. (Also see **How to Use the Right-Hand Calendar Pages, page 118.**)

			1		2		3	4	5		6		7	8
DAY OF YEAR	DAY OF MONTH	DAY OF WEEK	☀ RISES H. M.	RISE KEY	☀ SETS H. M.	SET KEY	LENGTH OF DAY H. M.	SUN FAST M.	SUN DECLINATION ° '	HIGH TIDE TIMES BOSTON	☾ RISES H. M.	RISE KEY	☾ SETS H. M.	SET KEY	☾ ASTRON. PLACE	☾ AGE

60	1	Fr.	6:20	D	5:34	C	11 14	4	7 s. 30	7¼	8	3:30	E	12:58	B	SAG	25
61	2	Sa.	6:18	D	5:35	C	11 17	4	7 s. 07	8¼	9	4:16	E	1:51	B	SAG	26
62	3	**F**	6:17	D	5:36	C	11 19	4	6 s. 44	9¼	9¾	4:56	E	2:47	B	CAP	27
63	4	M.	6:15	D	5:37	C	11 22	4	6 s. 21	10	10½	5:31	E	3:45	C	CAP	28

1. To calculate the sunrise time in your locale: Choose a day. Note its Sun Rise Key Letter. Find your (nearest) city on **page 238**. Add or subtract the minutes that correspond to the Sun Rise Key Letter to/from the sunrise time for Boston.†

EXAMPLE:

To calculate the sunrise time in Denver, Colorado, on day 1:

Sunrise, Boston, with Key Letter D (above)	6:20 A.M. ET
Value of Key Letter D for Denver (p. 238)	+ 11 minutes
Sunrise, Denver	6:31 A.M. MT

To calculate your sunset time, repeat, using Boston's sunset time and its Sun Set Key Letter value.

2. To calculate the length of day: Choose a day. Note the Sun Rise and Sun Set Key Letters. Find your (nearest) city on **page 238**. Add or subtract the minutes that correspond to the Sun Set Key Letter to/from Boston's length of day. *Reverse* the sign (e.g., minus to plus) of the Sun Rise Key Letter minutes. Add or subtract it to/from the first result.

EXAMPLE:

To calculate the length of day in Richmond, Virginia, on day 1:

Length of day, Boston (above)	11h.14m.
Sunset Key Letter C for Richmond (p. 242)	+ 25m.
	11h.39m.
Reverse sunrise Key Letter D for Richmond (p. 242, +17 to -17)	- 17m.
Length of day, Richmond	11h.22m.

3. Use Sun Fast to change sundial time to clock time. A sundial reads natural (Sun) time, which is neither Standard nor Daylight time. To calculate clock time on a sundial in Boston, subtract the minutes given in this column; add the minutes when preceded by an asterisk [*].

–Beth Krommes

† For locations where Daylight Saving Time is never observed, subtract 1 hour from results between the second Sunday of March and first Sunday of November.

To convert the time to your (nearest) city, use Key Letter C on **page 238**.

EXAMPLE:

To change sundial to clock time in Boston or Salem, Oregon, on day 1:

Sundial reading (Boston or Salem)	12:00 noon
Subtract Sun Fast (p. 116)	- 4 minutes
Clock time, Boston	11:56 A.M. ET**
Use Key Letter C for Salem (p. 241)	+ 27 minutes
Clock time, Salem	12:23 P.M. PT**

**Note: Add 1 hour to the results in locations where Daylight Saving Time is currently observed.

4. This column gives the degrees and minutes of the Sun from the celestial equator at noon ET.

5. This column gives the approximate times of high tide in Boston. For example, the first high tide occurs at 7:15 A.M. and the second occurs at 8:00 P.M. the same day. (A dash indicates that high tide occurs on or after midnight and is recorded on the next day.) Figures for calculating approximate high tide times for localities other than Boston are given in the **Tide Corrections** table on **page 236**.

6. To calculate the moonrise time in your locale: Choose a day. Note the Moon Rise Key Letter. Find your (nearest) city on **page 238**. Add or subtract the minutes that correspond to the Moon Rise Key Letter to/from the moonrise time given for Boston.

LONGITUDE OF CITY	CORRECTION MINUTES	LONGITUDE OF CITY	CORRECTION MINUTES
58°–76°	0	116°–127°	+4
77°–89°	+1	128°–141°	+5
90°–102°	+2	142°–155°	+6
103°–115°	+3		

(A dash indicates that the moonrise occurs on/after midnight and is recorded on the next day.) Find the longitude of your (nearest) city on **page 238**. Add a correction in minutes for your city's longitude (see table, bottom left). Use the same procedure with Boston's moonset time and the Moon Set Key Letter value to calculate the time of moonset in your locale.†

EXAMPLE:

To calculate the time of moonset in Lansing, Michigan, on day 1:

Moonset, Boston, with Key Letter B (p. 116)	12:58 P.M. ET
Value of Key Letter B for Lansing (p. 240)	+ 53 minutes
Correction for Lansing longitude, 84°33'	+ 1 minute
Moonset, Lansing	1:52 P.M. ET

7. This column gives the Moon's *astronomical* position among the constellations (not zodiac) at midnight. For *astrological* data, see **pages 224–227**.

Constellations have irregular borders; on successive nights, the midnight Moon may enter one, cross into another, and then move to a new area of the previous. It visits the 12 zodiacal constellations, as well as Auriga **(AUR),** a northern constellation between Perseus and Gemini; Cetus **(CET),** which lies south of the zodiac, just south of Pisces and Aries; Ophiuchus **(OPH),** primarily north of the zodiac but with a small corner between Scorpius and Sagittarius; Orion **(ORI),** whose northern limit first reaches the zodiac between Taurus and Gemini; and Sextans **(SEX),** which lies south of the zodiac except for a corner that just touches it near Leo.

8. This column gives the Moon's age: the number of days since the previous new Moon. (The average length of the lunar month is 29.53 days.) *(cont.)*

The Right-Hand Calendar Pages, 121 to 147

The Right-Hand Calendar Pages contain celestial events; religious observances; proverbs and poems; civil holidays; historical events; folklore; tide heights; weather prediction rhymes; Farmer's Calendar essays; and more.

A SAMPLE MONTH

	1	2	3	4	5	6	7	8	9	10

1	Fr.	ALL FOOLS' •	If you want to make a fool of yourself, you'll find a lot of people ready to help you.		*Flakes*	an inch long, who v
2	Sa.	Tap dancer Charles "Honi" Coles born, 1911 • Tides {9.5 9.0			*alive!*	in fresh water, pro
3	**B**	2nd S. of Easter •	Writer F. Scott Fitzgerald married Zelda Sayre, 1920		*Spring's*	pond across the i
4	M.	Annunciation^T • ♂♆☾ •	*Ben Hur* won 11 Academy Awards, 1960		*arrived!*	emerged a month (
5	Tu.	☾AT ☊ •	Blizzard left 27.2" snow, St. John's, Nfld., 1999 • Tides {10.8 10.8		*Or is this*	to spend the next 3
6	W.	☾ON EQ. • ♂♀☾ •	Twin mongoose lemurs born, Busch Gardens, Tampa, Fla., 2012		*warmth*	on land before ret their wet world. You can't mis

1. The bold letter is the Dominical Letter (from A to G), a traditional ecclesiastical designation for Sunday determined by the date on which the year's first Sunday falls. For 2024, the Dominical Letter is **G** through February. It then reverts to **F** for the rest of the year.

2. Civil holidays and astronomical events.

3. Religious feasts: A^T indicates a major feast that the church has this year temporarily transferred to a date other than its usual one.

4. Sundays and special holy days.

5. Symbols for notable celestial events. For example, ♂♆☾ on the 4th day means that a conjunction (♂) of Neptune (♆) and the Moon (☾) occurs.

6. Proverbs, poems, and adages.

7. Noteworthy historical events, folklore, and legends.

8. High tide heights, in feet, Boston, Massachusetts.

9. Weather prediction rhyme.

10. Farmer's Calendar essay.

Celestial Symbols

☉ Sun	⊕ Earth	♅ Uranus
○ ● ☾ Moon	♂ Mars	♆ Neptune
☿ Mercury	♃ Jupiter	♇ Pluto
♀ Venus	♄ Saturn	

♂ Conjunction (on the same celestial longitude)

☊ Ascending node

☋ Descending node

☍ Opposition (180 degrees from Sun)

PREDICTING EARTHQUAKES

Note the dates in the Right-Hand Calendar Pages when the Moon rides high or runs low. The date of the high begins the most likely 5-day period of earthquakes in the Northern Hemisphere; the date of the low indicates a similar 5-day period in the Southern Hemisphere. Also noted are the 2 days each month when the Moon is on the celestial equator, indicating the most likely time for earthquakes in either hemisphere.

EARTH AT PERIHELION AND APHELION

Perihelion: January 2, 2024 (EST). Earth will be 91,404,095 miles from the Sun. **Aphelion:** July 5, 2024 (EDT). Earth will be 94,510,539 miles from the Sun.

CALENDAR

Why We Have Seasons

The seasons occur because as Earth revolves around the Sun, its axis remains tilted at 23.5 degrees from the perpendicular. This tilt causes different latitudes on Earth to receive varying amounts of sunlight throughout the year.

In the Northern Hemisphere, the summer solstice marks the beginning of summer and occurs when the North Pole is tilted toward the Sun. The winter solstice marks the beginning of winter and occurs when the North Pole is tilted away from the Sun.

The equinoxes occur when the hemispheres equally face the Sun. At this time, the Sun rises due east and sets due west. The vernal equinox marks the beginning of spring; the autumnal equinox marks the beginning of autumn.

In the Southern Hemisphere, the seasons are the reverse of those in the Northern Hemisphere.

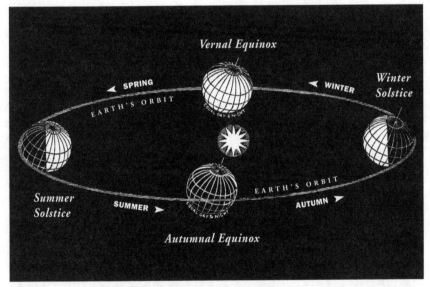

THE FIRST DAYS OF THE 2024 SEASONS

VERNAL (SPRING) EQUINOX:	March 19, 11:06 P.M. EDT
SUMMER SOLSTICE:	June 20, 4:51 P.M. EDT
AUTUMNAL (FALL) EQUINOX:	Sept. 22, 8:44 A.M. EDT
WINTER SOLSTICE:	Dec. 21, 4:21 A.M. EST

NOVEMBER 2023

SKY WATCH: Jupiter, in Aries, comes to opposition on the 3rd, rising at sunset; at its biggest and brightest of the year, the Giant World is visible all night. Saturn, in Aquarius, is also seen the entire night; any telescope using at least 30× magnification will capture its glorious rings. Uranus, in Aries, reaches opposition on the 13th, to the left of Jupiter, which is also in Aries. Binocular owners can easily find Uranus by looking for a green "star" halfway between Jupiter and the famous Pleiades star cluster. Since no star is green, identification should be easy. Not many meteors are expected when the Leonid shower peaks at night on the 18th and 19th. Look for the Moon to the right of Jupiter on the 24th.

☾ LAST QUARTER	5th day	3:37 A.M.
● NEW MOON	13th day	4:27 A.M.
☽ FIRST QUARTER	20th day	5:50 A.M.
○ FULL MOON	27th day	4:16 A.M.

After 2:00 A.M. on November 5, Eastern Standard Time is given.

GET THESE PAGES WITH TIMES SET TO YOUR ZIP CODE VIA ALMANAC.COM/2024.

DAY OF YEAR	DAY OF MONTH	DAY OF WEEK	☀ RISES H. M.	RISE KEY	☀ SETS H. M.	SET KEY	LENGTH OF DAY H. M.	SUN FAST M.	SUN DECLINATION ° '	HIGH TIDE TIMES BOSTON		☾ RISES H. M.	RISE KEY	☾ SETS H. M.	SET KEY	☾ ASTRON. PLACE	☾ AGE
305	1	W.	7:17	D	5:38	B	10 21	32	14 s. 29	2¼	2¼	8:10	A	11:43	E	TAU	18
306	2	Th.	7:18	D	5:36	B	10 18	32	14 s. 48	3	3	9:07	A	12:39	E	AUR	19
307	3	Fr.	7:20	D	5:35	B	10 15	32	15 s. 07	4	4	10:10	B	1:25	E	GEM	20
308	4	Sa.	7:21	D	5:34	B	10 13	32	15 s. 26	4¾	5	11:15	B	2:01	E	CAN	21
309	5	**A**	6:22	E	4:33	B	10 11	32	15 s. 44	4¾	4¾	11:19	B	1:29	E	CAN	22
310	6	M.	6:23	E	4:32	B	10 09	32	16 s. 02	5¾	5¾	—	-	1:53	E	LEO	23
311	7	Tu.	6:25	E	4:31	B	10 06	32	16 s. 20	6½	6¾	12:22	C	2:14	D	LEO	24
312	8	W.	6:26	E	4:29	B	10 03	32	16 s. 37	7½	7¾	1:24	C	2:32	D	LEO	25
313	9	Th.	6:27	E	4:28	B	10 01	32	16 s. 55	8¼	8½	2:26	D	2:50	C	VIR	26
314	10	Fr.	6:28	E	4:27	B	9 59	32	17 s. 12	8¾	9¼	3:29	D	3:09	C	VIR	27
315	11	Sa.	6:30	E	4:26	B	9 56	32	17 s. 28	9½	10	4:33	E	3:29	B	VIR	28
316	12	**A**	6:31	E	4:25	B	9 54	32	17 s. 45	10	10½	5:41	E	3:53	B	VIR	29
317	13	M.	6:32	E	4:24	B	9 52	32	18 s. 01	10¾	11¼	6:52	E	4:22	B	LIB	0
318	14	Tu.	6:33	E	4:23	B	9 50	31	18 s. 16	11½	—	8:04	E	4:59	A	SCO	1
319	15	W.	6:35	E	4:22	B	9 47	31	18 s. 32	12	12	9:15	E	5:46	A	OPH	2
320	16	Th.	6:36	E	4:22	B	9 46	31	18 s. 47	12¾	12¾	10:21	E	6:45	A	SAG	3
321	17	Fr.	6:37	E	4:21	B	9 44	31	19 s. 02	1½	1½	11:16	E	7:55	B	SAG	4
322	18	Sa.	6:38	E	4:20	B	9 42	31	19 s. 16	2½	2½	12:00	E	9:11	B	SAG	5
323	19	**A**	6:40	E	4:19	B	9 39	30	19 s. 30	3¼	3½	12:36	E	10:29	C	CAP	6
324	20	M.	6:41	E	4:18	B	9 37	30	19 s. 44	4¼	4½	1:04	E	11:45	C	CAP	7
325	21	Tu.	6:42	E	4:18	B	9 36	30	19 s. 57	5¼	5¾	1:29	D	—	-	AQU	8
326	22	W.	6:43	E	4:17	B	9 34	30	20 s. 10	6¼	6¾	1:51	D	1:01	D	AQU	9
327	23	Th.	6:44	E	4:16	B	9 32	29	20 s. 23	7¼	7¾	2:13	C	2:15	D	CET	10
328	24	Fr.	6:46	E	4:16	A	9 30	29	20 s. 35	8¼	8¾	2:36	C	3:29	E	PSC	11
329	25	Sa.	6:47	E	4:15	A	9 28	29	20 s. 47	9	9¾	3:02	B	4:44	E	ARI	12
330	26	**A**	6:48	E	4:15	A	9 27	28	20 s. 58	9¾	10½	3:33	B	6:00	E	ARI	13
331	27	M.	6:49	E	4:14	A	9 25	28	21 s. 09	10¾	11¼	4:11	A	7:15	E	TAU	14
332	28	Tu.	6:50	E	4:14	A	9 24	28	21 s. 20	11½	—	4:58	A	8:25	E	TAU	15
333	29	W.	6:51	E	4:13	A	9 22	27	21 s. 30	12	12¼	5:53	A	9:26	E	TAU	16
334	30	Th.	6:52	E	4:13	A	9 21	27	21 s. 40	12¾	1	6:54	A	10:17	E	GEM	17

NOVEMBER

NOVEMBER HATH 30 DAYS

The Frost Spirit comes! and the quiet lake shall feel
The torpid touch of his glazing breath.
–**John Greenleaf Whittier**

DAY OF MONTH	DAY OF WEEK	DATES, FEASTS, FASTS, ASPECTS, TIDE HEIGHTS, AND WEATHER	
1	W.	All Saints' • Boston Female Medical Col., 1st U.S. medical school for women, opened, Boston, Mass., 1848	*Flurries*
2	Th.	All Souls' • ☾ RIDES HIGH • 1st titanium mill opened, Toronto, Ohio, 1957 • {9.3 10.3	*again;*
3	Fr.	♃ AT ☍ • Bob Kane, co-creator of *Batman* comic, died, 1998 • Tides {8.8 9.7	*the bear*
4	Sa.	Sadie Hawkins Day • ♄ STAT. • Royal Montreal Golf Club founded, 1873	*makes*
5	**A**	**23rd S. af. P.** • **DAYLIGHT SAVING TIME ENDS, 2:00 A.M.** • Tides {8.2 9.0	*its den.*
6	M.	☾ AT APO. • 1st recorded sighting of supernova in Cassiopeia, 1572 • {8.2 8.8	*St. Martin's*
7	Tu.	**ELECTION DAY** • Singer-songwriter Leonard Cohen died, 2016 • {8.4 8.8	*summer,*
8	W.	Rodrigo Koxa surfed 80' wave, setting world record, Nazaré, Portugal, 2017 • Tides {8.7 8.9	*but*
9	Th.	☾ ON EQ. • ☌♀☾ • Alice Coachman, 1st Black woman to win Olympic gold medal, born, 1923	*showers*
10	Fr.	*If red the Sun begin his race, Be sure the rain will fall apace.* • Tides {9.5 9.2	*a bummer.*
11	Sa.	St. Martin of Tours • **VETERANS DAY** • ☾ AT ☋ • {9.9 9.3	*Veterans*
12	**A**	**24th S. af. P.** • Indian Summer • Tides {10.2 9.4	*we thank*
13	M.	**NEW** ● • ☌♂☾ • ⛢ AT ☍ • Tides {10.5 9.4	*as pull cords*
14	Tu.	☌☿☾ • UK's King Charles III born, 1948 • {10.7 —	*we yank*
15	W.	America Recycles Day • Astronomer Sir William Herschel born, 1738 • {9.4 10.8	*to start up*
16	Th.	☾ RUNS LOW • *Skylab 4* launched, 1973 • {9.3 10.8	*ye olde*
17	Fr.	St. Hugh of Lincoln • Deadly tornado outbreak spawned 55 in Ill. and Ind., 2013	*snowblower*
18	Sa.	St. Hilda of Whitby • ☌♂☉ • ☌♇☾ • Astronaut Alan Shepard born, 1923	*in temps*
19	**A**	**25th S. af. P.** • U.S. pres. Abraham Lincoln delivered Gettysburg Address, 1863	*getting*
20	M.	☌♄☾ • *Gratitude is the heart's memory.* • {9.1 10.0	*lower and*
21	Tu.	☾ AT PERIG. • *Nov. 19–21:* The "Long Storm" dropped 18" snow on N.Y.C., 1798 • {9.3 9.9	*lower.*
22	W.	☾ ON EQ. • ☌♆☾ • Wiley Post, 1st pilot to fly solo around world, born, 1898	*Time for*
23	Th.	St. Clement • **THANKSGIVING DAY** • Tides {10.2 9.9	*some turkey,*
24	Fr.	☾ AT ☊ • Baseball player Steve Yeager born, 1948 • Pilot reported UFO, north Baffin Island, Nunavut, 2018	*but*
25	Sa.	☌♃☾ • Naturalist Kenneth Brugger, finder of Mex. winter home of monarch butterflies, died, 1998	*rain*
26	**A**	**26th S. af. P.** • ☌⛢☾ • Thelma Chalifoux 1st Métis woman to become Canadian senator, Alta., 1997	
27	M.	**FULL BEAVER** ○ • *A soft answer turneth away wrath.* • Tides {11.3 9.8	*and snow*
28	Tu.	1st U.S. automobile race held, Chicago, Ill., 1895 • {11.2 —	*lurky.*
29	W.	☾ RIDES HIGH • Writer C. S. Lewis born, 1898 • {9.6 10.9	*Mild,*
30	Th.	St. Andrew • 1st solar eclipse known to be recorded (Ireland), 3340 B.C. • {9.3 10.5	*child!*

Farmer's Calendar

When nor'easters send Atlantic predator fish streaming south, winter flounder—aka mud dabs, blackbacks, lemon sole—begin their own migration, easing in from deep water to bays and estuaries from the Gulf of St. Lawrence to North Carolina. Protected from frigid water by "antifreeze" proteins in their blood, they'll spawn in winter, their eggs sinking unlike the buoyant offspring of most marine fish.

Winter flounder rest on the bottom, venturing higher in the water column less frequently than most members of the order. Early in their lives, their left eye migrates to the right side of their heads. Lying on their white blind sides, they're camouflaged against (or in) mud or sand. The first, and only, thing you're likely to see is their bulging eyes.

These fish lack the sharp teeth of their cousins, halibut and fluke, and their thick lips are permanently puckered, as if waiting for a kiss.

Few fish make better table fare, and now is the time to pursue them. Use small, long-shank hooks. Sea worms work best, but garden worms are nearly as effective and easier to come by. Flounders like bright colors, so paint your sinkers red.

DECEMBER 2023

SKY WATCH: All this month, Jupiter is visible at night. Saturn, now solely an evening star, stands on the meridian due south at nightfall, in Aquarius. A bright star far to Saturn's lower left is the 1st-magnitude star Fomalhaut. During December's first few mornings, Venus—a morning star—guides observers to Virgo's blue main star, Spica, to its right. The 13th brings the year's best meteor shower, the Geminids, under perfect, moonless, dark conditions. Rural observers can see a meteor a minute at any time of night. On the 17th, the Moon dangles below Saturn before moving on to meet Jupiter on the 21st and 22nd. Winter in the Northern Hemisphere begins with the solstice on the night of the 21st at 10:27 P.M. EST.

☽ LAST QUARTER	5th day 12:49 A.M.	☽ FIRST QUARTER	19th day 1:39 P.M.
● NEW MOON	12th day 6:32 P.M.	○ FULL MOON	26th day 7:33 P.M.

All times are given in Eastern Standard Time.

GET THESE PAGES WITH TIMES SET TO YOUR ZIP CODE VIA ALMANAC.COM/2024.

DAY OF YEAR	DAY OF MONTH	DAY OF WEEK	☀ RISES H.M.	RISE KEY	☀ SETS H.M.	SET KEY	LENGTH OF DAY H.M.	SUN FAST M.	SUN DECLINATION ° ′	HIGH TIDE TIMES BOSTON		☽ RISES H.M.	RISE KEY	☽ SETS H.M.	SET KEY	☽ ASTRON. PLACE	☽ AGE
335	1	Fr.	6:53	E	4:13	A	9 20	27	21 s. 49	1½	1¾	7:59	B	10:57	E	GEM	18
336	2	Sa.	6:54	E	4:12	A	9 18	26	21 s. 59	2½	2½	9:05	B	11:29	E	CAN	19
337	3	A	6:56	E	4:12	A	9 16	26	22 s. 07	3¼	3¼	10:08	C	11:55	E	LEO	20
338	4	M.	6:57	E	4:12	A	9 15	26	22 s. 15	4	4¼	11:11	C	12:17	D	LEO	21
339	5	Tu.	6:58	E	4:12	A	9 14	25	22 s. 23	5	5	—	-	12:36	D	LEO	22
340	6	W.	6:59	E	4:12	A	9 13	25	22 s. 30	5¾	6	12:12	D	12:54	D	VIR	23
341	7	Th.	6:59	E	4:12	A	9 13	24	22 s. 37	6½	7	1:14	D	1:12	C	VIR	24
342	8	Fr.	7:00	E	4:11	A	9 11	24	22 s. 44	7¼	7¾	2:17	E	1:31	C	VIR	25
343	9	Sa.	7:01	E	4:11	A	9 10	23	22 s. 50	8	8½	3:23	E	1:53	B	VIR	26
344	10	A	7:02	E	4:11	A	9 09	23	22 s. 55	8¾	9½	4:32	E	2:20	B	LIB	27
345	11	M.	7:03	E	4:12	A	9 09	23	23 s. 00	9½	10¼	5:44	E	2:54	B	LIB	28
346	12	Tu.	7:04	E	4:12	A	9 08	22	23 s. 05	10¼	11	6:57	E	3:37	A	SCO	0
347	13	W.	7:05	E	4:12	A	9 07	22	23 s. 09	11	11¾	8:07	E	4:33	A	OPH	1
348	14	Th.	7:05	E	4:12	A	9 07	21	23 s. 13	11¾	—	9:08	E	5:41	B	SAG	2
349	15	Fr.	7:06	E	4:12	A	9 06	21	23 s. 16	12½	12½	9:58	E	6:58	B	SAG	3
350	16	Sa.	7:07	E	4:13	A	9 06	20	23 s. 19	1¼	1½	10:37	E	8:17	C	CAP	4
351	17	A	7:08	E	4:13	A	9 05	20	23 s. 21	2¼	2¼	11:08	E	9:36	C	CAP	5
352	18	M.	7:08	E	4:13	A	9 05	19	23 s. 23	3	3¼	11:34	D	10:51	D	AQU	6
353	19	Tu.	7:09	E	4:14	A	9 05	19	23 s. 24	4	4¼	11:56	D	—	-	AQU	7
354	20	W.	7:09	E	4:14	A	9 05	18	23 s. 25	5	5¼	12:18	C	12:05	D	PSC	8
355	21	Th.	7:10	E	4:15	A	9 05	18	23 s. 26	6	6½	12:40	C	1:18	E	PSC	9
356	22	Fr.	7:10	E	4:15	A	9 05	17	23 s. 26	7	7½	1:04	B	2:31	E	ARI	10
357	23	Sa.	7:11	E	4:16	A	9 05	17	23 s. 25	7¾	8½	1:33	B	3:45	E	ARI	11
358	24	A	7:11	E	4:16	A	9 05	16	23 s. 24	8¾	9½	2:07	A	4:58	E	TAU	12
359	25	M.	7:12	E	4:17	A	9 05	16	23 s. 23	9½	10¼	2:50	A	6:09	E	TAU	13
360	26	Tu.	7:12	E	4:17	A	9 05	15	23 s. 21	10½	11	3:41	A	7:13	E	TAU	14
361	27	W.	7:12	E	4:18	A	9 06	15	23 s. 19	11¼	11¾	4:40	A	8:08	E	AUR	15
362	28	Th.	7:13	E	4:19	A	9 06	14	23 s. 16	11¾	—	5:44	B	8:53	E	GEM	16
363	29	Fr.	7:13	E	4:20	A	9 07	14	23 s. 12	12½	12½	6:50	B	9:28	E	CAN	17
364	30	Sa.	7:13	E	4:20	A	9 07	13	23 s. 09	1¼	1¼	7:55	C	9:56	E	CAN	18
365	31	A	7:13	E	4:21	A	9 08	13	23 s. 04	2	2	8:58	C	10:19	E	LEO	19

To use this page, see p. 116; for Key Letters, see p. 238. LIGHT = A.M. BOLD = P.M. 2024

DECEMBER

Hark! on the frozen ear of night, / The sleighs with silver bells—
On yonder hill top's snowy height, / The merry music swells.
–Richard George Holland

DAY OF MONTH	DAY OF WEEK	DATES, FEASTS, FASTS, ASPECTS, TIDE HEIGHTS, AND WEATHER	
1	Fr.	*Always put the saddle on the right horse.* • Tides {9.0 / 10.1	*C-c-c-cold*
2	Sa.	St. Viviana • Skier Bode Miller won his 33rd World Cup race, 2011 • {8.7 / 9.7	*and spitting,*
3	**A**	**1st S. of Advent** • *Pioneer 10* spacecraft's closest approach to Jupiter (EST), 1973	*snow*
4	M.	☾ at apo. • ☿ gr. elong. (21° east) • National Cookie Day (U.S.) • Tides {8.4 / 8.9	*showers*
5	Tu.	Six U.S. Navy planes (Flight 19 and Training 49) disappeared over Bermuda Triangle, 1945 • {8.4 / 8.7	*hitting,*
6	W.	St. Nicholas • ☾ on eq. • ♆ stat. • 1st U.S. presidential address via radio, 1923	*then*
7	Th.	St. Ambrose • Chanukah begins at sundown • NATIONAL PEARL HARBOR REMEMBRANCE DAY	*the*
8	Fr.	☾ at ☋ • Bank of Canada announced human rights activist Viola Desmond to appear on $10 note, 2016	*real*
9	Sa.	☌♀☾ • "Weary Willie" clown Emmett Kelly born, 1898 • {9.5 / 8.7	*heavy stuff.*
10	**A**	**2nd S. of Advent** • Treaty of Paris officially ended Spanish-American war, 1898	*Chill*
11	M.	Astronomer Annie Jump Cannon born, 1863 • Tides {10.3 / 9.0	*abating, more*
12	Tu.	OUR LADY OF GUADALUPE • NEW ● • ☌♂☾ • ☿ STAT.	*snow waiting.*
13	W.	St. Lucia • ☾ runs low • *Apollo 17*'s lunar rover reached 11.18 mph, setting record, 1972	*Enough!*
14	Th.	Halcyon Days begin. • ☌☿☾ • Canadian Capt. Paul Triquet's WWII valor earned him later Victoria Cross, 1943	
15	Fr.	☌♇☾ • Leaning Tower of Pisa reopened after 11 years of repair, Italy, 2001 • {9.4 / 11.2	*Flakes with*
16	Sa.	☾ at perig. • Boston Tea Party, 1773 • Tides {9.5 / 11.1	*mildness;*
17	**A**	**3rd S. of Advent** • ☌♄☾ • Tides {9.5 / 10.8	*snowstorm*
18	M.	*A fire hard to kindle indicates bad weather.* • Tides {9.6 / 10.4	*with wildness—*
19	Tu.	☌♆☾ • Beware the Pogonip. • Writer Emily Brontë died, 1848 • {9.7 / 10.0	*Oh, well!*
20	W.	Ember Day • ☾ on eq. • At 81+, Queen Elizabeth II became oldest monarch in UK history, 2007	*Clear*
21	Th.	St. Thomas • WINTER SOLSTICE • ☾ at ☊ • Tides {10.0 / 9.4	*sky*
22	Fr.	Ember Day • ☌♃☾ • ☿ in inf. ☌ • Tides {10.3 / 9.2	*for*
23	Sa.	Ember Day • ☌⛢☾ • *A Visit From St. Nicholas* 1st published, 1823 • {10.5 / 9.2	*Rudolph's*
24	**A**	**4th S. of Advent** • Entrepreneur Johns Hopkins died, 1873 • {10.7 / 9.2	*flight for*
25	M.	**Christmas** • 2.6" snow, Tucson, Ariz., 1987 • Tides {10.8 / 9.2	*Noël!*
26	Tu.	St. Stephen • BOXING DAY (CANADA) • FIRST DAY OF KWANZAA • FULL COLD ○ • ☾ rides high	
27	W.	St. John • ☌☿♂ • Aeronautics pioneer Sir George Cayley born, 1773	*Freezing and*
28	Th.	Holy Innocents • Endangered Species Act (U.S.) became law, 1973	*snow showers*
29	Fr.	Isaac Roberts's photo of Great Nebula in Andromeda (M31) 1st to show its spiral structure, 1888	*galore—*
30	Sa.	*One touch of nature makes the whole world kin.* –Shakespeare • {8.9 / 10.0	*Now we leap*
31	**A**	**1st S. af. Ch.** • ♃ stat. • Singer Donna Summer born, 1948	*to 2024!*

Farmer's Calendar

House mice, ship stowaways from Eurasia, infest human dwellings. Our cleaner, woodland-dwelling natives—white-footed mice—merely visit. If you live anywhere from Nova Scotia to Virginia and west to the Rockies, they are likely to enter your camp or house like poltergeists when the first frosts stiffen the grass.

Trying to block them is futile. By starlight, they always find openings unseen and unknown. You may see one of these creatures in the light of the dying fire, flowing over floor and hearth, pausing to preen its fur and tail, twitching its impossibly long whiskers, and fixing you with huge, obsidian eyes.

Your "polterguest" may even play music for you, especially if leaves have blown in through a door or window. For reasons not understood, they'll drum on them with their paws, creating a melodious buzz.

White-footed mice provide a service to forests by excreting spores of fungi that they eat. These fungi enhance the ability of trees to take up necessary nutrients.

Because these animals don't hibernate, they need a warm place. Beware: They'll poop, may chew soap, and can carry illnesses such as Lyme disease.

JANUARY

SKY WATCH: The year begins with Jupiter as the sky's brightest "star," high in the southeast at nightfall, while Saturn hovers in the lower half of the southwestern sky. Saturn's glorious rings—now almost edgewise to our view—can be seen through any telescope with more than 30× magnification; observe the Ringed Planet early, as it is too low to be seen after 7:00 P.M. Earth stands closest to the Sun (at perihelion) on the 2nd at 8:00 P.M. The Moon floats above Saturn on the 13th and below it on the 14th, before forming a close conjunction with Jupiter on the 18th. In the predawn sky, Venus, in Scorpius, is best seen in the east from 6:00 to 6:30 A.M., with Mercury to its lower left until the 27th. Both are extremely low, as is Mars when it joins Mercury on the morning of the 27th.

☽ **LAST QUARTER** 3rd day 10:30 P.M.	● **FIRST QUARTER** 17th day 10:53 P.M.	
● **NEW MOON** 11th day 6:57 A.M.	○ **FULL MOON** 25th day 12:54 P.M.	

All times are given in Eastern Standard Time.

GET THESE PAGES WITH TIMES SET TO YOUR ZIP CODE VIA ALMANAC.COM/2024.

DAY OF YEAR	DAY OF MONTH	DAY OF WEEK	☼ RISES H. M.	RISE KEY	☼ SETS H. M.	SET KEY	LENGTH OF DAY H. M.	SUN FAST M.	SUN DECLINATION ° '	HIGH TIDE TIMES BOSTON		☽ RISES H. M.	RISE KEY	☽ SETS H. M.	SET KEY	☽ ASTRON. PLACE	☽ AGE
1	1	M.	7:13	E	4:22	A	9 09	12	23 s. 00	2½	2¾	**10:00**	D	10:39	D	LEO	20
2	2	Tu.	7:13	E	4:23	A	9 10	12	22 s. 54	3¼	3½	**11:01**	D	10:58	D	LEO	21
3	3	W.	7:13	E	4:24	A	9 11	11	22 s. 49	4	4¼	—	-	11:15	C	VIR	22
4	4	Th.	7:13	E	4:25	A	9 12	11	22 s. 43	4¾	5¼	12:02	E	11:34	C	VIR	23
5	5	Fr.	7:13	E	4:26	A	9 13	11	22 s. 36	5½	6	1:05	E	11:54	B	VIR	24
6	6	Sa.	7:13	E	4:27	A	9 14	10	22 s. 29	6½	7	2:12	E	**12:18**	B	LIB	25
7	7	**G**	7:13	E	4:28	A	9 15	10	22 s. 22	7¼	8	3:21	E	**12:47**	B	LIB	26
8	8	M.	7:13	E	4:29	A	9 16	9	22 s. 14	8¼	8¾	4:34	E	**1:25**	A	SCO	27
9	9	Tu.	7:13	E	4:30	A	9 17	9	22 s. 06	9	9¾	5:46	E	**2:15**	A	OPH	28
10	10	W.	7:13	E	4:31	A	9 18	8	21 s. 57	9¾	10½	6:52	E	**3:19**	A	SAG	29
11	11	Th.	7:12	E	4:32	A	9 20	8	21 s. 48	10¾	11¼	7:48	E	**4:34**	B	SAG	0
12	12	Fr.	7:12	E	4:33	A	9 21	8	21 s. 38	11½	—	8:32	E	**5:56**	B	CAP	1
13	13	Sa.	7:12	E	4:34	A	9 22	7	21 s. 28	12¼	12¼	9:07	E	**7:18**	C	CAP	2
14	14	**G**	7:11	E	4:35	A	9 24	7	21 s. 18	1	1¼	9:36	E	**8:37**	D	AQU	3
15	15	M.	7:11	E	4:36	A	9 25	7	21 s. 07	1¾	2	10:00	D	**9:54**	D	AQU	4
16	16	Tu.	7:10	E	4:38	A	9 28	6	20 s. 56	2¾	3	10:22	C	**11:09**	E	PSC	5
17	17	W.	7:10	E	4:39	A	9 29	6	20 s. 44	3½	4	10:45	C	—	-	PSC	6
18	18	Th.	7:09	E	4:40	B	9 31	6	20 s. 32	4½	5	11:08	B	**12:23**	E	PSC	7
19	19	Fr.	7:09	E	4:41	B	9 32	5	20 s. 20	5½	6	11:35	B	**1:36**	E	ARI	8
20	20	Sa.	7:08	E	4:42	B	9 34	5	20 s. 07	6½	7¼	**12:07**	B	**2:49**	E	TAU	9
21	21	**G**	7:08	E	4:44	B	9 36	5	19 s. 54	7½	8¼	**12:46**	A	**4:00**	E	TAU	10
22	22	M.	7:07	E	4:45	B	9 38	4	19 s. 40	8½	9¼	**1:34**	A	**5:05**	E	TAU	11
23	23	Tu.	7:06	E	4:46	B	9 40	4	19 s. 26	9¼	10	**2:30**	A	**6:03**	E	AUR	12
24	24	W.	7:05	E	4:47	B	9 42	4	19 s. 12	10¼	10¾	**3:33**	A	**6:50**	E	GEM	13
25	25	Th.	7:05	E	4:49	B	9 44	4	18 s. 57	10¾	11½	**4:38**	B	**7:28**	E	CAN	14
26	26	Fr.	7:04	E	4:50	B	9 46	3	18 s. 42	11½	—	**5:43**	B	**7:58**	E	CAN	15
27	27	Sa.	7:03	E	4:51	B	9 48	3	18 s. 27	12	12¼	**6:47**	C	**8:23**	E	LEO	16
28	28	**G**	7:02	E	4:53	B	9 51	3	18 s. 12	12¾	12¾	**7:50**	C	**8:43**	D	LEO	17
29	29	M.	7:01	E	4:54	B	9 53	3	17 s. 56	1¼	1½	**8:51**	D	**9:02**	D	LEO	18
30	30	Tu.	7:00	E	4:55	B	9 55	3	17 s. 39	2	2¼	**9:51**	D	**9:20**	C	VIR	19
31	31	W.	6:59	E	4:56	B	9 57	3	17 s. 23	2½	2¾	**10:53**	E	**9:37**	C	VIR	20

JANUARY

JANUARY HATH 31 DAYS

We are standing on the threshold, we are in the opened door,
We are treading on a borderland we have never trod before.
–Anonymous

DAY OF MONTH	DAY OF WEEK	DATES, FEASTS, FASTS, ASPECTS, TIDE HEIGHTS, AND WEATHER	
1	M.	Holy Name • NEW YEAR'S DAY • ☾ AT APO. • ☿ STAT. • Tides {8.6/9.2	*New Year's*
2	Tu.	⊕ AT PERIHELION • *Luna-1,* 1st spacecraft to escape Earth's gravity, launched, 1959	*freeze,*
3	W.	☾ ON EQ. • Maya Angelou (American Women series) U.S. quarter released, 2022 • {8.6/8.5	*if you*
4	Th.	St. Elizabeth Ann Seton • ☾ AT ☋ • Teacher Louis Braille born, 1809 • {8.7/8.2	*please!*
5	Fr.	Twelfth Night • U.S. Brig. Gen. Zebulon Montgomery Pike born, 1779 • Tides {8.8/8.0	*Snow is*
6	Sa.	Epiphany • *At Twelfth Day, the days are lengthened a cock's stride.* • {9.0/8.0	*piling,*
7	G	1st S. af. Ep. • Orthodox Christmas (Julian) • Distaff Day • {9.3/8.1	*plow*
8	M.	Plough Monday • ☌♀☾ • Entertainer Elvis Presley born, 1935 • {9.8/8.4	*drivers*
9	Tu.	☌☿☾ • Runner Tom Longboat died, 1949 • Tides {10.2/8.7	*smiling.*
10	W.	☾ RUNS LOW • ☌♂☾ • *A good action is never thrown away.* • {10.7/9.1	*Let's all*
11	Th.	NEW ● • ☌♇☾ • Inventor Gail Borden died, 1874 • {11.2/9.5	*recall*
12	Fr.	☿ GR. ELONG. (24° WEST) • N.Y. Jets defeated Baltimore Colts, 16–7, in Super Bowl III, 1969	*a brave*
13	Sa.	St. Hilary • ☾ AT PERIG. • Discovery of 45,500-year-old painting in Sulawesi cave announced, 2021	
14	G	2nd S. af. Ep. • ☌♄☾ • Tides {10.1/11.5	*man's dream:*
15	M.	MARTIN LUTHER KING JR.'S BIRTHDAY • ☌♆☾ • 1st optical pulsar ID'd, 1969	*The King*
16	Tu.	☾ ON EQ. • Artist Andrew Wyeth died, 2009 • {10.4/10.6	*of*
17	W.	☾ AT ☊ • U.S. statesman Benjamin Franklin born, 1706 • Tides {10.4/10.0	*kindness*
18	Th.	☌♃☾ • Sale of pre-sliced bread banned in U.S. (law rescinded March 8), WWII, 1943	*reigns*
19	Fr.	National Popcorn Day • ☌♅☾ • Tides {10.2/8.9	*supreme.*
20	Sa.	☌♇☉ • 1st bridge in U.S. to cross Columbia River opened, Wenatchee, Wash., 1908 • {10.1/8.6	*A*
21	G	3rd S. af. Ep. • Confederate general Thomas "Stonewall" Jackson born, 1824	*brief*
22	M.	St. Vincent • ☾ RIDES HIGH • Tides {10.0/8.5	*reprieve,*
23	Tu.	Elizabeth Blackwell 1st woman to receive medical degree, 1849 • Tides {10.1/8.6	*then*
24	W.	Warmest January on record across globe at time, 2020 • Tides {10.1/8.7	*frigid*
25	Th.	Conversion of Paul • FULL WOLF ○ • January thaw typically begins about now.	*eves!*
26	Fr.	Sts. Timothy & Titus • Canadian Red Ensign approved as official flag for govt. buildings, 1924	*Oh,*
27	Sa.	☌☿♂ • ♅ STAT. • 113-lb. 6-oz. black grouper caught, Dry Tortugas, Fla., 1990	*to see*
28	G	Septuagesima • *Every hill has its valley.* • Tides {9.0/9.9	*some*
29	M.	☾ AT APO. • Entrepreneur Oprah Winfrey born, 1954 • Tides {9.0/9.6	*palm*
30	Tu.	☾ ON EQ. • Raccoons mate now. • Tides {9.0/9.3	*tree*
31	W.	☾ AT ☋ • 0°F, San Antonio, Tex., 1949 • Film producer Samuel Goldwyn died, 1974	*leaves!*

Farmer's Calendar

They can be smaller than chocolate sprinkles, smaller even than some coffee grounds. Under a warm January Sun, they stretch over the snow's surface as if some mad grocer had slashed bags of pepper and danced over woods and meadow. Watch closely, and you'll see them launch. They are wingless, harmless snow fleas. Not real fleas, they belong to a group of arthropods called "springtails"—of an order so successful that it has not changed much in 410 million years.

The name "springtail" derives from an appendage under their abdomen, which, when released, can catapult the creature 4 inches into the air—the equivalent of a human jumping across a football field. Throughout North America, they live in leaf litter, bark, and decaying logs—sometimes 100,000 per cubic yard of soil.

There is no "dead of winter," and snow is not sterile. There's an ecosystem on and in it. When even muted sunlight strikes snow during a winter thaw, springtails scurry up from the forest floor to graze on the algae, fungi, bacteria, and decaying organic matter on its surface. Then, when night falls, they all scurry back.

FEBRUARY

SKY WATCH: From the 11th through the 13th, the crescent Moon appears as a smile in dusk's fading twilight—in contrast to the upward-aiming archer's bow orientation in which it can be seen for the rest of the year. Saturn is now too low to observe, but Jupiter remains the night's brightest "star" until 11:00 P.M. A Valentine's Day gift is Jupiter hovering just to the left of the Moon on the 14th, when early risers can also observe Venus above Mars low in the brightening dawn twilight to the southeast. Earth's two nearest planetary neighbors (Venus and Mars) form a close morning conjunction in the southeast from the 20th to the 24th.

◗ **LAST QUARTER** 2nd day 6:18 P.M. ◐ **FIRST QUARTER** 16th day 10:01 A.M.
● **NEW MOON** 9th day 5:59 P.M. ○ **FULL MOON** 24th day 7:30 A.M.

All times are given in Eastern Standard Time.

GET THESE PAGES WITH TIMES SET TO YOUR ZIP CODE VIA ALMANAC.COM/2024.

DAY OF YEAR	DAY OF MONTH	DAY OF WEEK	☀ RISES H. M.	RISE KEY	☀ SETS H. M.	SET KEY	LENGTH OF DAY H. M.	SUN FAST M.	SUN DECLINATION ° '	HIGH TIDE TIMES BOSTON		☾ RISES H. M.	RISE KEY	☾ SETS H. M.	SET KEY	☾ ASTRON. PLACE	☾ AGE
32	1	Th.	6:58	E	4:58	B	10 00	2	17 s. 06	3¼	3½	11:57	E	9:56	B	VIR	21
33	2	Fr.	6:57	E	4:59	B	10 02	2	16 s. 49	4	4½	—	-	10:18	B	VIR	22
34	3	Sa.	6:56	E	5:00	B	10 04	2	16 s. 31	4¾	5½	1:03	E	10:44	B	LIB	23
35	4	**G**	6:55	E	5:02	B	10 07	2	16 s. 13	5¾	6¼	2:13	E	11:17	A	LIB	24
36	5	M.	6:54	D	5:03	B	10 09	2	15 s. 55	6½	7¼	3:23	E	11:59	A	SCO	25
37	6	Tu.	6:53	D	5:04	B	10 11	2	15 s. 37	7½	8¼	4:31	E	12:55	A	OPH	26
38	7	W.	6:51	D	5:06	B	10 15	2	15 s. 18	8½	9¼	5:32	E	2:05	B	SAG	27
39	8	Th.	6:50	D	5:07	B	10 17	2	14 s. 59	9½	10¼	6:22	E	3:24	B	SAG	28
40	9	Fr.	6:49	D	5:08	B	10 19	2	14 s. 40	10¼	11	7:02	E	4:48	C	CAP	0
41	10	Sa.	6:48	D	5:09	B	10 21	2	14 s. 21	11¼	11¾	7:33	E	6:11	C	CAP	1
42	11	**G**	6:47	D	5:11	B	10 24	2	14 s. 01	12	—	8:00	D	7:32	D	AQU	2
43	12	M.	6:45	D	5:12	B	10 27	2	13 s. 41	12½	1	8:24	D	8:51	D	AQU	3
44	13	Tu.	6:44	D	5:13	B	10 29	2	13 s. 21	1½	1¾	8:47	C	10:08	E	PSC	4
45	14	W.	6:43	D	5:15	B	10 32	2	13 s. 01	2¼	2¾	9:11	B	11:24	E	PSC	5
46	15	Th.	6:41	D	5:16	B	10 35	2	12 s. 40	3	3½	9:37	B	—	-	ARI	6
47	16	Fr.	6:40	D	5:17	B	10 37	2	12 s. 20	4	4½	10:08	B	12:39	E	ARI	7
48	17	Sa.	6:38	D	5:19	B	10 41	2	11 s. 59	5	5¾	10:45	A	1:52	E	TAU	8
49	18	**G**	6:37	D	5:20	B	10 43	2	11 s. 38	6	6¾	11:30	A	3:00	E	TAU	9
50	19	M.	6:36	D	5:21	B	10 45	2	11 s. 16	7	8	12:24	A	4:00	E	AUR	10
51	20	Tu.	6:34	D	5:22	B	10 48	2	10 s. 55	8¼	9	1:24	A	4:49	E	GEM	11
52	21	W.	6:33	D	5:24	B	10 51	2	10 s. 33	9	9¾	2:28	B	5:29	E	GEM	12
53	22	Th.	6:31	D	5:25	B	10 54	2	10 s. 12	10	10½	3:34	B	6:01	E	CAN	13
54	23	Fr.	6:30	D	5:26	B	10 56	3	9 s. 50	10½	11	4:38	C	6:27	E	LEO	14
55	24	Sa.	6:28	D	5:27	B	10 59	3	9 s. 28	11¼	11¾	5:41	C	6:49	D	LEO	15
56	25	**G**	6:27	D	5:29	B	11 02	3	9 s. 05	11¾	—	6:42	D	7:08	D	LEO	16
57	26	M.	6:25	D	5:30	B	11 05	3	8 s. 43	12¼	12½	7:43	D	7:26	C	VIR	17
58	27	Tu.	6:23	D	5:31	C	11 08	3	8 s. 20	12¾	1	8:44	E	7:43	C	VIR	18
59	28	W.	6:22	D	5:32	C	11 10	3	7 s. 58	1¼	1¾	9:47	E	8:01	C	VIR	19
60	29	Th.	6:20	D	5:34	C	11 14	4	7 s. 35	2	2¼	10:52	E	8:21	B	VIR	20

FEBRUARY

Outside the shivering ivy clings,
While on the hob the kettle sings.
–William Wilfred Campbell

DAY OF MONTH	DAY OF WEEK	DATES, FEASTS, FASTS, ASPECTS, TIDE HEIGHTS, AND WEATHER	
1	Th.	St. Brigid • Major snow and ice storm ended, Nashville, Tenn., 1951 • Tides {9.0 8.5	*This*
2	Fr.	Candlemas • Groundhog Day • *At Candlemas, Cold come to us.* • {8.9 8.1	*shortest*
3	Sa.	Writer Gertrude Stein born, 1874 • –81.4°F, Snag, Y.T., 1947 • {8.9 7.9	*month*
4	**G**	**Sexagesima** • Distribution of Canadian penny stopped, 2013 • {9.0 7.8	*will*
5	M.	St. Agatha • ☌☿♇ • Botanist John Lindley born, 1799 • Tides {9.3 7.9	*grow by*
6	Tu.	☾ runs low • Woodrow Wilson 1st U.S. president buried in D.C., 1924 • {9.7 8.3	*a day;*
7	W.	☌♀☾ • Basketball player Steve Nash born, 1974 • Tides {10.3 8.8	*pray icy*
8	Th.	☌☿☾ • ☌♂☾ • ☌♇☾ • Tides {10.9 9.4	*winds*
9	Fr.	NEW ● • The Beatles made their U.S. live TV debut, 1964 • Tides {11.4 10.0	*don't*
10	Sa.	LUNAR NEW YEAR (CHINA) • ☾ AT PERIG. • ☌♄☾ • {11.7 10.5	*blow us*
11	**G**	**Quinquagesima** • Barbara Harris 1st female bishop in Anglican Communion, 1989	*away!*
12	M.	☾ ON EQ. • ☌♆☾ • U.S. president Abraham Lincoln born, 1809 • {10.9 11.7	*Sun*
13	Tu.	Shrove Tuesday • ☾ AT ☊ • –2°F, Tallahassee, Fla., 1899 • {11.1 11.2	*sends*
14	W.	Ash Wednesday • VALENTINE'S DAY • ☌♂♇ • Tides {11.1 10.5	*love,*
15	Th.	NATIONAL FLAG OF CANADA DAY • ☌♃☾ • ☌⛢☾ • Social reformer Susan B. Anthony born, 1820	*but*
16	Fr.	73.2% of continental U.S. covered in snow, 2021 • Tides {10.5 9.1	*cold's*
17	Sa.	☌♀♇ • Winter's back breaks. • Artist Raphaelle Peale born, 1774 • {10.0 8.5	*the*
18	**G**	**1st. S. in Lent** • Auguste Bartholdi's statue design for "Liberty enlightening the world" patented, 1879	
19	M.	PRESIDENTS' DAY • ☾ RIDES HIGH • 1st N.Am. sighting of (beached) hoodwinker sunfish, Calif., 2019	*boss.*
20	Tu.	Film critic Gene Siskel died, 1999 • *If today will not, tomorrow may.* • Tides {9.5 8.3	*Heavens*
21	W.	Ember Day • 1st telephone directory published, New Haven, Conn., 1878 • {9.6 8.5	*above,*
22	Th.	☌♀♂ • U.S. president George Washington born, 1732 • Tides {9.8 8.7	*please*
23	Fr.	Ember Day • 1st mass Salk polio vaccine inoculation of children, Pittsburgh, Pa., 1954	*let us*
24	Sa.	St. Matthias • Ember Day • FULL SNOW ○ • Tides {10.0 9.2	*defrost!*
25	**G**	**2nd. S. in Lent** • ☾ AT APO. • Tides {9.9 —	*Sunshine*
26	M.	☾ ON EQ. • Skunks mate now. • 1st spacewalk outside ISS w/o crew member inside, 2004	*fizzles*
27	Tu.	Int'l Polar Bear Day • ☾ AT ☋ • 5-lb. 11-oz. Pacific bonefish caught, Honolulu, Hawaii, 2022	*in a*
28	W.	St. Romanus • ☌☿♄ • ☌♄☉ • ☿ IN SUP. ☌ • {9.5 9.3	*Leap Day*
29	Th.	LEAP DAY • *Leap year was ne'er a good sheep year.* • {9.4 8.9	*drizzle.*

Q: What is the difference between here and there? A: The letter "t"

Farmer's Calendar

Few mushrooms can be collected now. But almost anywhere in North America you are likely to encounter gelatinous fungi with the consistency of marmalade. Collectively, these particular jelly fungi are known as "witch's butter." If you find one in someone else's woods, you have nothing to worry about. But if it grows on your property—especially on your door frame—a witch has hexed you, and to rid yourself of the curse you must pierce and drain it with a sharp stick. Or so proclaim ancient texts.

Several species of witch's butter are edible: Yellow, or golden, jelly fungi (*Tremella mesenterica* and *Naematelia aurantia,* aka *T. aurantia*) prefer hardwood trees with attached bark and parasitize other fungi. Orange jelly fungus (*Dacrymyces chrysospermus,* aka *D. palmatus*) favors conifers, especially those without bark; instead of parasitizing fungi, it decomposes wood.

Witch's butter, known also by the endearing name of "yellow brain fungus," makes a superb base for soups. It has no taste of its own, however. So, after you have prudently dispelled the witch's hex by puncturing and draining it, do resist the temptation to eat it raw.

MARCH

SKY WATCH: Venus remains glued in place as a brilliant morning star all month, low in the southeast at around 6:30 A.M. Look to Venus's right on the 7th, from 5:45 to 6:00 A.M., to see the hair-thin waning crescent Moon—in between them is Mercury. At dawn on the 21st, Venus closely meets Saturn very low in the east; use binoculars for viewing. Between midnight and dawn on the 25th, a penumbral eclipse of the Moon occurs, but this is the type of eclipse in which the appearance of the full Moon doesn't noticeably change. On the 29th at 6:30 A.M., look for Saturn halfway between low and brilliant Venus and higher and much dimmer Mars. Spring begins with the vernal equinox on the 19th at 11:06 P.M. EDT.

☽ LAST QUARTER	3rd day 10:23 A.M.	☽ FIRST QUARTER	17th day 12:11 A.M.
● NEW MOON	10th day 5:00 A.M.	○ FULL MOON	25th day 3:00 A.M.

After 2:00 A.M. on March 10, Eastern Daylight Time is given.

GET THESE PAGES WITH TIMES SET TO YOUR ZIP CODE VIA ALMANAC.COM/2024.

DAY OF YEAR	DAY OF MONTH	DAY OF WEEK	☀ RISES H. M.	RISE KEY	☀ SETS H. M.	SET KEY	LENGTH OF DAY H. M.	SUN FAST M.	SUN DECLINATION ° '	HIGH TIDE TIMES BOSTON		☽ RISES H. M.	RISE KEY	☽ SETS H. M.	SET KEY	☽ ASTRON. PLACE	☽ AGE
61	1	Fr.	6:19	D	5:35	C	11 16	4	7 s. 12	2½	3	11:59	E	8:45	B	LIB	21
62	2	Sa.	6:17	D	5:36	C	11 19	4	6 s. 49	3¼	3¾	—	-	9:14	A	LIB	22
63	3	F	6:15	D	5:37	C	11 22	4	6 s. 26	4	4¾	1:08	E	9:51	A	SCO	23
64	4	M.	6:14	D	5:38	C	11 24	4	6 s. 03	5	5¾	2:16	E	10:40	A	OPH	24
65	5	Tu.	6:12	D	5:40	C	11 28	5	5 s. 40	6	6¾	3:18	E	11:41	A	SAG	25
66	6	W.	6:10	D	5:41	C	11 31	5	5 s. 17	7	8	4:11	E	12:54	B	SAG	26
67	7	Th.	6:09	C	5:42	C	11 33	5	4 s. 53	8	8¾	4:54	E	2:14	B	CAP	27
68	8	Fr.	6:07	C	5:43	C	11 36	5	4 s. 30	9	9¾	5:29	E	3:37	C	CAP	28
69	9	Sa.	6:05	C	5:44	C	11 39	6	4 s. 06	10	10½	5:58	E	5:00	D	AQU	29
70	10	F	7:04	C	6:46	C	11 42	6	3 s. 43	12	—	7:23	D	7:21	D	AQU	0
71	11	M.	7:02	C	6:47	C	11 45	6	3 s. 19	12¼	12¾	7:46	C	8:41	E	PSC	1
72	12	Tu.	7:00	C	6:48	C	11 48	6	2 s. 55	1¼	1½	8:10	C	10:01	E	PSC	2
73	13	W.	6:59	C	6:49	C	11 50	7	2 s. 32	2	2½	8:36	B	11:20	E	ARI	3
74	14	Th.	6:57	C	6:50	C	11 53	7	2 s. 08	2¾	3¼	9:06	B	—	-	ARI	4
75	15	Fr.	6:55	C	6:51	C	11 56	7	1 s. 44	3½	4¼	9:41	A	12:37	E	TAU	5
76	16	Sa.	6:53	C	6:53	C	12 00	7	1 s. 21	4½	5¼	10:25	A	1:50	E	TAU	6
77	17	F	6:52	C	6:54	C	12 02	8	0 s. 57	5½	6¼	11:17	A	2:54	E	TAU	7
78	18	M.	6:50	C	6:55	C	12 05	8	0 s. 33	6½	7½	12:16	A	3:48	E	GEM	8
79	19	Tu.	6:48	C	6:56	C	12 08	8	0 s. 09	7¾	8½	1:20	B	4:31	E	GEM	9
80	20	W.	6:46	C	6:57	C	12 11	9	0 N. 13	8¾	9½	2:25	B	5:05	E	CAN	10
81	21	Th.	6:45	C	6:58	C	12 13	9	0 N. 37	9¾	10¼	3:30	B	5:32	E	LEO	11
82	22	Fr.	6:43	C	6:59	C	12 16	9	1 N. 01	10½	11	4:33	C	5:55	E	LEO	12
83	23	Sa.	6:41	C	7:01	C	12 20	10	1 N. 24	11¼	11½	5:35	C	6:14	D	LEO	13
84	24	F	6:40	C	7:02	C	12 22	10	1 N. 48	11¾	—	6:36	D	6:32	D	VIR	14
85	25	M.	6:38	C	7:03	C	12 25	10	2 N. 11	12	12½	7:37	E	6:50	C	VIR	15
86	26	Tu.	6:36	C	7:04	C	12 28	10	2 N. 35	12¾	1	8:39	E	7:07	C	VIR	16
87	27	W.	6:34	C	7:05	C	12 31	11	2 N. 58	1¼	1½	9:44	E	7:27	B	VIR	17
88	28	Th.	6:33	C	7:06	D	12 33	11	3 N. 22	1¾	2¼	10:51	E	7:49	B	LIB	18
89	29	Fr.	6:31	C	7:07	D	12 36	11	3 N. 45	2¼	3	11:59	E	8:16	B	LIB	19
90	30	Sa.	6:29	C	7:08	D	12 39	12	4 N. 08	3	3½	—	-	8:50	A	SCO	20
91	31	F	6:27	C	7:10	D	12 43	12	4 N. 32	3¾	4½	1:06	E	9:34	A	OPH	21

MARCH

Not too hot nor yet too cold,
Graciously your charms unfold.
–**Eugene Field, of spring**

DAY OF MONTH	DAY OF WEEK	DATES, FEASTS, FASTS, ASPECTS, TIDE HEIGHTS, AND WEATHER	
1	Fr.	St. David • Director Ron Howard born, 1954 • Tides { 9.4 / 8.5	*Still*
2	Sa.	St. Chad • Mount Rainier became national park, Wash., 1899 • Tides { 9.3 / 8.2	*cold,*
3	F	**3rd S. in Lent** • 1st U.S. international airmail delivery, Vancouver, B.C., to Seattle, Wash., 1919	*still*
4	M.	☾ RUNS LOW • Composer Antonio Vivaldi born, 1678 • Comedian John Candy died, 1994	*wet?*
5	Tu.	St. Piran • 13 tornadoes struck Iowa, 2022 • Tides { 9.4 / 8.1	*You bet!*
6	W.	☌♇☾ • Toronto (Upper Canada) incorporated, 1834 • 4" snow in 24 hours, Milton Exp. Station, Fla., 1954	
7	Th.	St. Perpetua • Melvin Garlow 1st scheduled U.S. pilot to log 1,000,000 miles in jet planes, 1959	*Clocks*
8	Fr.	☌☿♆ • ☌♀☾ • ☌♂☾ • Baseball player Joe DiMaggio died, 1999	*ahead:*
9	Sa.	☌♄☾ • Hummingbirds migrate north now. • Tides { 11.4 / 10.7	*Don't forget!*
10	F	**DST BEGINS** • **RAMADAN BEGINS** • **NEW** ● • ☾ AT PERIG. • ☌☿☾ • ☌♆☾	
11	M.	☾ ON EQ. • ☾ AT ☊ • *A Raisin in the Sun* opened on Broadway, N.Y.C., 1959 • { 11.2 / 11.8	*Lawn*
12	Tu.	Inventor George Westinghouse died, 1914 • Tides { 11.6 / 11.5	*busy*
13	W.	☌♃☾ • Major auroral display visible as far south as Cuba, 1989 • { 11.7 / 11.0	*thawin';*
14	Th.	☌♅☾ • *Knowledge without practice makes but half an artist.* • Tides { 11.5 / 10.3	*look*
15	Fr.	Beware the ides of March. • Tides { 11.0 / 9.6	*for*
16	Sa.	Navigator Matthew Flinders born, 1774 • New Grand Ole Opry House opened, Nashville, Tenn., 1974	*shamrocks*
17	F	**5th S. in Lent** • **ST. PATRICK'S DAY** • ☾ RIDES HIGH • ☌♆☉	*upon!*
18	M.	**Orthodox Lent begins** • Daylilies returned to Earth via space shuttle *Discovery,* 1989	*Spring*
19	Tu.	St. Joseph • **VERNAL EQUINOX** • *A late spring is a great blessing.* • { 9.1 / 8.1	*has begun,*
20	W.	Alfred Einstein submitted his theory of general relativity to physics journal, 1916 • Tides { 9.2 / 8.3	*but*
21	Th.	☌♀♄ • Twitter co-founder Jack Dorsey sent out 1st tweet on platform, 2006 • { 9.3 / 8.6	*snowy*
22	Fr.	Nurse Col. Elizabeth Lawrie Smellie born, 1884 • Tides { 9.5 / 8.9	*showers*
23	Sa.	☾ AT APO. • Botanist John Bartram born, 1699 • Tides { 9.6 / 9.3	*not*
24	F	**Palm Sunday** • ☾ ON EQ. • ☿ GR. ELONG. (19° EAST) • { 9.7 / —	*yet*
25	M.	**FULL WORM** ○ • **ECLIPSE** ☾ • *Words are the wings of action.* • { 9.5 / 9.7	*done—*
26	Tu.	☾ AT ☋ • Poet Robert Frost born, 1874 • Tides { 9.7 / 9.6	*big*
27	W.	9.2-magnitude earthquake, Prince William Sound, Alaska, 1964 • Tides { 9.8 / 9.4	*earmuffs*
28	Th.	**Maundy Thursday** • Brewer August Anheuser Busch Jr. born, 1899	*for*
29	Fr.	**Good Friday** • *Mariner 10* completed 1st flyby of Mercury, 1974 • { 9.8 / 8.9	*the*
30	Sa.	Chipmunks emerge from hibernation now. • { 9.7 / 8.6	*Easter*
31	F	**Easter** • Nfld. became Canada's 10th province, 1949 • Tides { 9.6 / 8.3	*Bun!*

Farmer's Calendar

When the first chipmunk peeks over the rim of its winter burrow and scampers across your yard, spring can be only a few days away. In the eastern half of the country (except the extreme South), your harbinger will be the eastern chipmunk. In the West, it will be one of at least 20 species, all strikingly similar. The capacity of a chipmunk's cheeks is prodigious. One load was measured at 70 sunflower seeds, another at 12 acorns. So, it's easy for a chipmunk to empty and cache the entire contents of a bird feeder in 1 hour.

While chipmunks remain underground for most of the winter, they don't sleep through it. They have a bedroom in which they may sleep for several days before getting a snack from their pantry. Chipmunks are fastidious groomers; after eating they'll sit on their haunches, lick the inside of their paws, and rub their faces.

In the language of eastern chipmunks, loud "chips" may indicate alarm. "Chucking" warns of aerial predators. "Trills" indicate pursuit by a predator. But, when you hear an eastern chipmunk steadily chipping for several minutes, it's often simply saying, "I am a chipmunk, and I am here."

APRIL

SKY WATCH: On the 8th, a rare total solar eclipse can be seen from parts of Mexico, the U.S., and Canada. (See "Behold Nature's Grandest Event!," page 158.) Observers are strongly encouraged to travel to where it can be seen as a total eclipse rather than partial one. In early April, Jupiter sinks lower each nightfall until its close proximity to the horizon ends the gas giant's reign as an evening star. On the 6th, the waning crescent Moon forms a triangle with Saturn and Mars low in the east at 6:00 A.M. On the next morning, the thin crescent Moon stands to the right of dazzling Venus at 6:15 A.M. at a very low elevation, which will require an unobstructed view of the eastern horizon for observation.

◑ LAST QUARTER	1st day	11:15 P.M.	◐ FIRST QUARTER	15th day	3:13 P.M.
● NEW MOON	8th day	2:21 P.M.	○ FULL MOON	23rd day	7:49 P.M.

All times are given in Eastern Daylight Time.

GET THESE PAGES WITH TIMES SET TO YOUR ZIP CODE VIA ALMANAC.COM/2024.

DAY OF YEAR	DAY OF MONTH	DAY OF WEEK	☀ RISES H. M.	RISE KEY	☀ SETS H. M.	SET KEY	LENGTH OF DAY H. M.	SUN FAST M.	SUN DECLINATION ° '	HIGH TIDE TIMES BOSTON		☾ RISES H. M.	RISE KEY	☾ SETS H. M.	SET KEY	☾ ASTRON. PLACE	☾ AGE
92	1	M.	6:26	C	7:11	D	12 45	12	4 N. 55	4½	5¼	2:09	E	10:29	A	SAG	22
93	2	Tu.	6:24	C	7:12	D	12 48	12	5 N. 18	5½	6½	3:04	E	11:35	A	SAG	23
94	3	W.	6:22	C	7:13	D	12 51	13	5 N. 41	6½	7½	3:49	E	12:50	B	SAG	24
95	4	Th.	6:21	C	7:14	D	12 53	13	6 N. 04	7¾	8½	4:26	E	2:09	C	CAP	25
96	5	Fr.	6:19	C	7:15	D	12 56	13	6 N. 26	8¾	9½	4:56	E	3:30	C	AQU	26
97	6	Sa.	6:17	C	7:16	D	12 59	14	6 N. 49	9¾	10¼	5:22	D	4:50	D	AQU	27
98	7	**F**	6:15	B	7:17	D	13 02	14	7 N. 11	10¾	11	5:46	D	6:10	E	AQU	28
99	8	M.	6:14	B	7:19	D	13 05	14	7 N. 34	11½	—	6:09	C	7:30	E	PSC	0
100	9	Tu.	6:12	B	7:20	D	13 08	14	7 N. 56	12	12½	6:34	B	8:51	E	PSC	1
101	10	W.	6:10	B	7:21	D	13 11	15	8 N. 18	12¾	1¼	7:02	B	10:11	E	ARI	2
102	11	Th.	6:09	B	7:22	D	13 13	15	8 N. 40	1½	2	7:35	B	11:29	E	TAU	3
103	12	Fr.	6:07	B	7:23	D	13 16	15	9 N. 02	2¼	3	8:16	A	—	-	TAU	4
104	13	Sa.	6:06	B	7:24	D	13 18	15	9 N. 24	3¼	4	9:06	A	12:40	E	TAU	5
105	14	**F**	6:04	B	7:25	D	13 21	16	9 N. 45	4	4¾	10:04	A	1:40	E	AUR	6
106	15	M.	6:02	B	7:27	D	13 25	16	10 N. 07	5	6	11:08	A	2:28	E	GEM	7
107	16	Tu.	6:01	B	7:28	D	13 27	16	10 N. 28	6	7	12:14	B	3:06	E	CAN	8
108	17	W.	5:59	B	7:29	D	13 30	16	10 N. 49	7¼	8	1:20	B	3:36	E	CAN	9
109	18	Th.	5:58	B	7:30	D	13 32	17	11 N. 10	8¼	8¾	2:24	C	4:00	E	LEO	10
110	19	Fr.	5:56	B	7:31	D	13 35	17	11 N. 30	9	9½	3:26	C	4:20	D	LEO	11
111	20	Sa.	5:55	B	7:32	D	13 37	17	11 N. 51	10	10¼	4:27	D	4:39	D	LEO	12
112	21	**F**	5:53	B	7:33	D	13 40	17	12 N. 11	10¾	11	5:28	D	4:56	C	VIR	13
113	22	M.	5:51	B	7:34	D	13 43	17	12 N. 31	11¼	11½	6:30	E	5:14	C	VIR	14
114	23	Tu.	5:50	B	7:36	D	13 46	18	12 N. 51	12	—	7:35	E	5:33	B	VIR	15
115	24	W.	5:48	B	7:37	D	13 49	18	13 N. 11	12	12½	8:41	E	5:54	B	VIR	16
116	25	Th.	5:47	B	7:38	D	13 51	18	13 N. 30	12¾	1¼	9:50	E	6:20	B	LIB	17
117	26	Fr.	5:46	B	7:39	D	13 53	18	13 N. 49	1¼	1¾	10:58	E	6:51	A	SCO	18
118	27	Sa.	5:44	B	7:40	D	13 56	18	14 N. 08	2	2½	—	-	7:32	A	OPH	19
119	28	**F**	5:43	B	7:41	E	13 58	18	14 N. 27	2½	3¼	12:03	E	8:24	A	SAG	20
120	29	M.	5:41	B	7:42	E	14 01	18	14 N. 46	3½	4¼	1:00	E	9:26	B	SAG	21
121	30	Tu.	5:40	B	7:43	E	14 03	19	15 N. 04	4¼	5	1:48	E	10:37	B	SAG	22

Behold the Moon!—whose heavenly alchemy
Turns waves and clouds to silver.
–Park

DAY OF MONTH	DAY OF WEEK	DATES, FEASTS, FASTS, ASPECTS, TIDE HEIGHTS, AND WEATHER	
1	M.	Easter Monday • **ALL FOOLS'** • ☾ RUNS LOW • ☿ STAT. • Nunavut est., 1999	*Foolishly*
2	Tu.	*You can only take out of a bag what was already in it.* • Tides {9.5 {8.2	*assumin'*
3	W.	♂♀♅ • ♂☽☾ • Tsawwassen First Nation Final Agreement came into effect, 2009	*that soon*
4	Th.	North Atlantic Treaty signed, 1949 • Tides {9.9 {9.1	*we'll be*
5	Fr.	♂♂☾ • 26.9" snow, St. John's, Nfld., 1999 • Tides {10.4 {9.8	*bloomin'!*
6	Sa.	♂♄☾ • King Richard I, "the Lionheart," died, 1199 • Tides {10.8 {10.6	*As snow*
7	**F**	2nd S. of Easter • ☾ ON EQ. • ☾ AT PERIG. • ♂♀☾ • ♂♃☾	*reminds*
8	M.	Annunciation[T] • **NEW ●** • **ECLIPSE ☉** • ☾ AT ☊ • ♂☿☾	*us,*
9	Tu.	NASA introduced 1st seven astronauts to press, 1959 • Tides {11.3 {—	*winter's*
10	W.	♂♄ • ♂♃☾ • ♂♂☽ • Safety pin patented, 1849 • {12.0 {11.0	*not yet*
11	Th.	☿ IN INF. ♂ • *Clouds that thunder do not always rain.* • Tides {11.9 {10.6	*behind us.*
12	Fr.	Dr. Peter Safar, "father of CPR," born, 1924 • Poet Gary Soto born, 1952 • {11.5 {10.0	*With*
13	Sa.	☾ RIDES HIGH • U.S. president Thomas Jefferson born, 1743 • Tides {11.0 {9.4	*Tax*
14	**F**	**3rd S. of Easter** • 1st MLB game in Canada, Montreal Expos vs. St. Louis Cardinals, 1969	*Day*
15	M.	George H. Shull, plant geneticist and "father of hybrid corn," born, 1874 • Tides {9.7 {8.4	*looming,*
16	Tu.	Two giant pandas, gift to U.S. from China, arrived at National Zoo, D.C., 1972 • {9.2 {8.2	*last*
17	W.	Geraldine "Jerrie" Mock 1st woman to complete solo flight around world, 1964 • {9.0 {8.3	*snowbanks*
18	Th.	♂♀♀ • Banshee, world's longest inverted roller coaster (4,124'), opened, Mason, Ohio, 2014	*melt,*
19	Fr.	☾ AT APO. • *Little by little, one goes far.* • Tides {9.0 {8.9	*in the*
20	Sa.	♂♃☽ • 106°F, Del Rio, Tex., 1984 • Tides {9.2 {9.2	*chilliest*
21	**F**	**4th S. of Easter** • ☾ ON EQ. • Naturalist John Muir born, 1838 • {9.3 {9.5	*spring*
22	M.	Passover begins at sundown • **EARTH DAY** • ☾ AT ☊ • {9.4 {9.8	*we've*
23	Tu.	St. George • **FULL PINK ○** • Olympic snowboarder Chloe Kim born, 2000 • {9.4 {—	*ever*
24	W.	☿ STAT. • *The Old Farmer's Almanac* founder Robert B. Thomas born, 1766 • {10.0 {9.4	*felt.*
25	Th.	St. Mark • English statesman Oliver Cromwell born, 1599 • Tides {10.1 {9.2	*Dress*
26	Fr.	National Help a Horse Day (U.S.) • Geologist Eduard Suess died, 1914 • Tides {10.2 {9.1	*in*
27	Sa.	Poplars leaf out about now. • 27" snow in 24 hours, Minot, N.Dak., 1984	*layers*
28	**F**	**5th S. of Easter** • ☾ RUNS LOW • Tides {10.1 {8.7	*for*
29	M.	♂♂♅ • Jazz pianist/bandleader Duke Ellington born, 1899 • Tides {10.0 {8.6	*Passover*
30	Tu.	♂♇☾ • Franklin D. Roosevelt 1st U.S. president to appear on TV, 1939 • {9.9 {8.6	*prayers!*

Farmer's Calendar

In early spring, vernal pools—pockets of snowmelt and rain that vanish in the heat of summer—teem with life unseen by most woods wanderers. You can't be sure that you've found a vernal pool until you identify one of its obligate denizens such as fairy shrimp, of an order more ancient than dinosaurs. Under the dappled surface, you may see a translucent creature roughly an inch long materialize. Fairy shrimp glide along, swimming on their backs, breathing and rowing with 11 pairs of legs. They are there because fish are not. Ducks eat fairy shrimp but also serve to unknowingly transport their eggs to other vernal pools.

There are two kinds of eggs—one for times of plenty when males are scarce and one for occasions of low or no water. The first type, from unfertilized females of some species, quickly produce clones. The second, which are actually encysted embryos, are more common and result from male-female unions; these cysts remain viable for years. Development, drainage of wetlands, and other factors are causing the loss of vernal pools and consequent decline of fairy shrimp in much of North America.

MAY

SKY WATCH: This month's action is concentrated in the eastern sky during dawn's twilight. On the 1st at around 5:15 A.M., Saturn stands highest in the east, with Mercury below it and a dim, orange Mars halfway between them. On the 4th, Saturn and Mars stand on opposite sides of the thin, crescent Moon in the brightening twilight. Mars hovers to the upper right of the Moon on the 5th at 5:00 A.M. On the 6th at 5:15 A.M., an unobstructed view of the eastern horizon reveals Mercury to the lower right of the crescent Moon. On the evening of the 15th, the Moon is just above blue Spica, Virgo's brightest star. A gorgeous, super-close Saturn–Moon conjunction unfolds from 4:30 to 5:00 A.M. on the 31st.

☾ LAST QUARTER	1st day 7:27 A.M.	○ FULL MOON	23rd day 9:53 A.M.
● NEW MOON	7th day 11:22 P.M.	☾ LAST QUARTER	30th day 1:13 P.M.
☽ FIRST QUARTER	15th day 7:48 A.M.		

All times are given in Eastern Daylight Time.

GET THESE PAGES WITH TIMES SET TO YOUR ZIP CODE VIA ALMANAC.COM/2024.

DAY OF YEAR	DAY OF MONTH	DAY OF WEEK	☀ RISES H. M.	RISE KEY	☀ SETS H. M.	SET KEY	LENGTH OF DAY H. M.	SUN FAST M.	SUN DECLINATION ° '	HIGH TIDE TIMES BOSTON		☾ RISES H. M.	RISE KEY	☾ SETS H. M.	SET KEY	☾ ASTRON. PLACE	☾ AGE
122	1	W.	5:39	B	7:44	E	14 05	19	15 N. 22	5¼	6	2:26	E	11:53	B	CAP	23
123	2	Th.	5:37	B	7:46	E	14 09	19	15 N. 40	6¼	7	2:57	E	1:11	C	CAP	24
124	3	Fr.	5:36	B	7:47	E	14 11	19	15 N. 57	7¼	8	3:24	D	2:28	D	AQU	25
125	4	Sa.	5:35	B	7:48	E	14 13	19	16 N. 15	8½	9	3:47	D	3:45	D	AQU	26
126	5	**F**	5:33	B	7:49	E	14 16	19	16 N. 32	9½	9¾	4:10	C	5:03	E	PSC	27
127	6	M.	5:32	B	7:50	E	14 18	19	16 N. 48	10¼	10¾	4:33	C	6:22	E	PSC	28
128	7	Tu.	5:31	B	7:51	E	14 20	19	17 N. 05	11¼	11½	4:59	B	7:42	E	ARI	0
129	8	W.	5:30	B	7:52	E	14 22	19	17 N. 21	12	—	5:29	B	9:02	E	ARI	1
130	9	Th.	5:29	B	7:53	E	14 24	19	17 N. 37	12¼	1	6:07	A	10:18	E	TAU	2
131	10	Fr.	5:27	B	7:54	E	14 27	19	17 N. 52	1	1¾	6:53	A	11:25	E	TAU	3
132	11	Sa.	5:26	B	7:55	E	14 29	19	18 N. 08	2	2¾	7:49	A	—	-	AUR	4
133	12	**F**	5:25	B	7:56	E	14 31	19	18 N. 22	2¾	3½	8:53	A	12:20	E	GEM	5
134	13	M.	5:24	B	7:58	E	14 34	19	18 N. 37	3¾	4½	10:00	B	1:03	E	CAN	6
135	14	Tu.	5:23	B	7:59	E	14 36	19	18 N. 51	4½	5¼	11:07	B	1:36	E	CAN	7
136	15	W.	5:22	B	8:00	E	14 38	19	19 N. 05	5½	6¼	12:12	C	2:03	E	LEO	8
137	16	Th.	5:21	B	8:01	E	14 40	19	19 N. 19	6½	7¼	1:15	C	2:25	E	LEO	9
138	17	Fr.	5:20	B	8:02	E	14 42	19	19 N. 32	7½	8	2:17	D	2:44	D	LEO	10
139	18	Sa.	5:19	B	8:03	E	14 44	19	19 N. 45	8¼	8¾	3:18	D	3:02	C	VIR	11
140	19	**F**	5:18	B	8:04	E	14 46	19	19 N. 58	9¼	9½	4:19	E	3:19	C	VIR	12
141	20	M.	5:18	A	8:05	E	14 47	19	20 N. 11	10	10¼	5:23	E	3:37	C	VIR	13
142	21	Tu.	5:17	A	8:06	E	14 49	19	20 N. 23	10¾	10¾	6:29	E	3:58	B	VIR	14
143	22	W.	5:16	A	8:06	E	14 50	19	20 N. 34	11½	11½	7:37	E	4:22	B	LIB	15
144	23	Th.	5:15	A	8:07	E	14 52	19	20 N. 45	12¼	—	8:47	E	4:52	A	LIB	16
145	24	Fr.	5:14	A	8:08	E	14 54	19	20 N. 56	12¼	12¾	9:54	E	5:30	A	SCO	17
146	25	Sa.	5:14	A	8:09	E	14 55	19	21 N. 07	12¾	1½	10:55	E	6:19	A	OPH	18
147	26	**F**	5:13	A	8:10	E	14 57	19	21 N. 17	1½	2¼	11:46	E	7:19	A	SAG	19
148	27	M.	5:12	A	8:11	E	14 59	18	21 N. 27	2¼	3	—	-	8:28	B	SAG	20
149	28	Tu.	5:12	A	8:12	E	15 00	18	21 N. 36	3¼	4	12:27	E	9:44	B	CAP	21
150	29	W.	5:11	A	8:13	E	15 02	18	21 N. 46	4	4¾	1:00	E	11:00	C	CAP	22
151	30	Th.	5:11	A	8:13	E	15 02	18	21 N. 54	5	5¾	1:27	E	12:16	C	AQU	23
152	31	Fr.	5:10	A	8:14	E	15 04	18	22 N. 03	6	6¾	1:51	D	1:31	D	AQU	24

How pleasant the life of a bird must be,
Flitting about in each leafy tree.
–Mary Howitt

DAY OF MONTH	DAY OF WEEK	DATES, FEASTS, FASTS, ASPECTS, TIDE HEIGHTS, AND WEATHER	
1	W.	Sts. Philip & James • May Day • Goddard Space Flight Center established, Greenbelt, Md., 1959	*Buy*
2	Th.	St. Athanasius • Artist/scientist Leonardo da Vinci died, 1519 • Tides 9.9 / 9.2	*fresh*
3	Fr.	☌♄☾ • ♇ stat. • Legally blind Dale Davis bowled perfect game, Alta, Iowa, 2008	*flowers,*
4	Sa.	☾ on Eq. • ☌♂☾ • ☌♆☾ • Tides 10.2 / 10.4	*bake*
5	**F**	Rogation Sunday • Orthodox Easter • ☾ at perig. • ☾ at ☊ • 10.5 / 11.1	*a cake:*
6	M.	☌☿☾ • *Hindenburg* disaster, 1937 • Tides 10.6 / 11.6	*Celebrate,*
7	Tu.	New ● • ☌♀☾ • *A north wind with new Moon will hold until the full.*	*commemorate*
8	W.	St. Julian of Norwich • ☌♃☾ • ☌♅☾ • 10.6 / —	*Mom*
9	Th.	Ascension • ☿ Gr. Elong. (26° West) • Musician Billy Joel born, 1949 • 11.9 / 10.4	*on*
10	Fr.	Anna Jarvis organized Mother's Day observance at Andrews Methodist Episcopal Church, Grafton, Va., 1908	*her*
11	Sa.	Three • ☾ rides high • 2-day Dust Bowl storm blew silt from Great Plains to East Coast, 1934	*special*
12	**F**	Chilly • 1st S. af. Asc. • Mother's Day • Tides 10.7 / 9.2	*date.*
13	M.	Saints • ☌♅☉ • Cranberries in bud now. • 10.2 / 8.8	*Wetness*
14	Tu.	Lewis and Clark expedition began, 1804 • Singer Frank Sinatra died, 1998 • 9.6 / 8.6	*chills us*
15	W.	Mickey Mouse 1st appeared in test screening for short film *Plane Crazy,* 1928 • 9.2 / 8.5	*to the*
16	Th.	Mill River dam break caused deadly flash flood, western Mass., 1874 • Tides 8.9 / 8.6	*core;*
17	Fr.	☾ at apo. • Fire destroyed large section of riverfront, St. Louis, Mo., 1849 • 8.8 / 8.8	*we want*
18	Sa.	☾ on Eq. • ☌♀♅ • ☌♃☉ • Tides 8.7 / 9.1	*sun,*
19	**F**	Whit S. • Pentecost • ☾ at ☋ • Tides 8.8 / 9.4	*not rain*
20	M.	Victoria Day (Canada) • *It is better to begin in the evening than not at all.* • 8.9 / 9.7	*galore!*
21	Tu.	New National Gallery of Canada opened, Ottawa, Ont., 1988 • Tides 8.9 / 10.0	*Windswept*
22	W.	Ember Day • Canadian Space Agency launched 3rd astronaut recruitment campaign, 2008	*lakes are*
23	Th.	Vesak • Full Flower ○ • ☌♀♃ • Tides 9.1 / —	*flecked*
24	Fr.	Ember Day • Queen Victoria born, 1819 • Samuel Morse transmitted 1st telegraphic message, 1844	*with*
25	Sa.	St. Bede • Ember Day • ☾ runs low • Painter Rosa Bonheur died, 1899	*foam, as*
26	**F**	Trinity • 1st public elevator in Eiffel Tower opened, Paris, France, 1889 • 10.5 / 9.0	*thunder*
27	M.	Memorial Day, observed • ☌♇☾ • Reformer Julia Ward Howe born, 1819	*salutes*
28	Tu.	Hockey player Red Horner born, 1909 • Tides 10.5 / 9.1	*those*
29	W.	*Rebuke with soft words and hard arguments.* • 10.4 / 9.3	*who ne'er*
30	Th.	☌☿♅ • 2" hail, Deschutes, Grant, Umatilla counties, Oreg., 2020 • 10.2 / 9.6	*came*
31	Fr.	Visit. of Mary • ☌♄☾ • ☌♆☾ • Tides 10.1 / 9.9	*home.*

Farmer's Calendar

Robert Frost called them "sky flakes" and "flowers that fly and all but sing." Even when snow lingers on the greening earth, they start emerging from overwintering pupae to skip through woodlands, fields, marshes, prairies, and backyards from Atlantic to Pacific and tundra's edge to Gulf shores. They are azures—quarter-size butterflies dusted with cobalt scales.

Lepidopterists have recently discovered that what they'd been calling the "spring azure" may be at least a half-dozen species or subspecies. There is indeed a spring azure—one of our earliest emerging butterflies, whose flight period ends in May or early June and whose pupae go into diapause (a pause in development) until the following spring. Then there's the paler summer azure that, in most of its range, starts flying in May or June and produces up to three generations before its last flight period in autumn. Among other recently discovered varieties are the cherry gall azure, Appalachian azure, holly azure, and hops azure. If you see a diminutive blue butterfly during the flight periods of spring and summer azures, photograph it: You may have a new species.

JUNE

SKY WATCH: On the 1st at 4:30 A.M., look for the crescent Moon halfway between Saturn and Mars. Both planets share the same 1st-magnitude brightness. Due east on the mornings of the 2nd and 3rd, Mars is the bright orange "star" near the Moon at 4:30 A.M. After the 15th, Jupiter returns as a morning star due east at 4:30 A.M. On the 30th, Mars hovers halfway between the crescent Moon and brilliant Jupiter, a sight best seen at around 4:45 A.M. Summer in the Northern Hemisphere begins with the solstice on the 20th at 4:51 P.M. EDT. This is the day when the Sun is highest at midday, rises at its leftmost position, and sets at the year's rightmost spot on the horizon.

● **NEW MOON** 6th day 8:38 A.M.   ○ **FULL MOON** 21st day 9:08 P.M.
◑ **FIRST QUARTER** 14th day 1:18 A.M.   ◐ **LAST QUARTER** 28th day 5:53 P.M.

All times are given in Eastern Daylight Time.

GET THESE PAGES WITH TIMES SET TO YOUR ZIP CODE VIA ALMANAC.COM/2024.

DAY OF YEAR	DAY OF MONTH	DAY OF WEEK	☀ RISES H.M.	RISE KEY	☀ SETS H.M.	SET KEY	LENGTH OF DAY H.M.	SUN FAST M.	SUN DECLINATION ° '	HIGH TIDE TIMES BOSTON		☾ RISES H.M.	RISE KEY	☾ SETS H.M.	SET KEY	☾ ASTRON. PLACE	☾ AGE
153	1	Sa.	5:10	A	8:15	E	15 05	18	22 N. 11	7	7½	2:13	D	2:46	E	PSC	25
154	2	**F**	5:09	A	8:16	E	15 07	18	22 N. 18	8	8½	2:35	C	4:02	E	PSC	26
155	3	M.	5:09	A	8:16	E	15 07	17	22 N. 25	9	9½	2:59	B	5:19	E	ARI	27
156	4	Tu.	5:08	A	8:17	E	15 09	17	22 N. 32	10	10¼	3:27	B	6:38	E	ARI	28
157	5	W.	5:08	A	8:18	E	15 10	17	22 N. 39	11	11¼	4:00	A	7:55	E	TAU	29
158	6	Th.	5:08	A	8:19	E	15 11	17	22 N. 45	11¾	—	4:42	A	9:06	E	TAU	0
159	7	Fr.	5:08	A	8:19	E	15 11	17	22 N. 50	12	12¾	5:34	A	10:07	E	TAU	1
160	8	Sa.	5:07	A	8:20	E	15 13	16	22 N. 55	12¾	1½	6:35	A	10:56	E	GEM	2
161	9	**F**	5:07	A	8:20	E	15 13	16	23 N. 00	1½	2¼	7:42	B	11:34	E	GEM	3
162	10	M.	5:07	A	8:21	E	15 14	16	23 N. 05	2½	3¼	8:51	B	—	-	CAN	4
163	11	Tu.	5:07	A	8:21	E	15 14	16	23 N. 08	3¼	4	9:58	B	12:03	E	LEO	5
164	12	W.	5:07	A	8:22	E	15 15	16	23 N. 12	4	4¾	11:02	C	12:27	E	LEO	6
165	13	Th.	5:07	A	8:22	E	15 15	15	23 N. 15	5	5½	12:05	C	12:48	D	LEO	7
166	14	Fr.	5:07	A	8:23	E	15 16	15	23 N. 18	5¾	6¼	1:06	D	1:06	D	VIR	8
167	15	Sa.	5:07	A	8:23	E	15 16	15	23 N. 20	6¾	7¼	2:07	E	1:23	C	VIR	9
168	16	**F**	5:07	A	8:23	E	15 16	15	23 N. 22	7½	8	3:09	E	1:41	C	VIR	10
169	17	M.	5:07	A	8:24	E	15 17	15	23 N. 24	8½	8¾	4:14	E	2:00	B	VIR	11
170	18	Tu.	5:07	A	8:24	E	15 17	14	23 N. 25	9¼	9½	5:21	E	2:23	B	LIB	12
171	19	W.	5:07	A	8:24	E	15 17	14	23 N. 26	10	10¼	6:31	E	2:50	B	LIB	13
172	20	Th.	5:07	A	8:25	E	15 18	14	23 N. 26	11	11	7:40	E	3:25	A	SCO	14
173	21	Fr.	5:08	A	8:25	E	15 17	14	23 N. 26	11¾	11¾	8:44	E	4:10	A	OPH	15
174	22	Sa.	5:08	A	8:25	E	15 17	14	23 N. 25	12½	—	9:40	E	5:07	A	SAG	16
175	23	**F**	5:08	A	8:25	E	15 17	13	23 N. 24	12½	1¼	10:26	E	6:15	B	SAG	17
176	24	M.	5:08	A	8:25	E	15 17	13	23 N. 23	1¼	2	11:02	E	7:31	B	CAP	18
177	25	Tu.	5:09	A	8:25	E	15 16	13	23 N. 21	2	2¾	11:31	E	8:49	C	CAP	19
178	26	W.	5:09	A	8:25	E	15 16	13	23 N. 19	3	3½	11:56	D	10:06	C	AQU	20
179	27	Th.	5:09	A	8:25	E	15 16	12	23 N. 16	3¾	4½	—	-	11:22	D	AQU	21
180	28	Fr.	5:10	A	8:25	E	15 15	12	23 N. 13	4¾	5¼	12:18	D	12:37	D	PSC	22
181	29	Sa.	5:10	A	8:25	E	15 15	12	23 N. 10	5¾	6¼	12:40	C	1:51	E	PSC	23
182	30	**F**	5:11	A	8:25	E	15 14	12	23 N. 06	6¾	7¼	1:03	B	3:06	E	PSC	24

CALENDAR

JUNE

JUNE HATH 30 DAYS

Th' indented bean beneath its clay / Moves cautiously and slow,
Curves its white stem to meet the ray, / And hides its head below.
–Peter Sherston

DAY OF MONTH	DAY OF WEEK	DATES, FEASTS, FASTS, ASPECTS, TIDE HEIGHTS, AND WEATHER	
1	Sa.	☾ ON EQ. • ☾ AT ☊ • EF3 tornado struck western Mass., 2011 • {9.9 10.4	*Storming,*
2	**F**	**Corpus Christi** • ☾ AT PERIG. • ☌♂☾ • Tides {9.9 10.8	*then*
3	M.	*There is no general rule without some exception.* • {9.9 11.2	*warming!*
4	Tu.	☌☿♃ • ☌⛢☾ • ♀ IN SUP. ☌ • Tides {9.9 11.4	*Plants*
5	W.	St. Boniface • ☌☿☾ • ☌♃☾ • Tides {9.9 11.5	*now,*
6	Th.	NEW ● • ☌♀☾ • Canadian Nat'l Railway Co. incorporated, 1919 • D-Day, 1944	*forming,*
7	Fr.	☾ RIDES HIGH • *A good name keeps its luster in the dark.* • Tides {9.7 —	*school*
8	Sa.	Kathy Sullivan 1st woman to reach Challenger Deep, Mariana Trench, 2020 • {11.2 9.5	*bells*
9	**F**	**3rd S. af. P.** • Church of England fully adopted *Book of Common Prayer,* 1549	*ring:*
10	M.	Agriculturist David Lubin born, 1849 • Tides {10.5 9.1	*Caps*
11	Tu.	St. Barnabas • Shavuot begins at sundown • Actor DeForest Kelley died, 1999 • {10.1 8.9	*and*
12	W.	Little League 1st allowed girls, 1974 • Tides {9.6 8.8	*gowns*
13	Th.	Orthodox Ascension • Yellowstone Nat'l Park closed due to flooding and other hazards, Idaho/Mont./Wyo., 2022	*mean*
14	Fr.	St. Basil • FLAG DAY • ☾ ON EQ. • ☾ AT APO. • ☿ IN SUP. ☌	*everything!*
15	Sa.	☾ AT ☋ • Hinkle Tree planted, 79th U.S. Golf Open, Inverness Club, Toledo, Ohio, 1979	*Happy*
16	**F**	**4th S. af. P.** • FATHER'S DAY • Sea turtle biologist Archie Carr born, 1909	*dads*
17	M.	☌☿♀ • 1st successful kidney transplant, Evergreen Park, Ill., 1950 • Tides {8.4 9.4	*wear*
18	Tu.	Edward Fincke 1st U.S. astronaut in space during birth of his child, 2004 • Tides {8.4 9.7	*brand-*
19	W.	JUNETEENTH NATIONAL INDEPENDENCE DAY	*new*
20	Th.	SUMMER SOLSTICE • Singer Lionel Richie born, 1949 • {8.7 10.3	*ties;*
21	Fr.	FULL STRAWBERRY ○ • ☾ RUNS LOW • Astronomer William Morgan died, 1994	*summer*
22	Sa.	St. Alban • Actress Meryl Streep born, 1949 • 1st operational use of Canadarm, 1983	*arrives and*
23	**F**	**5th S. af. P.** • Orthodox Pentecost • Tides {10.8 9.2	*finally dries!*
24	M.	Nativ. John the Baptist • MIDSUMMER DAY • ☌♇☾	*Clouds*
25	Tu.	*Before the storm the crab his briny home / Sidelong forsakes, and strives on land to roam.* • {11.0 9.6	*loom in*
26	W.	Physicist William Thomson, Baron Kelvin, born, 1824 • Tides {10.9 9.8	*flashing skies,*
27	Th.	National Sunglasses Day (U.S.) • ☾ AT PERIG. • ☌♄☾ • {10.7 10.1	*and flowers*
28	Fr.	St. Irenaeus • ☾ ON EQ. • ☌♆☾ • Stonewall Riots began, N.Y.C., 1969	*bloom*
29	Sa.	Sts. Peter & Paul • ☾ AT ☊ • Chef Jordi Cruz Mas born, 1978 • {10.0 10.5	*before*
30	**F**	**6th S. af. P.** • Orthodox All Saints' • ♄ STAT. • Tides {9.7 10.7	*our eyes.*

Farmer's Calendar

The pileated, our largest woodpecker, which can knock 14-inch chips out of even live trees, has spent late winter and early spring mating and nest-building. Now both male and female are incubating eggs and taking care of the nestlings.

Throughout wooded North America, from Nova Scotia down through the eastern United States and west to the Pacific Coast from British Columbia to California, you may hear the maniacal laughter of this crow-size, scarlet-crested bird, which, along with the acorn woodpecker, served as the model for Walter Lantz's Woody Woodpecker.

If you pound a hollow tree with a stick, a male may fly in to defend his territory. When courting, the two birds do much bobbing, head-swinging, wing-flailing, and crest-raising. They'll meet on a limb or trunk; dance; bow; stretch their necks; appear to kiss; and inscribe lazy circles with fluttering, silver-lined wings. The pair mates for life, usually cutting a new nest hole each year. "Pileated," which means "capped," can be pronounced "pile" or "pill." Either way, reports ornithologist John Eastman, "will be wrong in whatever field group one happens to join."

JULY

SKY WATCH: On the morning of the 1st, the thin crescent Moon can be seen above Mars at 4:45 A.M. On the 2nd, the Moon stands between Jupiter and Mars due east at 4:45 A.M. On the 3rd, Jupiter is very close to the Moon, a lovely conjunction best seen due east between 4:45 and 5:00 A.M. On the 14th and 15th, Mars meets Uranus at 4:45 A.M., due east at a comfortable 30 degrees high. Use binoculars to enjoy the orange color of Mars and the green of Uranus, both seen to the right of the Pleiades and upper right of Jupiter. Mars and Jupiter steadily approach each other all month, culminating in the formation of a tight triangle with the crescent Moon on the 30th.

● **NEW MOON** 5th day 6:57 P.M.   ○ **FULL MOON** 21st day 6:17 A.M.

◑ **FIRST QUARTER** 13th day 6:49 P.M.   ◐ **LAST QUARTER** 27th day 10:52 P.M.

All times are given in Eastern Daylight Time.

GET THESE PAGES WITH TIMES SET TO YOUR ZIP CODE VIA ALMANAC.COM/2024.

DAY OF YEAR	DAY OF MONTH	DAY OF WEEK	☀ RISES H. M.	RISE KEY	☀ SETS H. M.	SET KEY	LENGTH OF DAY H. M.	SUN FAST M.	SUN DECLINATION ° ′	HIGH TIDE TIMES BOSTON	☽ RISES H. M.	RISE KEY	☽ SETS H. M.	SET KEY	☽ ASTRON. PLACE	☽ AGE
183	1	M.	5:11	A	8:25	E	15 14	12	23 N. 02	7¾ 8¼	1:28	B	4:23	E	ARI	25
184	2	Tu.	5:12	A	8:25	E	15 13	11	22 N. 57	8¾ 9	1:59	B	5:39	E	ARI	26
185	3	W.	5:13	A	8:24	E	15 11	11	22 N. 52	9¾ 10	2:37	A	6:51	E	TAU	27
186	4	Th.	5:13	A	8:24	E	15 11	11	22 N. 47	10¾ 11	3:24	A	7:55	E	TAU	28
187	5	Fr.	5:14	A	8:24	E	15 10	11	22 N. 41	11¾ 11¾	4:21	A	8:48	E	AUR	0
188	6	Sa.	5:14	A	8:23	E	15 09	11	22 N. 34	12½ —	5:26	A	9:30	E	GEM	1
189	7	**F**	5:15	A	8:23	E	15 08	11	22 N. 28	12½ 1¼	6:34	B	10:03	E	CAN	2
190	8	M.	5:16	A	8:23	E	15 07	11	22 N. 21	1¼ 2	7:42	B	10:29	E	CAN	3
191	9	Tu.	5:16	A	8:22	E	15 06	10	22 N. 13	2 2¾	8:49	C	10:51	D	LEO	4
192	10	W.	5:17	A	8:22	E	15 05	10	22 N. 06	2¾ 3¼	9:52	C	11:10	D	LEO	5
193	11	Th.	5:18	A	8:21	E	15 03	10	21 N. 58	3½ 4	10:54	D	11:27	C	LEO	6
194	12	Fr.	5:19	A	8:21	E	15 02	10	21 N. 49	4¼ 4¾	11:55	D	11:45	C	VIR	7
195	13	Sa.	5:20	A	8:20	E	15 00	10	21 N. 40	5 5½	12:56	E	—	-	VIR	8
196	14	**F**	5:20	A	8:20	E	15 00	10	21 N. 31	6 6¼	1:59	E	12:03	B	VIR	9
197	15	M.	5:21	A	8:19	E	14 58	10	21 N. 21	6¾ 7	3:04	E	12:24	B	VIR	10
198	16	Tu.	5:22	A	8:18	E	14 56	10	21 N. 11	7¾ 8	4:12	E	12:49	B	LIB	11
199	17	W.	5:23	A	8:17	E	14 54	10	21 N. 01	8½ 8¾	5:21	E	1:20	A	SCO	12
200	18	Th.	5:24	A	8:17	E	14 53	9	20 N. 50	9½ 9¾	6:28	E	2:00	A	OPH	13
201	19	Fr.	5:25	A	8:16	E	14 51	9	20 N. 39	10½ 10½	7:29	E	2:51	A	SAG	14
202	20	Sa.	5:26	A	8:15	E	14 49	9	20 N. 28	11¼ 11¼	8:19	E	3:56	A	SAG	15
203	21	**F**	5:26	A	8:14	E	14 48	9	20 N. 16	12 —	8:59	E	5:10	B	SAG	16
204	22	M.	5:27	B	8:13	E	14 46	9	20 N. 04	12 12¾	9:32	E	6:30	B	CAP	17
205	23	Tu.	5:28	B	8:13	E	14 45	9	19 N. 51	1 1½	9:59	D	7:50	C	CAP	18
206	24	W.	5:29	B	8:12	E	14 43	9	19 N. 39	1¾ 2½	10:22	D	9:09	D	AQU	19
207	25	Th.	5:30	B	8:11	E	14 41	9	19 N. 26	2¾ 3¼	10:44	C	10:25	D	AQU	20
208	26	Fr.	5:31	B	8:10	E	14 39	9	19 N. 12	3½ 4	11:07	C	11:41	E	PSC	21
209	27	Sa.	5:32	B	8:09	E	14 37	9	18 N. 58	4½ 5	11:32	B	12:57	E	PSC	22
210	28	**F**	5:33	B	8:08	E	14 35	9	18 N. 44	5½ 5¾	—	-	2:13	E	ARI	23
211	29	M.	5:34	B	8:06	E	14 32	9	18 N. 30	6½ 6¾	12:00	B	3:29	E	ARI	24
212	30	Tu.	5:35	B	8:05	E	14 30	9	18 N. 15	7½ 7¾	12:35	A	4:42	E	TAU	25
213	31	W.	5:36	B	8:04	E	14 28	9	18 N. 00	8½ 8¾	1:19	A	5:48	E	TAU	26

To use this page, see p. 116; for Key Letters, see p. 238. LIGHT = A.M. **BOLD = P.M.**

CALENDAR

THE SEVENTH MONTH • 2024 JULY JULY HATH 31 DAYS

All things on earth, in ocean, or in air
Do in the clouds some rude resemblance find.
–**John Askham**

DAY OF MONTH	DAY OF WEEK	DATES, FEASTS, FASTS, ASPECTS, TIDE HEIGHTS, AND WEATHER	
1	M.	**Canada Day** • ☌♂☾ • 18-month International Geophysical Year began, 1957	*Nighttime*
2	Tu.	☌♅☾ • ♆ stat. • Civil Rights Act (U.S.) signed into law, 1964 • {9.3 10.9	*brightening*
3	W.	Dog Days begin. • ☌♃☾ • *Dog days bright and clear Indicate a happy year.* • {9.2 11.0	*as*
4	Th.	**Independence Day** • ☾ rides high • Writer Nathaniel Hawthorne born, 1804	*fireworks*
5	Fr.	New ● • ⊕ at aphelion • 113°F (45°C), Midale and Yellow Grass, Sask., 1937	*boom,*
6	Sa.	☌♀☾ • Pirate "Capt. Kidd" arrested, Boston, Mass., 1699 • Tides {9.2 —	*joined*
7	**F**	**7th S. af. P.** • First of Muharram begins at sundown • ☌☿☾ • {10.8 9.2	*by*
8	M.	Armadillos mate now. • Chef Wolfgang Puck born, 1949 • {10.6 9.2	*lightning!*
9	Tu.	Traveling at 0.92 ft./sec., Bertie set record for fastest tortoise, Brasside, UK, 2014 • {10.3 9.1	*(Where's*
10	W.	*When a friend asks, there is no tomorrow.* • Tides {10.0 9.1	*the*
11	Th.	National Blueberry Muffin Day (U.S.) • Writer E. B. White born, 1899 • {9.6 9.1	*Moon?)*
12	Fr.	☾ on Eq. • ☾ at ☋ • ☾ at apo. • Webb telescope's 1st images released, 2022	*Storms*
13	Sa.	Cornscateous air is everywhere. • Tides {8.8 9.0	*will*
14	**F**	**8th S. af. P.** • Bastille Day • Folk singer Woody Guthrie born, 1912 • {8.5 9.1	*briefly*
15	M.	St. Swithin • ☌♂♅ • 3"-diameter hail fell, SE Conn., 1799 • {8.2 9.2	*brew,*
16	Tu.	Millennium Park opened, Chicago, Ill., 2004 • {8.1 9.4	*then*
17	W.	Montreal, Que., 1st Canadian city to host Summer Olympics, 1976 • Tides {8.1 9.6	*skies are*
18	Th.	Writer Jane Austen died, 1817 • Hockey player Jamie Benn born, 1989 • {8.3 10.0	*chiefly*
19	Fr.	☾ runs low • *By Love Possessed* 1st scheduled in-flight movie (TWA), 1961 • Tides {8.5 10.4	*blue,*
20	Sa.	"One giant leap for mankind," Apollo 11, 1969 • {8.9 10.8	*prompting*
21	**F**	**9th S. af. P.** • Full Buck ○ • ☌♇☾ • Actor Don Knotts born, 1924 • {9.3 —	
22	M.	St. Mary Magdalene • ☿ Gr. Elong. (27° East) • Tides {11.2 9.7	*pies*
23	Tu.	♇ at ☍ • Astronaut Eileen Collins 1st woman to command space shuttle mission, 1999 • {11.4 10.1	*and*
24	W.	☾ at perig. • ☌♄☾ • Black-eyed Susans in bloom now. • {11.4 10.4	*barbecue.*
25	Th.	Sts. James & Christopher • ☾ on Eq. • ☌♆☾ • {11.2 10.6	*Campers*
26	Fr.	St. Anne • ☾ at ☊ • Van McCoy's "The Hustle" topped U.S. charts amid hustle dance craze, 1975	*be*
27	Sa.	*Be silent and pass for a philosopher.* • Tides {10.4 10.8	*warned:*
28	**F**	**10th S. af. P.** • 1st public auction of Gorgosaurus dinosaur skeleton, 2022	*Watch*
29	M.	St. Martha • ☌♅☾ • Singer "Mama Cass" Elliot died, 1974 • {9.3 10.6	*out*
30	Tu.	☌♂☾ • ☌♃☾ • 33-lb. 8-oz. tripletail caught off Hilton Head, S.C., 2005 • {9.0 10.5	*for*
31	W.	St. Ignatius of Loyola • French became sole official language of Quebec, 1974 • Tides {8.8 10.4	*storms!*

Farmer's Calendar

The profusion of zucchini, eggplants, green peppers, basil leaves, tomatoes, onions, and other vegetables that ripen now render waste a common affliction. You can't eat all of these, so stew them into ratatouille, then freeze in several portions. Size matters with zucchini: It's inverse to quality. But don't compost the giant zucchini; hollow them out and stuff them with cooked ground beef, tomatoes, and onions; top with mozzarella cheese; and bake. Surplus beans can be blanched in boiling water for 3 minutes, plunged into ice water to arrest ripening enzymes, then frozen. Thawed and steamed, they'll taste almost fresh. Sauté surplus tomatoes with basil, garlic, and onions; freeze the stew. In the garden, onions started in January now have droopy brown stalks, which means that the bulbs are ready to harvest. Leave them in the sun for 2 days before storing them somewhere dark and cool for 2 weeks.

And always remember to put away tools—a painful lesson that Robert Frost learned only too well: "At the end of the row / I stepped on the toe / Of an unemployed hoe. / It rose in offense / And struck me a blow / In the seat of my sense."

AUGUST

SKY WATCH: On the 1st between 4:30 and 5:00 A.M., look for a lovely triangle in the east composed of Jupiter to the lower left; the orange Taurus star, Aldebaran, to the lower right; and Mars at the upper apex—all to the right of the crescent Moon. From the 1st through the 13th, Mars and Jupiter draw closer together in the predawn sky. From the 13th to the 16th, the two planets are wonderfully close, creating a glorious conjunction. On the 11th and 12th, the Perseid meteor shower is not affected by the Moon, which sets before midnight—just as the most intense meteors appear. On the 27th, look for the crescent Moon to the upper left of dazzling Jupiter in the east, especially between 4:30 and 5:30 A.M.

● **NEW MOON** 4th day 7:13 A.M.   ○ **FULL MOON** 19th day 2:26 P.M.
◐ **FIRST QUARTER** 12th day 11:19 A.M.   ◑ **LAST QUARTER** 26th day 5:26 A.M.

All times are given in Eastern Daylight Time.

GET THESE PAGES WITH TIMES SET TO YOUR ZIP CODE VIA ALMANAC.COM/2024.

DAY OF YEAR	DAY OF MONTH	DAY OF WEEK	☼ RISES H.M.	RISE KEY	☼ SETS H.M.	SET KEY	LENGTH OF DAY H.M.	SUN FAST M.	SUN DECLINATION ° '	HIGH TIDE TIMES BOSTON		☾ RISES H.M.	RISE KEY	☾ SETS H.M.	SET KEY	☾ ASTRON. PLACE	☾ AGE
214	1	Th.	5:37	B	8:03	E	14 26	9	17 N. 45	9¾	9¾	2:12	A	6:44	E	AUR	27
215	2	Fr.	5:38	B	8:02	E	14 24	10	17 N. 30	10½	10¾	3:14	A	7:28	E	GEM	28
216	3	Sa.	5:39	B	8:01	E	14 22	10	17 N. 14	11½	11½	4:21	B	8:04	E	CAN	29
217	4	**F**	5:40	B	7:59	E	14 19	10	16 N. 58	12¼	—	5:29	B	8:31	E	CAN	0
218	5	M.	5:41	B	7:58	E	14 17	10	16 N. 41	12¼	12¾	6:36	C	8:54	E	LEO	1
219	6	Tu.	5:42	B	7:57	E	14 15	10	16 N. 25	1	1½	7:41	C	9:14	D	LEO	2
220	7	W.	5:43	B	7:56	E	14 13	10	16 N. 08	1½	2	8:43	D	9:32	D	LEO	3
221	8	Th.	5:45	B	7:54	E	14 09	10	15 N. 51	2¼	2¾	9:44	D	9:49	C	VIR	4
222	9	Fr.	5:46	B	7:53	E	14 07	10	15 N. 33	3	3¼	10:45	E	10:07	C	VIR	5
223	10	Sa.	5:47	B	7:52	E	14 05	11	15 N. 15	3¾	4	11:47	E	10:26	B	VIR	6
224	11	**F**	5:48	B	7:50	E	14 02	11	14 N. 58	4½	4¾	12:50	E	10:49	B	VIR	7
225	12	M.	5:49	B	7:49	D	14 00	11	14 N. 39	5¼	5½	1:56	E	11:16	B	LIB	8
226	13	Tu.	5:50	B	7:47	D	13 57	11	14 N. 21	6	6¼	3:04	E	11:51	A	LIB	9
227	14	W.	5:51	B	7:46	D	13 55	11	14 N. 02	7	7¼	4:11	E	—	-	SCO	10
228	15	Th.	5:52	B	7:44	D	13 52	11	13 N. 44	8	8¼	5:14	E	12:37	A	OPH	11
229	16	Fr.	5:53	B	7:43	D	13 50	12	13 N. 25	9	9¼	6:08	E	1:34	A	SAG	12
230	17	Sa.	5:54	B	7:41	D	13 47	12	13 N. 05	9¾	10	6:53	E	2:44	B	SAG	13
231	18	**F**	5:55	B	7:40	D	13 45	12	12 N. 46	10¾	11	7:29	E	4:02	B	CAP	14
232	19	M.	5:56	B	7:38	D	13 42	12	12 N. 26	11½	11¾	7:58	E	5:24	C	CAP	15
233	20	Tu.	5:57	B	7:37	D	13 40	13	12 N. 06	12¼	—	8:24	D	6:45	C	AQU	16
234	21	W.	5:58	B	7:35	D	13 37	13	11 N. 46	12½	1¼	8:47	C	8:05	D	AQU	17
235	22	Th.	5:59	B	7:34	D	13 35	13	11 N. 26	1½	2	9:10	C	9:24	E	PSC	18
236	23	Fr.	6:00	B	7:32	D	13 32	13	11 N. 06	2¼	2¾	9:34	B	10:42	E	PSC	19
237	24	Sa.	6:01	B	7:31	D	13 30	14	10 N. 45	3¼	3½	10:02	B	12:01	E	ARI	20
238	25	**F**	6:02	B	7:29	D	13 27	14	10 N. 24	4¼	4½	10:35	A	1:19	E	ARI	21
239	26	M.	6:04	B	7:27	D	13 23	14	10 N. 03	5¼	5½	11:17	A	2:34	E	TAU	22
240	27	Tu.	6:05	B	7:26	D	13 21	15	9 N. 42	6¼	6½	—	-	3:42	E	TAU	23
241	28	W.	6:06	B	7:24	D	13 18	15	9 N. 21	7¼	7½	12:07	A	4:41	E	AUR	24
242	29	Th.	6:07	B	7:22	D	13 15	15	9 N. 00	8½	8¾	1:06	A	5:29	E	GEM	25
243	30	Fr.	6:08	B	7:21	D	13 13	15	8 N. 38	9½	9½	2:11	B	6:06	E	GEM	26
244	31	Sa.	6:09	B	7:19	D	13 10	16	8 N. 16	10¼	10½	3:19	B	6:35	E	CAN	27

AUGUST

AUGUST HATH 31 DAYS

'Twas summer, and parched by the merciless drouth,
The earth gaped with hope long deferred.
–**Abel Beach**

DAY OF MONTH	DAY OF WEEK	DATES, FEASTS, FASTS, ASPECTS, TIDE HEIGHTS, AND WEATHER	
1	Th.	Lammas Day • ☾ RIDES HIGH • U.S. Olympic gold medalist and diver Sammy Lee born, 1920	*Bees*
2	Fr.	*When it rains in August, it rains honey and wine.* • {8.9 10.4	*are*
3	Sa.	National Basketball Association formed from merger, 1949 • Tides {9.0 10.5	*humming,*
4	**F**	**11th S. af. P.** • NEW ● • ☿ STAT. • Tides {9.1 —	*thunder*
5	M.	**Civic Holiday (Canada)** • ☌☿☾ • ☌♀☾ • Tides {10.4 9.2	*rumbles—*
6	Tu.	**Transfiguration** • ☌☿♀ • Poet Alfred, Lord Tennyson, born, 1809	*school's*
7	W.	Explorer La Salle's *Griffon* launched on Great Lakes, to vanish later that year, 1679 • {10.1 9.3	*a-coming,*
8	Th.	**St. Dominic** • ☾ ON EQ. • ☾ AT ☋ • ☾ AT APO. • {9.8 9.4	*children*
9	Fr.	Ragweed in bloom. • Richard Nixon resigned as U.S. president, 1974 • Tides {9.5 9.3	*grumble.*
10	Sa.	**St. Lawrence** • Ground-breaking ceremony for St. Lawrence Seaway, 1954 • {9.1 9.3	*Humid*
11	**F**	**12th S. af. P.** • Dog Days end. • Tides {8.7 9.2	*days,*
12	M.	232-day MLB baseball strike began, 1994 • Gray squirrels have second litters now. • {8.3 9.1	*lightning*
13	Tu.	Filmmaker Sir Alfred Hitchcock born, 1899 • {8.1 9.2	*flashes,*
14	W.	☌♂♃ • 1st game of Canadian Football League, 1958 • Tides {7.9 9.3	*stay*
15	Th.	**Assumption** • ☾ RUNS LOW • Emperor Napoleon Bonaparte born, 1769	*away*
16	Fr.	Chemist Robert Bunsen died, 1899 • Tides {8.3 10.0	*from*
17	Sa.	Cat Nights commence. • ☌♇☾ • Hurricane Camille made landfall, Miss., 1969 • {8.7 10.6	*curbside*
18	**F**	**13th S. af. P.** • ☿ IN INF. ☌ • Explorer Meriwether Lewis born, 1774	*splashes!*
19	M.	FULL STURGEON ○ • *A mariner must have his eye upon rock and sands as well as upon the North Star.*	*Rain*
20	Tu.	☌♄☾ • Greatest global temperature differential in 1 day (250.2 degrees F, Calif. and Antarctica), 1992	*is*
21	W.	☾ ON EQ. • ☾ AT PERIG. • ☌♆☾ • Hawaii statehood, 1959 • {11.7 10.9	*soaking*
22	Th.	☾ AT ☊ • 1.7 earthquake near Rochester, N.H., 2021 • Tides {11.6 11.2	*but*
23	Fr.	Physician Antonia Novello, 1st woman and Hispanic to serve as U.S. Surgeon General, born, 1944	*puddles*
24	Sa.	**St. Bartholomew** • Pianist Louis Teicher born, 1924 • {10.8 11.2	*are*
25	**F**	**14th S. af. P.** • ☌⛢☾ • *Voyager 2* closest approach to Neptune, 1989	*fun,*
26	M.	Aviator Charles Lindbergh died, 1974 • Hummingbirds migrate south. • {9.6 10.6	*bullfrog's*
27	Tu.	☌♂☾ • ☌♃☾ • ☿ STAT. • Tides {9.0 10.3	*croaking*
28	W.	**St. Augustine of Hippo** • ☾ RIDES HIGH • Polymath Johann Wolfgang von Goethe born, 1749	*will*
29	Th.	**St. John the Baptist** • 13-lb. 3-oz. barred sand bass caught, Huntington Flats, Calif., 1988 • {8.6 10.0	*bring*
30	Fr.	*Good nature is the proper soil upon which virtue grows.* • Tides {8.6 10.0	*back*
31	Sa.	National Trail Mix Day • Actor Richard Gere born, 1949 • Tides {8.8 10.1	*the Sun.*

Farmer's Calendar

Chestnut-flanked and flecked with scarlet spots centered in azure halos, eastern brook trout are gaudy in any season. But as spawning approaches in August, the bellies of males turn sunrise-orange, and the ivory trim on the edges of their bottom fins gets even whiter. These fish are native to the eastern United States and Canada, but they've been stocked all across the continent. The brook trout's scientific name, *Salvelinus fontinalis,* means "dweller of springs." Look for it where cold water tumbles over mossy ledges and curls off through alder runs and boggy meadows. These are not true trout but descendants of oceangoing arctic char landlocked by glaciers.

Populations can adjust to fit the habitat. In big lakes like Superior and Nipigon, such trout can reach 10 pounds in weight. But no perennial rill is too small for these glacial relics: Adults can be no longer than your thumb. Walk along almost any high-country or north-country stream, and you'll see them. Or maybe when swamp maples blush and woodcock twitter, you'll find them paired up, hovering over gravel in water so clear that you can't tell where it stops and the air begins.

SEPTEMBER

SKY WATCH: On the 8th, Saturn comes to opposition. Surrounded by the dim stars of Aquarius, the planet's rings can be seen as almost edgewise this year. Any telescope using more than 30× magnification will capture its rings. Saturn leaves the far southern regions of the zodiac that it has inhabited for nearly a decade, causing it to be low in the sky and telescopically blurry for U.S. and Canadian observers. On the 17th, a strange partial lunar eclipse is visible from most of the U.S. and Canada. Even at the time of the Moon's maximum obscuration at 10:44 P.M., only 9 percent of it is dark. Fall begins with the autumnal equinox on the 22nd at 8:44 A.M. EDT.

● NEW MOON	2nd day	9:56 P.M.
○ FULL MOON	17th day	10:34 P.M.
◗ FIRST QUARTER	11th day	2:06 A.M.
◖ LAST QUARTER	24th day	2:50 P.M.

All times are given in Eastern Daylight Time.

GET THESE PAGES WITH TIMES SET TO YOUR ZIP CODE VIA ALMANAC.COM/2024.

DAY OF YEAR	DAY OF MONTH	DAY OF WEEK	☀ RISES H. M.	RISE KEY	☀ SETS H. M.	SET KEY	LENGTH OF DAY H. M.	SUN FAST M.	SUN DECLINATION ° '	HIGH TIDE TIMES BOSTON		☽ RISES H. M.	RISE KEY	☽ SETS H. M.	SET KEY	☽ ASTRON. PLACE	☽ AGE
245	1	**F**	6:10	B	**7:17**	D	13 07	16	7 N. 55	11	11¼	4:26	B	**6:59**	E	LEO	28
246	2	M.	6:11	B	**7:16**	D	13 05	16	7 N. 33	11¾	—	5:31	C	**7:20**	D	LEO	0
247	3	Tu.	6:12	C	**7:14**	D	13 02	17	7 N. 10	12	12¼	6:34	C	**7:38**	D	LEO	1
248	4	W.	6:13	C	**7:12**	D	12 59	17	6 N. 48	12½	1	7:35	D	**7:55**	C	VIR	2
249	5	Th.	6:14	C	**7:10**	D	12 56	17	6 N. 26	1¼	1½	8:36	E	**8:12**	C	VIR	3
250	6	Fr.	6:15	C	**7:09**	D	12 54	18	6 N. 04	1¾	2	9:37	E	**8:31**	B	VIR	4
251	7	Sa.	6:16	C	**7:07**	D	12 51	18	5 N. 41	2½	2¾	10:40	E	**8:52**	B	VIR	5
252	8	**F**	6:17	C	**7:05**	D	12 48	18	5 N. 18	3	3¼	11:45	E	**9:17**	B	LIB	6
253	9	M.	6:18	C	**7:03**	D	12 45	19	4 N. 56	3¾	4	12:51	E	**9:48**	A	LIB	7
254	10	Tu.	6:19	C	**7:02**	C	12 43	19	4 N. 33	4¾	4¾	1:57	E	**10:28**	A	SCO	8
255	11	W.	6:20	C	**7:00**	C	12 40	19	4 N. 10	5½	5¾	3:00	E	**11:19**	A	OPH	9
256	12	Th.	6:21	C	**6:58**	C	12 37	20	3 N. 47	6½	6¾	3:57	E	—	-	SAG	10
257	13	Fr.	6:23	C	**6:56**	C	12 33	20	3 N. 24	7½	7¾	4:45	E	**12:22**	A	SAG	11
258	14	Sa.	6:24	C	**6:55**	C	12 31	21	3 N. 01	8½	8¾	5:24	E	**1:34**	B	CAP	12
259	15	**F**	6:25	C	**6:53**	C	12 28	21	2 N. 38	9½	9¾	5:56	E	**2:53**	B	CAP	13
260	16	M.	6:26	C	**6:51**	C	12 25	21	2 N. 15	10¼	10½	6:23	D	**4:14**	C	AQU	14
261	17	Tu.	6:27	C	**6:49**	C	12 22	22	1 N. 52	11	11½	6:47	D	**5:35**	D	AQU	15
262	18	W.	6:28	C	**6:48**	C	12 20	22	1 N. 29	11¾	—	7:10	C	**6:56**	D	PSC	16
263	19	Th.	6:29	C	**6:46**	C	12 17	22	1 N. 05	12¼	12¾	7:34	C	**8:17**	E	PSC	17
264	20	Fr.	6:30	C	**6:44**	C	12 14	23	0 N. 42	1	1½	8:01	B	**9:38**	E	PSC	18
265	21	Sa.	6:31	C	**6:42**	C	12 11	23	0 N. 19	2	2¼	8:33	B	**11:00**	E	ARI	19
266	22	**F**	6:32	C	**6:41**	C	12 09	23	0 s. 04	3	3¼	9:13	A	**12:19**	E	TAU	20
267	23	M.	6:33	C	**6:39**	C	12 06	24	0 s. 27	3¾	4	10:01	A	**1:33**	E	TAU	21
268	24	Tu.	6:34	C	**6:37**	C	12 03	24	0 s. 50	4¾	5	10:58	A	**2:36**	E	TAU	22
269	25	W.	6:35	C	**6:35**	C	12 00	24	1 s. 14	6	6¼	—	-	**3:28**	E	AUR	23
270	26	Th.	6:36	C	**6:33**	C	11 57	25	1 s. 37	7	7¼	12:03	A	**4:08**	E	GEM	24
271	27	Fr.	6:37	C	**6:32**	C	11 55	25	2 s. 00	8	8¼	1:10	B	**4:40**	E	CAN	25
272	28	Sa.	6:39	C	**6:30**	C	11 51	25	2 s. 24	9	9¼	2:17	B	**5:05**	E	CAN	26
273	29	**F**	6:40	C	**6:28**	C	11 48	26	2 s. 47	10	10¼	3:23	C	**5:26**	D	LEO	27
274	30	M.	6:41	C	**6:26**	C	11 45	26	3 s. 10	10½	10¾	4:26	C	**5:45**	D	LEO	28

To use this page, see p. 116; for Key Letters, see p. 238. LIGHT = A.M. **BOLD = P.M.**   2024

THE NINTH MONTH · 2024 **SEPTEMBER** SEPTEMBER HATH 30 DAYS

Now the last load, now merry tune the pipe,
To celebrate the harvest—rich and ripe.
–**John Evans**

DAY OF MONTH	DAY OF WEEK	DATES, FEASTS, FASTS, ASPECTS, TIDE HEIGHTS, AND WEATHER	
1	**F**	**15th S. af. P.** • ☌☿☾ • ⛢ STAT. • Tides {9.0 / 10.1	*Labor*
2	M.	**Labor Day** • **NEW** ● • 103.3°F (39.6°C), Lytton, B.C., 2022 • Tides {9.2 / 10.1	*Day*
3	Tu.	Writer Sarah Orne Jewett born, 1849 • Astronaut Peggy Whitson spent 665 days in space over career, setting record, 2017	*is*
4	W.	☾ ON EQ. • ☿ GR. ELONG. (18° WEST) • Bob Barker began hosting *The Price is Right*, 1972 • {10.0 / 9.6	*mild*
5	Th.	☾ AT ☋ • ☾ AT APO. • ☌♀☾ • Tides {9.9 / 9.6	*and*
6	Fr.	"Yellow Day" in Northeast, due to yellow haze from Thumb Fire in Mich., 1881 • {9.6 / 9.6	*gray,*
7	Sa.	Nolan Ryan 1st to pitch baseball at more than 100 mph (100.8), 1974 • {9.3 / 9.6	*neighborhood*
8	**F**	**16th S. af. P.** • ♄ AT ☍ • Composer Richard Strauss died, 1949	*kids*
9	M.	Cranberry bog harvest begins, Cape Cod, Mass. • Tides {8.6 / 9.3	*have a*
10	Tu.	*When the rain is from the east, / It is for four-and-twenty hours at least.* • Tides {8.3 / 9.2	*last chance*
11	W.	**Patriot Day** • Explorer Henry Hudson anchored at Lenape island of Mannahatta (now Manhattan, N.Y.C.), 1609	
12	Th.	☾ RUNS LOW • Agricultural scientist Norman Ernest Borlaug died, 2009 • Tides {7.9 / 9.3	*to play.*
13	Fr.	International Chocolate Day • Tides {8.1 / 9.7	*Back to*
14	Sa.	Holy Cross • ☌♇☾ • Jasper Forest Park (later, Jasper Nat'l Park) established, Alta., 1907	*school,*
15	**F**	**17th S. af. P.** • Entomologist Frank Eugene Lutz born, 1879 • Tides {9.1 / 10.7	*it's rainy*
16	M.	Actress Lauren Bacall born, 1924 • Tides {9.9 / 11.2	*and cool.*
17	Tu.	**FULL HARVEST** ○ • **ECLIPSE** ☾ • ☌♄☾ • {10.6 / 11.5	*Here's*
18	W.	Ember Day • ☾ ON EQ. • ☾ AT ☊ • ☾ AT PERIG. • ☌♆☾ • {11.2 / —	*sun*
19	Th.	Astronomer Jean-Baptiste-Joseph Delambre born, 1749 • Tides {11.6 / 11.7	*instead,*
20	Fr.	Ember Day • ♆ AT ☍ • *He who will eat the kernel must crack the nut.* • {11.5 / 11.9	*as*
21	Sa.	St. Matthew • Ember Day • *MAVEN* spacecraft entered orbit around Mars, 2014 • {11.1 / 11.8	*leaves*
22	**F**	**18th S. af. P.** • **AUTUMNAL EQUINOX** • Harvest Home • ☌⛢☾ • {10.6 / 11.4	*turn*
23	M.	☌♃☾ • Judy Reed thought to be 1st Black woman to receive U.S. patent, 1884 • {9.9 / 10.9	*red,*
24	Tu.	☾ RIDES HIGH • Large meteoric fireball caught on video, N.C., 2021 • Tides {9.3 / 10.4	*then*
25	W.	☌♂☾ • Architect Francesco Borromini born, 1599 • Tides {8.8 / 9.9	*rain*
26	Th.	Woodchucks hibernate now. • Nurseryman John Chapman (aka "Johnny Appleseed") born, 1774	*will*
27	Fr.	St. Vincent de Paul • 33-lb. 4-oz. coho salmon caught, Salmon River, Pulaski, N.Y., 1989 • {8.5 / 9.6	*chase*
28	Sa.	Canada won Summit Series hockey game vs. Soviet Union, 6 to 5, 1972 • Tides {8.7 / 9.6	*you*
29	**F**	**19th S. af. P.** • *Fruit ripens not well in the shade.* • {9.0 / 9.7	*back*
30	M.	St. Michael[T] • ☿ IN SUP. ☌ • USS *Nautilus,* world's 1st nuclear submarine, commissioned, 1954	*to bed.*

Farmer's Calendar

Any morning now, your lawn may be draped with silver fabric so fine that it seems to have no mass. Chaucer called the phenomenon one of the unsolved mysteries of the universe. Subsequent investigators attributed it to evaporated dew. It took a pig to pin it down: "The baby spiders felt the warm updraft. One spider climbed to the top of the fence. Then it did something that came as a great surprise to Wilbur. The spider stood on its head, pointed its spinnerets in the air, and let loose a cloud of fine silk. The silk formed a balloon. As Wilbur watched, the spider let go of the fence and rose into the air." This passage from E. B. White's *Charlotte's Web* remains one of the best descriptions of how many juvenile spiders disperse.

Darwin observed silkriding spiderlings when his ship was 60 miles off Argentina. In May 1884, 9 months after one of the planet's most powerful volcanic explosions sterilized the island of Krakatoa, scientists found only one life form—a spider. Census traps mounted on airplanes have caught spiderlings at 15,000 feet. Occasionally, they'll ascend to the jet stream and cross oceans.

OCTOBER

SKY WATCH: On the 2nd, an annular solar eclipse resembling a ring of fire can be seen in Patagonia, the southernmost regions of Chile and Argentina. Venus returns as an evening star early in the month and hovers next to the waxing crescent Moon on the 5th. On the 14th, the Moon meets Saturn at nightfall and is visible throughout the night. Jupiter rises by 9:30 P.M. at midmonth and meets the Moon on the 20th. The Moon hovers above Mars starting at midnight on the 22nd and is to the left of Mars on the 23rd. From the 24th to the 28th, look for Venus, now brightening to magnitude –4.0, standing above Scorpius's famous orange-color "heart," Antares. With an unobstructed horizon, the pair can be seen low in the southwest at around 6:00 P.M.

● NEW MOON	2nd day 2:49 P.M.	○ FULL MOON	17th day 7:26 A.M.
☽ FIRST QUARTER	10th day 2:55 P.M.	☾ LAST QUARTER	24th day 4:03 A.M.

All times are given in Eastern Daylight Time.

GET THESE PAGES WITH TIMES SET TO YOUR ZIP CODE VIA ALMANAC.COM/2024.

DAY OF YEAR	DAY OF MONTH	DAY OF WEEK	☼ RISES H. M.	RISE KEY	☼ SETS H. M.	SET KEY	LENGTH OF DAY H. M.	SUN FAST M.	SUN DECLINATION ° '	HIGH TIDE TIMES BOSTON		☾ RISES H. M.	RISE KEY	☾ SETS H. M.	SET KEY	☾ ASTRON. PLACE	☾ AGE
275	1	Tu.	6:42	C	6:25	C	11 43	26	3 s. 34	11¼	11½	5:28	D	6:02	C	LEO	29
276	2	W.	6:43	C	6:23	C	11 40	27	3 s. 57	11¾	—	6:29	D	6:19	C	VIR	0
277	3	Th.	6:44	C	6:21	C	11 37	27	4 s. 20	12¼	12¼	7:30	E	6:37	C	VIR	1
278	4	Fr.	6:45	D	6:20	C	11 35	27	4 s. 43	12¾	1	8:32	E	6:57	B	VIR	2
279	5	Sa.	6:46	D	6:18	C	11 32	28	5 s. 06	1¼	1½	9:36	E	7:21	B	LIB	3
280	6	**F**	6:47	D	6:16	C	11 29	28	5 s. 29	2	2	10:42	E	7:50	A	LIB	4
281	7	M.	6:48	D	6:14	C	11 26	28	5 s. 52	2¾	2¾	11:47	E	8:26	A	SCO	5
282	8	Tu.	6:50	D	6:13	C	11 23	28	6 s. 15	3¼	3½	12:51	E	9:12	A	OPH	6
283	9	W.	6:51	D	6:11	C	11 20	29	6 s. 38	4¼	4¼	1:49	E	10:08	A	SAG	7
284	10	Th.	6:52	D	6:09	C	11 17	29	7 s. 00	5	5¼	2:39	E	11:15	B	SAG	8
285	11	Fr.	6:53	D	6:08	C	11 15	29	7 s. 23	6	6¼	3:20	E	—	-	SAG	9
286	12	Sa.	6:54	D	6:06	C	11 12	29	7 s. 45	7	7¼	3:53	E	12:29	B	CAP	10
287	13	**F**	6:55	D	6:05	B	11 10	30	8 s. 08	8	8¼	4:21	E	1:47	C	CAP	11
288	14	M.	6:56	D	6:03	B	11 07	30	8 s. 30	9	9¼	4:46	D	3:05	C	AQU	12
289	15	Tu.	6:58	D	6:01	B	11 03	30	8 s. 52	9¾	10¼	5:09	D	4:25	D	AQU	13
290	16	W.	6:59	D	6:00	B	11 01	30	9 s. 14	10½	11	5:33	C	5:45	E	PSC	14
291	17	Th.	7:00	D	5:58	B	10 58	31	9 s. 36	11½	—	5:58	B	7:06	E	PSC	15
292	18	Fr.	7:01	D	5:57	B	10 56	31	9 s. 58	12	12¼	6:28	B	8:29	E	ARI	16
293	19	Sa.	7:02	D	5:55	B	10 53	31	10 s. 19	12¾	1	7:05	A	9:52	E	ARI	17
294	20	**F**	7:04	D	5:54	B	10 50	31	10 s. 41	1¾	1¾	7:51	A	11:12	E	TAU	18
295	21	M.	7:05	D	5:52	B	10 47	31	11 s. 02	2½	2¾	8:47	A	12:23	E	TAU	19
296	22	Tu.	7:06	D	5:51	B	10 45	31	11 s. 23	3½	3¾	9:51	A	1:22	E	AUR	20
297	23	W.	7:07	D	5:49	B	10 42	32	11 s. 44	4½	4¾	10:59	B	2:07	E	GEM	21
298	24	Th.	7:08	D	5:48	B	10 40	32	12 s. 05	5½	5¾	—	-	2:42	E	CAN	22
299	25	Fr.	7:10	D	5:46	B	10 36	32	12 s. 25	6½	6¾	12:08	B	3:10	E	CAN	23
300	26	Sa.	7:11	D	5:45	B	10 34	32	12 s. 46	7½	7¾	1:14	C	3:32	E	LEO	24
301	27	**F**	7:12	D	5:43	B	10 31	32	13 s. 06	8½	8¾	2:18	C	3:51	D	LEO	25
302	28	M.	7:13	D	5:42	B	10 29	32	13 s. 26	9¼	9½	3:20	D	4:09	D	LEO	26
303	29	Tu.	7:14	D	5:41	B	10 27	32	13 s. 46	10	10¼	4:21	D	4:26	C	VIR	27
304	30	W.	7:16	D	5:39	B	10 23	32	14 s. 05	10¾	11	5:22	E	4:44	C	VIR	28
305	31	Th.	7:17	D	5:38	B	10 21	32	14 s. 25	11¼	11¾	6:24	E	5:03	B	VIR	29

To use this page, see p. 116; for Key Letters, see p. 238. LIGHT = A.M. BOLD = P.M.   2024

THE TENTH MONTH • 2024 **OCTOBER** OCTOBER HATH 31 DAYS

Thou, from whose unseen presence the leaves dead
Are driven, like ghosts from an enchanter fleeing.
–Percy Bysshe Shelley, of the west wind

DAY OF MONTH	DAY OF WEEK	DATES, FEASTS, FASTS, ASPECTS, TIDE HEIGHTS, AND WEATHER	
1	Tu.	☾ ON EQ. • Yosemite Nat'l Park established, 1890 • {9.5 9.8	*Witness autumn's*
2	W.	Rosh Hashanah begins at sundown • NEW ● • ECLIPSE ⊙ • ☾ AT ☋ • ☾ AT APO. • ☌☿☾	
3	Th.	Watch for banded woolly bear caterpillars now.	*convocation:*
4	Fr.	St. Francis of Assisi • World Animal Day • {9.6 9.9	*blue*
5	Sa.	☌♀☾ • Shawnee chief Tecumseh died (War of 1812), 1813 • Tides {9.4 9.9	*skies*
6	F	**20th S. af. P.** • Groundbreaking for Red River Floodway, Winnipeg, Man., 1962	*and*
7	M.	1st images rec'd of Moon's far side, 1959 • Tornado struck near Jenner, Alta., 2017 • {8.8 9.7	*leafy*
8	Tu.	Actress Sigourney Weaver born, 1949 • *The mill does not grind with water that is past.*	*conflagration.*
9	W.	☾ RUNS LOW • ♃ STAT. • Meteorite hit car in Peekskill, N.Y., 1992 • Tides {8.2 9.4	*A*
10	Th.	Little brown bats hibernate now. • Tides {8.1 9.4	*football*
11	Fr.	Yom Kippur begins at sundown • ☌♇☾ • ♇ STAT. • {8.2 9.5	*win,*
12	Sa.	NATIONAL FARMER'S DAY • Basketball player Wilt Chamberlain died, 1999	*congratulations!*
13	F	**21st S. af. P.** • TV personality Ed Sullivan died, 1974 • Tides {9.0 10.1	*Cool, with*
14	M.	COLUMBUS DAY, OBSERVED • INDIGENOUS PEOPLES' DAY • THANKSGIVING DAY (CANADA) • ☌♄☾	
15	Tu.	☾ ON EQ. • ☌♆☾ • Green Bay Packers/Denver Broncos played football in blizzard, Denver, Colo., 1984	
16	W.	Sukkoth begins at sundown • ☾ AT ☊ • ☾ AT PERIG. • Tides {11.2 11.2	*rain in*
17	Th.	St. Ignatius of Antioch • FULL HUNTER'S ○ • Composer Frederic Chopin died, 1849	*isolation,*
18	Fr.	St. Luke • St. Luke's little summer. • Tides {12.1 —	*then*
19	Sa.	☌♅☾ • Outdoorsman Eddie Bauer born, 1899 • Tides {11.1 12.1	*sun*
20	F	**22nd S. af. P.** • "Black Friday Storm" sank 4 ships on Lake Erie, 1916 • {10.7 11.9	*spreads*
21	M.	☾ RIDES HIGH • ☌♃☾ • Joseph Aspdin granted UK patent for Portland cement, 1824	*a warm*
22	Tu.	*The dews of the evening industriously shun, / They're the tears of the sky for the loss of the sun.* • {9.6 10.8	*sensation.*
23	W.	St. James of Jerusalem • ☌♂☾ • Musician Weird Al Yankovic born, 1959 • {9.1 10.1	*Stockpile*
24	Th.	Bar-tailed godwit flew 8,425 miles nonstop (Alaska to Tasmania), setting record, 2022 • {8.7 9.6	*candy*
25	Fr.	Frederic Edwin Church's "The Icebergs" auctioned for $2.5 million, setting record for U.S. paintings, 1979	*for*
26	Sa.	Timber rattlesnakes move to winter dens. • {8.6 9.2	*Halloween*
27	F	**23rd S. af. P.** • Nat'l Council of Women of Canada formed, Toronto, Ont., 1893	*Nation:*
28	M.	Sts. Simon & Jude • Discovery of 3.4-billion-yr.-old 1-cell fossils announced in *Science* journal, 1977	*Cool*
29	Tu.	☾ ON EQ. • ☾ AT ☋ • ☾ AT APO. • Tides {9.4 9.3	*night*
30	W.	*Fear has no understanding.* • Tides {9.7 9.3	*tricks bring*
31	Th.	All Hallows' Eve • Reformation Day • Nev. statehood, 1864	*consternation!*

Farmer's Calendar

From Newfoundland south to Delaware and northwest to Alaska the leaves of the quaking aspen, our most widely distributed tree, dance in the wind, glowing neon yellow as they catch the rays of the low-arcing Sun. Unlike other trees, aspens also photosynthesize through their bark, so they continue to produce energy and sugar in winter.

Seventy years is ancient for a quaking aspen tree. Aspens, however, should be thought of not as trees but as root systems. The "trees" are clones sent up by the main part of the organism. Inject dye or a radioactive isotope into one tree, and it will show up in another. From this perspective, the quaking aspen is the largest and heaviest organism on Earth. In Minnesota, one clone root system has been estimated to be 8,000 years old. In Utah, a 100-acre root system weighs an estimated 6,600 tons and is thought to be 80,000 years old.

Preferring moist sites, aspen doesn't do well in dry habitats such as Yellowstone National Park. So why is there so much of it there? Botanist Roy Renkin thinks that aspen got started in the park when the climate there was cold and wet—that is, during the last Ice Age.

CALENDAR

NOVEMBER

SKY WATCH: On the 1st, Mars, now a brilliant magnitude 0, rises at midnight just below the Gemini twins, Castor and Pollux, with dazzling Jupiter high above them. On the 10th, don't miss the very close conjunction of the Moon and Saturn, with the best viewing between 9:30 and 10:00 P.M. Jupiter, now rising at around 6:30 P.M., hangs just below the Moon on the 16th. On this same night, Uranus comes to opposition, at its closest and brightest appearance of the year. Just to the right of the famous Pleiades star cluster, Uranus's magnitude of 5.6 means that it can be seen as a faint star from dark rural sites, although binoculars make for easier viewing of its green color. On the 20th, Mars rises by 9:30 P.M. and hovers next to the Moon.

● NEW MOON	1st day 8:47 A.M.	○ FULL MOON	15th day	4:29 P.M.
◐ FIRST QUARTER	9th day 12:55 A.M.	◑ LAST QUARTER	22nd day	8:28 P.M.

After 2:00 A.M. on November 3, Eastern Standard Time is given.

GET THESE PAGES WITH TIMES SET TO YOUR ZIP CODE VIA ALMANAC.COM/2024.

DAY OF YEAR	DAY OF MONTH	DAY OF WEEK	☼ RISES H. M.	RISE KEY	☼ SETS H. M.	SET KEY	LENGTH OF DAY H. M.	SUN FAST M.	SUN DECLINATION °	'	HIGH TIDE TIMES BOSTON		☾ RISES H. M.	RISE KEY	☾ SETS H. M.	SET KEY	☾ ASTRON. PLACE	☾ AGE
306	1	Fr.	7:18	D	**5:37**	B	10 19	32	14 s.	44	11¾	—	7:27	E	**5:25**	B	VIR	0
307	2	Sa.	7:19	D	**5:36**	B	10 17	32	15 s.	03	12¼	**12½**	8:33	E	**5:53**	A	LIB	1
308	3	**F**	6:21	D	**4:34**	B	10 13	32	15 s.	21	1	**12**	8:39	E	**5:27**	A	SCO	2
309	4	M.	6:22	D	**4:33**	B	10 11	32	15 s.	40	12½	**12½**	9:44	E	**6:10**	A	SCO	3
310	5	Tu.	6:23	E	**4:32**	B	10 09	32	15 s.	58	1¼	**1¼**	10:44	E	**7:03**	A	OPH	4
311	6	W.	6:24	E	**4:31**	B	10 07	32	16 s.	16	2	**2**	11:36	E	**8:06**	A	SAG	5
312	7	Th.	6:26	E	**4:30**	B	10 04	32	16 s.	33	2¾	**2¾**	**12:18**	E	**9:16**	B	SAG	6
313	8	Fr.	6:27	E	**4:29**	B	10 02	32	16 s.	51	3¾	**3¾**	**12:53**	E	**10:30**	B	CAP	7
314	9	Sa.	6:28	E	**4:27**	B	9 59	32	17 s.	08	4½	**4¾**	**1:22**	E	**11:45**	C	CAP	8
315	10	**F**	6:29	E	**4:26**	B	9 57	32	17 s.	24	5½	**5¾**	**1:47**	D	—	-	AQU	9
316	11	M.	6:31	E	**4:25**	B	9 54	32	17 s.	41	6½	**7**	**2:10**	D	1:01	D	AQU	10
317	12	Tu.	6:32	E	**4:24**	B	9 52	32	17 s.	57	7½	**7¾**	**2:32**	C	2:18	D	PSC	11
318	13	W.	6:33	E	**4:24**	B	9 51	31	18 s.	13	8¼	**8¾**	**2:56**	C	3:36	E	PSC	12
319	14	Th.	6:34	E	**4:23**	B	9 49	31	18 s.	28	9¼	**9¾**	**3:23**	B	4:56	E	PSC	13
320	15	Fr.	6:36	E	**4:22**	B	9 46	31	18 s.	43	10	**10¾**	**3:56**	B	6:19	E	ARI	14
321	16	Sa.	6:37	E	**4:21**	B	9 44	31	18 s.	58	10¾	**11½**	**4:38**	A	7:42	E	TAU	15
322	17	**F**	6:38	E	**4:20**	B	9 42	31	19 s.	12	11¾	—	**5:30**	A	8:59	E	TAU	16
323	18	M.	6:39	E	**4:19**	B	9 40	30	19 s.	27	12½	**12½**	**6:32**	A	10:06	E	TAU	17
324	19	Tu.	6:40	E	**4:19**	B	9 39	30	19 s.	40	1¼	**1½**	**7:41**	B	10:59	E	GEM	18
325	20	W.	6:42	E	**4:18**	B	9 36	30	19 s.	54	2¼	**2¼**	**8:52**	B	11:39	E	GEM	19
326	21	Th.	6:43	E	**4:17**	B	9 34	30	20 s.	07	3	**3¼**	**10:01**	C	**12:11**	E	CAN	20
327	22	Fr.	6:44	E	**4:16**	B	9 32	29	20 s.	20	4	**4¼**	**11:07**	C	**12:35**	E	LEO	21
328	23	Sa.	6:45	E	**4:16**	A	9 31	29	20 s.	32	5	**5¼**	—	-	**12:56**	D	LEO	22
329	24	**F**	6:46	E	**4:15**	A	9 29	29	20 s.	44	6	**6¼**	12:11	C	**1:14**	D	LEO	23
330	25	M.	6:48	E	**4:15**	A	9 27	29	20 s.	55	6¾	**7**	1:12	D	**1:31**	C	VIR	24
331	26	Tu.	6:49	E	**4:14**	A	9 25	28	21 s.	07	7½	**8**	2:12	D	**1:49**	C	VIR	25
332	27	W.	6:50	E	**4:14**	A	9 24	28	21 s.	17	8¼	**8¾**	3:14	E	**2:08**	B	VIR	26
333	28	Th.	6:51	E	**4:13**	A	9 22	28	21 s.	28	9	**9½**	4:17	E	**2:29**	B	VIR	27
334	29	Fr.	6:52	E	**4:13**	A	9 21	27	21 s.	38	9½	**10¼**	5:22	E	**2:55**	B	LIB	28
335	30	Sa.	6:53	E	**4:13**	A	9 20	27	21 s.	47	10¼	**11**	6:29	E	**3:27**	A	LIB	29

 To use this page, see p. 116; for Key Letters, see p. 238. LIGHT = A.M. BOLD = P.M.

NOVEMBER

But the dinner—ah! the dinner—words are feeble to portray
What a culinary triumph is achieved Thanksgiving Day!
–**Horatio Alger Jr.**

DAY OF MONTH	DAY OF WEEK	DATES, FEASTS, FASTS, ASPECTS, TIDE HEIGHTS, AND WEATHER	
1	Fr.	All Saints' • NEW ● • Baseball player Fernando Valenzuela born, 1960	*Snowflakes*
2	Sa.	All Souls' • Sadie Hawkins Day • N.Dak. and S.Dak. statehood, 1889 • Tides {9.2 10.1	*fall*
3	**F**	24th S. af. P. • DAYLIGHT SAVING TIME ENDS, 2:00 A.M. • ☌☿☾ • {9.1 10.1	*on*
4	M.	☌♀☾ • Humorist Will Rogers born, 1879 • Tides {8.9 10.0	*people*
5	Tu.	ELECTION DAY • ☾ RUNS LOW • "Cotton candy" lobster caught, Casco Bay, Maine, 2021	*voting*
6	W.	*Sleep is the equalizer of all.* • Tides {8.5 9.8	*(for those*
7	Th.	☌♇☾ • 1st robot-assisted human hip replacement, 1992 • Tides {8.4 9.7	*up*
8	Fr.	Poet John Milton likely died, 1674 • Mont. statehood, 1889 • Tides {8.4 9.6	*north,*
9	Sa.	Canada joined the United Nations, 1945 • Tides {8.6 9.6	*a*
10	**F**	25th S. af. P. • ☌♄☾ • "Charmed quark" discovered, 1974 • {9.0 9.7	*decent*
11	M.	St. Martin of Tours • VETERANS DAY • ☌♆☾ • Wash. statehood, 1889	*coating).*
12	Tu.	Indian Summer • ☾ ON EQ. • ☾ AT ☊ • Tides {10.3 10.2	*Chills*
13	W.	1st modern-day cloud-seeding experiment, Mt. Greylock, Mass., 1946 • Tides {10.9 10.4	*retreat*
14	Th.	☾ AT PERIG. • Home improvement expert Chip Gaines born, 1974 • USS *Nimitz* "Tic Tac" UFO incident, off Calif., 2004	
15	Fr.	FULL BEAVER ○ • ☌⛢☾ • 1st U.S. poultry show began, Boston, Mass., 1849	*from sun*
16	Sa.	♄ STAT. • ⛢ AT ☍ • ☿ GR. ELONG. (23° EAST) • Tides {12.1 10.5	*serene,*
17	**F**	26th S. af. P. • ☌♃☾ • Sculptor Auguste Rodin died, 1917 • {12.0 —	*then*
18	M.	St. Hilda of Whitby • ☾ RIDES HIGH • Ballerina Evelyn Cisneros-Legate born, 1958	*rain*
19	Tu.	World's first surviving septuplets born, Des Moines, Iowa, 1997 • Tides {9.8 11.1	*and heat*
20	W.	☌♂☾ • *What has been, may be.* • Tides {9.4 10.5	*go to*
21	Th.	World Hello Day • N.C. statehood, 1789 • {9.0 9.9	*extremes!*
22	Fr.	Humane Society of the United States founded, 1954 • 15 tornadoes hit Ind., 1992 • {8.7 9.4	*Prepare*
23	Sa.	St. Clement • 1st smartphone (IBM Simon) introduced, COMDEX show, Las Vegas, Nev., 1992	*a feast,*
24	**F**	27th S. af. P. • Artist Henri de Toulouse-Lautrec born, 1864	*and as*
25	M.	☾ ON EQ. • ☾ AT ☋ • ☿ STAT. • Tides {8.8 8.6	*ice*
26	Tu.	☾ AT APO. • *Evening red and morning gray Help the traveler on his way.* • {9.0 8.6	*melts,*
27	W.	Mauna Loa eruption began, Hawaii, 2022 • {9.3 8.7	*do give*
28	Th.	THANKSGIVING DAY • Basketball game inventor James Naismith died, 1939 • {9.6 8.7	*thanks for*
29	Fr.	Entertainer Garry Shandling born, 1949 • Tides {9.8 8.8	*loosened*
30	Sa.	St. Andrew • Writer Lucy Maud Montgomery born, 1874 • {10.0 8.8	*belts!*

Farmer's Calendar

Most "traditional food" that we enjoy on Thanksgiving wasn't consumed by the Pilgrims. Turkey is a notable exception. The wild turkeys around Plimoth were the likely quarry of the "fowling" party dispatched in 1621 by Governor William Bradford in preparation for the 3-day (first Thanksgiving) event. The Pilgrims couldn't have eaten mashed potatoes because potatoes weren't cultivated in North America until the 1700s, and cranberry sauce and pumpkin pie wouldn't have been on the menu because sugar, flour, and butter were in short supply. Seafood was probably part of the feast. As colonist Edward Winslow reported, "In September, we can take a hogshead of eels in a night. . . . We have mussels . . . at our doors." Recently harvested corn, onions, beans, lettuce, spinach, cabbage, and carrots were probably served. Wampanoag guests contributed five deer.

In 1939, Franklin Roosevelt attempted to boost retail sales by moving Thanksgiving up a week. Such was the opposition to "Franksgiving," that in 1941 he reluctantly signed a bill codifying Thanksgiving on November's fourth Thursday instead.

DECEMBER

SKY WATCH: Venus, now a bright magnitude –4.2, is an evening star in the west from 5:00 to 6:30 P.M. On the 6th, look for Mercury low in the southeast at dawn, after which it remains visible until the 15th. Jupiter floats below the Moon on the 6th and is in opposition on the morning of the 7th, creating a conjunction with the Moon. Now at its brightest of the year, Jupiter rises at around 9:30 P.M. before hovering close to the Moon on the 14th. The Geminid meteor shower arrives on the 13th and is best seen before the Moon rises at around 1:00 A.M. On the 28th, Mercury hovers to the left of the crescent Moon in dawn's twilight. Winter in the Northern Hemisphere begins with the solstice on the 21st at 4:21 A.M. EST.

● NEW MOON	1st day	1:21 A.M.
◑ FIRST QUARTER	8th day	10:27 A.M.
○ FULL MOON	15th day	4:02 A.M.
◐ LAST QUARTER	22nd day	5:18 P.M.
● NEW MOON	30th day	5:27 P.M.

All times are given in Eastern Standard Time.

GET THESE PAGES WITH TIMES SET TO YOUR ZIP CODE VIA ALMANAC.COM/2024.

DAY OF YEAR	DAY OF MONTH	DAY OF WEEK	☼ RISES H.M.	RISE KEY	☼ SETS H.M.	SET KEY	LENGTH OF DAY H.M.	SUN FAST M.	SUN DECLINATION ° '	HIGH TIDE TIMES BOSTON		☽ RISES H.M.	RISE KEY	☽ SETS H.M.	SET KEY	☽ ASTRON. PLACE	☽ AGE
336	1	F	6:54	E	4:12	A	9 18	26	21 s. 56	11	11½	7:35	E	4:07	A	SCO	0
337	2	M.	6:55	E	4:12	A	9 17	26	22 s. 05	11½	—	8:37	E	4:58	A	OPH	1
338	3	Tu.	6:56	E	4:12	A	9 16	26	22 s. 13	12¼	12¼	9:32	E	5:59	A	SAG	2
339	4	W.	6:57	E	4:12	A	9 15	25	22 s. 21	1	1	10:18	E	7:08	B	SAG	3
340	5	Th.	6:58	E	4:12	A	9 14	25	22 s. 29	1¾	1¾	10:55	E	8:21	B	CAP	4
341	6	Fr.	6:59	E	4:12	A	9 13	24	22 s. 36	2½	2½	11:25	E	9:35	C	CAP	5
342	7	Sa.	7:00	E	4:11	A	9 11	24	22 s. 42	3¼	3½	11:51	D	10:49	C	AQU	6
343	8	F	7:01	E	4:11	A	9 10	24	22 s. 48	4¼	4½	12:13	D	—	-	AQU	7
344	9	M.	7:02	E	4:11	A	9 09	23	22 s. 54	5¼	5½	12:35	C	12:03	D	PSC	8
345	10	Tu.	7:03	E	4:12	A	9 09	23	22 s. 59	6	6½	12:57	C	1:17	E	PSC	9
346	11	W.	7:04	E	4:12	A	9 08	22	23 s. 04	7	7½	1:22	B	2:33	E	PSC	10
347	12	Th.	7:04	E	4:12	A	9 08	22	23 s. 08	8	8½	1:51	B	3:52	E	ARI	11
348	13	Fr.	7:05	E	4:12	A	9 07	21	23 s. 12	8¾	9½	2:27	B	5:13	E	ARI	12
349	14	Sa.	7:06	E	4:12	A	9 06	21	23 s. 15	9¾	10½	3:14	A	6:33	E	TAU	13
350	15	F	7:07	E	4:13	A	9 06	20	23 s. 18	10½	11¼	4:12	A	7:45	E	TAU	14
351	16	M.	7:07	E	4:13	A	9 06	20	23 s. 21	11½	—	5:19	A	8:45	E	AUR	15
352	17	Tu.	7:08	E	4:13	A	9 05	19	23 s. 23	12¼	12¼	6:31	B	9:32	E	GEM	16
353	18	W.	7:09	E	4:14	A	9 05	19	23 s. 24	1	1	7:43	B	10:08	E	CAN	17
354	19	Th.	7:09	E	4:14	A	9 05	18	23 s. 25	1¾	1¾	8:52	C	10:36	E	CAN	18
355	20	Fr.	7:10	E	4:15	A	9 05	18	23 s. 26	2½	2¾	9:57	C	10:58	E	LEO	19
356	21	Sa.	7:10	E	4:15	A	9 05	17	23 s. 26	3½	3½	11:00	D	11:18	D	LEO	20
357	22	F	7:11	E	4:16	A	9 05	17	23 s. 25	4¼	4½	—	-	11:36	D	VIR	21
358	23	M.	7:11	E	4:16	A	9 05	16	23 s. 25	5	5¼	12:01	D	11:53	C	VIR	22
359	24	Tu.	7:12	E	4:17	A	9 05	16	23 s. 23	5¾	6¼	1:02	E	12:11	C	VIR	23
360	25	W.	7:12	E	4:17	A	9 05	15	23 s. 21	6¾	7¼	2:04	E	12:31	B	VIR	24
361	26	Th.	7:12	E	4:18	A	9 06	15	23 s. 19	7½	8	3:08	E	12:55	B	LIB	25
362	27	Fr.	7:13	E	4:19	A	9 06	14	23 s. 16	8¼	9	4:14	E	1:25	A	LIB	26
363	28	Sa.	7:13	E	4:19	A	9 06	14	23 s. 13	9	9¾	5:21	E	2:02	A	SCO	27
364	29	F	7:13	E	4:20	A	9 07	13	23 s. 10	9¾	10½	6:26	E	2:49	A	OPH	28
365	30	M.	7:13	E	4:21	A	9 08	13	23 s. 05	10½	11¼	7:24	E	3:48	A	SAG	0
366	31	Tu.	7:13	E	4:22	A	9 09	13	23 s. 01	11¼	11¾	8:14	E	4:56	B	SAG	1

To use this page, see p. 116; for Key Letters, see p. 238. LIGHT = A.M. BOLD = P.M.

CALENDAR

THE TWELFTH MONTH · 2024 **DECEMBER** DECEMBER HATH 31 DAYS

Welcome all and make good cheer,
Welcome all another year.
–**Anonymous**

DAY OF MONTH	DAY OF WEEK	DATES, FEASTS, FASTS, ASPECTS, TIDE HEIGHTS, AND WEATHER	
1	F	1st S. of Advent • NEW ● • ☌☿☾ • {10.1 / 8.8	*Mulled*
2	M.	St. Viviana • ☾ RUNS LOW • Major League Baseball agreed to accept cowhide baseballs, 1974	*wine or*
3	Tu.	John Backus, who led team that designed FORTRAN programming language, born, 1924 • {8.8 / 10.3	*ciders*
4	W.	☌♀☾ • ☌♇☾ • Montreal Canadiens founded, 1909 • Tides {8.7 / 10.2	*warm*
5	Th.	☿ IN INF. ☌ • Chemist Hazel Bishop died, 1998 • Tides {8.7 / 10.2	*snowboard*
6	Fr.	St. Nicholas • *Joy that we can not share with others is only half enjoyed.* • {8.8 / 10.1	*riders,*
7	Sa.	St. Ambrose • NAT'L PEARL HARBOR REMEMBRANCE DAY • ☌♀♇ • ♂ STAT. • ♃ AT ☍	
8	F	2nd S. of Advent • ☌♄☾ • ♆ STAT.	*alpine sliders,*
9	M.	☾ ON EQ. • ☾ AT ☊ • ☌♆☾ • {9.6 / 9.6	*and cross-country*
10	Tu.	St. Eulalia • Colonel John P. Stapp attained 632 mph on rocket sled, 1954 • {10.0 / 9.6	*gliders.*
11	W.	Actress Rita Moreno born, 1931 • Statute of Westminster passed, 1931 • {10.5 / 9.6	*They're*
12	Th.	OUR LADY OF GUADALUPE • ☾ AT PERIG. • F3 waterspout-turned-tornado, Des Moines to Kent, Wash., 1969	*all*
13	Fr.	St. Lucia • ☌♅☾ • Royal charter for Dartmouth College (Hanover, N.H.) granted, 1769	*out in*
14	Sa.	Halcyon Days begin. • ☌♃☾ • U.S. president George Washington died, 1799 • {11.6 / 9.8	*frigid*
15	F	3rd S. of Advent • FULL COLD ○ • ☾ RIDES HIGH • ☿ STAT.	*air,*
16	M.	Discovery of 1st millipede species having more than 1,000 legs (1,306), announced, 2021 • {11.5 / —	*while*
17	Tu.	105.6°F national average set record for hottest day, Australia, 2019 • Tides {9.7 / 11.3	*others*
18	W.	Ember Day • ☌♂☾ • *How the Grinch Stole Christmas!* TV special 1st aired, 1966	*hibernate*
19	Th.	Beware the Pogonip. • Gustl, a terrier mix, undid 10 knots in 1 minute, setting record, 2012	*like*
20	Fr.	Ember Day • *When the night's darkest, the dawn is nearest.* • {9.0 / 9.8	*bears.*
21	Sa.	St. Thomas • Ember Day • WINTER SOLSTICE • Tides {8.9 / 9.3	*Raise*
22	F	4th S. of Advent • ☾ ON EQ. • ☾ AT ☋ • Tides {8.7 / 8.8	*a toast,*
23	M.	20-lb. 9-oz. southern flounder caught, Nassau Sound, Fla., 1983 • Tides {8.7 / 8.4	*give*
24	Tu.	☾ AT APO. • ☿ GR. ELONG. (22° WEST) • –57°F (–82°F old formula) wind chill, Chicago, Ill., 1983	*a cheer,*
25	W.	Christmas • Chanukah begins at sundown • Actor Humphrey Bogart born, 1899	*here's*
26	Th.	St. Stephen • BOXING DAY (CANADA) • FIRST DAY OF KWANZAA • {9.1 / 8.1	*wishing*
27	Fr.	St. John • Radio City Music Hall opened, N.Y.C., 1932 • Tides {9.3 / 8.2	*all*
28	Sa.	Holy Innocents • National Call a Friend Day (U.S.) • ☌☿☾ • Tides {9.6 / 8.3	*a*
29	F	1st S. af. Ch. • *Be it dry or be it wet, The weather'll always pay its debt.*	*grand*
30	M.	NEW ● • ☾ RUNS LOW • Musician Artie Shaw died, 2004 • Tides {10.2 / 8.7	*New*
31	Tu.	St. Sylvester • Educator Jaime Escalante born, 1930 • Tides {10.4 / 9.0	*Year!*

Farmer's Calendar

If you stand under wild American mistletoe, which grows from New Jersey to Florida and west through Texas, you may get something less welcome than a kiss. This is because the juicy white berries, now ripe, are relished by birds. The plant's seeds pass through avian digestive tracts, germinate on the bark of trees, and then send roots into sap-conducting tissues. But most mistletoe species are only partially parasitic; their evergreen leaves contain chlorophyll, which enables them to manufacture their own food once they have purloined water and nutrients from their host trees. In some of the range, foresters consider American mistletoe a pest because it can retard tree growth and break branches. However, ecologists recognize it as a keystone species because not only do many forest creatures forage on its leaves and shoots but also its berries help to sustain birds.

Ancient Europeans reasoned that because mistletoe stayed green in the dead of winter, it must provide shelter for woodland spirits—hence its use in rituals for fertility, health, peace, safety, and good luck.

HOLIDAYS AND OBSERVANCES

2024 HOLIDAYS
FEDERAL HOLIDAYS ARE LISTED IN BOLD.

JAN. 1: **New Year's Day**

JAN. 7: Orthodox Christmas (Julian)

JAN. 15: **Martin Luther King Jr.'s Birthday**

FEB. 1: First day of Black History Month

FEB. 2: Groundhog Day

FEB. 12: Abraham Lincoln's Birthday

FEB. 13: Mardi Gras *(Baldwin & Mobile counties, Ala.; La.)*

FEB. 14: Valentine's Day

FEB. 15: Susan B. Anthony's Birthday *(Fla.)*

FEB. 19: **Presidents' Day**

FEB. 22: George Washington's Birthday

FEB. 29: Leap Day

MAR. 2: Texas Independence Day

MAR. 5: Town Meeting Day *(Vt.)*

MAR. 8: International Women's Day

MAR. 10: Daylight Saving Time begins

MAR. 17: St. Patrick's Day
Evacuation Day *(Suffolk Co., Mass.)*

MAR. 25: Seward's Day *(Alaska)*

MAR. 31: César Chávez Day

APR. 2: Pascua Florida Day

APR. 15: Patriots Day *(Maine, Mass.)*

APR. 21: San Jacinto Day *(Tex.)*

APR. 22: Earth Day

APR. 26: National Arbor Day

MAY 1: First day of Asian American, Native Hawaiian, and Pacific Islander Heritage Month

MAY 5: Cinco de Mayo
Holocaust Remembrance Day begins at sundown

MAY 8: Truman Day *(Mo.)*

MAY 12: Mother's Day

MAY 18: Armed Forces Day

MAY 20: Victoria Day *(Canada)*

MAY 22: National Maritime Day

MAY 27: **Memorial Day, observed**

JUNE 1: First day of Pride Month

JUNE 5: World Environment Day

JUNE 6: D-Day

JUNE 11: King Kamehameha I Day *(Hawaii)*

JUNE 14: Flag Day

JUNE 16: Father's Day

JUNE 17: Bunker Hill Day *(Suffolk Co., Mass.)*

JUNE 19: **Juneteenth National Independence Day**

JUNE 20: West Virginia Day

JULY 1: Canada Day

JULY 4: **Independence Day**

JULY 20: Moon Day

JULY 24: Pioneer Day *(Utah)*

JULY 27: National Day of the Cowboy

AUG. 1: Colorado Day

AUG. 5: Civic Holiday *(parts of Canada)*

AUG. 16: Bennington Battle Day *(Vt.)*

AUG. 19: National Aviation Day

AUG. 26: Women's Equality Day

SEPT. 2: **Labor Day**

SEPT. 8: Grandparents Day

SEPT. 9: Admission Day *(Calif.)*

SEPT. 11: Patriot Day

SEPT. 15: First day of National Hispanic/Latinx Heritage Month

SEPT. 17: Constitution Day

SEPT. 21: International Day of Peace

SEPT. 30: National Day for Truth and Reconciliation *(Canada)*

OCT. 7: Child Health Day

OCT. 9: Leif Eriksson Day

OCT. 12: National Farmer's Day

OCT. 14: **Columbus Day, observed**
Indigenous Peoples' Day *(parts of U.S.)*
Thanksgiving Day *(Canada)*

OCT. 18: Alaska Day

OCT. 24: United Nations Day

OCT. 25: Nevada Day

OCT. 31: Halloween

NOV. 3: Daylight Saving Time ends

CALENDAR

NOV. 4: Will Rogers Day *(Okla.)*
NOV. 5: Election Day
NOV. 11: Veterans Day
      Remembrance Day *(Canada)*
NOV. 19: Discovery of Puerto Rico Day
NOV. 28: Thanksgiving Day
NOV. 29: Acadian Day *(La.)*

DEC. 7: National Pearl Harbor
      Remembrance Day
DEC. 15: Bill of Rights Day
DEC. 17: Wright Brothers Day
DEC. 25: Christmas Day
DEC. 26: Boxing Day *(Canada)*
      First day of Kwanzaa

Movable Religious Observances

JAN. 28: Septuagesima Sunday
FEB. 13: Shrove Tuesday
FEB. 14: Ash Wednesday
MAR. 10: Ramadan begins at sundown
MAR. 18: Orthodox Lent begins
MAR. 24: Palm Sunday
MAR. 29: Good Friday
MAR. 31: Easter
APR. 22: Passover begins at sundown
MAY 5: Orthodox Easter
     Rogation Sunday

MAY 9: Ascension Day
MAY 19: Whitsunday–Pentecost
MAY 26: Trinity Sunday
JUNE 2: Corpus Christi
JUNE 23: Orthodox Pentecost
OCT. 2: Rosh Hashanah begins at
    sundown
OCT. 11: Yom Kippur begins at sundown
DEC. 1: First Sunday of Advent
DEC. 25: Chanukah begins at sundown

CHRONOLOGICAL CYCLES

Dominical Letters **GF**
Epact **19**
Golden Number (Lunar Cycle) **11**
Roman Indiction **2**
Solar Cycle (Julian Calendar) **17**
Year of Julian Period **6737**

–Beth Krommes

ERAS

ERA	YEAR	BEGINS
Byzantine	7533	September 14
Jewish (A.M.)*	5785	October 2
Chinese (Lunar) [Year of the Dragon]	4722	February 10
Roman (A.U.C.)	2777	January 14
Nabonassar	2773	April 17
Japanese	2684	January 1
Grecian (Seleucidae)	2336	September 14 (or October 14)
Indian (Saka)	1946	March 21
Diocletian	1741	September 11
Islamic (Hegira)*	1446	July 7
Bahá'í*	181	March 19

*Year begins at sundown.

GLOSSARY OF ALMANAC ODDITIES

Many readers have expressed puzzlement over the rather obscure entries that appear on our **Right-Hand Calendar Pages, 121–147.** These "oddities" have long been fixtures in the Almanac, and we are pleased to provide some definitions. Once explained, they may not seem so odd after all!

EMBER DAYS: These are the Wednesdays, Fridays, and Saturdays that occur in succession following (1) the First Sunday in Lent; (2) Whitsunday–Pentecost; (3) the Feast of the Holy Cross, September 14; and (4) the Feast of St. Lucia, December 13. The word *ember* is perhaps a corruption of the Latin *quatuor tempora,* "four times." The four periods are observed by some Christian denominations for prayer, fasting, and the ordination of clergy.

Folklore has it that the weather on each of the 3 days foretells the weather for the next 3 months; that is, in September, the first Ember Day, Wednesday, forecasts the weather for October; Friday predicts November; and Saturday foretells December.

DISTAFF DAY (JANUARY 7): This was the day after Epiphany, when women were expected to return to their spinning following the Christmas holiday. A distaff is the staff that women used for holding the flax or wool in spinning. Hence, the term "distaff" refers to women's work or the maternal side of the family.

PLOUGH MONDAY (JANUARY): Traditionally, the first Monday after Epiphany was called Plough Monday because it was the day when men returned to their plough, or daily work, following the Christmas holiday. (Every few years, Plough Monday and Distaff Day fall on the same day.) It was customary at this time for farm laborers to draw a plough through the village, soliciting money for a "plough light,"

–Beth Krommes

which was kept burning in the parish church all year. This traditional verse captures the spirit of it:

> *Yule is come and Yule is gone,*
> *and we have feasted well;*
> *so Jack must to his flail again*
> *and Jenny to her wheel.*

THREE CHILLY SAINTS (MAY): Mamertus, Pancras, and Gervais were three early Christian saints whose feast days, on May 11, 12, and 13, respectively, are traditionally cold; thus they have come to be known as the Three Chilly Saints. An old French saying translates to "St. Mamertus, St. Pancras, and St. Gervais do not pass without a frost."

MIDSUMMER DAY (JUNE 24): To the farmer, this day is the midpoint of the growing season, halfway between planting and harvest. The Anglican Church considered it a "Quarter Day," one of the four major divisions of the liturgical year. It also marks the feast day of St. John the Baptist. (Midsummer Eve is an occasion for festivity and celebrates fertility.)

CORNSCATEOUS AIR (JULY): First used by early almanac makers, this term signifies warm, damp air. Although it signals ideal climatic conditions for growing corn, warm, damp air poses a danger to those affected by asthma and other respiratory problems.

DOG DAYS (JULY 3-AUGUST 11): These 40 days are traditionally the year's hottest and unhealthiest. They once coincided with the year's heliacal (at sunrise) rising of the Dog Star, Sirius. Ancient folks thought that the "combined heat" of Sirius and the Sun caused summer's swelter.

LAMMAS DAY (AUGUST 1): Derived from the Old English *hlaf maesse,* meaning "loaf mass," Lammas Day marked the beginning of the harvest. Traditionally, loaves of bread were baked from the first-ripened grain and brought to the churches to be consecrated. In Scotland, Lammastide fairs became famous as the time when trial marriages could be made. These marriages could end after a year with no strings attached.

CAT NIGHTS COMMENCE (AUGUST 17): This term harks back to the days when people believed in witches. An Irish legend says that a witch could turn into a cat and regain herself eight times, but on the ninth time (August 17), she couldn't change back and thus began her final life permanently as a cat. Hence the saying "A cat has nine lives."

HARVEST HOME (SEPTEMBER): In Britain and other parts of Europe, this marked the conclusion of the harvest and a period of festivals for feasting and thanksgiving. It was also a time to hold elections, pay workers, and collect rents. These festivals usually took place around the autumnal equinox. Certain groups in the United States, e.g., the Pennsylvania Dutch, have kept the tradition alive.

ST. LUKE'S LITTLE SUMMER (OCTOBER): This is a period of warm weather that occurs on or near St. Luke's feast day (usually October 18).

INDIAN SUMMER (NOVEMBER): A period of warm weather following a cold spell or a hard frost, Indian summer can occur between St. Martin's Day (November 11) and November 20. Although there are differing dates for its occurrence, for more than 230 years the Almanac has adhered to the saying "If All Saints' [November 1] brings out winter, St. Martin's brings out Indian summer." The term may have come from early North American indigenous peoples, some of whom believed that the condition was caused by a warm wind sent from the court of their southwestern god, Cautantowwit.

HALCYON DAYS (DECEMBER): This period of about 2 weeks of calm weather often follows the blustery winds at autumn's end. Ancient Greeks and Romans experienced this weather at about the time of the winter solstice (around December 21), when the halcyon, or kingfisher—having charmed the wind and waves so that waters were especially calm at this time—was thought to brood in a nest floating on the sea.

BEWARE THE POGONIP (DECEMBER): The word *pogonip* refers to frozen fog and was coined by North American indigenous peoples to describe the frozen fogs of fine ice needles that occur in the mountain valleys of the western United States and Canada. According to tradition, breathing the fog is injurious to the lungs. ∎

–Beth Krommes

Nature's Germ Killer
Stop a virus before it starts

Scientists have discovered a natural way to kill germs fast.

Now thousands of people are using it against viruses and bacteria that cause illness.

Colds, flu, and many other illnesses start when viruses get in your nose and multiply. If you don't stop them early, they spread and cause misery.

Hundreds of studies confirm copper kills germs like viruses, bacteria, and fungus almost instantly, just by touch.

That's why ancient Greeks and Egyptians used copper to purify water and heal wounds. They didn't know about germs. Now we do.

The National Institutes of Health and the American Society for Microbiology vouch for the power of copper to kill germs.

Scientists say copper's high conductance disrupts the electrical balance in a germ cell and destroys it in seconds.

The EPA recommends hospitals use copper for touch surfaces such as faucets and doorknobs. This cuts the spread of MRSA and other illnesses by over half, and saves lives.

The strong scientific evidence gave inventor Doug Cornell an idea. He made a smooth copper probe with a tip to fit in the bottom of the nostril where viruses collect.

New research: Copper kills bad germs in seconds.

When he felt a tickle in his nose like a cold about to start, he rubbed the copper gently in his nose for 60 seconds.

"It worked!" he exclaimed. "The cold never happened." That was 2012.

Now he's gone 11 years without a cold. "I used to get 2-3 bad colds every year. Now I use my CopperZap right away at any sign I am about to get sick."

After the initial success, he asked relatives and friends to try it. They all said it worked, so he patented CopperZap® and put it on the market.

Soon hundreds of people had tried it. 99% said copper worked if they used it right away at the first sign of bad germs, like a tickle in the nose or a scratchy throat.

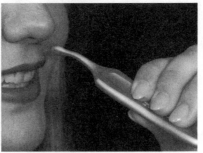

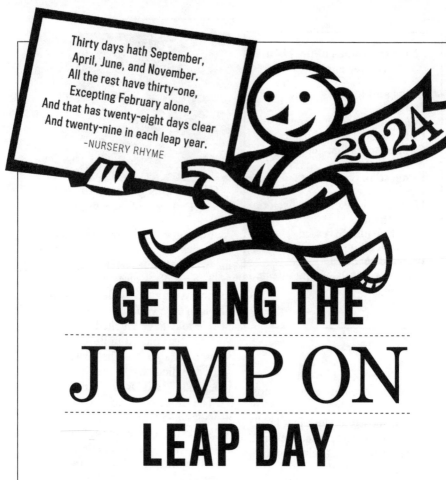

Thirty days hath September,
April, June, and November.
All the rest have thirty-one,
Excepting February alone,
And that has twenty-eight days clear
And twenty-nine in each leap year.

—NURSERY RHYME

GETTING THE
JUMP ON
LEAP DAY

BY TIM GOODWIN
ILLUSTRATIONS BY TIM ROBINSON

2024 IS A LEAP YEAR!

It is widely assumed that leap year—or, more specifically, Leap Day—appears on the calendar every 4 years and that an extra day is added to February in any year that is divisible by four.

Not exactly true. Leap years are defined by two general rules:

■ A year may be a leap year if it is evenly divisible by four, as is this year.

■ However, century years (those that are divisible by 100, such as 1900 or 2000) can not be leap years unless they are also divisible by 400. So, the years 1700, 1800, and 1900 were not leap years, while the year 2000 was.

The next year that is evenly divisible by four that will not have a Leap Day is the year 2100.

Why Have a Leap Day?

Julius Caesar introduced the Julian calendar in 46 B.C. It was created to replace the Roman calendar, which was initially a complicated lunar arrangement based on Moon phases. The Julian calendar was not perfect, though: It overestimated the length of the year by more than 11 minutes and installed leap years every 4 years, which was too often. By the mid-1500s, the Julian seasons had shifted by about 10 days.

In 1582, Pope Gregory XIII introduced the Gregorian calendar, currently used by much of the world, as a modification to the Julian calendar. Its first iteration contained 10 fewer days in October in order to realign with the solar year. (In 1752, Britain and her colonies adopted the Gregorian calendar, skipping 11 days in September to be in sync.) The Gregorian calendar also instituted the current criteria for adding leap days.

In the Gregorian calendar, a year has 365 days. But Earth's orbit around the Sun takes about 365.2422 days. If we didn't add the extra day (February 29) almost every 4 years, our calendar would once again get out of sync with the astronomical seasons.

A PROPOSAL PROPOSITION

According to legend, in the 5th century, Saint Brigid of Ireland asked Saint Patrick to grant women the right to propose marriage. The two negotiated, and it was agreed that women could propose on Leap Day. Some claim that Brigid then proposed to Patrick, who declined and then gave her a silk gown to soothe her broken heart.

Gifts for rejected proposals by women became the tradition. According to Scottish lore, a rejected proposal would entitle a woman to a kiss, a silk gown, or 12 pairs of gloves—the latter so that the woman could hide the fact that she was not wearing a ring. The legend grew, and the practice spread throughout Europe before eventually arriving in the United States.

(continued)

Leap Day Weather

Look up historical weather events for February 29, and you will find some extreme conditions.

- In 1956, the coldest temperature ever recorded in the United States on a Leap Day, -66°F, was measured at Hughes, Alaska.
- The hottest U.S. Leap Day on record occurred in the towns of Encinal, Mission, and Weslaco, Texas, where the temperature reached 100°F in 1940.
- On February 29, 1944, 33 inches of snow fell in Cisco Grove, California.
- Hawaii has recorded more than 10 inches of rain on eight different Leap Days, with the most (21 inches) falling in 1984, in Maui.
- In the early morning hours of February 29, 2012, an E4 tornado, reaching 180 miles per hour, destroyed more than 200 homes and about 25 businesses in the Harrisburg, Illinois, area. Eight people died and more than 100 were injured. The twister was part of the Leap Day Tornado Outbreak, when more than 30 tornadoes developed in Nebraska, Kansas, Missouri, Kentucky, Tennessee, and Illinois.

LEAP DAY BABIES

- Only one of every 1,461 births occurs on Leap Day.
- Peter Anthony Keogh was born in Ireland on Leap Day 1940. His son, Peter Eric, entered the world on February 29, 1964, in the United Kingdom. In 1996, Peter Eric's daughter, Bethany, became a Leap Day baby. This is the only documented case of three consecutive generations of one family being born on Leap Day.
- Karin Henriksen of Norway can lay claim to the title of the only mom on record to bear three children on Leap Days—Heidi in 1960; Olav, 1964; and Leif-Martin, 1968.
- Folks born on Leap Day are known as 29ers, leaplings, leapers, and leapsters.
- The Honor Society of Leap Year Day Babies connects leaplings around the world through social media and Leap Day events.
- During non–leap years, Leap Day birthdays are usually celebrated on February 28 or March 1.

Leap Year Odds and Ends

■ Anthony, New Mexico, and Anthony, Texas, share the title "Leap Year Capital of the World." These communities sit on the border between Texas and New Mexico. In 1988, Anthony (Texas) resident Mary Ann Brown, a leapling herself, led a campaign to encourage the governors of both states to issue proclamations recognizing the title. Since 1988, the communities have celebrated every Leap Year with a festival.

■ *La Bougie du Sapeur,* a French satirical publication that translates to "The Sapper's Candle," has been sold on newsstands across France every February 29 since 1980. It claims to be the least frequently published newspaper in the world because it is printed only during leap years. About 150,000 copies are sold every Leap Day.

■ Rare Disease Day was created on Leap Day in 2008 by the European Organisation for Rare Disease (February 29 being the rarest day). During non-leap years, Rare Disease Day is held on February 28.

■ Non-leap years always begin and end on the same day of the week. The first and last days of leap years are different.

DON'T BE CONFUSED

A leap second has nothing to do with a leap year or Leap Day. In fact, if necessary, a leap second can be added or subtracted at the end of June or December by the International Earth Rotation and Reference Systems Service to adjust Coordinated Universal Time (UTC) to align with the imprecise observed Universal Time (UT1). The first leap second was added on June 30, 1972. To date, no seconds have been subtracted. ■

Tim Goodwin, the Almanac's associate editor, hopes that everyone will consider leaping in the air at least once on Leap Day.

BEHOLD NATURE'S GRANDEST EVENT!

Here's how to make April 8, 2024, one of the most memorable days of your life.

BY BOB BERMAN

I shall only say that I have passed a varied and eventful life, that it has been my fortune to see earth, heavens, ocean, and man in most of their aspects; but never have I beheld any spectacle which so plainly manifested the majesty of the Creator or so forcibly taught the lesson of humility to man as a total eclipse of the Sun.

–from "The Eclipse," by James Fenimore Cooper, American writer (1789–1851)

Numerous surveys have probed the public's opinion on a very simple issue: What's the most impressive natural spectacle that you've ever seen?

People who have seen several notable events generally agree that a "Great Comet" ranks high, as does a meteor storm, when shooting stars explode across the sky every few seconds. Both are rare events, occurring only once every two, three, or more decades. A major display of the northern lights always makes the list, too.

But the ultimate sky show—the visual experience that's the best of the best—is, hands-down, a total eclipse of the Sun, which happens also to be the only such event that makes many observers weep with emotion.

One reason for this enthusiasm for solar eclipses is that they are brief and rare: Totality persists for just a few minutes ($7\frac{1}{2}$ minutes being its absolute—and only occasional—maximum duration), so a badly timed cloud can spoil everything. What's more, any given place on Earth sees a solar totality only once every 360 years, on average.

For example, Los Angeles was last in the path of a total solar eclipse in 1724, and the next one to occur there will not arrive until 3290. On the other hand, Carbondale, Illinois, was in the path of the recent total solar eclipse of 2017 and also happens to lie within the 115-mile-wide path of the 2024 totality. How, you might wonder, did the Carbondale area get so lucky? Blame it on the randomness of the universe.

On a global scale, the random and occasional occurrences of total solar eclipses means that relatively few people have seen one. This—and the fact that we all spend much of our lives going about the business of living and may have only a grade school knowledge of eclipses—means that many people are not aware of the vastly different types of eclipses. For instance, a lunar eclipse occurs when the Moon enters Earth's shadow—but which area of shadow? Earth's dark, Moon-obscuring umbra shadow or its outer, barely visible penumbral shadow? Each is a different event, a different experience for an observer.

Consider this: All four lunar eclipses in 2020 were of the penumbral variety, which is quite different from solar totality. This is why, after TV meteorologists and others that year urged people to go outdoors to see an "amazing lunar eclipse," most observers who gazed upward with high expectations were disappointed or perplexed: Nothing appeared to happen. Nobody had told them that during a penumbral eclipse, a full Moon undergoes no discernible change.

I n vivid contrast, at the ultimate and opposite point on the eclipse spectacularness spectrum, stands the event that will occur on April 8, 2024—a total solar eclipse. Conveniently, this one will be visible from along a path running from Mexico to Canada. In the United States, optimum viewing opportunities will first occur in south and central Texas before moving up through Arkansas and into the Ohio Valley, traversing Lakes Erie and Ontario, and crossing northern New York and New England. In Canada, the route will include large swaths of New Brunswick and Newfoundland.

Interestingly, this eclipse will unfold only 7 years after the spectacular 2017 U.S. totality. That event made millions of the people who observed it believers in the unique and compelling nature of the experience and

VIEWER, BEWARE!
Some publications and Web sites will say that the eclipse is visible from almost everywhere in eastern Canada and the eastern United States. In a way, this is true. However, outside the narrow, 115-mile-wide path of totality—say, on the northern part of the Island of Montreal, for example—only a partial eclipse will occur. Viewing this will require eye protection for the entire time and will not feature the glorious natural wonders such as prominences, the corona, and stars appearing in the daytime that are visible only where the eclipse is total. Thus, you should consider making every effort possible to travel, if necessary, to be within this grand event's enchanted path.

convinced many of those who saw it as a "partial" eclipse that they had missed the true glories of a full totality.

Speaking of "glories," many people are of the notion that the main attraction of a solar eclipse is an effect called "blackness at noon." The popularity of this belief was made clear by American writer James Fenimore Cooper in his memoir titled "The Eclipse," which was based on his observation of the totality viewable in his hometown of Cooperstown, New York, on June 16, 1806. He writes of being most moved by the darkness at midday. Absent are observations of the features that fascinate many of today's observers, such as "the diamond ring effect" (more on this in a moment) and coronal streamers, largely because the Sun's magnetic field and the streamers were unknown at the time.

A RADIANT "DIAMOND" OF SUNLIGHT IS SEEN IN THE MOMENTS AFTER TOTALITY DURING THE TOTAL SOLAR ECLIPSE ON AUGUST 21, 2017.

Today, those who presume that experiencing natural midday blackness is the most compelling reason to travel to put themselves in the eclipse's path miss a good portion (some would say the best parts) of the show—the unearthly glories that appear only during the event's total portion.

To wit, only in totality is there the opportunity to . . .

■ safely stare at the Sun directly or even through binoculars; with the naked eye, you can actually watch the Moon's 1-kilometer-per-second motion as it orbits Earth! (Direct viewing during the hours-long partial solar eclipse periods requires special filters or goggles to protect eyesight from retinal damage.)

■ see the famous "diamond ring"—the brief, surrealistically intense pinpoint of light just before and immediately after totality that appears wholly different from its appearance in photographs.

■ gaze at long, thin, ethereal "streamers" radiating from the Sun as it hides behind the inky-black Moon. These force-field lines reveal the solar magnetic field, the largest structure in the solar system that is normally invisible.

■ observe pink prominences resembling fiery geysers sprouting from the Sun's edge. These are the features most dramatically enhanced by those who take a minute to use binoculars at around totality's midpoint.

HOW TO PREPARE FOR A *REALLY* BIG SHOW

FOR VIEWING IN THE UNITED STATES:

■ Go to NASA's eclipse Web site: Solarsystem.nasa.gov /eclipses. Click on "Total Solar Eclipse April 8, 2024," click on "Where & When," and study the map showing the path of totality in an area that you can access. The event will be as well seen from U.S. cities as from rural areas. On April 8, more than 3 full minutes of totality will be visible from dozens of major cities, including Dallas, Texas; Hot Springs, Arkansas; Fairfield, Illinois; Evansville and Jasper, Indiana; Sandusky, Ohio; Erie, Pennsylvania; Buffalo, Niagara Falls, Rochester, and Watertown, New York; Burlington, Vermont; Pittsburg, New Hampshire; and Jackman, Maine. For a complete list of towns and cities in the path of totality, the exact local times of the eclipse, and the length of totality at each site, go to Nationaleclipse.com.

FOR VIEWING IN CANADA:

■ Go to the Royal Astronomical Society of Canada's New Brunswick site at RASCNB.ca and click on "2024 Solar Eclipse." Then click on the "interactive map" under "ECLIPSE PATH MAP" to find where the path of totality will be in an area that you can access. The event will be as well seen from Canadian cities as from rural areas. On April 8, certain parts of New Brunswick— in particular, Fredericton, Woodstock, Florenceville-Bristol, and Miramichi—will experience 100% totality, the complete coverage of the Sun. For a complete list of towns and cities in the path of totality, the exact local times of the eclipse, and the length of totality at each site, go to Eclipse2024.com.

FOR VIEWING IN BOTH:

■ Ideal weather conditions would be clear skies. For a real-time, 5-day forecast of conditions based on a specific zip or postal code, go to Almanac.com/Weather or Weather .gov for the U.S. or Almanac.ca/Weather for Canada. ■

Bob Berman, astronomy editor of *The Old Farmer's Almanac,* has led 11 solar eclipse expeditions and is the author of *The Sun's Heartbeat* (Little Brown, 2015).

ADVICE FOR VIEWERS EVERYWHERE

■ Contact a welding supply store and order several shade 12, 13, or 14 filters. Do not accept shade 10; it is more common than the others but not dark enough to keep your eyes safe while viewing the eclipse's partial phases.

■ If hotel accommodations or camping reservations are booked up, remember that you can see the event from the rooftop of a camper or a lawn chair on a highway pull-off or rest area. Study the maps!

■ Review the short-term weather forecast regularly.

■ Never use binoculars to view the Sun except during those few minutes of totality. During the rest of the eclipse–the partial phases–you would suffer permanent eye damage in a mere 1 or 2 seconds.

■ If you experience totality, count yourself among a select lucky few people in the world!

A HOME ON HALLOWED GROUND

How a potter's field in 1864 became
a sacred shrine 160 years later

BY JAMES EDWARD PETERS

Rising above the Potomac River overlooking Washington, D.C., stands Arlington House—the focal point of Arlington National Cemetery. New visitors to Arlington often ask, "Why did Robert E. Lee build his home in a cemetery?" The answer is complicated.

In 1759, George Washington married Martha Custis, a widow with two children, John and Patsy Custis. In 1781, while serving with Washington during the Revolution, 27-year-old John died, leaving a young widow with four children. To assist John's widow, George and Martha adopted two of John's children, 6-month-old George Washington Parke Custis and 2-year-old Eleanor Parke Custis.

Young George W. P. Custis spent his life watching and learning from his adoptive father as the latter managed the Mount Vernon plantation and served as the first U.S. president. In 1799, when Custis was just 18 years old, George Washington died. Custis quickly resolved to create a memorial to him.

When Martha died in 1802, Custis attempted to buy Mount Vernon as the memorial. However, Washington's nephew, Bushrod Washington, inherited the property and was unwilling to sell it. So, Custis chose to build his memorial on a 1,100-acre estate north of Mount Vernon that he had inherited from his natural father.

ARLINGTON HOUSE—THE HOME OF ROBERT E. LEE—IS THE FOCAL POINT OF ARLINGTON NATIONAL CEMETERY.

In 1802, he moved onto the site and began construction. It would take 16 years to complete Arlington House (named after the Earl of Arlington, who had given the Custis family their original land grant). During this period, Custis collected Washington memorabilia. The result was the most extensive assemblage of the first president's personal effects and historic artifacts in the country. The finished mansion was clearly visible from Washington, D.C. Its south wing housed the Washington collection, which visitors came in droves to view.

In 1804, Custis married Mary Lee Fitzhugh, a descendant of an old Virginia family. They had four children, but only one, Mary Anna Randolph Custis, lived to maturity.

Life at Arlington House provided Mary Custis with all of the luxuries that a young woman her age could have desired. Yet she knew that someday she would be entrusted with the preservation of the first president's living memorial.

Many young men sought to win the heart and hand of Mary Custis, but it was a distant cousin, Robert E. Lee, who captured her affections. Lee was the son of a former Virginia governor and an 1829 graduate of West Point. Their wedding on June 30, 1831, was the grandest event ever held at Arlington House, and Lee realized that with his marriage came shared custodial responsibility for the Washington memorabilia.

FOLLOWING THE CIVIL WAR, MORE AND MORE VETERANS CHOSE TO BE BURIED AT ARLINGTON.

Robert E. Lee's service in the U.S. Army often required him to be away for extended periods of time, so he took his family with him. In the fall of 1857, while commanding the 2nd U.S. Cavalry in Texas, Lee received word that his elderly father-in-law had died. As executor of his estate, Lee returned to Arlington, only to find that the property had been sorely neglected.

Lee worked diligently to restore Arlington. In October 1859, with the restoration done, Lee received an urgent message to report to the War Department in Washington. There he was offered command of a detachment to apprehend John Brown, who had seized the federal arsenal at Harper's Ferry, Virginia. Lee accepted the command and captured Brown, earning considerable recognition and accelerating his return to duty.

In February 1860, Lee resumed his assignment in Texas. There he heard widespread talk of secession and bitterly argued against it. By December 1860, South Carolina had seceded, to be followed by Texas on February 1, 1861. Lee was ordered back to Washington.

Events unfolded rapidly after Southern soldiers fired on Fort Sumter, South Carolina, on April 12, 1861. President Abraham Lincoln called for 75,000 volunteers, and Lee was offered command of the new Union army being raised. When Virginia seceded, Lee struggled with what he should do and what would become of Arlington House.

Finally, on April 20, 1861, Lee submitted his letter of resignation from the U.S. Army, stating, "Save in defense of my native State, I never desire again to draw my sword." But events intervened. The Virginia governor summoned Lee to Richmond, Virginia, where he accepted the command of the Virginia militia and ultimately the Confederate Army.

As war seemed imminent, Lee wrote his wife that the family should leave Arlington and stay with relatives in southern Virginia. Following her departure, Arlington House was occupied by Union soldiers.

Early in the war, fighting centered on Washington, forcing it to become a city of hospitals where many wounded soldiers were treated and many died. Soon burial space became scarce, so President Lincoln directed Secretary of War Edwin Stanton to establish the necessary burial grounds.

Stanton and his ally, Quartermaster General Montgomery Meigs, had long considered Lee a traitor, so they conspired to appropriate 200 acres surrounding Arlington House to be used as a military cemetery. After the land was designated as such on June 15, 1864, burials began almost immediately; most were of unknowns, former enslaved persons, or soldiers whose families could not afford to bring their remains home.

In April 1865, after Lee's surrender at Appomattox, he and his wife, wanting desperately to recover their home and the Washington collection, made discreet yet unsuccessful attempts to do so.

Lee never returned to Arlington House. Instead, he became president of Washington College (today Washington and Lee University) in Lexington, Virginia. When he died in 1870, he was buried in the college chapel. Mrs. Lee died in 1873.

The Washington collection? It had been moved to the National Archives early in the war after articles started disappearing as troops trafficked in and around the estate. Today, it is part of the Smithsonian's collection.

Under the terms of George W. Custis's will, the title to Arlington was passed to his daughter and then to her eldest son, George W. Custis Lee. In 1877, Custis Lee sued the United States for the return of Arlington House, claiming that it had been illegally confiscated. After a lengthy court battle, in 1882 the Supreme Court ordered the government to return the property. Custis Lee could have ordered the government to disinter more than 17,000 remains, dismantle army forts, and close the encampment of former enslaved persons located on the estate. Instead, he accepted compensation of $150,000.

Following the Civil War, more and more veterans chose to be buried at Arlington. In 1914, the installation of a Confederate Monument made Arlington a truly national cemetery. The Unknown Soldier from WWI was interred in 1921, followed by Unknowns from WWII, Korea, and Vietnam.

Robert E. Lee's home? It is not in the cemetery. In 1925, Arlington House was designated as the Robert E. Lee Memorial, separated from the cemetery, and placed under the jurisdiction of the National Park Service.

So, during the 160 years since its controversial creation, Arlington National Cemetery has been transformed from a hastily created potter's field to America's most sacred national shrine.

(continued)

NOTABLE DEPARTED

Today there are nearly 400,000 veterans and eligible dependents buried at Arlington. Among them we find presidents and paupers, officers and enlisted personnel, justices and former enslaved persons. Here are a few—all connected to the military but often better known for other reasons.

ASTRONAUTS: There are more than 30 astronauts buried at Arlington, including John Glenn, Virgil "Gus" Grissom, Pete Conrad, Dick Scobee, Michael Smith, and Laurel Clark. The un-identified commingled remains of the crews of the Shuttle *Challenger* and the Shuttle *Columbia* are buried beneath the monuments honoring their respective missions.

ABNER DOUBLEDAY: first Union soldier to fire a return shot at Fort Sumter; a hero at Gettysburg; credited with inventing baseball, although he never claimed to have done so; general, U.S. Army.

JOHN GREEN: reinterred Revolutionary War veteran; born 1730; longest-deceased person in the cemetery; colonel, 10th Virginia Volunteers.

DASHIELL HAMMETT: author of *The Maltese Falcon* and *The Thin Man;* WWII veteran; sergeant, U.S. Army.

GRACE HOPPER: Navy pioneer computer programmer; highest-ranking woman buried at Arlington; rear admiral, U.S. Navy.

DANIEL "CHAPPIE" JAMES JR.: Korean and Vietnam wars pilot with 179 combat missions; first Black four-star (full) general; U.S. Air Force.

MICHAEL KILIAN: *Chicago Tribune* correspondent; mystery novelist; co-writer of the *Dick Tracy* comic strip; corporal, U.S. Army.

JOE LOUIS: heavyweight boxing champion; WWII veteran; sergeant, U.S. Army.

LEE MARVIN: Academy Award–winning actor, *Cat Ballou,* 1966; Purple Heart recipient; WWII veteran; private 1st class, U.S. Marine Corps.

Photos, clockwise from top: Facebook; The National WWII Museum; Wikimedia; Wikimedia

GLENN MILLER: Big Band leader who went missing in action when his plane disappeared in WWII; although not buried at Arlington, he has an official memorial headstone reserved for MIAs; major, U.S. Army Air Forces.

AUDIE MURPHY: most decorated WWII serviceman, with 28 medals, including Congressional Medal of Honor, three Purple Hearts, and honors from Belgium and France; starred in 40 movies, including his memoir film, *To Hell and Back;* major, U.S. Army.

MAUREEN O'HARA: Irish-American actress who starred in more than 50 movies; wife of Brig. Gen. Charles Blair, U.S. Air Force.

JAMES PARKS: only person buried at Arlington who was born on the property (1843); enslaved there until after the Civil War; remained as a maintenance person until his death in 1929; granted special permission to be buried there because of his lifelong service to the cemetery.

ROBERT PEARY and **MATTHEW HENSON:** along with several Inuit guides, first to reach the North Pole, on April 6, 1909; Peary was a navy rear admiral. Henson was not a veteran and thus ineligible for Arlington, but in 1988 President Ronald Reagan authorized his reinterment near Peary.

VINNIE REAM: 18-year-old sculptress who in 1866 received a commission from the United States Congress to create a memorial statue of President Abraham Lincoln; the resulting sculpture stands in the U.S. Capitol rotunda; wife of Brig. Gen. Richard Hoxie, U.S. Army.

FRANK REYNOLDS: Peabody Award–winning ABC News anchor; WWII veteran; Purple Heart recipient; staff sergeant, U.S. Army.

SULLIVAN BROTHERS: five young men from Waterloo, Iowa, who became celebrities when they enlisted together and were all assigned to the USS *Juneau* in WWII. Sadly, all five were lost at sea when the *Juneau* was torpedoed on Nov. 13, 1942. A memorial headstone marks the cenotaph (empty grave) of each man; U.S. Navy. ∎

James Edward Peters has been researching and lecturing on Arlington National Cemetery for over 40 years. He is the author of *Arlington National Cemetery: Shrine to America's Heroes,* 3rd Edition (Woodbine House, 2008).

MEMORABLE
OLYMPIC
MOMENTS

WHEN IT COMES TO GOLD AND GLORY, OLYMPIC ATHLETES GET THEIR RIGHTFUL SHARE, BUT COULD IT BE THAT THEIR BACKGROUND STORIES ARE THE REAL WINNERS?

BY KRISTIN KRAUSE · ILLUSTRATIONS BY KELLY ALDER

While the Olympic motto of "Faster, Higher, Stronger" promises great athletic accomplishments, the Games' human tales of sportsmanship, sacrifice, and character often remind us that the quadrennial sports extravaganza can mean much more than just going for the gold. In celebration of the 2024 Summer Olympics in Paris, we present some little-known side stories from past Olympiads.

STROKE OF GENIUS

Thirteen-year-old Alfréd Hajós resolved to become a good swimmer after witnessing his father drown in the Danube. Five years later, in 1896, the young Hungarian traveled to Athens to compete in the first modern Olympiad. The swimming competitions were held in the Mediterranean Sea, whose temperature in early April was only 55°F—cold enough to make limbs numb and clumsy from hypothermia. Hajós smeared his body with grease to fend off the cold and fought through waves up to 12 feet high in two events—the 100- and 1,200-meter freestyle contests—on the same day. He won both.

At the 1924 Games in Paris, Hajós won again—a silver medal for architecture. Yes, architecture. From 1912 to 1952, Olympic competitions included fine arts. Medals were awarded for architecture, literature, music, painting, and sculpture.

FAIR PLAY

During the 1936 Berlin Games, two close friends, Shuhei Nishida and Sueo Oe, tied for second place in the pole vault. Officials demanded a tiebreaker to determine the silver and bronze medal winners, but Nishida and Oe declined. Nishida was awarded the silver because he had cleared the height in fewer attempts, but it didn't matter. When the athletes returned to Japan, they had their medals cut in half to create two new ones, each half-silver and half-bronze. These became known as "the Medals of Friendship."

DUCKING OUT

Australian phenom Henry Robert "Bobby" Pearce dominated the 1928 Olympic rowing trials in Amsterdam. However, a complication arose during his quarterfinal race. Hearing shouts from the bank, he turned to see a mother duck and her ducklings crossing the racecourse ahead of him. Pearce stopped to let them pass, winning the adoration of the Dutch spectators. The pause allowed his competitor to take the lead, but Pearce caught up and won the match. After defeating the eventual silver medalist by 9.8 seconds in the finals—a huge margin for the 2,000-meter race—he would go on to win Olympic gold again in Los Angeles in 1936. *(continued)*

GOLDEN GIRL

Europe had not yet recovered from WWII when the Games were held in London in 1948. Food was rationed, and athletes had to bring their own towels. In these "Austerity Games," 30-year-old Fanny Blankers-Koen of Holland, mother of two, won four gold medals in track and field while pregnant with her third child. At this time, married female athletes were rare and mothers unheard of. Newspapers said she was too old to compete, criticized her for leaving her children at home, and dubbed her the "Flying Housewife." Nonetheless, her wins made her the most successful athlete of that Olympiad.

LIKE **FATHER**, LIKE **SON**

In 1924, canoeist Bill Havens learned that his wife was due to give birth during the Paris Olympics. Reluctantly, he resigned his place on the United States Olympic team to be present at the birth of his son Frank. The team, which included Bill's brother Bud, paddled to glory without him, winning three gold, one silver, and two bronze medals in six events.

Twenty-eight years later, at the 1952 Olympics in Helsinki, the gold medal in the 10,000-meter single-blade canoeing event was won by Frank Havens. In a telegram to his father (and coach), Frank wrote, "Dear Dad, thanks for waiting around for me to get born in 1924. I'm coming home with the gold medal that you should have won. Your loving son, Frank."

LIFESAVER

At the 1988 Games in Seoul, Canadian sailor Lawrence Lemieux was racing through rough seas, in second place in his race, when he heard cries of distress. The boat of two sailors from Singapore, competing in a different race, had capsized, and the men were in danger of being swept out to sea. Lemieux changed course to come to their aid, knowing that he could get to them more quickly than any rescue boats could. Although he ended up finishing in 21st place after diverting to ensure their safety, his gallantry did not go unnoticed: The International Olympic Committee later awarded him the Pierre de Coubertin medal for sportsmanship.

RUNNING INTO HISTORY

In 1904, St. Louis, Missouri, concurrently hosted both the Olympics and the World's Fair. At the time of this, its third modern iteration, the Olympiad was still relatively unknown, so to increase participation, the organizers allowed anybody to compete. That year's marathon is remembered for a number of interesting moments, including:

■ Len Taunyane and Jan Mashiani, two members of South Africa's Tswana tribe who were in St. Louis to perform in the World's Fair, decided to enter the road race. In so doing, they became the first Black Africans to compete in the Olympics. Running barefoot, they finished ninth and twelfth, respectively, even though Taunyane was chased a mile off course by dogs.

■ Cuba's first Olympian, Félix Carvajal, traveled to New Orleans by boat, then walked and hitchhiked the 670 miles to St. Louis. His running outfit consisted of a beret, a long-sleeve shirt, long pants, and dress shoes. Another entrant cut the trousers off at the knees for him so that he would not overheat. During the race, Carvajal seemed unhurried: He stopped to chat with spectators and, one time, to pick and eat apples from a roadside tree. The fruit upset his stomach, so he lay down and took a nap. When he woke up, he continued running, eventually—remarkably—finishing fourth.

■ The race took place with temperatures in the 90s. Water was available only at the 6- and 12-mile marks of the 24.85-mile course. (The chief organizer of the Games supported research on the effects of dehydration on the body.) American Thomas Hicks begged his handlers for water. Instead, they gave him a mixture of strychnine and raw egg whites (and later, brandy). Strychnine, a form of rat poison, was believed to be a stimulant when taken in small doses. This marked the first recorded use of performance-enhancing drugs in the modern Olympics. (Strychnine is poison. Do not consume, inhale, or inject it into your body.)

■ American Fred Lorz also struggled in the heat, so he rode 11 miles in a car, waving at spectators. After it broke down, he jumped out, finished the race, and was declared the winner by the none-the-wiser officials. Then, as President Theodore Roosevelt's daughter Alice was presenting him the gold medal, he was abruptly disqualified. An hour later, the dehydrated Hicks, half-dead in the arms of his trainers, lurched across the finish line, to be declared the winner. His time of 3:28 remains the slowest winning marathon mark in Olympic history. ■

Kristin Krause is a scientist, teacher, author, and mom who enjoys history's odd moments. She watches the Olympics with her family in Maine.

SIMPLE STEPS TO
SEED-STARTING
SUCCESS

Learning to grow your own seedlings is one of the most valuable gardening skills that you can acquire. By starting with seeds, you can choose from a huge selection of interesting varieties that are not available as seedlings. Growing your own seedlings also allows you to control timing. You can kick-start spring by starting cool-season plants like broccoli and lettuce indoors in late winter. Then switch to starting tomatoes, peppers, and summer crops in midspring. Plan on another flurry of seed-starting activity in summer, as you get ready to stock your fall garden with spinach, kale, and kohlrabi. In addition to having the seedlings that you want when you want them, you will save a ton of money by growing your own.

HOW SEEDS GERMINATE

Seeds are plants in a deep dormant state. When triggered by moisture, temperature, and sometimes light, specialized cells inside the seeds wake up and start to grow. Stored nutrients are sent to the embryo, which holds the basic

WHAT REALLY GOES ON INSIDE
AWAKENING SEEDS AND WHY YOU SHOULD
START YOUR OWN SEEDLINGS INDOORS

BY BARBARA PLEASANT

botanic structures for roots, stem, and leaves. Fast-germinating seeds for vegetables like cucumbers and tomatoes have well-developed embryos, but seeds of the carrot and onion families do not. Their tiny embryos must grow before the seeds can sprout, so they take longer to emerge.

Priming seeds by soaking them in water for a few hours and then drying them on paper towels before planting often improves the germination of older seeds, but too much water, for too long, can be deadly.

Germination requires oxygen because until leaves emerge to synthesize solar energy, seeds combine oxygen with their stored food reserves to grow new cells. When you force out soil oxygen with too much water, seeds struggle or rot.

SPECIAL SOIL FOR STARTERS

As soon as they sprout, seedlings must defend themselves from fungi and bacteria, particularly those that live in soil. To prevent potential problems, buy a fresh bag of organic seed-starting mix every spring and keep it indoors, closed and dry, between uses. Most seed-starting mixes are composed of peat moss, coconut coir, and vermiculite or perlite, materials that are hospitable to plant roots but not to soilborne diseases.

You can make your own seed-starting mix from rich, fluffy compost that has been placed in a heatproof pan, tightly covered, and heated to 150°F in the oven for 30 minutes to kill pathogens and weed seeds, but you should still add perlite or vermiculite to help the

mixture to hold air. Made from naturally occurring minerals, vermiculite alone forms a moist, semi-sterile barrier when spread in a thin layer over germinating seeds.

CHOOSING RELIABLE CONTAINERS

The most common seed-starting containers are plastic cell packs like those used for bedding plants. These clean up quickly in warm, soapy water; can be watered easily from the top or the bottom; and can be reused several times. Three-ounce paper cups with holes punched in the bottom also work well, and you can write the names of the varieties right on the cups. Be careful with peat pellets, which hold too much water and not enough nutrients, and peat pots, which form a dry, acidic barrier that frustrates plant roots.

When you are ready to plant, fill containers halfway with moist seed-starting mix, dribble in a teaspoon or so of water, add enough mix to fill to the top, and then water again. Tamp down the soil with your finger to eliminate air pockets. Plant seeds at their proper depth in the seed-starting mix, spray with water from a pump spray bottle, cover the tops with a thin layer of vermiculite, and spritz again.

Plastic domes are used to retain surface moisture until the seeds germinate, but a damp, folded newspaper placed directly over the planted seeds works just as well. If you are starting only a few seeds, place the planted containers on a plate or in a baking pan that you enclose loosely in a plastic produce bag. Remove the bag when the seedlings start to sprout.

SIMULATING WARM SUN

Once seedlings are equipped with leaves, they switch to light as their primary energy source. To simulate sunshine, grow your veggie seedlings under bright light from a fluorescent or LED light fixture. Inexpensive shop lights from a building supply store, suspended over seedlings, will meet this need. (There is little difference in seedlings' performance under fluorescent and LED lights. Super-efficient broad-spectrum LED plant lights that glow pink seem to have a comforting effect on stressed seedlings, yet they also thrive under fluorescent fixtures, which give off a little heat, like a gentle Sun.)

As soon as little sprouts appear, keep your seedlings under lights for 12 hours a day. Adjust the height of the lights as the seedlings grow. Fluorescent lights should be less than 2 inches from the tops of the plants, while LEDs should be at least 4 inches from the highest leaves. (If you can not raise or lower the lights, raise or lower the containers by putting books or the like under them.)

Seeds germinate best when temperatures range between 75°F during the day and 65°F at night. When growing seedlings in a cool space like a basement, add modest bottom heat to your seedling setup with a seed-heating mat or electric heating pad. You can use food cans or books to hold a tray of seedlings over a heating pad set at its lowest setting.

THINNING AND FEEDING

A week or so after germination, seedlings develop their first true leaf, a sign that roots are also making good progress. This is the best time to thin seedlings by nipping out the weakest ones with little scissors. Or, separate and replant the seedlings into containers filled with regular potting soil, a step which is called "pricking out."

To do this, remove the mass of seedings from its container and place it on its side. Then use your fingers to lift individual seedlings, touching only their seedling leaves. Gently slip seedlings into their new containers, press lightly to firm soil around the roots, water well, and return the seedlings to the same position under lights where they were before. New growth should resume in a day or two.

As the seedlings grow and roots fill the containers, the plants use up soil-borne nutrients. Keep them well nourished by using a water-soluble plant food mixed at half the rate recommended on the package every other time you water. Make a habit of lifting seedling containers to judge their weight. Very light containers are likely to be too dry, while heavy ones are loaded with water.

Learning to grow your own seedlings takes practice, but the life force locked away in every seed wants you to be successful. After all, only the luckiest seeds will get to be planted and cared for by you! ■

Barbara Pleasant is the author of many best-selling garden books, including *Starter Vegetable Gardens* (Storey Publishing, 2022).

WANT TO **GROW** *A*

Say hello to your new old flame!

Plants are seldom collected and cultivated for the purpose of performing party tricks. Yes, many put on a show, with gorgeous blooms, sensuous foliage, and/or seductive scents. But the real showstopper may be the gas plant: It emits a flammable oil that, under the right conditions, can be ignited for a brief but glorious flare-up.

In its extinguished state, this horticultural curiosity—a member of the citrus family native to Europe and Asia— might not immediately spark your interest. The perennial gas plant (*Dictamnus albus,* aka dittany) forms broad and dense clumps of glossy, aromatic, dark-green leaves that emerge from the earth in early spring. Footlong spikes of pure-white flowers develop in early summer. When

rubbed or crushed, the gas plant's leaves release a pleasant, lemony fragrance— but beware and touch with care (wear gloves): The aromatic oil can trigger an allergic reaction or photoreactive burn in some people.

The gas plant grows from 2 to 4 feet tall, needs very little care (just well-draining soil in full sun), and is exceptionally hardy— to Zone 3. Because it is taprooted, it can

SUREFIRE SENSATION?

WHEN CONDITIONS ARE JUST RIGHT, STRIKE A MATCH NEAR THE FLOWER STEM, JUST BELOW THE BLOOMS— AND *POOF!*

179

A GAS PLANT CAN TAKE SEVERAL YEARS TO MATURE, BUT ONCE IT'S ESTABLISHED, IT WILL LAST FOR DECADES.

be tricky to grow in containers and fares poorly if divided. The species can produce pink or purple flowers, but these are less common than white, which are magnificent in an all-white garden or mixed bed.

The flowers are your cue to prepare for the spectacle. Timing is critical: Still, sultry conditions are essential. (Wind would disperse the plant's volatile oils.) When conditions are just right, strike a match near the flower stem, just below the blooms—and *poof!* In only a second or two, a burst of flame travels upward (without harm to the plant), and then disappears! Each flambeau passes out quickly but not so fast that it can not be caught on camera. The flame does not leap to an adjacent stem; you must ignite each one. As you can imagine, the

pyrotechnic effect is especially dramatic after sunset.

Propagation of the gas plant is best achieved with seeds and patience. Fading flowers develop into curious ornamental seedpods, hard and woody to the touch (crafty sorts will note that these could easily be dried for everlasting arrangements). The pods hold beautiful, shiny, black oval seeds, each kept in place by an intriguing spring mechanism. When ripe, the bulging pods split or shoot out the seeds to fall where they may—or into a bag that you arrange on or near the pod. A gas plant can take several years to mature, but once it's established, it will last for decades: "Instances are known where *D. fraxinella* has outlived father, son, and grandson in the same spot without increase," says Henderson's *Handbook of Plants, 1890*. That's a long-running show! ■

–*Cynthia Van Hazinga, with Almanac editors*

WALKING FISH, BEANSTALKS
THAT STING, AND JUMPING WORMS?
YOU'LL NOT FIND THESE IN
A MOVIE OR THE METAVERSE—
THEY'RE RIGHT OUTSIDE.
BY JEFF HELSDON
ILLUSTRATIONS BY KRISTIN KEST

WILD THINGS *THAT*

NORTHERN SNAKEHEADS

Sharp teeth and an aggressive eating habit earned the northern snakehead the name "frankenfish." As if that weren't bad enough, it also has a lunglike organ that allows it to survive out of water for up to 4 days. Still not alarmed? This freshwater freak can travel *across dry land* by moving its head and back fins in opposite directions.

Native to Siberia, China, and Korea and first reported in California in 1997, the northern snakehead is suspected to have gained a finhold in North America after being released into the wild illegally by people who bought them from pet shops or live fish markets. The first breeding population in the U.S. was found in the Potomac River in Maryland in 2002. Populations are now established in New York, Pennsylvania, Virginia, and Maryland. In Canada, there were

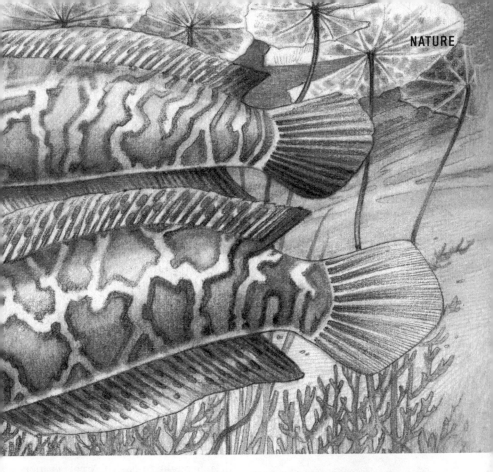

WREAK HAVOC

no known breeding populations as of the summer 2022, despite a few reports of individual fish catches.

The highly adaptable northern snakehead can live in lakes, rivers, wetlands, and smaller streams. It prefers shallow, slow-moving water and has a diverse diet: When young, it preys on plankton, insects, and small fish. As it grows, it begins to also feed on small reptiles and birds and mammals up to a third of its size. Well-fed and unchallenged (it has no natural enemies in North America and can outcompete native fish for both food and habitat), the northern snakehead can mature to 3 feet in length and weigh 19 pounds.

Its torpedo-shape body, scale-clad head, and large single dorsal and anal fins distinguish it from native burbot, bowfin, and eels. Report any suspected encounter with a northern snakehead immediately to a state or local fish and/or wildlife management agency. *(continued)*

GIANT HOGWEED

Giant hogweed, which can reach a height of more than 18 feet, evokes the mythical beanstalk grown from a bean by Jack in the classic children's story, but this monster works only black magic.

On contact with human skin, the clear sap of giant hogweed can burn and sting, causing dermatitis. After exposure to sunlight, the contacted flesh can develop blisters that leave scars for years.

It is no kinder to kindred flora, shading out native plants and in turn degrading wildlife habitat.

This biennial nuisance is a member of the carrot family (Apiaceae), which is a scary clan as it includes both delicious and deadly plants. The giant hogweed takes 2 to 5 years to flower, at which time it can produce up to 120,000 seeds before dying. Its winged seeds are spread by wind and waterways.

Native to Eurasia, giant hogweed was first brought to North America more than 100 years ago as an ornamental for gardens. It has since spread across all Canadian provinces except the Prairies, as well as into U.S. states from New England south to the Carolinas, the U.S. Midwest, and Oregon and Washington.

Manual removal is one method of control—but with a few provisos: Protective clothing should be worn. If the plant is in flower, extra care should be taken to ensure that no seeds fall off. Flowers should be placed in a black garbage bag (sealed closed) for a week to ensure their demise; they should not be burned or composted. Sightings should be reported to local branches of an invasive species network.

JUMPING WORMS

What looks like a common earthworm, thrashes wildly about like a snake and leaps when disturbed, and can shed a portion of its tail to escape?

A jumping worm.

Native to China, Korea, and Japan, the "jumping worm" can be any of several Asian worm species. These creepy crawlers were first introduced to North America in the early 1900s. Spread through mulch and soil on plants, they have begun appearing in forests in more recent years, particularly in the midwestern and northeastern United States.

Jumping worms live in the top layer of soil. Driven by an insatiable hunger, they eat forest leaf litter and remove nutrients from the soil, while leaving behind castings (feces) on the surface of the soil that wash away and/or won't penetrate deep into it where roots can access them. The worms' presence makes soil susceptible to erosion and creates an environment in which many plants and even trees can't live.

When mature, jumping worms can reach 4 to 8 inches in length. A telltale sign that differentiates them from earthworms is a milky white ring (clitellum). One known enemy is Old Man Winter: Jumping worms die during the first frost, but their eggs overwinter in the soil before hatching in April and May. Jumping worms mature in 60 days. Adults reproduce in late summer.

Authorities advise destroying mature jumping worms by drowning them in alcohol, vinegar, or soapy water or putting them into a sealed plastic bag that is then left in the sun. Consult with a state or local natural resources department if you see or catch any jumping worms. ■

Jeff Helsdon is a freelance writer and photographer based in Ontario. He writes for several publications in the United States and Canada, including *Ontario Out of Doors.*

CURES, **CHARMS,** OINTMENTS, and **PRESCRIBED** UNDERTAKINGS

FOR BRIEF RELIEF IN A WORLD OF HURT

ILLUSTRATIONS BY TIM ROBINSON

In ancient Egypt, c. 2500 B.C., the treatment for a wound—a sign that an individual had been visited by evil spirits—involved donkey feces. Records from the period indicate that it worked; modern science (c. 2015) suggests that the manure's efficacy derives from antibacterial agents and probiotics in the animal's digestive system.

Over time, physicians learned of the antibiotic effect of other substances—herbs, minerals, milk, and water—and washed wounds with them. By 400 B.C., Greek physician Hippocrates (c. 460–375 B.C.) had added wine or vinegar to that list of options.

In the centuries since, folk remedies or traditional medicine have proliferated around the globe primarily because they were perceived—or proven—to be effective. You may know a few and may have tried these or others. Nonetheless, we advise that you not try these at home and instead just read on. Whether you call them science or superstition, these medical treatments are amazing.

THE GOAT

UNITED KINGDOM

In the year 410, cancer patients in the United Kingdom were treated with an ointment of goat's gall bladder and honey, while people experiencing "half-dead disease," aka a stroke, were encouraged to inhale the smoke of a burning pine tree. (In the late 1700s, smoke again found favor as a nostrum, this time when delivered to the rectum. The "smoke enema" was believed to stimulate respiration, especially in a drowning victim; relieve headaches, hernias, and stomach cramps, the latter especially if administered while the patient consumed chicken broth; and cure cholera and typhoid.)

Meanwhile, charmers prescribed cures for warts, a common ailment. One still in use involves rubbing the wart with a piece of raw meat before burying it. The expectation is that as the meat deteriorates, so too will the wart.

By the late 19th century, people in the UK with tumors or an enlarged thyroid gland (goiter) were told that they would be restored to health if they touched a hangman's hand, while those who had been bitten by a mad dog would seek relief by holding the key of a church door. Baldness was reputedly cured by sleeping on stones, and fevers were broken by the consumption of willow tree tea (the latter may indeed have been efficacious, as willow contains salicin, a chemical similar to aspirin).   *(continued)*

UKRAINE

In Ukraine, the way to bring a fever down was to drink tea spiked with honey and alcohol while standing in ankle-deep hot water. A straight shot of hard liquor taken with a raw egg was the solution for an ulcer. A cloth soaked in cognac and warm water and then pressed against the neck was said to eliminate a sore throat, while for a stuffy nose, you were advised to bring a pot of chopped garlic to a boil and then stand over it and inhale the fumes.

INDIA, GHANA, AND THE DOMINICAN REPUBLIC

The antidote for a common cold or cough varies around the world: In India, it's a cup of boiling milk with 1 teaspoonful of turmeric. In Ghana, halves of a peeled onion are placed on either side of a child's bed to absorb toxins from the air. In the Dominican Republic, the fix is a tea made by boiling four halves of passion fruit and two halves of onion in water, straining the liquid, and then sweetening the concoction with honey before imbibing it.

ITALY

Farmers in Italy's South Tyrol district have been easing aches and pains in hay baths for centuries. Legend has it that the practice began some 300 years ago when local farmers fell asleep in a meadow. Upon waking, they found that their discomforts had vanished. The farmers capitalized on this happy accident by inviting people to lie in holes in the ground, after which the farmers covered them with dry hay. Today, visitors to area spas can replicate this experience indoors by lying on an air mattress or water bed for 20 minutes while covered in boiled mountain grass. This, locals say, opens pores and stimulates metabolism—albeit most effectively with a week's worth of treatments.

TURKEY

In Turkey, folks suffering from rheumatism would soak in a barley bath. They might eat hedgehog meat to eliminate eczema, consume one pigeon egg per day for 40 days to cure asthma, lay a round slice of lemon on their forehead to cure a headache, relieve an earache with water dripping from a leek, or inhale the ashes of a burnt eggshell to stanch a nosebleed. *(continued)*

UNITED STATES

In the United States, people who experienced "jerking fits" (epileptic seizures) were advised to swallow the heart of a rattlesnake. (When worn around the waist, rattlesnake skin was thought to prolong life.) High blood pressure could supposedly be lowered if green Spanish moss was tucked into a person's shoes. An eel skin tied around the head diffused a headache; tied into the hair, it stimulated growth. A toothache would go away if a splinter from a pine tree that had been struck by lightning was used to pick the tooth. In the Ozarks, wounds were disinfected with turpentine or kerosene; chapped skin was moisturized with possum fat, mutton tallow, or beeswax; and congestion broke up when onion and mustard poultices were applied to the chest.

SOUTH AMERICA

In South America, Incas found a use for every part of the native molle tree (*Schinus molle,* aka Peruvian pepper): The sap had a laxative effect, the resin healed wounds, and teas made from its leaves and bark repaired a panoply of ailments.

CANADA

In Canada, fever, pneumonia, or a cold was treated with a goose fat–and-mustard plaster on the chest. Hot ashes bound in cloth and wrapped around the neck helped to relieve a sore throat. Bleeding wounds were bound in birch bark, and a combination of spruce pitch and grease was applied to skin rashes and burns. Plant parts—roots, stems, leaves, and berries—were used to make teas for a variety of conditions: asthma, diarrhea, headache, muscle or menstrual cramps, sore throat, stomachache— even labor contractions.

SOUTHEAST ASIA

A cure for almost any cold, flu, or headache in Southeast Asia was "coining" (*cao gio,* pronounced "gow yaw"), or catching the wind.

This was based on the popular belief that a body's blood contained too much wind, which needed to be released in order for the body to be relieved.

The procedure itself involved applying warm oil to the chest, back, or shoulders and then rubbing a coin over the skin until the pressure caused red marks— which were taken to be the cue for the wind to exit. ■

–Almanac editors

191

WHEN THE RAT
TRICKED THE CAT

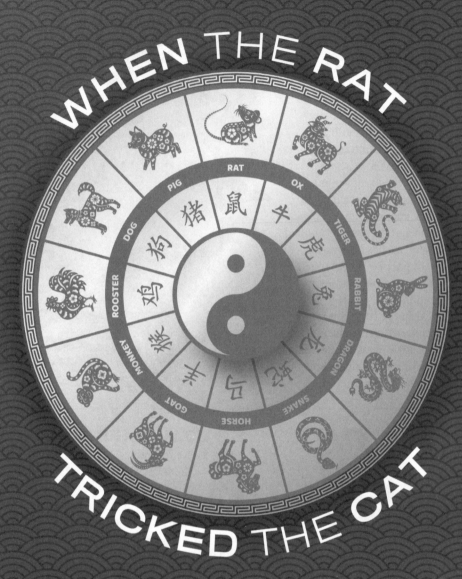

This simple explanation of the Chinese zodiac provides valuable insight into an important part of Chinese culture that has thrived for more than two millennia.

BY TEAM CHINEASY

WHAT IS THE CHINESE ZODIAC?

In the traditional Chinese calendar, each year is denoted by one of 12 animals, and the 12 animals together are known as the Chinese zodiac. The animals appear in the following order: Rat, Ox, Tiger, Rabbit, Dragon, Snake, Horse, Goat, Monkey, Rooster, Dog, and Pig. Each animal begins a year, after which the cycle is repeated again and again. 2024 brings us the Year of the Dragon.

ONE POSSIBLE ORIGIN OF THE CHINESE ZODIAC

There are several versions of how these 12 animals were chosen. One popular story involves a race held by the Jade Emperor, one of the most influential gods in the traditional Chinese religion. In ancient China, recording time—years, months, days, or hours— was not an easy task. According to legend, the Jade Emperor decided to use animals to form calendar years, thus developing an easy way to allow Chinese people to keep track of years.

Yet, even the clever Jade Emperor could not decide which animals should be included. As a solution, he declared on his birthday that he would be holding a swimming race on the river for all of the animals. The goal would be to swim across the river, with the first 12 animals to reach the opposite riverbank to be honored accordingly as the zodiac signs.

Water sports wasn't a fair competition for every species. Some animals were not good at swimming at all; among these were close friends the Cat and the Rat. So, these two decided to ask a favor of the Ox, who was known to be kind, gentle, and a sturdy vessel to cross waters. The kind Ox eventually agreed to take the Cat and the Rat across the river.

In the early morning of the day of the competition, the devious Rat deliberately failed to wake up the Cat. Even worse, the Rat lied to the Ox, telling him that the Cat was dropping out of the race. The Rat then urged the Ox to take only itself across the river. The Ox, ever kind and gentle, agreed to carry the Rat. After numerous splashes and struggles in the water by all, 12 animals were finally nearly ready to complete the crossing.

Each in its turn struggled ashore. Just before the finish line, as the Ox approached the riverbank, the sneaky Rat jumped ahead, stealing the title of winner. The rest followed, in this order: Ox, Tiger, Rabbit, Dragon, Snake, Horse, Goat, Monkey, Rooster, Dog, and Pig.

Poor Cat, having missed the race altogether, was bitter. It blamed the Rat for destroying the trust between them and thus started chasing it. This is why and when the vindictive Cat and the guilty Rat became enemies. Although we know that cats had not been introduced into China by the time the zodiac was established, a story ending like this brings a modern twist to this interesting folktale.

HOW THE CHINESE ZODIAC INFLUENCES PEOPLE'S LIVES

For thousands of years, the Chinese zodiac has influenced people on many levels. The earliest literature that mentions the zodiac dates from the Qin dynasty (c. 220 B.C.), with an ancient storyline featuring the Dragon as a Bug.

The Chinese zodiac is often regarded as the Chinese horoscope divided by years rather than months, as in Western astrology. Each zodiac is associated with different personalities. The zodiac is still in use today as a social indicator for people. Some Chinese people believe that their Chinese signs must be compatible in order for them to get along with others. Theories have been developed to predict one's personality, fortune, and significant life decisions, such as career and marriage, based on the characteristics attributed to each animal of the zodiac.

Moreover, many Chinese people firmly believe that their marriage's happiness (or unhappiness) is determined by the perfect match of a couple's zodiac. Most Chinese also believe that children born into a certain zodiac year will have better luck and fortune than others. For example, many families dream of having a Dragon child, as Dragon babies will supposedly have a prosperous career and good fortune.

Although the Chinese zodiac might seem to have had a mysterious beginning, it has asserted a remarkable influence on Chinese people's lives and decisions for more than 2,000 years. It is deeply rooted in Chinese culture. ∎

Chineasy (Chineasy .com) is a globally recognized, awardwinning brand in the field of language education.

ANIMAL SIGNS OF THE CHINESE ZODIAC

The animal designations of the Chinese zodiac follow a 12-year cycle and are always used in the same sequence. The Chinese year of 354 days begins 3 to 7 weeks into the western 365-day year, so the animal designation changes at that time, rather than on January 1. This year, the Lunar New Year in China starts on February 10.

RAT

Ambitious and sincere, you can be generous with your money. Compatible with the dragon and the monkey. Your opposite is the horse.

1936	1948	1960
1972	1984	1996
2008	2020	2032

OX OR BUFFALO

A leader, you are bright, patient, and cheerful. Compatible with the snake and the rooster. Your opposite is the goat.

1937	1949	1961
1973	1985	1997
2009	2021	2033

TIGER

Forthright and sensitive, you possess great courage. Compatible with the horse and the dog. Your opposite is the monkey.

1938	1950	1962
1974	1986	1998
2010	2022	2034

RABBIT OR HARE

Talented and affectionate, you are a seeker of tranquility. Compatible with the goat and the pig. Your opposite is the rooster.

1939	1951	1963
1975	1987	1999
2011	2023	2035

DRAGON

Robust and passionate, your life is filled with complexity. Compatible with the monkey and the rat. Your opposite is the dog.

1928	1940	1952
1964	1976	1988
2000	2012	2024

SNAKE

Strong-willed and intense, you display great wisdom. Compatible with the rooster and the ox. Your opposite is the pig.

1929	1941	1953
1965	1977	1989
2001	2013	2025

HORSE

Physically attractive and popular, you like the company of others. Compatible with the tiger and the dog. Your opposite is the rat.

1930	1942	1954
1966	1978	1990
2002	2014	2026

GOAT OR SHEEP

Aesthetic and stylish, you enjoy being a private person. Compatible with the pig and the rabbit. Your opposite is the ox.

1931	1943	1955
1967	1979	1991
2003	2015	2027

MONKEY

Persuasive, skillful, and intelligent, you strive to excel. Compatible with the dragon and the rat. Your opposite is the tiger.

1932	1944	1956
1968	1980	1992
2004	2016	2028

ROOSTER OR COCK

Seeking wisdom and truth, you have a pioneering spirit. Compatible with the snake and the ox. Your opposite is the rabbit.

1933	1945	1957
1969	1981	1993
2005	2017	2029

DOG

Generous and loyal, you have the ability to work well with others. Compatible with the horse and the tiger. Your opposite is the dragon.

1934	1946	1958
1970	1982	1994
2006	2018	2030

PIG OR BOAR

Gallant and noble, your friends will remain at your side. Compatible with the rabbit and the goat. Your opposite is the snake.

1935	1947	1959
1971	1983	1995
2007	2019	2031

THE **BEST BREAD**

BY SUSAN PEERY

This quirky, smelly way of making bread is a true American treasure and produces a loaf that tastes remarkably good. The recipes and techniques (and loaf's common name, "salt-rising bread") harken back to the early 1800s, before commercial yeast or other leavening was available, when settlers moving across the Appalachian Mountains simply had to make do. If they had a potato, some cornmeal, flour, and a way to keep a bread starter warm, they could make loaves of a peculiar taste, texture, and appearance that were almost addictive to their families.

Today, old cookbooks from West Virginia to Minnesota and Montana and onward to California testify to the tenacity of this recipe. Bread gurus James Beard and Bernard Clayton included it (with cautionary advice) in their books. Two women who grew up in the heart of Appalachia, Genevieve "Jenny" Bardwell and Susan Ray Brown, have even written an entire book, *Salt Rising Bread* (St. Lynn's Press, 2016), about this finicky, distinctive bread and its rich folklore.

ABOUT THE NAME

It is not salt that makes the bread rise. (Only a small amount of salt is used.) I found two explanations, both reasonable. One is that bakers would warm a pan of rock salt and nestle a jar of starter into the salt to keep it warm overnight. The second is that the term "salt rising" is a variation of "salt raisin'," which in turn is a corruption of "saleratus," a naturally occurring mineral that was a precursor to baking soda, a pinch of which is found in most salt-rising bread recipes.

ABOUT THE SMELL

The starter for this bread develops a rather alarming odor somewhere between the stenches of sweaty old sneakers and overripe cheese. "Stinky feet" is a common descriptor. The more fermentation you get, the better—and the smellier. One family member described it as "dog breath after the dog has been in the compost pile." The

FOR
TOASTING

WHEN EVERYTHING WORKS PERFECTLY, IT TAKES ABOUT 18 HOURS TO GO FROM STARTER TO FINISHED BREAD.

rising dough retains much of the smell. But once the bread is baking, it starts to smell "better," and the bread itself is delicious, with a slight hint of cheese. Aficionados claim that it makes the best toast ever.

WHAT CAUSES THE ODOR?

The microbe that enlivens the starter, *Clostridium perfringens,* is naturally present in the potato and/or cornmeal and is the source of the smell. It multiplies quickly and creates hydrogen gas (just as yeast-generated dough creates carbon dioxide). The scalding-hot liquid used to make the starter wipes out any natural yeasts and leaves only the *Clostridium* microbes to leaven the bread.

YOU WILL NEED . . .

1. Patience. When everything works perfectly, it takes about 18 hours to go from starter to finished bread. One of my efforts took 26 hours. You will know after 5 to 6 hours whether your starter works (i.e., starts to get foamy). At this point, if nothing is bubbling in the jar, give up and start over. It is better to throw out a couple of cups of starter than to prolong the agony and never end up with a loaf of bread. I had one total failure out of five attempts.

2. Heat. The starter and the rising dough need to be held at 100°F or slightly above. This can be hard to achieve. The strategy that worked best for me was to make the starter in the late afternoon, put it in the oven with just the oven light on and a pan of hot (boiling) water on the rack below the starter, and then renew the hot water before going to bed. By bedtime, the starter should have started to foam up. (If not, see Step 1, "Patience.") You may end up devising other ways to maintain a steady 100° to 110°F temperature. Use an oven thermometer to make sure that the oven is warm enough.

SALT-RISING BREAD

This is an adaptation of James Beard's recipe in Beard on Bread *(Knopf, 1995). Keep in mind that the dough is not as elastic as with a yeast-based dough, nor does it rise into a dome shape.*

STARTER:
1 medium white potato, scrubbed and sliced thin
2 tablespoons good-quality cornmeal
1 teaspoon sugar
½ teaspoon salt
1½ cups boiling water

■ Into a large jar, deep ceramic or glass bowl, or heatproof quart jar, put the potato, cornmeal, sugar, and salt. Pour the boiling water into the jar. Cover loosely with a plate and place in the oven inside a larger pan, to catch any drips. Pour more boiling water into a shallow pan set on the rack below the jar of starter. Turn the oven light on. Replace the water in the lower pan with more boiling water, if needed, to keep the starter warm at around 100° to 110°F.

■ After about 12 hours, the starter will have a layer of foam on top as much as an inch thick. This is a good sign. (If no foam appears after about 6 hours, discard and start over.)

■ Pour the jarful of foamy liquid through a strainer into a large mixing bowl or the bowl of a stand mixer. Pour another ½ cup of warm (100° to 110°F or above) water over the potatoes in the strainer and press down on them to extract as much liquid starter as possible into the bowl. Discard potatoes.

DOUGH:
5 cups unbleached, all-purpose flour, divided
½ cup warm (about 100°F) whole milk
1 tablespoon melted butter, plus more to brush on top
1 teaspoon salt
¼ teaspoon baking soda

■ Into the bowl with the starter, put 2 cups of flour, milk, butter, salt, and baking soda. Using a wooden spoon (or dough hook if using a stand mixer), mix well until smooth. Gradually add up to 3 more cups of flour until a soft dough is formed. Turn out onto a floured board and knead until smooth, adding up to ½ cup of flour if needed. Divide the dough and shape into two equal loaves. Place the loaves in well-greased 8x4-inch loaf pans and brush them with melted butter.

■ Cover and let rise in a warm place until the dough has risen to the top of the pans. The dough will be flat, not domed. This may take at least 4 to 5 hours.

■ Bake at 375°F for about 40 minutes, or until loaves are golden and pull away from the pan. The loaves will be flat-topped. Cool slightly before slicing.
Makes 2 loaves. ■

Susan Peery is a regular contributor to Almanac publications.

FOOD

(continued from page 71)

GINGER GREMOLATA BAKED SALMON

GREMOLATA:
½ cup salted, roasted pistachios, finely chopped
½ cup fresh cilantro, chopped
¼ cup fresh mint, chopped
3 tablespoons freshly grated ginger
2 tablespoons chopped chives
2 tablespoons agave syrup or honey
1 tablespoon lemon zest
1 tablespoon fresh lemon juice

SALMON:
1 salmon fillet (1 lb.), cut into two pieces
2 tablespoons olive oil
½ teaspoon salt
½ teaspoon freshly ground black pepper

■ *For gremolata:* In a bowl, combine all ingredients. Cover and set aside.

■ *For salmon:* Preheat oven to 425°F. Line a baking sheet with aluminum foil or parchment paper.

■ Pat salmon dry. Brush with olive oil. Place on prepared baking sheet, skin side down. Season with salt and pepper.

■ Bake for 12 to 14 minutes, or until salmon registers an internal temperature of 145°F on a meat thermometer.

■ *To serve:* Stir gremolata, then equally divide over tops of salmon portions.

Makes 4 servings.

–Sharyn LaPointe Hill, Las Cruces, New Mexico

THAI GINGER MEATBALL SALAD

DRESSING:
¼ cup honey
¼ cup vegetable oil
3 tablespoons fresh lime juice
2 tablespoons smooth peanut butter
1½ tablespoons teriyaki sauce
1 tablespoon freshly grated ginger
1 teaspoon sesame oil

MEATBALLS:
1½ pounds ground chicken breast
½ cup chopped fresh cilantro, plus more for garnish
2 tablespoons freshly grated ginger
1½ tablespoons teriyaki sauce
2 tablespoons vegetable oil

SALAD:
4 cups coleslaw mix
1 cup matchstick carrots
4 scallions, chopped

■ *For dressing:* In the bowl of a food processor or blender, combine all ingredients. Pulse until well combined. Set aside.

■ *For meatballs:* In a bowl, combine chicken, cilantro, ginger, and teriyaki sauce. Use hands or a small cookie scoop to form mixture into 1- to 1½-inch meatballs.

■ In a large skillet over medium-high heat, warm oil. Working in batches, cook meatballs for 10 to 15 minutes, or until cooked through. Add more oil as needed. Set meatballs aside and keep warm.

■ *For salad:* In a bowl, toss together coleslaw, carrots, scallions, and dressing. Mix until well combined.

■ *To serve:* Divide coleslaw mixture onto individual plates and top with meatballs. Garnish with cilantro.

Makes 4 to 6 servings.

–Arlene Erlbach, Morton Grove, Illinois

GINGER PEACH CRISP WITH GINGER-INFUSED WHIPPED CREAM

WHIPPED CREAM:
1 cup heavy whipping cream
2 tablespoons minced candied ginger or 1 tablespoon fresh ginger, roughly chopped
2 tablespoons confectioners' sugar

CRISP:
4 to 5 large peaches, peeled, pitted, and sliced
1 teaspoon cornstarch
½ cup old-fashioned oats
¼ cup almond flour

2 tablespoons brown sugar
1 tablespoon minced candied ginger or
½ tablespoon freshly grated ginger
1 teaspoon ground cinnamon
⅛ teaspoon ground nutmeg
⅛ teaspoon salt
4 tablespoons (½ stick) cold unsalted
butter, cut into pieces

■ *For whipped cream:* In a saucepan over medium heat, bring cream and ginger to a simmer. Reduce heat to low and cook for 10 minutes, stirring often. Turn off heat, cover, and allow to cool in the pan. Once cooled, place in the refrigerator until very cold. This may take several hours.

■ *For crisp:* Preheat oven to 350°F. Grease an oven-safe 7x5-inch baking dish or two small cast-iron skillets.

■ Toss peaches with cornstarch. Place them evenly into prepared baking dish.

■ In a bowl, combine oats, flour, brown sugar, ginger, cinnamon, nutmeg, and salt. With a fork or pastry cutter, cut in butter until all ingredients are incorporated and no pockets of dry oats or flour remain. Spread over peaches.

■ Bake for 30 to 35 minutes, or until top is dark golden brown and peach juices are bubbling. Move to a wire rack to cool.

■ *To serve:* While crisp is cooling, strain ginger pieces out of cream. In a bowl, combine cream and confectioners' sugar. Beat until soft peaks form. Top each serving with whipped cream.

Makes 4 servings.

–Kristen Streepey, Geneva, Illinois

GINGER SWIRL BUNS

FILLING:
8 ounces (1 package) cream cheese,
softened
½ cup confectioners' sugar
2 tablespoons freshly grated ginger
BUNS:
2¼ cups lukewarm (105° to 115°F) water

2 tablespoons molasses
1 package (2¼ teaspoons) active dry yeast
6 cups all-purpose flour, divided
⅓ cup sugar
2 tablespoons canola oil
2¼ teaspoons salt
1 tablespoon freshly grated ginger
FROSTING:
4 ounces (½ package) cream cheese,
softened
2 tablespoons butter, softened
1¼ cups confectioners' sugar
½ teaspoon vanilla extract

■ *For filling:* Beat together all ingredients until smooth. Store in refrigerator until 30 minutes before using.

■ *For buns:* Line a baking sheet with parchment paper.

■ Into the bowl of a mixer with a dough hook, add water, molasses, and yeast. Allow mixture to bubble. Add 2 cups of flour, sugar, oil, salt, and ginger. Mix well. Add remaining 4 cups of flour, slowly, until dough comes away from sides of bowl. Place in a greased bowl, cover with a cloth. Let rise until doubled. Punch down, cover with a cloth, then let rise again until doubled.

■ On a lightly floured surface, roll dough into a long rectangle. Spread filling to edges of dough, leaving one long edge bare. Roll to bare edge and pinch seam to seal. Cut into 2-inch sections and lay cut side down on prepared baking sheet. Cover with cloth and let rise.

■ Preheat oven to 350°F. Bake for 20 to 25 minutes, or until golden. Cool slightly.

■ *For frosting:* Beat cream cheese and butter until smooth. Slowly add in confectioners' sugar, then vanilla. Beat until smooth. Spread over warm buns.

Makes 12 buns.

–Sandy Metzler, Kelowna, British Columbia ■

HOW WE PREDICT THE WEATHER

We derive our weather forecasts from a secret formula that was devised by the founder of this Almanac, Robert B. Thomas, in 1792. Thomas believed that weather on Earth was influenced by sunspots, which are magnetic storms on the surface of the Sun.

Over the years, we have refined and enhanced this formula with state-of-the-art technology and modern scientific calculations. We employ three scientific disciplines to make our long-range predictions: solar science, the study of sunspots and other solar activity; climatology, the study of prevailing weather patterns; and meteorology, the study of the atmosphere. We predict weather trends and events by comparing solar patterns and historical weather conditions with current solar activity.

Our forecasts emphasize temperature and precipitation deviations from averages, or normals. These are based on 30-year statistical averages prepared by government meteorological agencies and updated every 10 years. Our forecasts are based on the tabulations that span the period 1991 through 2020.

The borders of the 16 weather regions of the contiguous states **(page 205)** are based primarily on climatology and the movement of weather systems. For example, while the average weather in Richmond, Virginia, and Boston, Massachusetts, is very different (although both are in Region 2), both areas tend to be affected by the same storms and high-pressure centers and have weather deviations from normal that are similar.

We believe that nothing in the universe happens haphazardly and that there is a cause-and-effect pattern to all phenomena. However, although neither we nor any other forecasters have as yet gained sufficient insight into the mysteries of the universe to predict the weather with total accuracy, our results are almost always very close to our traditional claim of 80%.

WEATHER PHOBIAS

FEAR OF	PHOBIA
Clouds	Nephophobia
Cold	Cheimatophobia Frigophobia Psychrophobia
Dampness, moisture	Hygrophobia
Daylight, sunshine	Heliophobia Phengophobia
Extreme cold, frost, ice	Cryophobia Pagophobia
Floods	Antlophobia
Fog	Homichlophobia Nebulaphobia
Heat	Thermophobia
Hurricanes, tornadoes	Lilapsophobia
Lightning, thunder	Astraphobia Brontophobia Keraunophobia
Northern lights, southern lights	Auroraphobia
Rain	Ombrophobia Pluviophobia
Snow	Chionophobia
Thunder	Ceraunophobia Tonitrophobia
Wind	Ancraophobia Anemophobia

HOW ACCURATE WAS OUR FORECAST LAST WINTER?

Our accuracy in forecasting the direction of precipitation departure from normal for a representative city in each region was 100%. Our forecast for a very wet winter in California was very accurate, as was our prediction of a colder winter from the Rockies through the northern Plains and upper Midwest. The heart of the cold was in the West, and while there were some brief bursts of predicted extreme cold from the Great Lakes to the Northeast, winter was very warm throughout that area. Overall, our accuracy rate in forecasting the direction of temperature departure for a representative city in each region was 39%, a reflection of how abnormal recent weather patterns have been. This makes last winter's total accuracy rate 70%, slightly below our traditional average rate of 80%.

Last winter was a season of snowfall extremes. Our forecast for a snowy winter was correct from eastern Washington through the northern Rockies and northern Plains, where Bismarck, North Dakota, ended up having one of its snowiest winters on record. Another big forecasting victory occurred across the high terrain in the West, from northern Arizona into California's Sierra Nevada, where snowfall ended up being well above normal and Mammoth Mountain had its snowiest season on record. From the southern Plains through the Ohio and Tennessee valleys and into the mid-Atlantic, snowfall underperformed our above-normal forecast. While it was a largely snowless winter from Washington, D.C., to Boston, snowfall did end up near or above normal across portions of northern New England. In Alaska, which did end up mostly snowier, our forecast for a drier-than-normal winter was correct in eastern areas around Juneau.

The table below shows how the actual average precipitation differed from our forecast for November through March for one city in each region. On average, these actual winter precipitation results differed from our forecasts by 0.28 inch.

REGION/ CITY	Nov.-Mar. Monthly Precip. Change vs. Normal (in.) PREDICTED	ACTUAL	REGION/ CITY	Nov.-Mar. Monthly Precip. Change vs. Normal (in.) PREDICTED	ACTUAL
1. Concord, NH	0.6	0.6	**10.** Des Moines, IA	0.2	0.4
2. Hartford, CT	0.8	0.5	**11.** Houston, TX	−0.2	−0.01
3. Roanoke, VA	0.6	1.0	**12.** Amarillo, TX	−0.05	−0.5
4. Savannah, GA	−0.4	−0.3	**13.** Salt Lake City, UT	0.7	0.7
5. Miami, FL	0.8	1.6	**14.** Tucson, AZ	0.1	0.1
6. Detroit, MI	0.5	0.5	**15.** Portland, OR	−0.1	−0.03
7. Charleston, WV	−0.3	−0.5	**16.** Fresno, CA	1.84	1.8
8. Nashville, TN	−0.2	−0.3	**17.** Juneau, AK	−0.49	−0.7
9. International Falls, MN	0.1	0.1	**18.** Honolulu, HI	−2.59	−0.4

WEATHER

WEATHER REGIONS

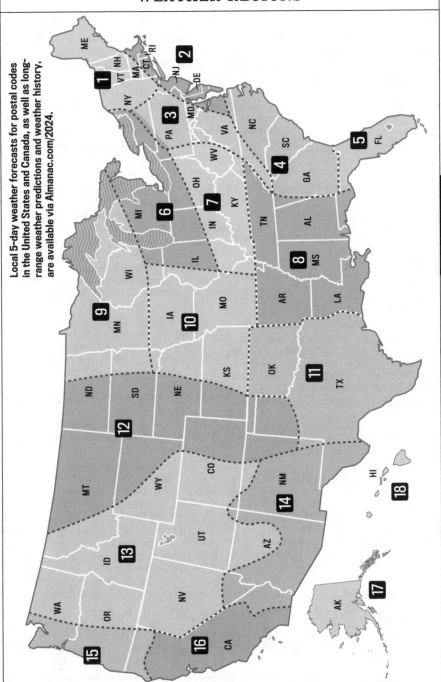

Local 5-day weather forecasts for postal codes in the United States and Canada, as well as long-range weather predictions and weather history, are available via Almanac.com/2024.

WEATHER

NORTHEAST

SUMMARY: Winter temperatures will be above normal, as will be precipitation and snowfall. The coldest periods will occur in mid- to late November, early to mid-January, and early to mid-February, while the snowiest stretches will arrive in mid- to late November, mid-December, and early to mid-January. **April** and **May** will be warmer and wetter than normal. **Summer** temperatures will be above normal, with rainfall below normal. The hottest periods will be in early June and mid-July. **September** and **October** temperatures will average near normal, while rainfall will be below normal.

NOV. 2023: Temp. 37.5° (3° below avg. north, avg. south); precip. 1.5" (1.5" below avg.). 1–4 Sunny, warm. 5–11 Showers, mild. 12–15 Sunny north, flurries south; cold. 16–26 Snowy, very cold. 27–30 Flurries north, sunny south; mild.

DEC. 2023: Temp. 32° (2° above avg.); precip. 4" (0.5" above avg.). 1–5 Flurries north, snowy south; cold. 6–14 Snowy north, sunny before ice and rain south; mild. 15–18 Sunny, then snowstorm; mild. 19–23 Sunny, chilly. 24–26 Rainy, very warm. 27–31 Snowy, chilly.

JAN. 2024: Temp. 26° (3° above avg. north, 1° below south); precip. 5.5" (1" above avg. north, 3" above south). 1–14 Snowstorms, very cold. 15–25 Snowy north, rain and snow south; mild. 26–31 Flurries north, sunny south; chilly.

FEB. 2024: Temp. 20° (3° below avg.); precip. 3.5" (1" above avg.). 1–12 Flurries, then sunny; frigid. 13–19 Snow showers north, rainy south; mild. 20–22 Flurries north, sunny south; mild. 23–29 Rainy, mild.

MAR. 2024: Temp. 37° (3° above avg.); precip. 2" (1" below avg.). 1–4 Snow north, showers south; mild. 5–10 Flurries, chilly. 11–18 Sunny, then showers; warm. 19–21 Sunny, chilly. 22–31 Rain and snow showers, cool.

APR. 2024: Temp. 46° (1° above avg.); precip. 2.5" (0.5" below avg.). 1–3 Snow, chilly. 4–10 Sunny north, showers south; cool. 11–18 Sunny; chilly, then mild. 19–27 Scattered showers, mild. 28–30 Sunny, cool.

MAY 2024: Temp. 61° (4° above avg.); precip. 4.5" (1" above avg.). 1–4 Sunny, warm. 5–16 Scattered showers, mild. 17–18 Heavy rain, cool. 19–24 Rainy, mild. 25–28 Sunny, warm. 29–31 Isolated t-storms, mild.

JUNE 2024: Temp. 65° (1° below avg.); precip. 2" (2" below avg.). 1–4 A few t-storms, warm. 5–11 Showers north, sunny south; becoming hot. 12–14 Sunny, cool. 15–19 Showers north, sunny south; cool. 20–26 T-storms, mild. 27–30 Sunny, cool.

JULY 2024: Temp. 74° (4° above avg.); precip. 2.5" (1.5" below avg.). 1–5 T-storms north, sunny south; mild. 6–8 Sunny, hot. 9–11 T-storms, cool. 12–18 Sunny, becoming hot. 19–28 T-storms, warm. 29–31 T-storms north, sunny south; cool.

AUG. 2024: Temp. 67° (avg.); precip. 6" (3" above avg. north, 1" above south). 1–12 Rainy periods, cool. 13–15 Isolated showers, cool. 16–27 Scattered t-storms, warm. 28–31 Sunny, then heavy rain; warm.

SEPT. 2024: Temp. 62° (1° above avg.); precip. 3.5" (avg.). 1–5 Isolated showers north, sunny south; cool. 6–15 Scattered showers, cool. 16–20 Sunny; cool, then mild. 21–30 Rainy periods, mild.

OCT. 2024: Temp. 48° (1° below avg.); precip. 2.5" (1.5" below avg.). 1–5 Showers, chilly. 6–10 Isolated showers north, sunny south; cool. 11–16 Showers north, sunny south; warm. 17–22 Isolated showers, cool. 23–27 Sunny, then rainy; mild. 28–31 Sunny, cool.

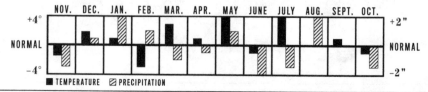

ATLANTIC CORRIDOR

SUMMARY: Winter temperatures, precipitation, and snowfall will all be above normal. The coldest spell will run from late January into mid-February, while the snowiest periods will occur in late December, late January, and mid-February. **April** and **May** will be warmer and wetter than normal. **Summer** will be hotter than average, while rainfall will be below normal in the north and above normal in the south. The hottest periods will be in early July, late July into early August, and late August. Watch for a tropical storm in late August. **September** and **October** will be slightly cooler than normal, with near-normal precipitation.

Boston
Providence
Hartford
New York
Philadelphia
Atlantic City
Baltimore
Washington, D.C.
Richmond

NOV. 2023: Temp. 49° (avg. north, 4° above south); precip. 3.5" (avg. north, 1" above south). 1–8 Sunny north, showers south; mild. 9–11 Rainy, warm. 12–13 Sunny, mild. 14–19 Showers north, sunny south; chilly. 20–23 Snow, then rain; chilly. 24–30 Rainy, mild.

DEC. 2023: Temp. 43° (2° above avg.); precip. 5.5" (2" above avg.). 1–3 Snow north, rain south; turning cold. 4–8 Sunny, chilly. 9–18 Rainy periods; cold, then mild. 19–23 Sunny, chilly. 24–27 Rainy, warm. 28–31 Snow and rain; cold, then warm.

JAN. 2024: Temp. 36° (1° below avg.); precip. 6.5" (3" above avg.). 1–7 Rain and snow, cold. 8–12 Snow showers north, sunny south; cold. 13–14 Heavy rain, mild. 15–25 Rain and snow, mild. 26–31 Sunny, then snowstorm; cold.

FEB. 2024: Temp. 32° (3° below avg.); precip. 6" (3" above avg.). 1–10 Sunny north, snowy south; very cold. 11–13 Snowstorm, very cold. 14–19 Rainy, mild. 20–25 Sunny, mild. 26–29 Rainy, mild.

MAR. 2024: Temp. 48° (4° above avg.); precip. 2" (2" below avg.). 1–7 Showers; mild, then chilly. 8–16 Sunny, warm. 17–18 Rain, mild. 19–21 Sunny, chilly. 22–29 Rainy; warm, then chilly. 30–31 Sunny, chilly.

APR. 2024: Temp. 55° (2° above avg.); precip. 3" (0.5" below avg.). 1–9 Showers, cool. 10–18 Sunny, mild. 19–28 Scattered showers, mild. 29–30 Sunny, mild.

MAY 2024: Temp. 66° (3° above avg.); precip. 5" (1.5" above avg.). 1–4 Sunny, warm. 5–10 Showers, then sunny; warm. 11–15 Showers, then sunny; mild. 16–31 Showers; chilly, then mild.

JUNE 2024: Temp. 70° (2° below avg.); precip. 2" (2" below avg.). 1–5 Sunny, then t-storms; warm, then cool. 6–9 Sunny, cool. 10–17 Scattered t-storms, cool. 18–22 Sunny, cool. 23–30 Showers, then sunny; cool.

JULY 2024: Temp. 80° (3° above avg.); precip. 4" (avg.). 1–7 Sunny north, t-storms south; cool, then hot. 8–11 Showers north, sunny south; hot. 12–20 Scattered t-storms, warm. 21–31 A few t-storms, hot.

AUG. 2024: Temp. 76° (1° above avg.); precip. 6.5" (1" above avg. north, 4" above south). 1–6 Heavy t-storms; hot, then cool. 7–12 Sunny, then showers; cool. 13–23 Sunny, then showers; warm. 24–28 Scattered t-storms, hot. 29–31 Tropical storm threat, warm.

SEPT. 2024: Temp. 69° (avg.); precip. 5" (1" above avg.). 1–7 Sunny, then showers; mild. 8–13 Sunny, cool. 14–21 Showers, then sunny; cool. 22–30 Rainy, warm.

OCT. 2024: Temp. 56° (1° below avg.); precip. 3" (1" below avg.). 1–6 Rainy, cool. 7–15 Sunny; cool, then warm. 16–24 A few showers, cool. 25–27 Rainy, warm. 28–31 Sunny, mild.

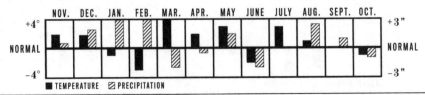

	NOV.	DEC.	JAN.	FEB.	MAR.	APR.	MAY	JUNE	JULY	AUG.	SEPT.	OCT.
+4°												+3"
NORMAL												NORMAL
-4°												-3"

■ TEMPERATURE ▨ PRECIPITATION

APPALACHIANS

Elmira
Scranton
Harrisburg
Frederick
Roanoke
Asheville

SUMMARY: Winter temperatures will be below normal, with above-normal precipitation and snowfall. The coldest period will run from early January through mid-February, while the snowiest spells will occur in late December, mid- to late January, and early to mid-February. **April** and **May** temperatures will be near normal, with rainfall slightly above normal. **Summer** temperatures will average below normal, as will precipitation. The hottest periods will arrive in early July and early and late August. **September** and **October** temperatures will be below average, while precipitation will be greater than normal.

NOV. 2023: Temp. 46° (avg. north, 4° above south); precip. 3" (1" below avg. north, 1" above south). 1–7 Sunny, then showers north; warm. 8–11 Rainy, warm. 12–18 Scattered showers, cool. 19–22 Snow showers north, sunny south; chilly. 23–30 Rainy periods, warm.

DEC. 2023: Temp. 37° (1° below avg.); precip. 5" (1.5" above avg.). 1–4 Rain, then sunny; turning cold. 5–18 Rain and snow showers, chilly. 19–22 Sunny, cold. 23–31 Snowy north, rain south; cold.

JAN. 2024: Temp. 28° (3° below avg.); precip. 5" (1.5" above avg.). 1–13 Snowy north, rainy south; cold. 14–21 Periods of snow, cold. 22–29 Flurries north, sunny south; cold. 30–31 Snowstorm, cold.

FEB. 2024: Temp. 26° (4° below avg.); precip. 4.5" (2" above avg.). 1–10 Snow showers north, flurries south; very cold. 11–12 Snowstorm, very cold. 13–17 Rainy, mild. 18–20 Rain, then snow; chilly. 21–24 Sunny, mild. 25–29 Rainy, mild.

MAR. 2024: Temp. 41° (1° above avg. north, 1" above south); precip. 3" (1" below avg. north, 1" above south). 1–8 Rain and snow north, showers south; mild. 9–15 Sunny, warm. 16–17 Rain, heavy south; warm. 18–21 Sunny, chilly. 22–25 Showers north, sunny south; warm. 26–31 Rainy, chilly.

APR. 2024: Temp. 50° (1° below avg.); precip. 4" (avg.). 1–3 Rain and snow north, sunny south; chilly. 4–9 Showers, cool. 10–14 Sunny, cool. 15–21 Rainy periods, mild. 22–24 Sunny, cool. 25–30 Showers, then sunny; cool.

MAY 2024: Temp. 62° (1° above avg.); precip. 5" (1" above avg.). 1–5 Sunny north, rainy south; very warm. 6–11 Showers north, sunny south; mild. 12–21 Rainy periods; mild, then chilly. 22–31 Showers, warm.

JUNE 2024: Temp. 66° (3° below avg.); precip. 3.5" (1" below avg.). 1–4 Sunny north, t-storms south; warm. 5–14 Sunny north, isolated t-storms south; cool. 15–21 Showers, then sunny; warm, then cool. 22–27 T-storms, cool. 28–30 Sunny, cool.

JULY 2024: Temp. 74° (avg.); precip. 2.5" (1" below avg.). 1–4 Sunny north, t-storms south; cool. 5–12 Isolated t-storms, hot. 13–20 Rainy periods; cool, then warm. 21–31 Showers, then sunny; warm.

AUG. 2024: Temp. 72° (avg.); precip. 4.5" (1" above avg.). 1–10 T-storms, then sunny; hot, then very cool. 11–19 Rainy periods, warm. 20–25 Sunny north, t-storms south; hot. 26–31 T-storms, warm.

SEPT. 2024: Temp. 63° (2° below avg.); precip. 6" (2" above avg.). 1–5 Sunny, cool. 6–11 Showers, then sunny; warm, then cool. 12–15 Heavy rain, cool. 16–19 Sunny, cool. 20–30 Rainy periods; warm, then cool.

OCT. 2024: Temp. 53° (1° below avg.); precip. 3.5" (avg.). 1–6 Rainy, cool. 7–15 Sunny, cool. 16–21 Isolated showers, cool. 22–25 Sunny north, showers south; mild. 26–31 Rain, then sunny; cool.

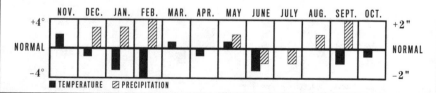

SOUTHEAST

SUMMARY: Winter temperatures will be above normal, as will be precipitation and snowfall. The coldest periods will arrive in late December and early and mid-February, with the best chances for snow occurring in late January and mid-February. **April** and **May** will be warmer and wetter than normal. **Summer** temperatures will be cooler than normal, with the hottest periods in late June, early July, and late July into mid-August. Rainfall will be above normal in the east and below normal in the west. Watch for a hurricane in late August. **September** and **October** will be slightly cooler than normal, with normal precipitation.

NOV. 2023: Temp. 61° (5° above avg.); precip. 4" (1" above avg.). 1–8 Showers, then sunny; warm. 9–15 Showers, then sunny north, sunny south; warm. 16–22 Rainy periods north, sunny before showers south; mild. 23–30 Rainy periods, then sunny; warm.

DEC. 2023: Temp. 49° (avg.); precip. 4.5" (0.5" above avg.). 1–5 A few showers, turning cold. 6–14 Isolated showers north, sunny south; turning warm. 15–17 Sunny, then rain, heavy south; mild. 18–23 Sunny, cool. 24–28 Rain, then sunny; turning very cold. 29–31 Rain, milder.

JAN. 2024: Temp. 45° (2° below avg.); precip. 5.5" (1" above avg.). 1–4 Showers, then sunny; cold. 5–11 Rainy, then sunny; chilly. 12–14 Rainy, warm. 15–24 Rainy periods, cold. 25–31 Snow showers and flurries north, showers south; cold.

FEB. 2024: Temp. 46° (1° below avg.); precip. 5" (avg. east, 2" above west). 1–2 Snow showers north, sunny south; cold. 3–9 Sunny, turning warm. 10–12 Snowstorm, very cold. 13–18 Rainy; cold, then warmer. 19–23 Sunny, mild. 24–29 Rainy, mild.

MAR. 2024: Temp. 57° (1° above avg.); precip. 3.5" (1" below avg.). 1–7 Rainy periods, mild. 8–13 Sunny; cold, then warm. 14–17 Rainy, mild. 18–26 Sunny; chilly, then warm. 27–31 Showers, then sunny; cool.

APR. 2024: Temp. 66° (2° above avg.); precip. 4.5" (1" above avg.). 1–7 Rainy periods, heavy north; mild. 8–17 Sunny; cool, then warm.

18–20 Rain, mild. 21–25 Sunny, cool. 26–30 A few showers, warm.

MAY 2024: Temp. 73° (1° above avg.); precip. 7" (5" above avg. east, 1" above west). 1–7 Rainy periods, heavy south; warm. 8–10 Sunny, mild. 11–17 Scattered t-storms, warm. 18–21 Rainy north, sunny south; cool. 22–31 Scattered t-storms, warm.

JUNE 2024: Temp. 77° (2° below avg.); precip. 2.5" (2" below avg.). 1–7 Sunny north, isolated t-storms south; warm. 8–10 T-storms, cool. 11–22 Scattered t-storms, cool. 23–30 Isolated t-storms, then sunny; hot.

JULY 2024: Temp. 83° (avg.); precip. 4.5" (1" above avg. east, 1" below west). 1–5 Scattered t-storms, warm. 6–10 Sunny, becoming hot. 11–18 T-storms, heavy rain south; mild. 19–31 Sunny, isolated t-storms; hot.

AUG. 2024: Temp. 82° (1° above avg.); precip. 6.5" (2" above avg.). 1–11 T-storms, then sunny; hot, then cool. 12–14 Sunny, hot. 15–26 T-storms, isolated east; warm. 27–31 Hurricane threat east, sunny west; warm.

SEPT. 2024: Temp. 74° (1° below avg.); precip. 7" (2" above avg.). 1–11 Sunny north, scattered t-storms south; cool. 12–15 Rain, heavy south; mild. 16–19 Isolated showers, cool. 20–28 T-storms; warm, then cool. 29–30 Sunny, cool.

OCT. 2024: Temp. 65° (avg.); precip. 1" (2" below avg.). 1–6 Showers north, sunny south; cool. 7–15 Sunny, turning warm. 16–20 Showers, then sunny; cool. 21–24 Sunny, warm. 25–31 Rainy, then sunny; turning cool.

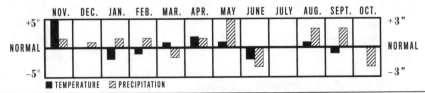

FLORIDA

Jacksonville
Orlando
Tampa
Miami

SUMMARY: Winter will be warmer than normal, with the coldest temperatures in late December, late January, and early February. Winter rainfall will be above normal in the north and below normal in the south. **April** and **May** will be warmer and wetter than normal. **Summer** will bring above-normal temperatures and below-normal rainfall. The hottest periods will be in late June and early July. Watch for a hurricane in late August. **September** and **October** will be slightly cooler and drier than normal.

NOV. 2023: Temp. 75° (6° above avg.); precip. 1.5" (1" below avg.). 1–6 Scattered showers, very warm. 7–14 Sunny north, a few showers south; warm. 15–22 Sunny, very warm. 23–30 Scattered showers, warm.

DEC. 2023: Temp. 66° (1° above avg.); precip. 3.5" (1" above avg.). 1–5 Scattered showers, turning chilly. 6–13 Sunny, cool. 14–24 Rainy periods, then sunny; mild. 25–28 Rain, then sunny; cold. 29–31 Isolated showers, warm.

JAN. 2024: Temp. 59° (2° below avg.); precip. 4.5" (3" above avg. north, 1" above south). 1–8 Rainy periods, heavy north; cold. 9–12 Sunny, mild. 13–20 Rainy, colder. 21–27 Isolated showers, then sunny; cold. 28–31 Rain north, sunny south; mild.

FEB. 2024: Temp. 61° (1° below avg.); precip. 2.5" (2" above avg. north, 1" below south). 1–9 Sunny; very cold, then warmer. 10–14 Sunny, cool. 15–18 Rainy, mild. 19–24 Sunny; cold, then warmer. 25–29 Rainy periods, mild.

MAR. 2024: Temp. 67° (1° below avg.); precip. 0.5" (2" below avg.). 1–4 Isolated showers, cool. 5–15 Sunny, cool. 16–21 Showers, then sunny; cool. 22–27 Sunny, warmer. 28–31 Isolated showers, mild.

APR. 2024: Temp. 75° (2° above avg.); precip. 5" (avg. north, 5" above south). 1–7 Showers north, sunny south; warm. 8–16 Sunny, mild. 17–18 Rain, very heavy south; mild. 19–27 Isolated showers, mild. 28–30 T-storms, warm.

MAY 2024: Temp. 78° (avg.); precip. 6.5" (5" above avg. north, 1" below south). 1–7 T-storms with heavy rain north, sunny south; warm. 8–12 Sunny north, t-storms south; cool. 13–17 T-storms north, sunny south; mild. 18–20 Sunny, cool. 21–31 Scattered t-storms, warm.

JUNE 2024: Temp. 83° (avg.); precip. 4" (3" below avg.). 1–11 Isolated t-storms, mild. 12–18 Sunny, warm. 19–22 Sunny north, t-storms south; mild. 23–26 Sunny, hot. 27–30 Scattered t-storms, warm.

JULY 2024: Temp. 85° (1° above avg.); precip. 6" (1" below avg.). 1–12 T-storms, isolated south; hot. 13–18 Scattered t-storms, warm. 19–21 Sunny, warm. 22–31 Scattered t-storms; hot north, warm south.

AUG. 2024: Temp. 83° (avg.); precip. 7" (1" below avg.). 1–6 T-storms north, sunny south; mild. 7–11 Isolated t-storms, warm. 12–24 Sunny north, t-storms south; warm. 25–28 Hurricane threat north, t-storms south; warm. 29–31 Sunny, warm.

SEPT. 2024: Temp. 80° (1° below avg.); precip. 9.5" (2" above avg.). 1–8 T-storms, warm. 9–13 Isolated t-storms, warm. 14–23 T-storms; warm north, cool south. 24–30 Sunny north, isolated t-storms south; warm, then cooler.

OCT. 2024: Temp. 76° (avg.); precip. 1.5" (3" below avg.). 1–5 Sunny, mild. 6–11 Sunny north, scattered showers south; mild. 12–16 Isolated showers, warm. 17–23 Sunny, mild. 24–27 Showers, warm. 28–31 Sunny, mild.

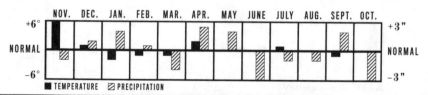

| | NOV. | DEC. | JAN. | FEB. | MAR. | APR. | MAY | JUNE | JULY | AUG. | SEPT. | OCT. |

+6° NORMAL -6°   +3" NORMAL -3"

■ TEMPERATURE ▨ PRECIPITATION

LOWER LAKES

SUMMARY: Winter will be colder than normal, with the coldest periods in early and late December and from January through mid-February. Precipitation and snowfall will average above normal, with the snowiest periods occurring from late December through most of January and in mid-February. **April** and **May** temperatures will be above normal, while precipitation will be slightly below normal.

Summer temperatures will be warmer than normal in the east and cooler than normal in the west, with the hottest periods in early and mid-July. Rainfall will be above normal. **September** and **October** will be cooler than normal, with precipitation above normal in the east and below normal in the west.

NOV. 2023: Temp. 42° (1° above avg.); precip. 2.5" (1" below avg. east, 1" above west). 1–4 Sunny, mild. 5–12 Showers, then sunny; mild. 13–18 Flurries, chilly. 19–23 Snow, then sunny; chilly. 24–30 Rain and snow east, snowstorms west; cool.

DEC. 2023: Temp. 32° (2° below avg.); precip. 4" (1" above avg.). 1–7 Snow showers east, sunny west; very cold. 8–16 Rain and snow, then sunny; chilly. 17–25 Snowstorm, rainy periods; cold, then mild. 26–31 Lake snows east, sunny west; very cold.

JAN. 2024: Temp. 24.5° (2° below avg. east, 5° below west); precip. 3.5" (0.5" above avg.). 1–12 Periods of snow, heavy west; cold. 13–17 Rain and snow east, heavy snow west; chilly. 18–27 Snowy periods, cold. 28–31 Lake snows east, sunny west; frigid.

FEB. 2024: Temp. 25° (3° below avg.); precip. 2" (avg.). 1–12 Lake snows, frigid. 13–16 Rainy, milder. 17–20 Snowstorm east, flurries west; chilly. 21–29 Rainy periods, mild.

MAR. 2024: Temp. 39° (3° above avg. east, 1° below west); precip. 3.5" (0.5" above avg.). 1–6 Snow showers, then rain; turning warm. 7–9 Flurries, cold. 10–15 Sunny east, rain west; warm. 16–20 Rain, then snow; colder. 21–31 Rain, then snow; turning chilly.

APR. 2024: Temp. 49° (avg.); precip. 4" (avg.). 1–3 Snow, then sunny; cold. 4–7 Rain, heavy west; milder. 8–12 Sunny, mild. 13–18

Scattered showers, warm. 19–26 Showers, cool. 27–30 Sunny, warmer.

MAY 2024: Temp. 61° (2° above avg.); precip. 3" (avg. east, 2" below west). 1–4 Sunny, very warm. 5–8 Showers, cooler. 9–13 Sunny, mild. 14–23 Rainy, cool. 24–27 Sunny, warm. 28–31 T-storms, warm.

JUNE 2024: Temp. 66° (1° below avg.); precip. 3.5" (0.5" below avg.). 1–9 T-storms, then sunny; cool, then warm. 10–13 Sunny east, t-storms west; cool. 14–20 Sunny, cool. 21–27 T-storms, cool. 28–30 Sunny, cool.

JULY 2024: Temp. 73.5° (3° above avg. east, avg. west); precip. 5.5" (2" above avg.). 1–9 T-storms, hot. 10–14 Sunny, mild. 15–18 T-storms, hot. 19–31 Scattered t-storms, warm.

AUG. 2024: Temp. 69° (1° below avg.); precip. 5" (1" above avg.). 1–10 Scattered showers, cool. 11–15 Sunny east, t-storms west; mild. 16–22 T-storms, mild. 23–31 Scattered t-storms east, sunny west; warm.

SEPT. 2024: Temp. 61° (1° below avg. east, 2" below west); precip. 3" (2" above avg. east, 2" below west). 1–7 Sunny, then rain, heavy east; cool. 8–16 Isolated showers east, sunny west; mild. 17–23 Sunny, warm. 24–30 Showers; warm, then cool.

OCT. 2024: Temp. 52° (1° below avg.); precip. 1.5" (1.5" below avg.). 1–10 Isolated showers, cool. 11–14 Sunny, warm. 15–20 Showers; warm, then cooler. 21–31 Scattered showers, cool.

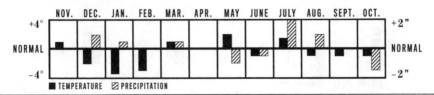

OHIO VALLEY

Pittsburgh
Cincinnati
Louisville • Charleston

SUMMARY: Winter will be colder than normal, with above-normal precipitation and snowfall. The coldest spells will occur in late December, early January, and late January through mid-February. The snowiest periods will be in late December through mid-January and late January through mid-February. **April** and **May** temperatures will be warmer than normal in the east and cooler than normal in the west. Precipitation will average slightly below normal. **Summer** will be cooler than normal, with rainfall below average in the east and above average in the west. The hottest periods will be late July and early August. **September** and **October** will be cooler than normal, with above-normal precipitation.

NOV. 2023: Temp. 48° (3° above avg.); precip. 5" (1" above avg. east, 3" above west). 1–4 Sunny, turning warm. 5–10 Rainy periods, mild. 11–15 Sunny, cool. 16–21 Rainy periods, cool. 22–25 Sunny, mild. 26–30 Rainy, mild.

DEC. 2023: Temp. 38° (1° below avg.); precip. 5.5" (2.5" above avg.). 1–4 Heavy rain, then flurries; chilly. 5–8 Sunny, mild. 9–16 Showers, then sunny; mild. 17–21 Snow showers east, sunny west; colder. 22–25 Rainy, milder. 26–31 Snowy, colder.

JAN. 2024: Temp. 30° (4° below avg.); precip. 4.5" (1" above avg.). 1–9 Snow east, sunny west; very cold. 10–15 Rain, then snow; milder. 16–27 Snowy, cold. 28–31 Sunny, then snow; frigid.

FEB. 2024: Temp. 32° (3° below avg.); precip. 4.5" (1" above avg.). 1–4 Snow, then sunny; frigid. 5–12 Rain and snow, cold. 13–18 Rainy, mild. 19–29 Rain, then sunny; mild.

MAR. 2024: Temp. 46° (3° above avg. east, 1° below west); precip. 4" (0.5" below avg.). 1–7 Rain and snow, mild. 8–14 Sunny; cold, then mild. 15–20 Rain, then snow; turning cold. 21–26 Rainy, warm. 27–31 Showers, colder.

APR. 2024: Temp. 56° (2° above avg. east, 2° below west); precip. 4" (avg.). 1–8 Rainy; cold, then warm. 9–16 Sunny, turning warm. 17–24 Showers, then sunny; turning cool. 25–30 Rain, then sunny; cool.

MAY 2024: Temp. 64° (2° above avg. east, 2° below west); precip. 3.5" (0.5" below avg.). 1–8 Showers; warm, then cool. 9–13 Sunny, mild. 14–25 Rainy periods, cool. 26–31 Sunny, then showers; mild.

JUNE 2024: Temp. 70° (2° below avg.); precip. 3" (1.5" below avg.). 1–8 Rainy, then sunny; turning cooler. 9–17 Isolated t-storms, warm. 18–21 Sunny, cool. 22–30 T-storms east, sunny west; cool.

JULY 2024: Temp. 76° (1° above avg. east, 1° below west); precip. 5" (1" below avg. east, 3" above west). 1–8 T-storms; cool, then warm. 9–14 Sunny, cool. 15–22 Periods of rain, heavy west; warm. 23–31 Sunny, hot.

AUG. 2024: Temp. 74° (avg.); precip. 4.5" (2" above avg. east, avg. west). 1–3 T-storms, hot. 4–10 Showers, then sunny; cool. 11–22 Showers, then sunny; turning warm. 23–28 Sunny, warm. 29–31 Isolated showers, cooler.

SEPT. 2024: Temp. 66° (2° below avg.); precip. 6.5" (2" above avg. east, 5" above west). 1–5 Sunny; cool, then warmer. 6–7 Rain, heavy west; cool. 8–12 Sunny, mild. 13–20 Showers, then sunny; cool. 21–30 Rainy periods, cool.

OCT. 2024: Temp. 58° (avg.); precip. 1.5" (1" below avg.). 1–8 Rainy, then sunny; cool. 9–14 Sunny, warm. 15–25 Isolated showers; cool, then warm. 26–31 Sunny, cool.

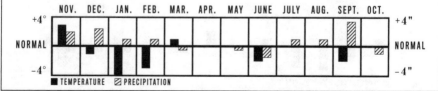

WEATHER

DEEP SOUTH

SUMMARY: Winter will be colder than normal in the north and warmer than normal in the south, with the coldest periods in late December, early January, late January, and early February. Precipitation and chances for snow will be above normal, with the best threats for snow in the north in mid- and late January and mid-February. **April** and **May** will be warmer and wetter than normal. **Summer** will be hotter and drier than normal, with the hottest periods in late June, late July, and much of August. Watch for a hurricane in early July and a tropical storm in mid-July. **September** and **October** temperatures will average near normal, with rainfall above normal in the north and below normal in the south. Watch for a hurricane in early September.

NOV. 2023: Temp. 58° (4° above avg.); precip. 7.5" (3" above avg.). 1–6 Sunny; cool, then warm. 7–10 Heavy rain north, showers south; warm. 11–14 Sunny, mild. 15–25 Rainy periods, then sunny; warm. 26–30 Heavy rain, mild.

DEC. 2023: Temp. 49° (1° below avg.); precip. 7" (4" above avg. north, avg. south). 1–8 Rain, then sunny; cool. 9–13 Showers, warmer. 14–18 Showers, cool. 19–21 Sunny, cool. 22–31 Rainy periods, chilly.

JAN. 2024: Temp. 43° (4° below avg.); precip. 7.5" (2" above avg.). 1–8 Sunny, then rainy; cold. 9–13 Rain; chilly north, warm south. 14–21 Snow north, showers south; cool. 22–25 Sunny, cold. 26–31 Snowstorm north, rain south; cold.

FEB. 2024: Temp. 47.5° (2° below avg. north, 1° above south); precip. 6.5" (avg. north, 2" above south). 1–3 Flurries north, sunny south; cold. 4–9 Sunny, warmer. 10–18 Snowstorms north, rain south; cold, then warm. 19–29 Rainy periods, mild.

MAR. 2024: Temp. 59° (2° above avg.); precip. 7" (1" above avg.). 1–3 Showers, cool. 4–11 Sunny, mild. 12–16 Rainy, warm. 17–22 Showers north, sunny south; chilly, then warm. 23–31 Rain, then sunny; mild.

APR. 2024: Temp. 67° (3° above avg.); precip. 7.5" (3" above avg. north, 1" above south). 1–6 Rain north, sunny south; mild. 7–13 Sunny, warm. 14–20 T-storms, warm. 21–25 Sunny, cool. 26–30 Rain, then sunny; cool north,

warm south.

MAY 2024: Temp. 73° (1° above avg.); precip. 6" (1" above avg.). 1–6 Sunny, then t-storms; warm. 7–10 Sunny, warm. 11–16 T-storms, warm. 17–27 Sunny, then t-storms; warm. 28–31 Isolated t-storms, warm.

JUNE 2024: Temp. 79° (avg.); precip. 2" (3.5" below avg.). 1–12 Sunny, warm. 13–17 T-storms, warm. 18–26 Sunny, warm. 27–30 Isolated t-storms, hot.

JULY 2024: Temp. 82° (avg.); precip. 6" (1" above avg.). 1–3 Isolated t-storms, warm. 4–6 Hurricane threat, warm. 7–14 Scattered t-storms, hot. 15–25 Scattered t-storms, tropical storm threat west; warm. 26–31 Sunny, hot.

AUG. 2024: Temp. 82° (1° above avg.); precip. 5.5" (2" above avg. north, 1" below south). 1–5 Scattered t-storms, hot. 6–10 Sunny, cooler. 11–16 Scattered t-storms, hot. 17–21 Rainy, cool. 22–31 Isolated t-storms, hot.

SEPT. 2024: Temp. 76° (1° below avg.); precip. 6" (3" above avg. north, avg. south). 1–3 Sunny, warm. 4–6 Hurricane threat, warm. 7–14 Scattered t-storms, cooler. 15–18 Sunny, cool. 19–22 T-storms east, sunny west; warmer. 23–30 Sunny; warm, then cool.

OCT. 2024: Temp. 67° (1° above avg.); precip. 2" (1" below avg.). 1–8 Sunny, cool. 9–14 Sunny, very warm. 15–20 T-storms, then sunny; cooler. 21–25 Showers, warm. 26–31 Sunny, cooler.

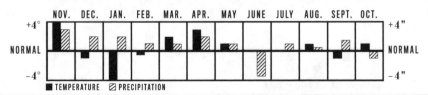

UPPER MIDWEST

SUMMARY: Winter temperatures will be below normal, with the coldest periods in mid- to late November, most of December, early and late January, and early February. Precipitation and snowfall will be above normal. The snowiest periods will be in late November, mid- to late December, mid-January, and early February. **April** and **May** temperatures will be below normal, while precipitation will be below normal in the east and near normal in the west. **Summer** will be warmer than normal, with rainfall above normal in the east and below normal in the west. The hottest periods will be in early, mid-, and late July, interspersed with cool spells. **September** and **October** will have near-normal temperatures and below-normal precipitation.

WEATHER

NOV. 2023: Temp. 25° (5° below avg.); precip. 3" (1" above avg.). 1–5 Sunny, then rain and snow showers; turning colder. 6–11 Periods of rain and snow, cold. 12–15 Flurries, frigid. 16–22 Snowy periods, cold. 23–30 Sunny, then snowy periods; very cold.

DEC. 2023: Temp. 15° (4° below avg.); precip. 0.5" (0.5" below avg.). 1–10 Sunny; frigid, then milder. 11–22 Periods of snow, turning colder. 23–25 Snow showers, chilly east; sunny, frigid west. 26–31 Sunny, bitter cold.

JAN. 2024: Temp. 8° (5° below avg.); precip. 1" (avg.). 1–4 Sunny, frigid. 5–10 Snowy periods east, flurries west; bitter cold. 11–18 Snow showers, not as cold. 19–23 Snowy periods, chilly. 24–31 Flurries, very cold.

FEB. 2024: Temp. 8° (4° below avg.); precip. 2" (1" above avg.). 1–8 Snowy periods, bitter cold. 9–13 Flurries, turning milder. 14–18 Periods of rain and snow, turning colder. 19–22 Sunny, chilly. 23–29 Periods of rain and snow, turning colder.

MAR. 2024: Temp. 25° (3° below avg.); precip. 2.5" (1.5" above avg. east, 0.5" above west). 1–10 Flurries, then sunny; frigid, then mild. 11–15 Showery, mild. 16–20 Snowy periods east, sunny west; very cold. 21–27 Rain and snow showers, chilly. 28–31 Flurries, cold.

APR. 2024: Temp. 40° (1° below avg.); precip. 2" (1" below avg. east, 1" above west). 1–3 Snow showers, cold. 4–6 Rain and snow showers, cold. 7–12 Sunny, turning warmer. 13–18 A few t-storms east, rainy periods

west; warm. 19–30 A few showers, chilly.

MAY 2024: Temp. 52° (2° below avg.); precip. 2.5" (1" below avg.). 1–4 Showery; mild east, chilly west. 5–9 Sunny, chilly. 10–16 Rainy; chilly, then milder. 17–20 Showery, cool. 21–23 T-storms, warm. 24–31 Showery, cool.

JUNE 2024: Temp. 63° (1° below avg.); precip. 4" (0.5" above avg.). 1–3 Rainy, mild east; a few showers, cool west. 4–10 Sunny, then heavy t-storms; turning warm. 11–19 Showers, cool. 20–26 Rainy periods, mild. 27–30 Sunny, cool.

JULY 2024: Temp. 72° (3° above avg.); precip. 3.5" (1" above avg. east, 1" below west). 1–6 Sunny, then scattered t-storms, heavy east; hot. 7–11 Sunny, cool. 12–17 A few t-storms, very warm. 18–20 Showers, cool. 21–31 A few t-storms, turning hot.

AUG. 2024: Temp. 65° (1° above avg.); precip. 4.5" (1" above avg.). 1–6 Rainy periods east, sunny west; cool. 7–12 Isolated showers, cool. 13–21 A few t-storms; warm, turning cool. 22–26 T-storms, warm. 27–31 Showers, turning cool.

SEPT. 2024: Temp. 60° (1° above avg.); precip. 1" (2" below avg.). 1–6 Sunny, then rainy periods; cool. 7–12 Sunny; warm, turning cool. 13–23 Isolated showers, then sunny; warm. 24–30 A few showers, chilly.

OCT. 2024: Temp. 46° (1° below avg.); precip. 3.5" (1" above avg.). 1–6 Showers, chilly. 7–10 Sunny, turning mild. 11–15 Rainy, mild. 16–22 Rain and snow showers east, sunny west; chilly. 23–26 Rain and snow, turning cold. 27–31 Rain and snow showers, cold.

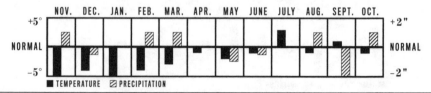

HEARTLAND

SUMMARY: Winter will be colder than normal, with the coldest periods in early and late December, early and late January, and early February. Precipitation and snowfall will be slightly above normal. The snowiest periods will be in late December and early to mid-January. **April** and **May** will be warmer than normal, with near-normal precipitation. **Summer** will be hotter and drier than normal, with the hottest periods in early and late July and early and mid-August. **September** and **October** will be warmer than normal, with below-average precipitation.

NOV. 2023: Temp. 42° (3° below avg. north, 1° above south); precip. 4" (2" above avg.). 1–3 Sunny, warm. 4–10 Rainy periods, turning chilly. 11–14 Sunny, cold. 15–18 Isolated showers, chilly. 19–30 Periods of rain and snow, cold north; showers, mild south.

DEC. 2023: Temp. 32° (3° below avg.); precip. 0.5" (1" below avg.). 1–12 Sunny; frigid, turning mild. 13–21 Isolated showers, turning colder. 22–31 Snowy periods; mild, then bitter cold.

JAN. 2024: Temp. 24° (6° below avg.); precip. 1" (avg.). 1–6 Sunny, then snowstorm; bitter cold. 7–9 Flurries, cold. 10–15 Rain and snow showers, mild. 16–23 Snowy periods, very cold. 24–31 Sunny, then snowy; frigid.

FEB. 2024: Temp. 28° (4° below avg.); precip. 2.5" (0.5" above avg.). 1–5 Snowy periods, then sunny; frigid. 6–11 Flurries; mild, then very cold. 12–15 Rain and snow showers, mild. 16–22 Sunny north, showers south; chilly. 23–29 Rain and snow showers, turning cold.

MAR. 2024: Temp. 43° (1° below avg.); precip. 3.5" (2" above avg. north, avg. south). 1–4 Flurries, cold. 5–9 Sunny, mild. 10–15 Rainy periods, mild. 16–20 Periods of rain and snow, cold. 21–23 Rainy, mild. 24–31 Rain and snow north, showers south; cold.

APR. 2024: Temp. 55° (avg.); precip. 4.5" (1" above avg.). 1–4 Rain, heavy south; chilly. 5–10 Sunny, turning warm. 11–18 Rainy periods, warm. 19–23 A few showers, chilly. 24–26 Rain, some heavy; cool. 27–30 Sunny, warm.

MAY 2024: Temp. 65° (1° above avg.); precip. 4" (1" below avg.). 1–2 Sunny, warm. 3–5 T-storms, turning cool. 6–10 Sunny, turning warm. 11–13 T-storms, warm. 14–18 Sunny, cool. 19–27 A few t-storms, then sunny; warm. 28–31 T-storms, some heavy; warm.

JUNE 2024: Temp. 73° (avg.); precip. 4" (1" below avg.). 1–2 T-storms; cool north, hot south. 3–9 A few t-storms, then sunny; hot. 10–16 Isolated t-storms, hot. 17–25 Sunny, then a few t-storms; cool. 26–30 Showers, cool.

JULY 2024: Temp. 78° (avg.); precip. 3" (1" below avg.). 1–8 A few t-storms, turning hot. 9–16 Sunny, warm. 17–25 T-storms; warm, turning cool. 26–31 Sunny, hot.

AUG. 2024: Temp. 76° (1° above avg.); precip. 4" (0.5" above avg.). 1–9 A few t-storms; hot, turning cool. 10–15 T-storms, hot. 16–25 Sunny, then a few t-storms; turning hot. 26–28 Sunny, warm. 29–31 T-storms north, sunny south; warm.

SEPT. 2024: Temp. 69° (1° above avg.); precip. 1" (2.5" below avg.). 1–5 Sunny, then isolated t-storms; warm. 6–16 Sunny, cool. 17–26 Isolated showers; warm, turning cool. 27–30 Sunny, cool.

OCT. 2024: Temp. 59° (2° above avg.); precip. 3" (1" above avg. north, 1" below south). 1–7 Sunny, turning chilly. 8–15 Rainy periods, very warm. 16–22 Sunny, turning warm. 23–25 Showers, turning cool. 26–31 Isolated showers, chilly.

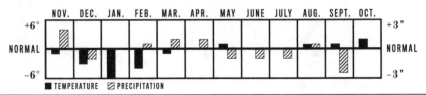

TEXAS-OKLAHOMA

SUMMARY: Winter will be colder than normal north and warmer south. It will be coldest in early and late December, early and late January, and mid-February. Precipitation and snow will be above normal. Best snow chances (north) will occur in late December and late January. **April** and **May** will be cool north and warm south, with more rain than usual. **Summer** will be cooler than normal north, hotter south, and hottest in late June, late July, and mid-August. Rainfall will be above normal, with tropical storms possible in mid-July and late August. **September** and **October** will be warmer than normal, with less rain than normal north and more south. Expect a tropical storm in mid-September.

NOV. 2023: Temp. 59.5° (avg. north, 5° above south); precip. 4" (1" above avg.). 1-6 Sunny, then isolated showers; warm. 7-9 Rainy, chilly north; a few showers, warm south. 10-15 Showers, cool. 16-19 Rain, some heavy south; warm. 20-25 Sunny; cool, then warm. 26-30 Sunny north, showers south; chilly.

DEC. 2023: Temp. 48° (3° below avg.); precip. 2.5" (1" below avg. north, 1" above south). 1-5 Sunny, very cold. 6-10 Sunny north, showers south; chilly. 11-18 Sunny, mild. 19-22 Showers, warm. 23-31 Rainy periods, some snow north; quite cold.

JAN. 2024: Temp. 46.5° (5° below avg. north, 2° below south); precip. 4" (1.5" above avg.). 1-4 Flurries north, rainy south; cold. 5-8 Sunny, cold. 9-13 Rainy, mild. 14-30 Rainy periods, some snow north; cold. 31 Sunny, cold.

FEB. 2024: Temp. 49° (4° below avg. north, avg. south); precip. 0.5" (1" below avg.). 1-8 Sunny; cold, then mild. 9-14 Rain and snow showers north, showers south; very cold. 15-22 Sunny, chilly north; isolated showers, warm south. 23-29 Showers, then sunny; mild.

MAR. 2024: Temp. 61° (1° above avg.); precip. 4.5" (2" above avg.). 1-7 Sunny, turning warm. 8-15 Rainy periods, some heavy; turning warm. 16-22 Sunny; cool, then warm. 23-31 A few t-storms, then sunny; turning cool.

APR. 2024: Temp. 68° (1° below avg. north, 3° above south); precip. 5.5" (2.5" above avg.). 1-9 Isolated t-storms, then sunny; turning warm. 10-14 T-storms, warm. 15-19 Sunny,

warm. 20-30 T-storms, then sunny; cool north, warm south.

MAY 2024: Temp. 73° (1° below avg.); precip. 6" (1" above avg.). 1-4 Sunny, then t-storms; warm. 5-12 Sunny; cool, then warm. 13-19 T-storms, then sunny; turning cooler. 20-29 Scattered t-storms, some heavy; warm. 30-31 Sunny, hot.

JUNE 2024: Temp. 80° (avg.); precip. 4" (3" above avg. north, 2" below south). 1-2 A few t-storms, warm. 3-12 Sunny; cool, then hot. 13-19 Heavy t-storms OK, isolated t-storms TX; warm. 20-30 Sunny, then t-storms; hot.

JULY 2024: Temp. 82.5° (1° below avg. north, 2° above south); precip. 3.5" (2" below avg. north, 3" above south). 1-8 Sunny north, a few t-storms south; warm. 9-16 Scattered t-storms, warm. 17-19 Tropical storm threat. 20-24 A few t-storms, warm. 25-31 Sunny OK, a few t-storms TX; hot.

AUG. 2024: Temp. 81° (1° below avg.); precip. 3.8" (avg. north, 2.5" above south). 1-5 Scattered t-storms, warm. 6-18 Isolated t-storms, hot. 19-21 Tropical storm threat. 22-31 Sunny, then a few t-storms; warm.

SEPT. 2024: Temp. 76° (1° below avg.); precip. 4" (2" below avg. north, 3" above south). 1-9 Sunny north, a few t-storms south; warm. 10-12 Tropical storm threat. 13-24 Isolated t-storms, then sunny; turning hot. 25-30 Sunny, warm.

OCT. 2024: Temp. 71° (3° above avg.); precip. 1.5" (2" below avg.). 1-7 Sunny; cool, then warm. 8-15 T-storms, very warm. 16-22 Sunny, warm. 23-31 T-storms to sunny; cool.

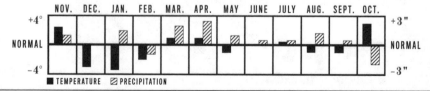

Get your local forecast via Almanac.com/2024.

HIGH PLAINS

SUMMARY: Winter will be colder than normal, with the coldest periods in late November, late December, and early to mid-January, as well as early February in the north only. Precipitation and snowfall will be slightly above normal, with the snowiest periods in late November, mid-December, and mid-January. **April** and **May** will be cooler and drier than normal in the north and warmer and wetter in the south. **Summer** will be hot, with the hottest periods in late June, mid-July, and late August. Rainfall will be below normal in the north and above normal in the south. **September** and **October** will be warmer and drier than normal.

NOV. 2023: Temp. 32.5° (7° below avg. north, 2° below south); precip. 2" (1" above avg.). 1–12 Periods of rain and snow, cold. 13–17 Sunny; frigid north, turning mild south. 18–24 Snowy periods, cold. 25–30 Snowstorm, then sunny; frigid.

DEC. 2023: Temp. 24° (5° below avg.); precip. 0.3" (0.2" below avg.). 1–10 Flurries; bitter cold, then mild. 11–21 Snowy periods, turning cold north; sunny, mild south. 22–31 Flurries, then sunny; bitter cold.

JAN. 2024: Temp. 23° (7° below avg. north, 3° below south); precip. 0.7" (0.2" above avg.). 1–8 Snow showers, frigid. 9–19 Snowy periods, cold. 20–31 Flurries; bitter cold north, turning mild south.

FEB. 2024: Temp. 26° (5° below avg. north, 3° above south); precip. 1" (0.5" above avg.). 1–8 Snow showers, frigid north; sunny, warm south. 9–23 Snowy periods, cold north; rain and snow showers, warm south. 24–29 Sunny, turning warm.

MAR. 2024: Temp. 39° (avg.); precip. 1.2" (0.2" above avg.). 1–9 Rain and snow showers, then sunny; turning warm. 10–15 Periods of rain and snow, chilly. 16–22 Flurries, chilly. 23–31 Rain and snow, then sunny; cold.

APR. 2024: Temp. 49° (3° below avg. north, 3° above south); precip. 1.5" (0.5" below avg. north, 0.5" above south). 1–6 Periods of rain and snow, cold. 7–11 Sunny, warm. 12–18 Isolated showers; chilly north, warm south. 19–27 Rain and snow showers, chilly. 28–30 A few showers; chilly north, warm south.

MAY 2024: Temp. 57° (1° below avg.); precip. 2.5" (1.5" below avg. north, 1.5" above south). 1–6 Rain and snow showers, cold. 7–12 Sunny, then a few showers; warm. 13–19 Isolated showers north, rainy periods south; cool. 20–25 Showers, cool. 26–31 Sunny, then a few t-storms; warm.

JUNE 2024: Temp. 69° (1° above avg.); precip. 2.5" (avg.). 1–6 Sunny, turning hot. 7–13 Isolated t-storms, turning cool. 14–18 Scattered t-storms, warm. 19–30 A few t-storms, hot.

JULY 2024: Temp. 74° (1° above avg.); precip. 1.5" (avg. north, 1" below south). 1–4 Sunny, hot. 5–10 A few t-storms, warm. 11–16 Sunny, then isolated t-storms; hot. 17–31 Scattered t-storms; cooler, turning hot.

AUG. 2024: Temp. 70° (1° below avg.); precip. 3.3" (0.5" below avg. north, 3" above south). 1–8 Scattered t-storms, turning cool. 9–13 Sunny north, t-storms south; warm. 14–21 A few t-storms, some heavy south; cool. 22–31 Sunny, turning hot.

SEPT. 2024: Temp. 67° (4° above avg.); precip. 0.5" (1" below avg.). 1–7 Isolated t-storms; hot, turning cool. 8–18 Sunny, warm. 19–30 Isolated t-storms, then sunny; warm.

OCT. 2024: Temp. 50° (1° above avg.); precip. 0.5" (0.5" below avg.). 1–7 Isolated showers, then sunny; turning cool. 8–14 A few showers, cool. 15–20 Sunny, very warm. 21–31 Periods of rain and snow, chilly.

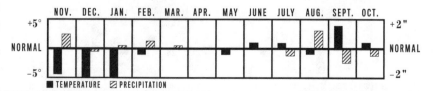

INTERMOUNTAIN

SUMMARY: Winter will be colder than normal, with the coldest periods in early and late November, late December, and late January. Precipitation will be below normal in the north and above normal in the south. Snowfall will be above normal, with the snowiest periods in mid- to late November, early and late January, and mid-February. **April** and **May** will be warmer than normal, with near-normal precipitation. **Summer** will be hotter than normal, with the hottest periods in mid- to late July and late August. Rainfall will be above normal in the north and below normal in the south. **September** and **October** will be quite warm, with below-normal rainfall.

NOV. 2023: Temp. 38° (3° below avg.); precip. 2" (avg. north, 2" above south). 1–8 Sunny north, periods of rain and snow south; cold. 9–16 Snowy periods, cold north; sunny, warm south. 17–27 Periods of rain and snow, chilly. 28–30 Sunny north, snowstorm south; very cold.

DEC. 2023: Temp. 29° (4° below avg.); precip. 1.5" (1" below avg. north, 1" above south). 1–6 Snow showers north, sunny south; cold. 7–9 Sunny, cold. 10–14 Flurries north, rain and snow south; chilly. 15–19 Flurries north, sunny south; mild. 20–31 Snow showers, bitter cold.

JAN. 2024: Temp. 29° (5° below avg.); precip. 2" (0.5" above avg.). 1–3 Snowy, cold. 4–11 Periods of rain and snow, then snowstorm; mild, turning cold. 12–26 Snowy periods, bitter cold. 27–31 Flurries, cold.

FEB. 2024: Temp. 34.5° (0.5° below avg.); precip. 2" (avg.). 1–7 Rain and snow showers, mild north; sunny, cold south. 8–13 Rain and snow showers, chilly. 14–16 Snowstorm, cold. 17–29 Rain and snow showers, turning mild.

MAR. 2024: Temp. 43° (1° below avg.); precip. 1.5" (0.5" below avg. north, 0.5" above south). 1–7 Sunny, warm. 8–11 A few showers, mild. 12–14 Sunny, warm north; rain and snow, cold south. 15–19 Sunny, mild. 20–31 Rain and snow, then sunny; turning warm.

APR. 2024: Temp. 51° (1° above avg.); precip. 1" (0.5" above avg. north, 0.5" below south).

1–5 Periods of rain and snow, chilly. 6–12 Sunny, then a few showers; warm. 13–24 A few showers north, sunny south; chilly, turning warm. 25–30 Showers, mild.

MAY 2024: Temp. 59° (1° above avg.); precip. 1" (0.5" below avg. north, 0.5" above south). 1–2 Rainy, cold. 3–11 Sunny, warm. 12–15 Sunny north, rainy periods south; warm. 16–21 A few showers, turning cold. 22–31 Isolated showers; warm, then cooler.

JUNE 2024: Temp. 67° (avg.); precip. 0.3" (0.2" below avg.). 1–6 Showers, then sunny; turning hot. 7–12 A few showers, cool. 13–22 Sunny, turning hot. 23–30 Isolated t-storms, warm.

JULY 2024: Temp. 77° (3° above avg.); precip. 0.3" (0.2" below avg.). 1–12 Sunny; cool, turning hot. 13–16 Isolated t-storms, warm. 17–31 Sunny, then isolated t-storms; turning hot.

AUG. 2024: Temp. 72° (1° below avg.); precip. 1.3" (1" above avg. north, 0.5" below south). 1–3 Sunny, warm. 4–8 Scattered t-storms, turning cool. 9–16 Isolated t-storms, cool. 17–20 Sunny, warm. 21–27 A few t-storms north, sunny south; cool. 28–31 Sunny, hot.

SEPT. 2024: Temp. 70° (6° above avg.); precip. 0.4" (0.6" below avg.). 1–4 Isolated t-storms, warm. 5–17 Sunny, very warm. 18–30 Isolated showers, quite warm.

OCT. 2024: Temp. 53° (1° above avg.); precip. 1" (avg.). 1–7 Sunny, warm. 8–16 Rainy periods, cool. 17–31 Isolated showers; warm, turning cool.

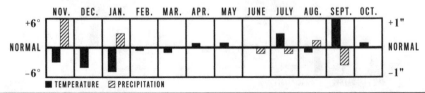

DESERT SOUTHWEST

SUMMARY: Winter will be colder than normal, with the coldest periods in late November, early and late December, and late January. Precipitation will be above normal, as will be snowfall in most areas that normally receive snow, with the snowiest periods in mid- to late January and mid-February. **April** and **May** will bring

temperatures near normal in the east and above normal in the west. Precipitation will be above normal. **Summer** will be hot, with rainfall below normal in the east and above normal in the west. The hottest periods will occur in early and mid-June as well as early and late July. **September** and **October** will be warmer and drier than normal.

NOV. 2023: Temp. 57° (2° above avg. east, 2° below west); precip. 1" (avg. east, 1" above west). 1–7 A few showers; warm east, cool west. 8–13 Sunny, cool. 14–18 Showers; warm east, cool west. 19–23 Sunny, cool. 24–30 Isolated showers, turning chilly.

DEC. 2023: Temp. 46° (2° below avg.); precip. 1" (0.5" above avg.). 1–8 Sunny, chilly. 9–12 Rainy periods, cool. 13–20 Sunny, mild. 21–31 Isolated showers, chilly.

JAN. 2024: Temp. 45° (4° below avg.); precip. 1.5" (1" above avg.). 1–7 Isolated showers, cool. 8–11 Rainy, mild. 12–15 Sunny, chilly. 16–26 Rain and snow showers, very cold. 27–31 Sunny, cold.

FEB. 2024: Temp. 51° (1° below avg.); precip. 0.4" (0.2" above avg. east, 0.3" below west). 1–7 Sunny, mild. 8–16 Rain and snow showers east, sunny west; turning chilly. 17–23 Sunny east, isolated showers west; chilly. 24–29 Sunny, turning warm.

MAR. 2024: Temp. 58° (2° below avg.); precip. 0.7" (0.2" below avg. east, 0.5" above west). 1–10 Isolated showers, mild. 11–14 Sunny east, rainy west; cool. 15–21 Sunny, then a few showers; chilly. 22–31 Isolated showers, chilly.

APR. 2024: Temp. 68° (2° above avg.); precip. 0.5" (avg.). 1–2 A few showers, cool. 3–13 Sunny, turning warm. 14–24 Isolated showers, then sunny; warm. 25–30 Isolated showers, cool.

MAY 2024: Temp. 73.5° (2° below avg. east, 1° above west); precip. 1" (0.5" above avg.). 1–6 Showers, then sunny; cool. 7–12 A few showers, mild. 13–24 Scattered t-storms east, sunny west; warm. 25–31 Isolated t-storms, cool east; sunny, hot west.

JUNE 2024: Temp. 85° (avg.); precip. 0.5" (avg.). 1–9 Isolated t-storms, then sunny; turning hot. 10–21 Sunny; cool, turning hot. 22–30 A few t-storms east, sunny west; warm.

JULY 2024: Temp. 91° (3° above avg.); precip. 1" (0.5" below avg.). 1–8 Sunny, hot. 9–14 Scattered t-storms, warm. 15–31 Sunny, then isolated t-storms; hot.

AUG. 2024: Temp. 86.5° (1° above avg. east, 2° below west); precip. 2" (avg. east, 1" above west). 1–2 Isolated t-storms, hot. 3–12 Scattered t-storms, some heavy; warm. 13–31 Sunny; hot east, warm west.

SEPT. 2024: Temp. 83° (1° above avg. east, 5° above west); precip. 0.3" (0.7" below avg.). 1–4 Sunny, hot. 5–14 A few showers, cool east; isolated t-storms, hot west. 15–30 Sunny, hot.

OCT. 2024: Temp. 70° (1° above avg.); precip. 0.3" (0.7" below avg.). 1–11 Sunny, warm. 12–15 Isolated showers, turning cool. 16–29 Sunny; warm, turning chilly. 30–31 A few showers, cool.

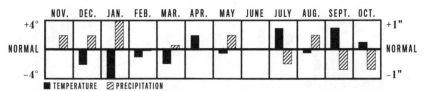

WEATHER

PACIFIC NORTHWEST

Seattle
Portland
Eugene
Eureka

SUMMARY: Winter temperatures will be colder than normal, with below-normal precipitation and snowfall. The coldest periods will be in mid-November, late December, and mid-January. The snowiest periods will occur in mid- to late December and mid-January. **April** and **May** will be warmer than normal, with near-normal rainfall. **Summer** temperatures will be below normal in the north and above normal in the south, with the hottest periods in early to mid-July. Precipitation will be slightly above normal. **September** and **October** will be warmer than normal, with rainfall near normal in the north and above normal in the south.

WEATHER

NOV. 2023: Temp. 44° (4° below avg.); precip. 5" (1" below avg.). 1–7 Rainy, then sunny; cold. 8–19 Rainy periods, then sunny; cold. 20–30 Periods of rain; mild, turning cold.

DEC. 2023: Temp. 40° (4° below avg.); precip. 3" (4" below avg.). 1–4 Rainy, cool. 5–12 Isolated showers, chilly. 13–17 Rain and snow showers north, sunny south; chilly. 18–31 Sunny, then isolated rain and snow showers; frigid.

JAN. 2024: Temp. 41° (3° below avg.); precip. 5" (1" below avg.). 1–7 Rainy periods; chilly north, mild south. 8–11 Sunny, cold. 12–20 Showers, mixed with snow north; cold. 21–25 Sunny, cold. 26–31 Rainy, mixed with snow north; turning mild.

FEB. 2024: Temp. 46° (2° above avg.); precip. 6.5" (2" above avg.). 1–6 Rainy, mild. 7–16 Sunny, then rainy periods; chilly. 17–29 Periods of rain, turning mild.

MAR. 2024: Temp. 50° (3° above avg.); precip. 1.5" (2.5" below avg.). 1–6 Sunny, warm. 7–11 Showers, mild. 12–18 Sunny, warm. 19–31 Rainy periods; chilly, turning mild.

APR. 2024: Temp. 53° (2° above avg.); precip. 5" (1.5" above avg.). 1–11 Rainy periods, cool. 12–21 Sunny, then showers; turning warm. 22–30 Sunny, then rainy; warm, then chilly.

MAY 2024: Temp. 58° (2° above avg.); precip. 0.5" (1.5" below avg.). 1–2 A few showers, chilly. 3–18 Sunny, warm. 19–21 Scattered showers, cool. 22–28 Sunny, turning hot. 29–31 Showers north, sunny south; cool.

JUNE 2024: Temp. 60° (1° below avg.); precip. 0.5" (1" below avg.). 1–6 Sunny, turning cool. 7–12 A few showers, cool. 13–22 Sunny, turning warm. 23–30 Scattered showers, then sunny; warm.

JULY 2024: Temp. 67° (1° above avg.); precip. 0.4" (0.3" below avg. north, 0.2" above south). 1–4 A few t-storms, warm. 5–13 Sunny, turning hot. 14–31 Sunny, warm.

AUG. 2024: Temp. 68.5° (1° below avg. north, 4° above south); precip. 2.5" (1.5" above avg.). 1–5 Sunny, warm. 6–15 Scattered t-storms; cool north, warm south. 16–19 Sunny, warm. 20–31 Rainy periods; cool north, warm south.

SEPT. 2024: Temp. 66° (4° above avg.); precip. 0.5" (1" below avg.). 1–7 Showers, then sunny; turning very warm. 8–16 Sunny, warm. 17–20 Isolated showers, mild. 21–30 Sunny, warm.

OCT. 2024: Temp. 59° (4° above avg.); precip. 6" (1" above avg. north, 4" above south). 1–5 Sunny, warm. 6–13 Rainy periods, turning chilly. 14–21 Sunny, then rainy; warm. 22–29 Sunny, then rainy periods; cool, then warm. 30–31 Sunny, warm.

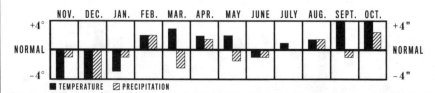

	NOV.	DEC.	JAN.	FEB.	MAR.	APR.	MAY	JUNE	JULY	AUG.	SEPT.	OCT.	
+4°													+4"
NORMAL													NORMAL
-4°													-4"

■ TEMPERATURE ▨ PRECIPITATION

PACIFIC SOUTHWEST

SUMMARY: Winter will be cooler and wetter than normal, with above-normal mountain snows. The coldest temperatures will occur in early and late November, early and late December, and late January. The stormiest periods will be in early and late January, early to mid-February, and mid-March. **April** and **May** will be warmer and drier than normal. **Summer** temperatures will be above normal, with slightly above-normal rainfall. The hottest periods will be in early June and early and late July. **September** and **October** will be warmer and wetter than normal.

NOV. 2023: Temp. 57° (2° below avg.); precip. 1.5" (0.5" above avg.). 1–7 Sunny, then rainy periods; turning chilly. 8–11 Sunny, cool. 12–17 Rainy periods, cool. 18–23 Sunny, cool. 24–30 Scattered showers, then sunny; turning cold.

DEC. 2023: Temp. 54° (1° below avg.); precip. 2" (1.5" below avg. north, 1.5" above south). 1–8 Sunny; cool north, turning warm south. 9–12 Rainy, cool. 13–26 Sunny, chilly. 27–31 Isolated showers north, rainy south; turning mild.

JAN. 2024: Temp. 55° (1° below avg.); precip. 5" (2" above avg.). 1–6 Rainy, then sunny; warm. 7–11 Rainy periods, some heavy; turning cool. 12–22 Sunny, then a few showers; chilly. 23–31 Rainy periods, then sunny; chilly.

FEB. 2024: Temp. 56° (avg.); precip. 3.3" (1.5" above avg. north, 1" below south). 1–5 Sunny, turning mild. 6–16 Rainy periods, some heavy north; chilly. 17–24 Showers, cool. 25–29 Sunny, warm.

MAR. 2024: Temp. 59° (1° above avg.); precip. 3.5" (avg. north, 2" above south). 1–5 Sunny, warm. 6–9 Showers, turning cool. 10–14 Isolated showers north, rainy south; cool. 15–22 Sunny, then rainy periods; mild. 23–31 Sunny, turning warm.

APR. 2024: Temp. 62° (1° above avg.); precip. 0.5" (0.5" below avg.). 1–4 Isolated showers, cool. 5–10 Sunny, then isolated showers; warm. 11–14 Sunny, cool. 15–20 A few showers, turning warm. 21–30 Sunny, then a few showers; turning cool.

MAY 2024: Temp. 66.5° (4° above avg. north, 1° above south); precip. 0.1" (0.4" below avg.). 1–6 Sunny, turning hot. 7–21 Sunny inland; A.M. sprinkles, P.M. sun coast; warm. 22–31 Sunny, very warm north; sprinkles, turning cool south.

JUNE 2024: Temp. 70° (1° below avg. north, 3° above south); precip. 0.1" (avg.). 1–6 Sunny, hot. 7–13 Sunny; cool north, warm south. 14–23 Sprinkles, cool north; sunny, warm south. 24–30 Sunny inland; A.M. clouds, P.M. sun coast; cool.

JULY 2024: Temp. 74° (2° above avg.); precip. 0.1" (0.1" above avg.). 1–15 Sunny, then isolated showers; warm. 16–27 Sunny, hot inland; A.M. clouds, P.M. sun, warm coast. 28–31 Sunny, warm.

AUG. 2024: Temp. 73° (1° above avg.); precip. 0" (avg.). 1–4 Sunny, warm. 5–14 Sunny inland; A.M. clouds, P.M. sun coast; mild. 15–24 Sunny; warm coast, cool inland. 25–31 Sunny, warm.

SEPT. 2024: Temp. 76° (4° above avg.); precip. 0.1" (avg.). 1–12 Sunny, turning hot. 13–21 Sunny, warm. 22–30 Isolated showers, then sunny; warm.

OCT. 2024: Temp. 67° (1° above avg.); precip. 1.5" (1" above avg.). 1–10 Sunny, warm. 11–16 Rainy periods, then sunny; cool. 17–19 Rainy north, sunny south; mild. 20–31 Sunny, then a few showers; mild.

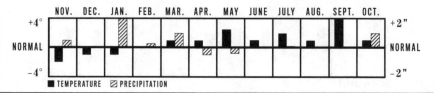

ALASKA

SUMMARY: Winter temperatures will be milder than normal, with the coldest periods in mid-December, late January, and early to mid-February. Precipitation will be slightly below normal, while snowfall will be slightly above normal. The snowiest periods will be in late November, mid-December, mid- to late January, and early March. **April** and **May** will be warmer than normal, with above-normal precipitation. **Summer** will be warmer than normal, with precipitation above normal in the north and below normal in the south. The hottest periods will be in early and mid-August. **September** and **October** will be milder than normal, with above-normal precipitation.

KEY: north (N), central (C), south (S), panhandle (P), elsewhere (EW).

NOV. 2023: Temp. 15° N, 43° S (11° above avg. N, 6° above S); precip. 0.4" N, 6" S (avg. N, 1" above S). 1–6 Periods of rain and snow, warm. 7–10 Clear, cold N; showers, mild S. 11–15 Rain and snow showers, warm. 16–18 Clear, chilly. 19–30 Flurries N, snowy periods C, periods of rain and snow EW; warm.

DEC. 2023: Temp. –1° N, 36° S (4° above avg.); precip. 0.2" N, 5" S (avg). 1–6 Flurries; cold N, mild EW. 7–20 Clear N, snowy periods EW; cold. 21–25 A few flurries; cold P, mild EW. 26–31 Snowy periods P, clear EW; quite mild.

JAN. 2024: Temp. –5° N, 34° S (5° above avg.); precip. 0.2" N, 4" S (avg. N, 1" below S). 1–7 Rain and snow P, clear EW; mild. 8–20 A few snow showers N+C, periods of rain and snow S; mild. 21–31 Flurries N, snowy periods C+S; bitter cold.

FEB. 2024: Temp. –14° N, 28° S (3° below avg.); precip. 0.1" N, 3" S (0.1" below avg. N, 1" below S). 1–14 A few snow showers P, clear EW; frigid. 15–20 Clear; mild N, cold EW. 21–29 Snow showers P, clear EW; cold N+C, mild EW.

MAR. 2024: Temp. –5° N, 40° S (6° above avg.); precip. 0.5" N, 5" S (avg). 1–7 Flurries, turning cold N; periods of rain and snow, mild S. 8–14 Clear, cold N; snowy periods, mild S. 15–20 Periods of rain and snow, mild. 21–31 Clear, then some rain and snow; cold N+P, mild EW.

APR. 2024: Temp. 10° N, 47° S (6° above avg.); precip. 1.2" N, 3.5" S (0.5" above avg.). 1–8 Sunny, cold N; a few showers, mild S. 9–20 Sunny, then rain and snow showers; mild. 21–30 Sunny N, a few showers C+S; warm.

MAY 2024: Temp. 26.5° N, 51° EW (4° above avg.); precip. 0.6" N, 3" S (avg.). 1–15 A few showers; mild N+P, chilly C+S. 16–23 Isolated showers N+S, rainy periods C+P; turning warm. 24–31 Rainy, cool P; sunny, warm EW.

JUNE 2024: Temp. 35° N, 58.5° EW (1° below avg. N, 3° above EW); precip. 2.2" N, 5" S (1.5" above avg.). 1–13 Showers; mild S, cool EW. 14–22 Isolated showers N, rainy periods EW; turning cool. 23–30 Rainy periods; warm, turning cool.

JULY 2024: Temp. 44.5° N, 59.5° EW (2° above avg.); precip. 0.7" N, 4.0" S (0.5" below avg.). 1–3 Showers, cool. 4–12 Sunny N, isolated showers C, rainy periods EW; mild, then cool. 13–20 A few showers; turning cool N, warm S. 21–31 A few showers N, rainy periods EW; turning cool.

AUG. 2024: Temp. 45.5° N, 61° EW (4° above avg.); precip. 0.7" N, 4" S (0.5" below avg. N, 1.5" below S). 1–11 Isolated showers N+P, rainy periods C+S; quite warm. 12–23 Showers N+C, sunny EW; very warm. 24–31 A few showers, mild.

SEPT. 2024: Temp. 39.5° N, 60° EW (5° above avg.); precip. 1.1" N, 7.5" S (avg.). 1–4 Turning rainy P, sunny EW; warm. 5–11 Showers; cool N+C, mild S. 12–21 Sunny N, rainy periods EW; mild. 22–30 Rain and snow showers N, rainy periods EW, some heavy P; mild.

OCT. 2024: Temp. 26° N, 49° S (6° above avg.); precip. 1" N, 7.5" S (0.5" above avg.). 1–7 Rain and snow showers N, rainy periods EW; quite mild. 8–16 Rain and snow showers N, a few showers S; turning cool S, mild EW. 17–31 Periods of rain and snow, turning mild.

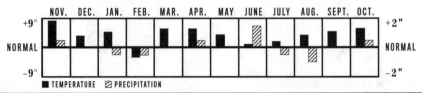

HAWAII

SUMMARY: Winter will be cooler than normal, with the coolest periods in mid-December through early January and early February. Rainfall will be above normal, with the stormiest periods in early November in the east and early January and mid-February throughout. **April** and **May** will be warmer than normal in the east and cooler than normal in the west. Rainfall will be below normal. **Summer** will be cooler and drier than normal, with the hottest periods in mid-July and late August. **September** and **October** will be warmer than normal, with the hottest periods in early and late September and early October. Rainfall will be below normal.

KEY: east (E), central (C), west (W). Note: Temperature and precipitation are substantially based upon topography. The detailed forecast focuses on the Honolulu–Waikiki area and provides general trends elsewhere.

NOV. 2023: Temp. 77.5° (1° above avg. E, 1° below W); precip. 2.5" (avg.). 1–10 Heavy rain E, scattered showers C+W; cool. 11–15 Rain E, isolated showers C+W; warm. 16–25 Showers E, sunny C+W; mild. 26–30 Rain, cool.

DEC. 2023: Temp. 73° (2° below avg.); precip. 2.3" (4" below avg. E+W, 1" below C). 1–13 Rainy periods, mild. 14–20 Sunny E+C, showers W; cool. 21–31 Sunny, cool.

JAN. 2024: Temp. 73° (2° below avg. E, 2° above W); precip. 6.5" (8" above avg. E, 4" above C+W). 1–8 Periods of heavy rain, chilly. 9–15 Showers, heavy E; milder. 16–26 Showers E, sunny C+W; cool E+C, mild W. 27–31 Scattered showers; mild, turning cool.

FEB. 2024: Temp. 72° (1° below avg.); precip. 6" (8" above avg. E, 4" above C+W). 1–11 Periods of rain, cool. 12–18 Rain, very heavy E; mild. 19–29 Showers E, sunny C+W; mild.

MAR. 2024: Temp. 74° (avg.); precip. 1" (5" below avg. E+W, 1" below C). 1–14 Showers E+W, sunny C; mild. 15–24 Scattered showers, cool. 25–31 Scattered showers E+W, sunny C; warm.

APR. 2024: Temp. 75.5° (1° above avg. E, 1° below W); precip. 0.2" (0.5" below avg.). 1–5 Showers, warm. 6–16 Showers, then sunny; mild. 17–30 Showers E+W, sunny C; cool, then warm.

MAY 2024: Temp. 77° (avg.); precip. 0.2" (2.5" below avg. E+W, 0.5" below C). 1–9 Showers, isolated C+W; warm. 10–23 Scattered showers E+W, sunny C; mild. 24–31 Isolated showers E, sunny C+W; warm.

JUNE 2024: Temp. 79.5° (avg.); precip. 0.9" (5" above avg. E, 0.5" above C+W). 1–13 Daily showers, heavy W; warm. 14–30 Showers E+W, sunny C; warm.

JULY 2024: Temp. 80° (1° below avg.); precip. 0.2" (3" below avg. E, 0.3" below C+W). 1–6 Isolated showers E, sunny C+W; cool. 7–18 Showers E+W, sunny C; very warm. 19–31 Showers, isolated C+W; warm.

AUG. 2024: Temp. 81.5° (avg.); precip. 0.2" (5" below avg. E, 0.4" below C+W). 1–9 Showers and t-storms E+W, sunny C; warm. 10–15 Sunny, warm. 16–23 Isolated showers E+W, sunny C; warm. 24–31 Showers, turning very warm.

SEPT. 2024: Temp. 82.5° (1° above avg.); precip. 0.3" (4" below avg. E, 0.5" below C+W). 1–5 Showers E, sunny C+W; very warm. 6–13 Isolated showers, warm. 14–30 Daily showers E+W, isolated C; warm.

OCT. 2024: Temp. 81° (1° above avg.); precip. 1.5" (5" below avg. E, 0.5" below C+W). 1–14 Daily showers E+W, sunny C; very warm. 15–22 Isolated showers E+W, sunny C; warm. 23–26 Showers, warm. 27–31 Showers E, sunny C+W; warm.

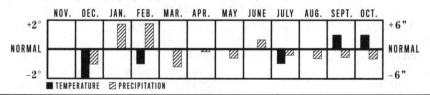

SECRETS OF THE ZODIAC

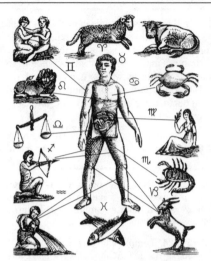

The Man of the Signs

Ancient astrologers believed that each astrological sign influenced a specific part of the body. The first sign of the zodiac—Aries—was attributed to the head, with the rest of the signs moving down the body, ending with Pisces at the feet.

♈ Aries, head	**ARI**	*Mar. 21–Apr. 20*
♉ Taurus, neck	**TAU**	*Apr. 21–May 20*
♊ Gemini, arms	**GEM**	*May 21–June 20*
♋ Cancer, breast	**CAN**	*June 21–July 22*
♌ Leo, heart	**LEO**	*July 23–Aug. 22*
♍ Virgo, belly	**VIR**	*Aug. 23–Sept. 22*
♎ Libra, reins	**LIB**	*Sept. 23–Oct. 22*
♏ Scorpio, secrets	**SCO**	*Oct. 23–Nov. 22*
♐ Sagittarius, thighs	**SAG**	*Nov. 23–Dec. 21*
♑ Capricorn, knees	**CAP**	*Dec. 22–Jan. 19*
♒ Aquarius, legs	**AQU**	*Jan. 20–Feb. 19*
♓ Pisces, feet	**PSC**	*Feb. 20–Mar. 20*

ASTROLOGY VS. ASTRONOMY

Astrology is a tool we use to plan events according to the placements of the Sun, the Moon, and the planets in the 12 signs of the zodiac. In astrology, the planetary movements do not cause events; rather, they explain the path, or "flow," that events tend to follow. *The Moon's astrological place is given on the next page.* **Astronomy** is the study of the actual placement of the known planets and constellations. The Moon's astronomical place is given in the **Left-Hand Calendar Pages, 120–146.** *(The placement of the planets in the signs of the zodiac is not the same astrologically and astronomically.)*

The dates in the **Best Days** table, **pages 226–227,** are based on the astrological passage of the Moon.

WHEN MERCURY IS RETROGRADE

Sometimes the other planets appear to be traveling backward through the zodiac; this is an illusion. We call this illusion *retrograde motion.*

Mercury's retrograde periods can cause our plans to go awry. However, intuition is high during these periods and coincidences can be extraordinary.

When Mercury is retrograde, stay flexible, allow more time for travel, and don't sign contracts. Review projects and plans but wait until Mercury is direct again to make final decisions.

Mercury will be retrograde from December 13, 2023–January 1, 2024, and during April 1–24, August 4–27, and November 25–December 15, 2024.

–Celeste Longacre

GARDENING BY THE MOON'S SIGN

USE CHART ON NEXT PAGE TO FIND THE BEST DATES FOR THE FOLLOWING GARDEN TASKS . . .

PLANT, TRANSPLANT, AND GRAFT: Cancer, Scorpio, Pisces, or Taurus
HARVEST: Aries, Leo, Sagittarius, Gemini, or Aquarius
BUILD/FIX FENCES OR GARDEN BEDS: Capricorn

CONTROL INSECT PESTS, PLOW, AND WEED: Aries, Gemini, Leo, Sagittarius, or Aquarius
PRUNE: Aries, Leo, or Sagittarius. During a waxing Moon, pruning encourages growth; during a waning Moon, it discourages it.

SETTING EGGS BY THE MOON'S SIGN

Chicks take about 21 days to hatch. Those born under a waxing Moon in Cancer, Scorpio, or Pisces are healthier and mature faster. To ensure that chicks are born during these times, "set eggs" (place eggs in an incubator or under a hen) 21 days before the desired hatching dates.

EXAMPLE:
The Moon is new on April 8 and full on April 23 (EDT). Between these dates, the Moon is in the sign of Cancer on April 14 and 15. To have chicks born on April 14, count back 21 days; set eggs on March 24.

Below are the best days to set eggs in 2024, using only the fruitful dates between the new and full Moons and counting back 21 days:

JAN.: 2, 3, 20, 21, 29, 30   **APR.:** 2, 20, 21, 30   **JULY:** 21, 22   **OCT.:** 11, 12, 20, 21
FEB.: 18, 25–27   **MAY:** 1, 17–19, 27, 28   **AUG.:** 17, 18, 26, 27   **NOV.:** 16, 17
MAR.: 24, 25   **JUNE:** 14, 15, 23–25   **SEPT.:** 13–15, 23, 24   **DEC.:** 13–15, 22, 23

The Moon's Astrological Place, 2023–24

	NOV.	DEC.	JAN.	FEB.	MAR.	APR.	MAY	JUNE	JULY	AUG.	SEPT.	OCT.	NOV.	DEC.
1	GEM	LEO	VIR	LIB	SCO	CAP	AQU	ARI	TAU	CAN	LEO	VIR	SCO	SAG
2	CAN	LEO	VIR	SCO	SAG	CAP	AQU	ARI	GEM	CAN	VIR	LIB	SCO	SAG
3	CAN	LEO	LIB	SCO	SAG	AQU	PSC	TAU	GEM	LEO	VIR	LIB	SAG	CAP
4	LEO	VIR	LIB	SAG	SAG	AQU	PSC	TAU	GEM	LEO	LIB	SCO	SAG	CAP
5	LEO	VIR	SCO	SAG	CAP	PSC	ARI	GEM	CAN	LEO	LIB	SCO	CAP	AQU
6	LEO	LIB	SCO	CAP	CAP	PSC	ARI	GEM	CAN	VIR	LIB	SCO	CAP	AQU
7	VIR	LIB	SCO	CAP	AQU	ARI	TAU	CAN	LEO	VIR	SCO	SAG	CAP	PSC
8	VIR	LIB	SAG	AQU	AQU	ARI	TAU	CAN	LEO	LIB	SCO	SAG	AQU	PSC
9	LIB	SCO	SAG	AQU	PSC	TAU	GEM	CAN	VIR	LIB	SAG	CAP	AQU	ARI
10	LIB	SCO	CAP	PSC	PSC	TAU	GEM	LEO	VIR	LIB	SAG	CAP	PSC	ARI
11	LIB	SAG	CAP	PSC	ARI	GEM	CAN	LEO	VIR	SCO	SAG	AQU	PSC	TAU
12	SCO	SAG	AQU	ARI	ARI	GEM	CAN	VIR	LIB	SCO	CAP	AQU	ARI	TAU
13	SCO	CAP	AQU	ARI	TAU	GEM	LEO	VIR	LIB	SAG	CAP	AQU	ARI	TAU
14	SAG	CAP	PSC	TAU	TAU	CAN	LEO	VIR	SCO	SAG	AQU	PSC	TAU	GEM
15	SAG	CAP	PSC	TAU	GEM	CAN	LEO	LIB	SCO	SAG	AQU	PSC	TAU	GEM
16	CAP	AQU	ARI	TAU	GEM	LEO	VIR	LIB	SCO	CAP	PSC	ARI	GEM	CAN
17	CAP	AQU	ARI	GEM	CAN	LEO	VIR	SCO	SAG	CAP	PSC	ARI	GEM	CAN
18	AQU	PSC	TAU	GEM	CAN	VIR	LIB	SCO	SAG	AQU	ARI	TAU	CAN	LEO
19	AQU	PSC	TAU	CAN	CAN	VIR	LIB	SAG	CAP	AQU	ARI	TAU	CAN	LEO
20	PSC	ARI	GEM	CAN	LEO	VIR	LIB	SAG	CAP	PSC	TAU	GEM	LEO	VIR
21	PSC	ARI	GEM	LEO	LEO	LIB	SCO	SAG	AQU	PSC	TAU	GEM	LEO	VIR
22	PSC	TAU	GEM	LEO	VIR	LIB	SCO	CAP	AQU	ARI	GEM	CAN	LEO	VIR
23	ARI	TAU	CAN	LEO	VIR	SCO	SAG	CAP	PSC	ARI	GEM	CAN	VIR	LIB
24	ARI	GEM	CAN	VIR	VIR	SCO	SAG	AQU	PSC	TAU	CAN	LEO	VIR	LIB
25	TAU	GEM	LEO	VIR	LIB	SCO	CAP	AQU	ARI	TAU	CAN	LEO	LIB	SCO
26	TAU	CAN	LEO	LIB	LIB	SAG	CAP	PSC	ARI	GEM	CAN	VIR	LIB	SCO
27	GEM	CAN	LEO	LIB	SCO	SAG	CAP	PSC	ARI	GEM	LEO	VIR	LIB	SCO
28	GEM	CAN	VIR	LIB	SCO	CAP	AQU	ARI	TAU	CAN	LEO	VIR	SCO	SAG
29	CAN	LEO	VIR	SCO	SCO	CAP	AQU	ARI	TAU	CAN	VIR	LIB	SCO	SAG
30	CAN	LEO	LIB	—	SAG	AQU	PSC	TAU	GEM	LEO	VIR	LIB	SAG	CAP
31	—	DEC	VIR	LIB	—	SAG	—	PSC	—	GEM	LEO	—	SCO	—	CAP

BEST DAYS FOR 2024

This chart is based on the Moon's sign and shows the best days each month for certain activities. –*Celeste Longacre*

	JAN.	FEB.	MAR.	APR.	MAY	JUNE	JULY	AUG.	SEPT.	OCT.	NOV.	DEC.
Quit smoking	2, 7	4, 29	6, 29	7, 28	5, 24	1, 28	25, 30	22, 26	22, 30	19, 29	16, 25	22, 27
Bake	23, 24	19, 20	17–19	14, 15	11, 12	7–9	5, 6	1, 2, 28, 29	24–26	22, 23	18, 19	16, 17
Brew	5–7	2, 3, 29	1, 27–29	23–25	21, 22	17, 18	14–16	11, 12	7, 8	4–6, 31	1, 2, 28, 29	25–27
Dry fruit, vegetables, or meat	8, 9, 26, 27	4, 5	2–4, 30, 31	26, 27	5, 6	1, 2, 28, 29	25–27	3, 22, 23	1, 27, 28	24, 25	20–22	18, 19
Make jams or jellies	14, 15	10, 11	9, 10	5, 6	3, 4, 30, 31	26, 27	23, 24	20, 21	16, 17	14, 15	10, 11	7, 8
Can, pickle, or make sauerkraut	5–7	2, 3, 29	1, 27–29	5, 6, 24, 25	3, 4, 30, 31	26, 27	23, 24	1, 2, 28, 29	24–26	22, 23	28, 29	25–27
Begin diet to lose weight	2, 7	4, 29	6, 29	7, 28	5, 24	1, 28	25, 30	22, 26	22, 30	19, 29	16, 25	22, 27
Begin diet to gain weight	15, 20	12, 16	15, 24	11, 21	13, 18	15, 19	12, 17	8, 13	4, 9	7, 16	3, 12	9, 12
Cut hair to encourage growth	18, 19	14–16	13, 14	9, 10	18–20	14–16	12, 13	8–10	4, 5	13–15	10, 11, 14	11–13
Cut hair to discourage growth	3, 4, 30, 31	1, 26–28	26	5, 6	3, 4	3, 4, 30	28, 29	24, 25	20, 21	29, 30	25–27	23, 24
Perm hair	12, 13	8, 9	7, 8	3, 4, 30	1, 2, 28, 29	24, 25	21, 22	18, 19	14, 15	11–13	8, 9	5, 6
Color hair	18, 19	14–16	13, 14	9, 10	7, 8	3, 4, 30	1, 28, 29	24, 25	20, 21	18, 19	14, 15	11–13
Straighten hair	8, 9	4, 5	2–4, 30, 31	26, 27	23, 24	19–21	17, 18	13–15	9–11	7, 8	3, 4, 30	1, 2, 28, 29
Have dental care	1, 2, 28, 29	24, 25	22–24	18–20	16, 17	12–14	9–11	6, 7	2, 3, 29, 30	1, 26–28	23, 24	20–22
Start projects	12	10	11	9	8	7	6	5	3	3	2	2, 31
End projects	24	23	24	22	22	20	20	18	16	16	14	14
Demolish	5–7	2, 3, 29	1, 27–29	23–25	21, 22	17, 18	14–16	11, 12	7, 8	4–6, 31	1, 2, 28, 29	25–27
Lay shingles	25–27	21–23	20, 21	16, 17	13–15	10, 11	7, 8	3–5, 30, 31	1, 27, 28	24, 25	20–22	18, 19
Paint	3, 4, 30, 31	14–16	13, 14	9, 10	7, 8	15, 16	12, 13	8–10	4–6	2, 3, 29, 30	25–27	23, 24
Wash windows	16, 17	12, 13	11, 12	7, 8	5, 6	1, 2, 28, 29	25–27	22, 23	18, 19	16, 17	12, 13	9, 10
Wash floors	14, 15	10, 11	9, 10	5, 6	3, 4, 30, 31	26, 27	23, 24	20, 21	16, 17	14, 15	10, 11	7, 8
Go camping	8, 9	4, 5	2–4, 30, 31	26, 27	23, 24	19–21	17, 18	13–15	9–11	7, 8	3, 4, 30	1, 2, 28, 29

	JAN.	FEB.	MAR.	APR.	MAY	JUNE	JULY	AUG.	SEPT.	OCT.	NOV.	DEC.
Entertain	25–27	21–23	20, 21	16, 17	13–15	10, 11	7, 8	3–5, 30, 31	1, 27, 28	24, 25	20–22	18, 19
Travel for pleasure	25–27	21–23	20, 21	16, 17	13–15	10, 11	7, 8	3–5, 30, 31	1, 27, 28	24, 25	20–22	18, 19
Get married	3, 4, 30, 31	1, 26–28	25, 26	21, 22	18–20	15, 16	12, 13	8–10	4–6	2, 3, 29, 30	25–27	23, 24
Ask for a loan	5–7	2, 3, 29	1, 27, 28	5, 6	5, 6	3, 4, 30	1, 28, 29	24, 25	20, 21	18, 19, 31	28, 29	25–27
Buy a home	18, 19	14–16	13, 14	23	8, 21, 22	17, 18	14–16	11, 12	7, 8	4–6	1, 2	11–13
Move (house/household)	20–22	17, 18	15, 16	11–13	9, 10	5, 6	2–4, 30, 31	26, 27	22, 23	20, 21	16, 17	14, 15
Advertise to sell	18, 19	14–16	13, 14	9, 10	7, 8, 21, 22	17, 18	14–16	11, 12	7, 8	4–6	1, 2	11–13
Mow to promote growth	14, 15	10, 11	17–19	14, 15	11, 12	17, 18	14–16	11, 12	7, 8	4–6	1, 2	7, 8
Mow to slow growth	5–7	2, 3, 29	1, 27–29	24, 25	3, 4, 30, 31	26, 27	23, 24	28, 29	24, 25	22, 23	28, 29	25–27
Plant aboveground crops	14, 15, 23, 24	10, 11	13, 14	14, 15	11, 12	17, 18	14–16	11, 12	7, 8	4–6	1, 2, 10, 11	7, 8
Plant belowground crops	5–7	2, 3, 29	1, 27–29	5, 6	3, 4, 30, 31	26, 27	23, 24	1, 2, 28, 29	24–26	1, 26–28	18, 19, 28, 29	25–27
Destroy pests and weeds	16, 17	12, 13	11, 12	7, 8	5, 6	1, 2, 28, 29	25–27	22, 23	18, 19	16, 17	12, 13	9, 10
Graft or pollinate	23, 24	19, 20	17–19	14, 15	11, 12	7–9	5, 6	1, 2, 28, 29	24–26	22, 23	18, 19	16, 17
Prune to encourage growth	16, 17	12, 13	11, 12	16, 17	13–15	10, 11	7, 8	13–15	9–11	7, 8	3, 4	9, 10
Prune to discourage growth	26, 27	4, 5	2–4, 30, 31	26, 27	5, 6	1, 2, 28, 29	25–27	3, 30, 31	1, 27, 28	24, 25	20–22	28, 29
Pick fruit	1, 2, 28, 29	24, 25	22–24	18–20	16, 17	12–14	9–11	6, 7	2, 3, 29, 30	1, 26–28	23, 24	20–22
Harvest aboveground crops	18, 19	14–16	22–24	9, 10	16, 17	12–14	9–11	6, 7	12, 13	9, 10	5–7	11–13
Harvest belowground crops	1, 2, 28, 29	6, 7, 25	5, 6	1, 2, 28, 29	25–27	3, 4, 30	1, 28, 29	24, 25	29, 30	26–28	23, 24	21, 22
Cut hay	16, 17	12, 13	11, 12	7, 8	5, 6	1, 2, 28, 29	25–27	22, 23	18, 19	16, 17	12, 13	9, 10
Begin logging, set posts, pour concrete	10, 11	6, 7	5, 6	1, 2, 28, 29	25–27	22, 23	19, 20	16, 17	12, 13	9, 10	5–7	3, 4, 30, 31
Purchase animals	23, 24	19, 20	17–19	14, 15	11, 12	7–9	5, 6	1, 2, 28, 29	24–26	22, 23	18, 19	16, 17
Breed animals	5–7	2, 3, 29	1, 27–29	23–25	21, 22	17, 18	14–16	11, 12	7, 8	4–6, 31	1, 2, 28, 29	25–27
Wean	2, 7	4, 29	6, 29	7, 28	5, 24	1, 28	25, 30	22, 26	22, 30	19, 29	16, 25	22, 27
Castrate animals	12, 13	8, 9	7, 8	3, 4, 30	1, 2, 28, 29	24, 25	21, 22	18, 19	14, 15	11–13	8, 9	5, 6
Slaughter livestock	5–7	2, 3, 29	1, 27–29	23–25	21, 22	17, 18	14–16	11, 12	7, 8	4–6, 31	1, 2, 28, 29	25–27

BEST FISHING DAYS AND TIMES

The best times to fish are when the fish are naturally most active. The Sun, Moon, tides, and weather all influence fish activity. For example, fish tend to feed more at sunrise and sunset, and also during a full Moon (when tides are higher than average). However, most of us go fishing simply when we can get the time off. But there are best times, according to fishing lore:

■ One hour before and one hour after high tides, and one hour before and one hour after low tides. The times of high tides for Boston are given on **pages 120–146;** also see **pages 236–237.** (Inland, the times for high tides correspond with the times when the Moon is due south. Low tides are halfway between high tides.)

GET TIDE TIMES AND HEIGHTS NEAREST TO YOUR LOCATION VIA ALMANAC.COM/2024.

■ During the "morning rise" (after sunup for a spell) and the "evening rise" (just before sundown and the hour or so after).

■ During the rise and set of the Moon.

■ Just before the arrival of a storm, although the falling barometric pressure will eventually slow down their feeding. Angling can also be good when the pressure is either steady or on the rise 1 to 2 days after a storm. High pressure accompanying clear weather can bring on sluggishness and reduced activity.

■ When there is a hatch of flies—caddis flies or mayflies, commonly.

■ When the breeze is from a westerly quarter, rather than from the north or east.

■ When the water is still or slightly rippled, rather than during a wind.

THE BEST FISHING DAYS FOR 2024, WHEN THE MOON IS BETWEEN NEW AND FULL

January 11–25
February 9–24
March 10–25
April 8–23
May 7–23
June 6–21
July 5–21
August 4–19
September 2–17
October 2–17
November 1–15
December 1–15, 30, 31

Dates based on Eastern Time.

HOW TO ESTIMATE THE WEIGHT OF A FISH

Measure the fish from the tip of its nose to the tip of its tail. Then measure its girth at the thickest portion of its midsection.

The weight of a fat-bodied fish (bass, salmon) =
(length x girth x girth)/800

The weight of a slender fish (trout, northern pike) =
(length x girth x girth)/900

EXAMPLE: If a trout is 20 inches long and has a 12-inch girth, its estimated weight is
(20 x 12 x 12)/900 =
2,880/900 = 3.2 pounds

SALMON

TROUT

CATFISH

GESTATION AND MATING TABLES

	PROPER AGE OR WEIGHT FOR FIRST MATING	PERIOD OF FERTILITY (YRS.)	NUMBER OF FEMALES FOR ONE MALE	PERIOD OF GESTATION (DAYS) AVERAGE	RANGE
CATTLE: Cow	15–18 mos.[1]	10–14		283	279–290[2] 262–300[3]
Bull	1 yr., well matured	10–12	50[4] / thousands[5]		
GOAT: Doe	10 mos. or 85–90 lbs.	6		150	145–155
Buck	well matured	5	30		
HORSE: Mare	3 yrs.	10–12		336	310–370
Stallion	3 yrs.	12–15	40–45[4] / record 252[5]		
PIG: Sow	5–6 mos. or 250 lbs.	6		115	110–120
Boar	250–300 lbs.	6	50[6] / 35–40[7]		
RABBIT: Doe	6 mos.	5–6		31	30–32
Buck	6 mos.	5–6	30		
SHEEP: Ewe	1 yr. or 90 lbs.	6		147 / 151[8]	142–154
Ram	12–14 mos., well matured	7	50–75[6] / 35–40[7]		
CAT: Queen	12 mos.	6		63	60–68
Tom	12 mos.	6	6–8		
DOG: Bitch	16–18 mos.	8		63	58–67
Male	12–16 mos.	8	8–10		

[1]Holstein and beef: 750 lbs.; Jersey: 500 lbs. [2]Beef; 8–10 days shorter for Angus. [3]Dairy. [4]Natural. [5]Artificial. [6]Hand-mated. [7]Pasture. [8]For fine wool breeds.

INCUBATION PERIOD OF POULTRY (DAYS)

Chicken	21
Duck	26–32
Goose	30–34
Guinea	26–28
Turkey	28

AVERAGE LIFE SPAN OF ANIMALS IN CAPTIVITY (YEARS)

Cat (domestic)	14	Goose (domestic)	20
Chicken (domestic)	8	Horse	22
Dog (domestic)	13	Pig	12
Duck (domestic)	10	Rabbit	6
Goat (domestic)	14	Turkey (domestic)	10

	ESTRAL/ESTROUS CYCLE (INCLUDING HEAT PERIOD) AVERAGE	RANGE	LENGTH OF ESTRUS (HEAT) AVERAGE	RANGE	USUAL TIME OF OVULATION	WHEN CYCLE RECURS IF NOT BRED
Cow	21 days	18–24 days	18 hours	10–24 hours	10–12 hours after end of estrus	21 days
Doe goat	21 days	18–24 days	2–3 days	1–4 days	Near end of estrus	21 days
Mare	21 days	10–37 days	5–6 days	2–11 days	24–48 hours before end of estrus	21 days
Sow	21 days	18–24 days	2–3 days	1–5 days	30–36 hours after start of estrus	21 days
Ewe	16½ days	14–19 days	30 hours	24–32 hours	12–24 hours before end of estrus	16½ days
Queen cat		15–21 days	3–4 days, if mated	9–10 days, in absence of male	24–56 hours after coitus	Pseudo-pregnancy
Bitch	24 days	16–30 days	7 days	5–9 days	1–3 days after first acceptance	Pseudo-pregnancy

PLANTING BY THE MOON'S PHASE

ACCORDING TO THIS AGE-OLD PRACTICE, CYCLES OF THE MOON AFFECT PLANT GROWTH.

Plant annual flowers and vegetables that bear crops above ground during the light, or waxing, of the Moon: from the day the Moon is new to the day it is full.

Plant flowering bulbs, biennial and perennial flowers, and vegetables that bear crops below ground during the dark, or waning, of the Moon: from the day after it is full to the day before it is new again.

The Planting Dates columns give the safe periods for planting in areas that receive frost. (See **page 232** for frost dates in your area.) The Moon Favorable columns give the best planting days within the Planting Dates based on the Moon's phases for 2024. (See **pages 120–146** for the exact days of the new and full Moons.)

The dates listed in this table are meant as general guidelines only. For seed-sowing dates based on frost dates in your local area, go to **Almanac.com/2024.**

Aboveground crops are marked *.
(E) means early; (L) means late.

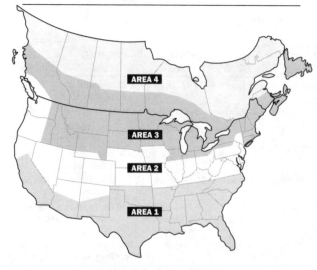

* Barley	
* Beans	(E)
	(L)
Beets	(E)
	(L)
* Broccoli plants	(E)
	(L)
* Brussels sprouts	
* Cabbage plants	
Carrots	(E)
	(L)
* Cauliflower plants	(E)
	(L)
* Celery plants	(E)
	(L)
* Collards	(E)
	(L)
* Corn, sweet	(E)
	(L)
* Cucumbers	
* Eggplant plants	
* Endive	(E)
	(L)
* Kale	(E)
	(L)
Leek plants	
* Lettuce	
* Muskmelons	
* Okra	
Onion sets	
* Parsley	
Parsnips	
* Peas	(E)
	(L)
* Pepper plants	
Potatoes	
* Pumpkins	
Radishes	(E)
	(L)
* Spinach	(E)
	(L)
* Squashes	
Sweet potatoes	
* Swiss chard	
* Tomato plants	
Turnips	(E)
	(L)
* Watermelons	
* Wheat, spring	
* Wheat, winter	

AREA 1		AREA 2		AREA 3		AREA 4	
PLANTING DATES	MOON FAVORABLE	PLANTING DATES	MOON FAVORABLE	PLANTING DATES	MOON FAVORABLE	PLANTING DATES	MOON FAVORABLE
2/15-3/7	2/15-24	3/15-4/7	3/15-25	5/15-6/21	5/15-23, 6/6-21	6/1-30	6/6-21
3/15-4/7	3/15-25	4/15-30	4/15-23	5/7-6/21	5/7-23, 6/6-21	5/30-6/15	6/6-15
8/7-31	8/7-19	7/1-21	7/5-21	6/15-7/15	6/15-21, 7/5-15	–	–
2/7-29	2/7-8, 2/25-29	3/15-4/3	3/26-4/3	4/25-5/15	4/25-5/6	5/25-6/10	5/25-6/5
9/1-30	9/1, 9/18-30	8/15-31	8/20-31	7/15-8/15	7/22-8/3	6/15-7/8	6/22-7/4
2/15-3/15	2/15-24, 3/10-15	3/7-31	3/10-25	5/15-31	5/15-23	6/1-25	6/6-21
9/7-30	9/7-17	8/1-20	8/4-19	6/15-7/7	6/15-21, 7/5-7	–	–
2/11-3/20	2/11-24, 3/10-20	3/7-4/15	3/10-25, 4/8-15	5/15-31	5/15-23	6/1-25	6/6-21
2/11-3/20	2/11-24, 3/10-20	3/7-4/15	3/10-25, 4/8-15	5/15-31	5/15-23	6/1-25	6/6-21
2/15-3/7	2/25-3/7	3/7-31	3/7-9, 3/26-31	5/15-31	5/24-31	5/25-6/10	5/25-6/5
8/1-9/7	8/1-3, 8/20-9/1	7/7-31	7/22-31	6/15-7/21	6/22-7/4	6/15-7/8	6/22-7/4
2/15-3/7	2/15-24	3/15-4/7	3/15-25	5/15-31	5/15-23	6/1-25	6/6-21
8/7-31	8/7-19	7/1-8/7	7/5-21, 8/4-7	6/15-7/21	6/15-21, 7/5-21	–	–
2/15-29	2/15-24	3/7-31	3/10-25	5/15-6/30	5/15-23, 6/6-21	6/1-30	6/6-21
9/15-30	9/15-17	8/15-9/7	8/15-19, 9/2-7	7/15-8/15	7/15-21, 8/4-15	–	–
2/11-3/20	2/11-24, 3/10-20	3/7-4/7	3/10-25	5/15-31	5/15-23	6/1-25	6/6-21
9/7-30	9/7-17	8/15-31	8/15-19	7/1-8/7	7/5-21, 8/4-7	–	–
3/15-31	3/15-25	4/1-17	4/8-17	5/10-6/15	5/10-23, 6/6-15	5/30-6/20	6/6-20
8/7-31	8/7-19	7/7-21	7/7-21	6/15-30	6/15-21	–	–
3/7-4/15	3/10-25, 4/8-15	4/7-5/15	4/8-23, 5/7-15	5/7-6/20	5/7-23, 6/6-20	5/30-6/15	6/6-15
3/7-4/15	3/10-25, 4/8-15	4/7-5/15	4/8-23, 5/7-15	6/1-30	6/6-21	6/15-30	6/15-21
2/15-3/20	2/15-24, 3/10-20	4/7-5/15	4/8-23, 5/7-15	5/15-31	5/15-23	6/1-25	6/6-21
8/15-9/7	8/15-19, 9/2-7	7/15-8/15	7/15-21, 8/4-15	6/7-30	6/7-21	–	–
2/11-3/20	2/11-24, 3/10-20	3/7-4/7	3/10-25	5/15-31	5/15-23	6/1-15	6/6-15
9/7-30	9/7-17	8/15-31	8/15-19	7/1-8/7	7/5-21, 8/4-7	6/25-7/15	7/5-15
2/15-4/15	2/25-3/9, 3/26-4/7	3/7-4/7	3/7-9, 3/26-4/7	5/15-31	5/24-31	6/1-25	6/1-5, 6/22-25
2/15-3/7	2/15-24	3/1-31	3/10-25	5/15-6/30	5/15-23, 6/6-21	6/1-30	6/6-21
3/15-4/7	3/15-25	4/15-5/7	4/15-23, 5/7	5/15-6/30	5/15-23, 6/6-21	6/1-30	6/6-21
4/15-6/1	4/15-23, 5/7-23	5/25-6/15	6/6-15	6/15-7/10	6/15-21, 7/5-10	6/15-7/7	6/15-21, 7/5-7
2/1-29	2/1-8, 2/25-29	3/1-31	3/1-9, 3/26-31	5/15-6/7	5/24-6/5	6/1-25	6/1-5, 6/22-25
2/20-3/15	2/20-24, 3/10-15	3/1-31	3/10-25	5/15-31	5/15-23	6/1-15	6/6-15
1/15-2/4	1/26-2/4	3/7-31	3/7-9, 3/26-31	4/1-30	4/1-7, 4/24-30	5/10-31	5/24-31
1/15-2/7	1/15-25	3/7-31	3/10-25	4/15-5/7	4/15-23, 5/7	5/15-31	5/15-23
9/15-30	9/15-17	8/7-31	8/7-19	7/15-31	7/15-21	7/10-25	7/10-21
3/1-20	3/10-20	4/1-30	4/8-23	5/15-6/30	5/15-23, 6/6-21	6/1-30	6/6-21
2/10-29	2/25-29	4/1-30	4/1-7, 4/24-30	5/1-31	5/1-6, 5/24-31	6/1-25	6/1-5, 6/22-25
3/7-20	3/10-20	4/23-5/15	4/23, 5/7-15	5/15-31	5/15-23	6/1-30	6/6-21
1/21-3/1	1/26-2/8, 2/25-3/1	3/7-31	3/7-9, 3/26-31	4/15-30	4/24-30	5/15-6/5	5/24-6/5
10/1-21	10/1, 10/18-21	9/7-30	9/18-30	8/15-31	8/20-31	7/10-31	7/22-31
2/7-3/15	2/9-24, 3/10-15	3/15-4/20	3/15-25, 4/8-20	5/15-31	5/15-23	6/1-25	6/6-21
10/1-21	10/2-17	8/1-9/15	8/4-19, 9/2-15	7/17-9/7	7/17-21, 8/4-19, 9/2-7	7/20-8/5	7/20-21, 8/4-5
3/15-4/15	3/15-25, 4/8-15	4/15-30	4/15-23	5/15-6/15	5/15-23, 6/6-15	6/1-30	6/6-21
3/23-4/7	3/26-4/7	4/21-5/9	4/24-5/6	5/15-6/15	5/24-6/5	6/1-30	6/1-5, 6/22-30
2/7-3/15	2/9-24, 3/10-15	3/15-4/15	3/15-25, 4/8-15	5/1-31	5/7-23	5/15-31	5/15-23
3/7-21	3/10-21	4/7-30	4/8-23	5/15-31	5/15-23	6/1-15	6/6-15
1/20-2/15	1/26-2/8	3/15-31	3/26-31	4/7-30	4/7, 4/24-30	5/10-31	5/24-31
9/1-10/15	9/1, 9/18-10/1	8/1-20	8/1-3, 8/20	7/1-8/15	7/1-4, 7/22-8/3	–	–
3/15-4/7	3/15-25	4/15-5/7	4/15-23, 5/7	5/15-6/30	5/15-23, 6/6-21	6/1-30	6/6-21
2/15-29	2/15-24	3/1-20	3/10-20	4/7-30	4/8-23	5/15-6/10	5/15-23, 6/6-10
10/15-12/7	10/15-17, 11/1-15, 12/1-7	9/15-10/20	9/15-17, 10/2-17	8/11-9/15	8/11-19, 9/2-15	8/5-30	8/5-19

FROSTS AND GROWING SEASONS

Dates given are normal averages (from 1991–2020) for a light freeze; local weather and topography may cause variations. The possibility of frost occurring after the spring dates and before the fall dates is 30 percent. The classification of freeze temperatures is usually based on their effect on plants. **Light freeze:** 29° to 32°F—tender plants killed. **Moderate freeze:** 25° to 28°F—widely destructive to most plants. **Severe freeze:** 24°F and colder—heavy damage to most plants.

–dates courtesy of National Centers for Environmental Information

STATE	CITY	GROWING SEASON (DAYS)	LAST SPRING FROST	FIRST FALL FROST	STATE	CITY	GROWING SEASON (DAYS)	LAST SPRING FROST	FIRST FALL FROST
AK	Juneau	171	Apr. 26	Oct. 15	NC	Fayetteville	212	Apr. 5	Nov. 4
AL	Mobile	269	Mar. 3	Nov. 28	ND	Bismarck	126	May 19	Sept. 23
AR	Pine Bluff	230	Mar. 22	Nov. 8	NE	Omaha	174	Apr. 23	Oct. 15
AZ	Phoenix	354*	Jan. 9	Dec. 30	NE	North Platte	131	May 16	Sept. 25
AZ	Tucson	309*	Feb. 2	Dec. 9	NH	Concord	136	May 15	Sept. 29
CA	Eureka	268	Mar. 4	Nov. 28	NJ	Newark	211	Apr. 6	Nov. 4
CA	Sacramento	281*	Feb. 17	Nov. 26	NM	Carlsbad	223	Mar. 27	Nov. 6
CO	Denver	154	May 4	Oct. 6	NM	Los Alamos	149	May 9	Oct. 6
CO	Grand Junction	159	May 3	Oct. 10	NV	Las Vegas	292*	Feb. 11	Dec. 1
CT	Hartford	165	Apr. 27	Oct. 10	NY	Albany	159	May 2	Oct. 9
DE	Wilmington	199	Apr. 13	Oct. 30	NY	Syracuse	158	May 5	Oct. 11
FL	Orlando	337*	Jan. 30	Jan. 3**	OH	Akron	174	Apr. 30	Oct. 22
FL	Tallahassee	238	Mar. 19	Nov. 13	OH	Cincinnati	179	Apr. 23	Oct. 20
GA	Athens	217	Mar. 31	Nov. 4	OK	Lawton	206	Apr. 7	Oct. 31
GA	Savannah	253	Mar. 12	Nov. 21	OK	Tulsa	207	Apr. 5	Oct. 30
IA	Atlantic	142	May 6	Sept. 26	OR	Pendleton	155	Apr. 30	Oct. 3
IA	Cedar Rapids	155	May 4	Oct. 7	OR	Portland	260	Mar. 6	Nov. 22
ID	Boise	166	Apr. 30	Oct. 14	PA	Franklin	160	May 9	Oct. 17
IL	Chicago	193	Apr. 17	Oct. 28	PA	Williamsport	167	May 1	Oct. 16
IL	Springfield	177	Apr. 20	Oct. 15	RI	Kingston	148	May 8	Oct. 4
IN	Indianapolis	172	Apr. 26	Oct. 16	SC	Charleston	305*	Feb. 17	Dec. 20
IN	South Bend	159	May 7	Oct. 14	SC	Columbia	235	Mar. 21	Nov. 12
KS	Topeka	182	Apr. 19	Oct. 19	SD	Rapid City	144	May 9	Oct. 1
KY	Lexington	185	Apr. 20	Oct. 23	TN	Memphis	229	Mar. 24	Nov. 9
LA	Monroe	238	Mar. 14	Nov. 8	TN	Nashville	206	Apr. 6	Oct. 30
LA	New Orleans	311*	Feb. 8	Dec. 17	TX	Amarillo	184	Apr. 20	Oct. 22
MA	Boston	208	Apr. 8	Nov. 3	TX	Denton	235	Mar. 21	Nov. 12
MA	Worcester	167	Apr. 29	Oct. 14	TX	San Antonio	267	Mar. 2	Nov. 25
MD	Baltimore	192	Apr. 16	Oct. 26	UT	Cedar City	119	May 31	Sept. 28
ME	Portland	160	May 1	Oct. 9	UT	Spanish Fork	162	May 2	Oct. 12
MI	Lansing	151	May 7	Oct. 6	VA	Norfolk	239	Mar. 23	Nov. 18
MI	Marquette	152	May 15	Oct. 15	VA	Richmond	204	Apr. 9	Oct. 31
MN	Duluth	129	May 19	Sept. 26	VT	Burlington	158	May 3	Oct. 9
MN	Willmar	149	May 4	Oct. 1	WA	Seattle	246	Mar. 12	Nov. 14
MO	Jefferson City	193	Apr. 14	Oct. 25	WA	Spokane	158	May 1	Oct. 7
MS	Columbia	243	Mar. 13	Nov. 12	WI	Green Bay	148	May 7	Oct. 3
MS	Tupelo	218	Mar. 30	Nov. 4	WI	Sparta	133	May 15	Sept. 26
MT	Fort Peck	135	May 13	Sept. 26	WV	Parkersburg	186	Apr. 20	Oct. 24
MT	Helena	132	May 15	Sept. 25	WY	Casper	105	June 1	Sept. 15

*In leap years, add 1 day   **In following year

TABLE OF MEASURES

LINEAR
1 hand = 4 inches
1 link = 7.92 inches
1 span = 9 inches
1 foot = 12 inches
1 yard = 3 feet
1 rod = 5½ yards
1 mile = 320 rods = 1,760 yards = 5,280 feet
1 international nautical mile = 6,076.1155 feet
1 knot = 1 nautical mile per hour
1 fathom = 2 yards = 6 feet
1 furlong = ⅛ mile = 660 feet = 220 yards
1 league = 3 miles = 24 furlongs
1 chain = 100 links = 22 yards

SQUARE
1 square foot = 144 square inches
1 square yard = 9 square feet
1 square rod = 30¼ square yards = 272¼ square feet = 625 square links
1 square chain = 16 square rods
1 acre = 10 square chains = 160 square rods = 43,560 square feet
1 square mile = 640 acres = 102,400 square rods

CUBIC
1 cubic foot = 1,728 cubic inches
1 cubic yard = 27 cubic feet
1 cord = 128 cubic feet
1 U.S. liquid gallon = 4 quarts = 231 cubic inches
1 imperial gallon = 1.20 U.S. gallons = 0.16 cubic foot
1 board foot = 144 cubic inches

DRY
2 pints = 1 quart
4 quarts = 1 gallon
2 gallons = 1 peck
4 pecks = 1 bushel

LIQUID
4 gills = 1 pint
63 gallons = 1 hogshead
2 hogsheads = 1 pipe or butt
2 pipes = 1 tun

KITCHEN
3 teaspoons = 1 tablespoon
16 tablespoons = 1 cup
1 cup = 8 ounces
2 cups = 1 pint
2 pints = 1 quart
4 quarts = 1 gallon

AVOIRDUPOIS
(for general use)
1 ounce = 16 drams
1 pound = 16 ounces
1 short hundredweight = 100 pounds
1 ton = 2,000 pounds
1 long ton = 2,240 pounds

APOTHECARIES'
(for pharmaceutical use)
1 scruple = 20 grains
1 dram = 3 scruples
1 ounce = 8 drams
1 pound = 12 ounces

METRIC CONVERSIONS

LINEAR
1 inch = 2.54 centimeters
1 centimeter = 0.39 inch
1 meter = 39.37 inches
1 yard = 0.914 meter
1 mile = 1.61 kilometers
1 kilometer = 0.62 mile

SQUARE
1 square inch = 6.45 square centimeters
1 square yard = 0.84 square meter
1 square mile = 2.59 square kilometers

1 square kilometer = 0.386 square mile
1 acre = 0.40 hectare
1 hectare = 2.47 acres

CUBIC
1 cubic yard = 0.76 cubic meter
1 cubic meter = 1.31 cubic yards

HOUSEHOLD
½ teaspoon = 2.46 mL
1 teaspoon = 4.93 mL
1 tablespoon = 14.79 mL
¼ cup = 59.15 mL

⅓ cup = 78.86 mL
½ cup = 118.29 mL
¾ cup = 177.44 mL
1 cup = 236.59 mL
1 liter = 1.057 U.S. liquid quarts
1 U.S. liquid quart = 0.946 liter
1 U.S. liquid gallon = 3.78 liters
1 gram = 0.035 ounce
1 ounce = 28.349 grams
1 kilogram = 2.2 pounds
1 pound = 0.45 kilogram

TO CONVERT CELSIUS AND FAHRENHEIT: $°C = (°F − 32)/1.8$; $°F = (°C × 1.8) + 32$

TIDAL GLOSSARY

APOGEAN TIDE: A monthly tide of decreased range that occurs when the Moon is at apogee (farthest from Earth).

CURRENT: Generally, a horizontal movement of water. Currents may be classified as tidal and nontidal. Tidal currents are caused by gravitational interactions between the Sun, Moon, and Earth and are part of the same general movement of the sea that is manifested in the vertical rise and fall, called tide. Nontidal currents include the permanent currents in the general circulatory systems of the sea as well as temporary currents arising from more pronounced meteorological variability.

DIURNAL TIDE: A tide with one high water and one low water in a tidal day of approximately 24 hours.

MEAN LOWER LOW WATER: The arithmetic mean of the lesser of a daily pair of low waters, observed over a specific 19-year cycle called the National Tidal Datum Epoch.

NEAP TIDE: A tide of decreased range that occurs twice a month, when the Moon is in quadrature (during its first and last quarters, when the Sun and the Moon are at right angles to each other relative to Earth).

PERIGEAN TIDE: A monthly tide of increased range that occurs when the Moon is at perigee (closest to Earth).

RED TIDE: Toxic algal blooms caused by several genera of dinoflagellates that usually turn the sea red or brown. These pose a serious threat to marine life and may be harmful to humans.

RIP CURRENT: A potentially dangerous, narrow, intense, surf-zone current flowing outward from shore.

SEMIDIURNAL TIDE: A tide with one high water and one low water every half-day. East Coast tides, for example, are semidiurnal, with two highs and two lows during a tidal day of approximately 24 hours.

SLACK WATER (SLACK): The state of a tidal current when its speed is near zero, especially the moment when a reversing current changes direction and its speed is zero.

SPRING TIDE: A tide of increased range that occurs at times of syzygy each month. Named not for the season of spring but from the German *springen* ("to leap up"), a spring tide also brings a lower low water.

STORM SURGE: The local change in the elevation of the ocean along a shore due to a storm, measured by subtracting the astronomic tidal elevation from the total elevation. It typically has a duration of a few hours and is potentially catastrophic, especially on low-lying coasts with gently sloping offshore topography.

SYZYGY: The nearly straight-line configuration that occurs twice a month, when the Sun and the Moon are in conjunction (on the same side of Earth, at the new Moon) and when they are in opposition (on opposite sides of Earth, at the full Moon). In both cases, the gravitational effects of the Sun and the Moon reinforce each other, and tidal range is increased.

TIDAL BORE: A tide-induced wave that propagates up a relatively shallow and sloping estuary or river with a steep wave front.

TSUNAMI: Sometimes mistakenly called a "tidal wave," a tsunami is a series of long-period waves caused by an underwater earthquake or volcanic eruption. In open ocean, the waves are small and travel at high speed; as they near shore, some may build to more than 30 feet high, becoming a threat to life and property.

VANISHING TIDE: A mixed tide of considerable inequality in the two highs and two lows, so that the lower high (or higher low) may appear to vanish. ■

TIDE CORRECTIONS

Many factors affect tides, including the shoreline, time of the Moon's southing (crossing of the meridian), and the Moon's phase. The High Tide Times column on the **Left-Hand Calendar Pages, 120–146,** lists the times of high tide at Commonwealth Pier in Boston (MA) Harbor. The heights of some of these tides, reckoned from Mean Lower Low Water, are given on the **Right-Hand Calendar Pages, 121–147.** Use the table below to calculate the approximate times and heights of high tide at the places shown. Apply the time difference to the times of high tide at Boston and the height difference to the heights at Boston. A more detailed and accurate tide calculator for the United States and Canada can be found via **Almanac.com/2024.**

EXAMPLE:

The conversion of the times and heights of the tides at Boston to those at Cape Fear, North Carolina, is given below:

High tide at Boston	11:45 A.M.
Correction for Cape Fear	– 3 55
High tide at Cape Fear	7:50 A.M.
Tide height at Boston	11.6 ft.
Correction for Cape Fear	– 5.0 ft.
Tide height at Cape Fear	6.6 ft.

Estimations derived from this table are *not* meant to be used for navigation. *The Old Farmer's Almanac* accepts no responsibility for errors or any consequences ensuing from the use of this table.

TIDAL SITE	TIME (H. M.)	HEIGHT (FT.)	TIDAL SITE	TIME (H. M.)	HEIGHT (FT.)
CANADA			Cape Cod Canal		
Alberton, PE	*–5 45	–7.5	East Entrance	–0 01	–0.8
Charlottetown, PE	*–0 45	–3.5	West Entrance	–2 16	–5.9
Halifax, NS	–3 23	–4.5	Chatham Outer Coast	+0 30	–2.8
North Sydney, NS	–3 15	–6.5	Inside	+1 54	**0.4
Saint John, NB	+0 30	+15.0	Cohasset	+0 02	–0.07
St. John's, NL	–4 00	–6.5	Cotuit Highlands	+1 15	**0.3
Yarmouth, NS	–0 40	+3.0	Dennis Port	+1 01	**0.4
MAINE			Duxbury–Gurnet Point	+0 02	–0.3
Bar Harbor	–0 34	+0.9	Fall River	–3 03	–5.0
Belfast	–0 20	+0.4	Gloucester	–0 03	–0.8
Boothbay Harbor	–0 18	–0.8	Hingham	+0 07	0.0
Chebeague Island	–0 16	–0.6	Hull	+0 03	–0.2
Eastport	–0 28	+8.4	Hyannis Port	+1 01	**0.3
Kennebunkport	+0 04	–1.0	Magnolia–Manchester	–0 02	–0.7
Machias	–0 28	+2.8	Marblehead	–0 02	–0.4
Monhegan Island	–0 25	–0.8	Marion	–3 22	–5.4
Old Orchard Beach	0 00	–0.8	Monument Beach	–3 08	–5.4
Portland	–0 12	–0.6	Nahant	–0 01	–0.5
Rockland	–0 28	+0.1	Nantasket Beach	+0 04	–0.1
Stonington	–0 30	+0.1	Nantucket	+0 56	**0.3
York	–0 09	–1.0	Nauset Beach	+0 30	**0.6
NEW HAMPSHIRE			New Bedford	–3 24	–5.7
Hampton	+0 02	–1.3	Newburyport	+0 19	–1.8
Portsmouth	+0 11	–1.5	Oak Bluffs	+0 30	**0.2
Rye Beach	–0 09	–0.9	Onset–R.R. Bridge	–2 16	–5.9
MASSACHUSETTS			Plymouth	+0 05	0.0
Annisquam	–0 02	–1.1	Provincetown	+0 14	–0.4
Beverly Farms	0 00	–0.5	Revere Beach	–0 01	–0.3

TIDAL SITE	TIME (H. M.)	HEIGHT (FT.)	TIDAL SITE	TIME (H. M.)	HEIGHT (FT.)
Rockport	−0 08	−1.0	**PENNSYLVANIA**		
Salem	0 00	−0.5	Philadelphia	+2 40	−3.5
Scituate	−0 05	−0.7	**DELAWARE**		
Wareham	−3 09	−5.3	Cape Henlopen	−2 48	−5.3
Wellfleet	+0 12	+0.5	Rehoboth Beach	−3 37	−5.7
West Falmouth	−3 10	−5.4	Wilmington	+1 56	−3.8
Westport Harbor	−3 22	−6.4	**MARYLAND**		
Woods Hole			Annapolis	+6 23	−8.5
Little Harbor	−2 50	**0.2	Baltimore	+7 59	−8.3
Oceanographic			Cambridge	+5 05	−7.8
Institute	−3 07	**0.2	Havre de Grace	+11 21	−7.7
RHODE ISLAND			Point No Point	+2 28	−8.1
Bristol	−3 24	−5.3	Prince Frederick–		
Narragansett Pier	−3 42	−6.2	Plum Point	+4 25	−8.5
Newport	−3 34	−5.9	**VIRGINIA**		
Point Judith	−3 41	−6.3	Cape Charles	−2 20	−7.0
Providence	−3 20	−4.8	Hampton Roads	−2 02	−6.9
Sakonnet	−3 44	−5.6	Norfolk	−2 06	−6.6
Watch Hill	−2 50	−6.8	Virginia Beach	−4 00	−6.0
CONNECTICUT			Yorktown	−2 13	−7.0
Bridgeport	+0 01	−2.6	**NORTH CAROLINA**		
Madison	−0 22	−2.3	Cape Fear	−3 55	−5.0
New Haven	−0 11	−3.2	Cape Lookout	−4 28	−5.7
New London	−1 54	−6.7	Currituck	−4 10	−5.8
Norwalk	+0 01	−2.2	Hatteras		
Old Lyme–			Inlet	−4 03	−7.4
Highway Bridge	−0 30	−6.2	Kitty Hawk	−4 14	−6.2
Stamford	+0 01	−2.2	Ocean	−4 26	−6.0
Stonington	−2 27	−6.6	**SOUTH CAROLINA**		
NEW YORK			Charleston	−3 22	−4.3
Coney Island	−3 33	−4.9	Georgetown	−1 48	**0.36
Fire Island Light	−2 43	**0.1	Hilton Head	−3 22	−2.9
Long Beach	−3 11	−5.7	Myrtle Beach	−3 49	−4.4
Montauk Harbor	−2 19	−7.4	St. Helena–		
New York City–Battery	−2 43	−5.0	Harbor Entrance	−3 15	−3.4
Oyster Bay	+0 04	−1.8	**GEORGIA**		
Port Chester	−0 09	−2.2	Jekyll Island	−3 46	−2.9
Port Washington	−0 01	−2.1	St. Simon's Island	−2 50	−2.9
Sag Harbor	−0 55	−6.8	Savannah Beach		
Southampton–			River Entrance	−3 14	−5.5
Shinnecock Inlet	−4 20	**0.2	Tybee Light	−3 22	−2.7
Willets Point	0 00	−2.3	**FLORIDA**		
NEW JERSEY			Cape Canaveral	−3 59	−6.0
Asbury Park	−4 04	−5.3	Daytona Beach	−3 28	−5.3
Atlantic City	−3 56	−5.5	Fort Lauderdale	−2 50	−7.2
Bay Head–Sea Girt	−4 04	−5.3	Fort Pierce Inlet	−3 32	−6.9
Beach Haven	−1 43	**0.24	Jacksonville–		
Cape May	−3 28	−5.3	Railroad Bridge	−6 55	**0.1
Ocean City	−3 06	−5.9	Miami Harbor Entrance	−3 18	−7.0
Sandy Hook	−3 30	−5.0	St. Augustine	−2 55	−4.9
Seaside Park	−4 03	−5.4			

*VARIES WIDELY; ACCURATE ONLY TO WITHIN 1½ HOURS. CONSULT LOCAL TIDE TABLES FOR PRECISE TIMES AND HEIGHTS.
**WHERE THE DIFFERENCE IN THE HEIGHT COLUMN IS SO MARKED, THE HEIGHT AT BOSTON SHOULD BE MULTIPLIED BY THIS RATIO.

TIME CORRECTIONS

Astronomical data for Boston (42°22' N, 71°3' W) is given on **pages 104, 106, 108–109,** and **120–146.** Use the Key Letters shown on those pages with this table to find the number of minutes that you must add to or subtract from Boston time to get the correct time for your city. (Times are approximate.) For more information on the use of Key Letters, see **How to Use This Almanac, page 116.**

GET TIMES SIMPLY AND SPECIFICALLY: Download astronomical times calculated for your zip code and presented as Left-Hand Calendar Pages via **Almanac.com/2024.**

TIME ZONES CODES represent standard time. Atlantic is –1, Eastern is 0, Central is 1, Mountain is 2, Pacific is 3, Alaska is 4, and Hawaii-Aleutian is 5.

STATE	CITY	NORTH LATITUDE °	NORTH LATITUDE ′	WEST LONGITUDE °	WEST LONGITUDE ′	TIME ZONE CODE	A	B	C	D	E
AK	Anchorage	61	10	149	59	4	–46	+27	+71	+122	+171
AK	Cordova	60	33	145	45	4	–55	+13	+55	+103	+149
AK	Fairbanks	64	48	147	51	4	–127	+2	+61	+131	+205
AK	Juneau	58	18	134	25	4	–76	–23	+10	+49	+86
AK	Ketchikan	55	21	131	39	4	–62	–25	0	+29	+56
AK	Kodiak	57	47	152	24	4	0	+49	+82	+120	+154
AL	Birmingham	33	31	86	49	1	+30	+15	+3	–10	–20
AL	Decatur	34	36	86	59	1	+27	+14	+4	–7	–17
AL	Mobile	30	42	88	3	1	+42	+23	+8	–8	–22
AL	Montgomery	32	23	86	19	1	+31	+14	+1	–13	–25
AR	Fort Smith	35	23	94	25	1	+55	+43	+33	+22	+14
AR	Little Rock	34	45	92	17	1	+48	+35	+25	+13	+4
AR	Texarkana	33	26	94	3	1	+59	+44	+32	+18	+8
AZ	Flagstaff	35	12	111	39	2	+64	+52	+42	+31	+22
AZ	Phoenix	33	27	112	4	2	+71	+56	+44	+30	+20
AZ	Tucson	32	13	110	58	2	+70	+53	+40	+24	+12
AZ	Yuma	32	43	114	37	2	+83	+67	+54	+40	+28
CA	Bakersfield	35	23	119	1	3	+33	+21	+12	+1	–7
CA	Barstow	34	54	117	1	3	+27	+14	+4	–7	–16
CA	Fresno	36	44	119	47	3	+32	+22	+15	+6	0
CA	Los Angeles-Pasadena-Santa Monica	34	3	118	14	3	+34	+20	+9	–3	–13
CA	Palm Springs	33	49	116	32	3	+28	+13	+1	–12	–22
CA	Redding	40	35	122	24	3	+31	+27	+25	+22	+19
CA	Sacramento	38	35	121	30	3	+34	+27	+21	+15	+10
CA	San Diego	32	43	117	9	3	+33	+17	+4	–9	–21
CA	San Francisco-Oakland-San Jose	37	47	122	25	3	+40	+31	+25	+18	+12
CO	Craig	40	31	107	33	2	+32	+28	+25	+22	+20
CO	Denver-Boulder	39	44	104	59	2	+24	+19	+15	+11	+7
CO	Grand Junction	39	4	108	33	2	+40	+34	+29	+24	+20
CO	Pueblo	38	16	104	37	2	+27	+20	+14	+7	+2
CO	Trinidad	37	10	104	31	2	+30	+21	+13	+5	0
CT	Bridgeport	41	11	73	11	0	+12	+10	+8	+6	+4
CT	Hartford-New Britain	41	46	72	41	0	+8	+7	+6	+5	+4
CT	New Haven	41	18	72	56	0	+11	+8	+7	+5	+4
CT	New London	41	22	72	6	0	+7	+5	+4	+2	+1
CT	Norwalk-Stamford	41	7	73	22	0	+13	+10	+9	+7	+5
CT	Waterbury-Meriden	41	33	73	3	0	+10	+9	+7	+6	+5
DC	Washington	38	54	77	1	0	+35	+28	+23	+18	+13
DE	Wilmington	39	45	75	33	0	+26	+21	+18	+13	+10

STATE	CITY	NORTH LATITUDE °	NORTH LATITUDE ′	WEST LONGITUDE °	WEST LONGITUDE ′	TIME ZONE CODE	KEY LETTERS (MINUTES) A	B	C	D	E
FL	Fort Myers	26	38	81	52	0	+87	+63	+44	+21	+4
FL	Jacksonville	30	20	81	40	0	+77	+58	+43	+25	+11
FL	Miami	25	47	80	12	0	+88	+57	+37	+14	−3
FL	Orlando	28	32	81	22	0	+80	+59	+42	+22	+6
FL	Pensacola	30	25	87	13	1	+39	+20	+5	−12	−26
FL	St. Petersburg	27	46	82	39	0	+87	+65	+47	+26	+10
FL	Tallahassee	30	27	84	17	0	+87	+68	+53	+35	+22
FL	Tampa	27	57	82	27	0	+86	+64	+46	+25	+9
FL	West Palm Beach	26	43	80	3	0	+79	+55	+36	+14	−2
GA	Atlanta	33	45	84	24	0	+79	+65	+53	+40	+30
GA	Augusta	33	28	81	58	0	+70	+55	+44	+30	+19
GA	Macon	32	50	83	38	0	+79	+63	+50	+36	+24
GA	Savannah	32	5	81	6	0	+70	+54	+40	+25	+13
HI	Hilo	19	44	155	5	5	+94	+62	+37	+7	−15
HI	Honolulu	21	18	157	52	5	+102	+72	+48	+19	−1
HI	Lanai City	20	50	156	55	5	+99	+69	+44	+15	−6
HI	Lihue	21	59	159	23	5	+107	+77	+54	+26	+5
IA	Davenport	41	32	90	35	1	+20	+19	+17	+16	+15
IA	Des Moines	41	35	93	37	1	+32	+31	+30	+28	+27
IA	Dubuque	42	30	90	41	1	+17	+18	+18	+18	+18
IA	Waterloo	42	30	92	20	1	+24	+24	+24	+25	+25
ID	Boise	43	37	116	12	2	+55	+58	+60	+62	+64
ID	Lewiston	46	25	117	1	3	−12	−3	+2	+10	+17
ID	Pocatello	42	52	112	27	2	+43	+44	+45	+46	+46
IL	Cairo	37	0	89	11	1	+29	+20	+12	+4	−2
IL	Chicago-Oak Park	41	52	87	38	1	+7	+6	+6	+5	+4
IL	Danville	40	8	87	37	1	+13	+9	+6	+2	0
IL	Decatur	39	51	88	57	1	+19	+15	+11	+7	+4
IL	Peoria	40	42	89	36	1	+19	+16	+14	+11	+9
IL	Springfield	39	48	89	39	1	+22	+18	+14	+10	+6
IN	Fort Wayne	41	4	85	9	0	+60	+58	+56	+54	+52
IN	Gary	41	36	87	20	1	+7	+6	+4	+3	+2
IN	Indianapolis	39	46	86	10	0	+69	+64	+60	+56	+52
IN	Muncie	40	12	85	23	0	+64	+60	+57	+53	+50
IN	South Bend	41	41	86	15	0	+62	+61	+60	+59	+58
IN	Terre Haute	39	28	87	24	0	+74	+69	+65	+60	+56
KS	Fort Scott	37	50	94	42	1	+49	+41	+34	+27	+21
KS	Liberal	37	3	100	55	1	+76	+66	+59	+51	+44
KS	Oakley	39	8	100	51	1	+69	+63	+59	+53	+49
KS	Salina	38	50	97	37	1	+57	+51	+46	+40	+35
KS	Topeka	39	3	95	40	1	+49	+43	+38	+32	+28
KS	Wichita	37	42	97	20	1	+60	+51	+45	+37	+31
KY	Lexington-Frankfort	38	3	84	30	0	+67	+59	+53	+46	+41
KY	Louisville	38	15	85	46	0	+72	+64	+58	+52	+46
LA	Alexandria	31	18	92	27	1	+58	+40	+26	+9	−3
LA	Baton Rouge	30	27	91	11	1	+55	+36	+21	+3	−10
LA	Lake Charles	30	14	93	13	1	+64	+44	+29	+11	−2
LA	Monroe	32	30	92	7	1	+53	+37	+24	+9	−1
LA	New Orleans	29	57	90	4	1	+52	+32	+16	−1	−15
LA	Shreveport	32	31	93	45	1	+60	+44	+31	+16	+4
MA	Brockton	42	5	71	1	0	0	0	0	0	−1
MA	Fall River-New Bedford	41	42	71	9	0	+2	+1	0	0	−1
MA	Lawrence-Lowell	42	42	71	10	0	0	0	0	0	+1
MA	Pittsfield	42	27	73	15	0	+8	+8	+8	+8	+8
MA	Springfield-Holyoke	42	6	72	36	0	+6	+6	+6	+5	+5
MA	Worcester	42	16	71	48	0	+3	+2	+2	+2	+2

TIME CORRECTIONS

STATE	CITY	NORTH LATITUDE °	NORTH LATITUDE '	WEST LONGITUDE °	WEST LONGITUDE '	TIME ZONE CODE	A	B	C	D	E
MD	Baltimore	39	17	76	37	0	+32	+26	+22	+17	+13
MD	Hagerstown	39	39	77	43	0	+35	+30	+26	+22	+18
MD	Salisbury	38	22	75	36	0	+31	+23	+18	+11	+6
ME	Augusta	44	19	69	46	0	−12	−8	−5	−1	0
ME	Bangor	44	48	68	46	0	−18	−13	−9	−5	−1
ME	Eastport	44	54	67	0	0	−26	−20	−16	−11	−8
ME	Ellsworth	44	33	68	25	0	−18	−14	−10	−6	−3
ME	Portland	43	40	70	15	0	−8	−5	−3	−1	0
ME	Presque Isle	46	41	68	1	0	−29	−19	−12	−4	+2
MI	Cheboygan	45	39	84	29	0	+40	+47	+53	+59	+64
MI	Detroit-Dearborn	42	20	83	3	0	+47	+47	+47	+47	+47
MI	Flint	43	1	83	41	0	+47	+49	+50	+51	+52
MI	Ironwood	46	27	90	9	1	0	+9	+15	+23	+29
MI	Jackson	42	15	84	24	0	+53	+53	+53	+52	+52
MI	Kalamazoo	42	17	85	35	0	+58	+57	+57	+57	+57
MI	Lansing	42	44	84	33	0	+52	+53	+53	+54	+54
MI	St. Joseph	42	5	86	26	0	+61	+61	+60	+60	+59
MI	Traverse City	44	46	85	38	0	+49	+54	+57	+62	+65
MN	Albert Lea	43	39	93	22	1	+24	+26	+28	+31	+33
MN	Bemidji	47	28	94	53	1	+14	+26	+34	+44	+52
MN	Duluth	46	47	92	6	1	+6	+16	+23	+31	+38
MN	Minneapolis-St. Paul	44	59	93	16	1	+18	+24	+28	+33	+37
MN	Ortonville	45	19	96	27	1	+30	+36	+40	+46	+51
MO	Jefferson City	38	34	92	10	1	+36	+29	+24	+18	+13
MO	Joplin	37	6	94	30	1	+50	+41	+33	+25	+18
MO	Kansas City	39	1	94	20	1	+44	+37	+33	+27	+23
MO	Poplar Bluff	36	46	90	24	1	+35	+25	+17	+8	+1
MO	St. Joseph	39	46	94	50	1	+43	+38	+35	+30	+27
MO	St. Louis	38	37	90	12	1	+28	+21	+16	+10	+5
MO	Springfield	37	13	93	18	1	+45	+36	+29	+20	+14
MS	Biloxi	30	24	88	53	1	+46	+27	+11	−5	−19
MS	Jackson	32	18	90	11	1	+46	+30	+17	+1	−10
MS	Meridian	32	22	88	42	1	+40	+24	+11	−4	−15
MS	Tupelo	34	16	88	34	1	+35	+21	+10	−2	−11
MT	Billings	45	47	108	30	2	+16	+23	+29	+35	+40
MT	Butte	46	1	112	32	2	+31	+39	+45	+52	+57
MT	Glasgow	48	12	106	38	2	−1	+11	+21	+32	+42
MT	Great Falls	47	30	111	17	2	+20	+31	+39	+49	+58
MT	Helena	46	36	112	2	2	+27	+36	+43	+51	+57
MT	Miles City	46	25	105	51	2	+3	+11	+18	+26	+32
NC	Asheville	35	36	82	33	0	+67	+55	+46	+35	+27
NC	Charlotte	35	14	80	51	0	+61	+49	+39	+28	+19
NC	Durham	36	0	78	55	0	+51	+40	+31	+21	+13
NC	Greensboro	36	4	79	47	0	+54	+43	+35	+25	+17
NC	Raleigh	35	47	78	38	0	+51	+39	+30	+20	+12
NC	Wilmington	34	14	77	55	0	+52	+38	+27	+15	+5
ND	Bismarck	46	48	100	47	1	+41	+50	+58	+66	+73
ND	Fargo	46	53	96	47	1	+24	+34	+42	+50	+57
ND	Grand Forks	47	55	97	3	1	+21	+33	+43	+53	+62
ND	Minot	48	14	101	18	1	+36	+50	+59	+71	+81
ND	Williston	48	9	103	37	1	+46	+59	+69	+80	+90
NE	Grand Island	40	55	98	21	1	+53	+51	+49	+46	+44
NE	Lincoln	40	49	96	41	1	+47	+44	+42	+39	+37
NE	North Platte	41	8	100	46	1	+62	+60	+58	+56	+54
NE	Omaha	41	16	95	56	1	+43	+40	+39	+37	+36
NH	Berlin	44	28	71	11	0	−7	−3	0	+3	+7
NH	Keene	42	56	72	17	0	+2	+3	+4	+5	+6

Get local rise, set, and tide times via Almanac.com/2024.

STATE	CITY	NORTH LATITUDE °	NORTH LATITUDE '	WEST LONGITUDE °	WEST LONGITUDE '	TIME ZONE CODE	KEY LETTERS (MINUTES) A	B	C	D	E
NH	Manchester-Concord	42	59	71	28	0	0	0	+1	+2	+3
NH	Portsmouth	43	5	70	45	0	–4	–2	–1	0	0
NJ	Atlantic City	39	22	74	26	0	+23	+17	+13	+8	+4
NJ	Camden	39	57	75	7	0	+24	+19	+16	+12	+9
NJ	Cape May	38	56	74	56	0	+26	+20	+15	+9	+5
NJ	Newark-East Orange	40	44	74	10	0	+17	+14	+12	+9	+7
NJ	Paterson	40	55	74	10	0	+17	+14	+12	+9	+7
NJ	Trenton	40	13	74	46	0	+21	+17	+14	+11	+8
NM	Albuquerque	35	5	106	39	2	+45	+32	+22	+11	+2
NM	Gallup	35	32	108	45	2	+52	+40	+31	+20	+11
NM	Las Cruces	32	19	106	47	2	+53	+36	+23	+8	–3
NM	Roswell	33	24	104	32	2	+41	+26	+14	0	–10
NM	Santa Fe	35	41	105	56	2	+40	+28	+19	+9	0
NV	Carson City-Reno	39	10	119	46	3	+25	+19	+14	+9	+5
NV	Elko	40	50	115	46	3	+3	0	–1	–3	–5
NV	Las Vegas	36	10	115	9	3	+16	+4	–3	–13	–20
NY	Albany	42	39	73	45	0	+9	+10	+10	+11	+11
NY	Binghamton	42	6	75	55	0	+20	+19	+19	+18	+18
NY	Buffalo	42	53	78	52	0	+29	+30	+30	+31	+32
NY	New York	40	45	74	0	0	+17	+14	+11	+9	+6
NY	Ogdensburg	44	42	75	30	0	+8	+13	+17	+21	+25
NY	Syracuse	43	3	76	9	0	+17	+19	+20	+21	+22
OH	Akron	41	5	81	31	0	+46	+43	+41	+39	+37
OH	Canton	40	48	81	23	0	+46	+43	+41	+38	+36
OH	Cincinnati-Hamilton	39	6	84	31	0	+64	+58	+53	+48	+44
OH	Cleveland-Lakewood	41	30	81	42	0	+45	+43	+42	+40	+39
OH	Columbus	39	57	83	1	0	+55	+51	+47	+43	+40
OH	Dayton	39	45	84	10	0	+61	+56	+52	+48	+44
OH	Toledo	41	39	83	33	0	+52	+50	+49	+48	+47
OH	Youngstown	41	6	80	39	0	+42	+40	+38	+36	+34
OK	Oklahoma City	35	28	97	31	1	+67	+55	+46	+35	+26
OK	Tulsa	36	9	95	60	1	+59	+48	+40	+30	+22
OR	Eugene	44	3	123	6	3	+21	+24	+27	+30	+33
OR	Pendleton	45	40	118	47	3	–1	+4	+10	+16	+21
OR	Portland	45	31	122	41	3	+14	+20	+25	+31	+36
OR	Salem	44	57	123	1	3	+17	+23	+27	+31	+35
PA	Allentown-Bethlehem	40	36	75	28	0	+23	+20	+17	+14	+12
PA	Erie	42	7	80	5	0	+36	+36	+35	+35	+35
PA	Harrisburg	40	16	76	53	0	+30	+26	+23	+19	+16
PA	Lancaster	40	2	76	18	0	+28	+24	+20	+17	+13
PA	Philadelphia-Chester	39	57	75	9	0	+24	+19	+16	+12	+9
PA	Pittsburgh-McKeesport	40	26	80	0	0	+42	+38	+35	+32	+29
PA	Reading	40	20	75	56	0	+26	+22	+19	+16	+13
PA	Scranton-Wilkes-Barre	41	25	75	40	0	+21	+19	+18	+16	+15
PA	York	39	58	76	43	0	+30	+26	+22	+18	+15
RI	Providence	41	50	71	25	0	+3	+2	+1	0	0
SC	Charleston	32	47	79	56	0	+64	+48	+36	+21	+10
SC	Columbia	34	0	81	2	0	+65	+51	+40	+27	+17
SC	Spartanburg	34	56	81	57	0	+66	+53	+43	+32	+23
SD	Aberdeen	45	28	98	29	1	+37	+44	+49	+54	+59
SD	Pierre	44	22	100	21	1	+49	+53	+56	+60	+63
SD	Rapid City	44	5	103	14	2	+2	+5	+8	+11	+13
SD	Sioux Falls	43	33	96	44	1	+38	+40	+42	+44	+46
TN	Chattanooga	35	3	85	19	0	+79	+67	+57	+45	+36
TN	Knoxville	35	58	83	55	0	+71	+60	+51	+41	+33
TN	Memphis	35	9	90	3	1	+38	+26	+16	+5	–3
TN	Nashville	36	10	86	47	1	+22	+11	+3	–6	–14

STATE/PROVINCE	CITY	NORTH LATITUDE °	′	WEST LONGITUDE °	′	TIME ZONE CODE	KEY LETTERS (MINUTES) A	B	C	D	E
TX	Amarillo	35	12	101	50	1	+85	+73	+63	+52	+43
TX	Austin	30	16	97	45	1	+82	+62	+47	+29	+15
TX	Beaumont	30	5	94	6	1	+67	+48	+32	+14	0
TX	Brownsville	25	54	97	30	1	+91	+66	+46	+23	+5
TX	Corpus Christi	27	48	97	24	1	+86	+64	+46	+25	+9
TX	Dallas–Fort Worth	32	47	96	48	1	+71	+55	+43	+28	+17
TX	El Paso	31	45	106	29	2	+53	+35	+22	+6	−6
TX	Galveston	29	18	94	48	1	+72	+52	+35	+16	+1
TX	Houston	29	45	95	22	1	+73	+53	+37	+19	+5
TX	McAllen	26	12	98	14	1	+93	+69	+49	+26	+9
TX	San Antonio	29	25	98	30	1	+87	+66	+50	+31	+16
UT	Kanab	37	3	112	32	2	+62	+53	+46	+37	+30
UT	Moab	38	35	109	33	2	+46	+39	+33	+27	+22
UT	Ogden	41	13	111	58	2	+47	+45	+43	+41	+40
UT	Salt Lake City	40	45	111	53	2	+48	+45	+43	+40	+38
UT	Vernal	40	27	109	32	2	+40	+36	+33	+30	+28
VA	Charlottesville	38	2	78	30	0	+43	+35	+29	+22	+17
VA	Danville	36	36	79	23	0	+51	+41	+33	+24	+17
VA	Norfolk	36	51	76	17	0	+38	+28	+21	+12	+5
VA	Richmond	37	32	77	26	0	+41	+32	+25	+17	+11
VA	Roanoke	37	16	79	57	0	+51	+42	+35	+27	+21
VA	Winchester	39	11	78	10	0	+38	+33	+28	+23	+19
VT	Brattleboro	42	51	72	34	0	+4	+5	+5	+6	+7
VT	Burlington	44	29	73	13	0	0	+4	+8	+12	+15
VT	Rutland	43	37	72	58	0	+2	+5	+7	+9	+11
VT	St. Johnsbury	44	25	72	1	0	−4	0	+3	+7	+10
WA	Bellingham	48	45	122	29	3	0	+13	+24	+37	+47
WA	Seattle-Tacoma–Olympia	47	37	122	20	3	+3	+15	+24	+34	+42
WA	Spokane	47	40	117	24	3	−16	−4	+4	+14	+23
WA	Walla Walla	46	4	118	20	3	−5	+2	+8	+15	+21
WI	Eau Claire	44	49	91	30	1	+12	+17	+21	+25	+29
WI	Green Bay	44	31	88	0	1	0	+3	+7	+11	+14
WI	La Crosse	43	48	91	15	1	+15	+18	+20	+22	+25
WI	Madison	43	4	89	23	1	+10	+11	+12	+14	+15
WI	Milwaukee	43	2	87	54	1	+4	+6	+7	+8	+9
WI	Oshkosh	44	1	88	33	1	+3	+6	+9	+12	+15
WI	Wausau	44	58	89	38	1	+4	+9	+13	+18	+22
WV	Charleston	38	21	81	38	0	+55	+48	+42	+35	+30
WV	Parkersburg	39	16	81	34	0	+52	+46	+42	+36	+32
WY	Casper	42	51	106	19	2	+19	+19	+20	+21	+22
WY	Cheyenne	41	8	104	49	2	+19	+16	+14	+12	+11
WY	Sheridan	44	48	106	58	2	+14	+19	+23	+27	+31

CANADA

STATE/PROVINCE	CITY	NORTH LATITUDE °	′	WEST LONGITUDE °	′	TIME ZONE CODE	KEY LETTERS (MINUTES) A	B	C	D	E
AB	Calgary	51	5	114	5	2	+13	+35	+50	+68	+84
AB	Edmonton	53	34	113	25	2	−3	+26	+47	+72	+93
BC	Vancouver	49	13	123	6	3	0	+15	+26	+40	+52
MB	Winnipeg	49	53	97	10	1	+12	+30	+43	+58	+71
NB	Saint John	45	16	66	3	−1	+28	+34	+39	+44	+49
NS	Halifax	44	38	63	35	−1	+21	+26	+29	+33	+37
NS	Sydney	46	10	60	10	−1	+1	+9	+15	+23	+28
ON	Ottawa	45	25	75	43	0	+6	+13	+18	+23	+28
ON	Peterborough	44	18	78	19	0	+21	+25	+28	+32	+35
ON	Thunder Bay	48	27	89	12	0	+47	+61	+71	+83	+93
ON	Toronto	43	39	79	23	0	+28	+30	+32	+35	+37
QC	Montreal	45	28	73	39	0	−1	+4	+9	+15	+20
SK	Saskatoon	52	10	106	40	1	+37	+63	+80	+101	+119

Get local rise, set, and tide times via Almanac.com/2024.

PRODUCE WEIGHTS AND MEASURES

VEGETABLES

ASPARAGUS: 1 pound = 3 cups chopped

BEANS (STRING): 1 pound = 4 cups chopped

BEETS: 1 pound (5 medium) = 2½ cups chopped

BROCCOLI: 1 pound = 6 cups chopped

CABBAGE: 1 pound = 4½ cups shredded

CARROTS: 1 pound = 3½ cups sliced or grated

CELERY: 1 pound = 4 cups chopped

CUCUMBERS: 1 pound (2 medium) = 4 cups sliced

EGGPLANT: 1 pound = 4 cups chopped = 2 cups cooked

GARLIC: 1 clove = 1 teaspoon chopped

LEEKS: 1 pound = 4 cups chopped = 2 cups cooked

MUSHROOMS: 1 pound = 5 to 6 cups sliced = 2 cups cooked

ONIONS: 1 pound = 4 cups sliced = 2 cups cooked

PARSNIPS: 1 pound = 1½ cups cooked, puréed

PEAS: 1 pound whole = 1 to 1½ cups shelled

POTATOES: 1 pound (3 medium) sliced = 2 cups mashed

PUMPKIN: 1 pound = 4 cups chopped = 2 cups cooked and drained

SPINACH: 1 pound = ¾ to 1 cup cooked

SQUASHES (SUMMER): 1 pound = 4 cups grated = 2 cups sliced and cooked

SQUASHES (WINTER): 2 pounds = 2½ cups cooked, puréed

SWEET POTATOES: 1 pound = 4 cups grated = 1 cup cooked, puréed

SWISS CHARD: 1 pound = 5 to 6 cups packed leaves = 1 to 1½ cups cooked

TOMATOES: 1 pound (3 or 4 medium) = 1½ cups seeded pulp

TURNIPS: 1 pound = 4 cups chopped = 2 cups cooked, mashed

FRUIT

APPLES: 1 pound (3 or 4 medium) = 3 cups sliced

BANANAS: 1 pound (3 or 4 medium) = 1¾ cups mashed

BERRIES: 1 quart = 3½ cups

DATES: 1 pound = 2½ cups pitted

LEMON: 1 whole = 1 to 3 tablespoons juice; 1 to 1½ teaspoons grated zest

LIME: 1 whole = 1½ to 2 tablespoons juice

ORANGE: 1 medium = 6 to 8 tablespoons juice; 2 to 3 tablespoons grated zest

PEACHES: 1 pound (4 medium) = 3 cups sliced

PEARS: 1 pound (4 medium) = 2 cups sliced

RHUBARB: 1 pound = 2 cups cooked

STRAWBERRIES: 1 quart = 4 cups sliced

GENERAL STORE CLASSIFIEDS

For advertising information and rates, go to Almanac.com/Advertising
or call RJ Media at 212-986-0016. The 2025 edition closes on April 30, 2024.

ASTROLOGY

REV. BUSH—I remove all ritual work, clear all negative energy. Heal all sickness. Call: 252-458-6864.

REV. BLACK, VOODOO HEALER. Removes evil influences, bad luck, sickness that doctors can't cure. Call: 252-366-4078.

SOPHIA GREEN. Don't tell me, I'll tell you! Helps all problems—Reunites lovers. Guaranteed! Call: 956-878-7053.

ATTENTION: SISTER LIGHT
Spartanburg, South Carolina
One FREE READING when you call.
I will help you with all problems.
Call: 864-576-9397

FREE READING
PSYCHIC SPIRITUALIST ROSELLA
Solves ALL problems. I don't judge.
Specializing: Divorce, Fear, Court Cases,
Spiritual Soul Cleansing.
Don't worry about tomorrow!
Call: 586-215-3838

PSYCHIC HANNAH • NEW YORK PSYCHIC
30 years' experience. Calls out your enemies.
Image Candles—Lucky Charms.
One Free Question!
Call: 347-448-6189

REVEREND EVETTE
Answers ALL questions. Solves life's problems. Need Help Desperately?
CALL IMMEDIATELY!
Does what others claim! 100% Guaranteed!
P.O. Box 80322, Chattanooga, TN, 37414
Call: 423-894-6699

BUSINESS OPPORTUNITIES

$800 WEEKLY POTENTIAL! Process HUD/FHA refunds from home. Free information available. Call: 860-357-1599.

CATALOGS & BOOKS

Catalog $4.00. Lyra Cartoons,
Juvenile Books, Armadillo Squirrel Kits,
Famous Doll Monster Poster from
the Top Archives
Armadillo Astronomy Theory.
3 Eastern Lane,
West Gardiner, Maine 04345

CLAIRVOYANT

CLAIRVOYANT PROPHETIC PSYCHIC. Intuitive, Love, Body, Ancestral Readings. Gives answers! Dreams, Colors, Numbers, Names. Call: 904-862-9520.

HEALTH

MACULAR DEGENERATION?

Restore
Lost Vision!

No need to travel.

Call for free booklet:
888-838-3937

Also helps RP, Stargardt

JEWELRY

WWW.AZUREGREEN.NET Jewelry, Amulets, Incense, Oils, Statuary, Gifts, Herbs, Candles, Gemstones. 8,000 Items. Wholesale inquiries welcome.

PERSONALS

ASIAN WOMEN! Overseas Penpals. Romance! Free brochure (send SASE). P.I.C., Box 4601-OFA, Thousand Oaks, CA 91359. Call today: 805-492-8040. www.pacisl.com

PSYCHIC READINGS

ANGEL PSYCHIC
MEDIUM CLAIRVOYANT
Spiritual - Positive Energy
*Accurate *Honest *Healing
Call: 323-466-3684
www.TruePsychicReader.com

(continued)

2023 ESSAY CONTEST WINNERS
"A Funny Thing That Happened to Me"

We received hundreds of amusing anecdotes and stories.
Thank you to all who submitted entries.

First Prize: $300

I had two short hours until my wedding. People milled around my dad's house getting dressed and making last-minute preparations. My youngest sister scurried into my bedroom and wanted to know if my shoes were polished. Huh? I had other things on my mind, so I shrugged and pointed to the closet. She snatched the shoes and promised to return right away. An hour later, in stocking feet, I found my sister and the shoes. She said that the polish was still wet and insisted that she help me put them on. Worried about other things, I shrugged and agreed. They didn't seem any more polished than before. She knelt, slipped them on on my feet one shoe at a time, and tied the laces.

Fast-forward an hour: My bride, Nancy, and I walked down the aisle at St. Stephen's and knelt before the priest. The majority of those in the front two rows started chuckling. The priest hesitated a couple of seconds, waiting for them to calm down. As it turns out, they chuckled because my sister had used fluorescent pink fingernail polish to write on the soles of my shoes: "Save Me" and "Help Me".

–Bruce Kubec, Longwood, Florida

Second Prize: $200

My son was 6 years old, about halfway through first grade, and he was in that magical stage when learning to read permeated every aspect of his life: reading street signs, reading posters in store windows, reading cereal boxes. He would focus, squint, and silently mouth the printed letters, then decode them into language. He'd do it again and again, the ratio of success creeping up with practice.

So it was that Mom had an evening meeting and my son and I headed to a local family restaurant for dinner. The menu became his prized focus, a small universe of words and pictures, puzzles to be solved, a playground for exercising his current favorite sport. He got "french fries" and "ice cream," but stumbled on "spaghetti" and "appetizer."

Then, as we neared the end of our dinner, a look of concern wrinkled his face. He scanned the dining room with mild confusion. His eyes lingered on an adjoining, smaller dining area. Finally, he asked, "Do we have to go there if we get ice cream?" I asked what he meant. He then pointed to the menu and read, "It says here, 'Leave room for dessert.'"

–Rick Schnable, Dover, New Hampshire

Third Prize: $100

The night before Thanksgiving one year, my husband sent our young daughters out to the freezer in the garage with instructions to bring in the turkey to defrost. They came back to report that there was no turkey. He told them to look again, adding that it was smaller than usual. They came back with a shrink-wrapped Cornish game hen, asking, "Is this really our turkey?" He assured them that it was, explaining that he'd learned about a new product called Expand-O Turkey.

They put the wrapped bird in the sink with water, and he assured them that—like their fun bath sponges—it would be full size by morning. After they were asleep, he cut open the shrink-wrap to look like it had burst wide open, wrapped up the game hen, and returned it to the freezer.

Before they awoke, he took our real turkey from a cooler where it had been defrosting, removed its shrink-wrap, and placed it in the sink. The game hen's torn tiny shrink wrap was placed in the water to await the girls' discovery. Their eyes widened at the scene. Expand-O Turkey was amazing. They spread the word far and wide.

–Cindy Dobrez, Grand Haven, Michigan

Honorable Mention

We were on the road to the Renaissance Festival in Sterling, New York. Upon arriving, my husband and I walked into the wooded grounds and made a beeline for the food stands—pulled pork pockets with creamy coleslaw; turkey legs; strawberry shortcake with whipped cream; and much more. We chose our desired delicacy, and off we ran to see the sights.

Except that I don't run. I can't even walk quickly. I have multiple sclerosis and walk with a limp. Climbing stairs is especially difficult, and this festival had plenty of stairs built into the ground. I was ascending one set of stairs as a woman going down stopped me. "How's the leg?" she asked. I did a quick memory jog: "Do I know her? Apparently, she knows me and knows that I have MS. Is she from church? The neighborhood?"

I didn't know, but I answered her: "The leg's a little weak, but I'm sure it'll get better." She nodded, smiling strangely at me. She went along her merry way, as I lifted a huge 1-pound turkey leg to my mouth.

–Geraldine Bereziuk-Lowrey,
Buffalo, New York

ANNOUNCING THE 2024 ESSAY CONTEST TOPIC:
THE BEST MONEY I EVER SPENT
SEE CONTEST RULES ON PAGE 251.

MADDENING MIND-MANGLERS

TENNESSEE TEASERS FOR '24

In the following lists, which does not belong?

1. hail, ice, icicle, rain, snow, water

2. bow, dessert, invalid, row, tear, wind, wound

3. badminton, pickleball, racquetball, squash, tennis

4. 7, 17, 27, 37, 47, 67, 97

–Morris Bowles, Cane Ridge, Tennessee

5. BALL AND BAT

A baseball and baseball bat cost a total of $1.20. The bat cost a dollar more than the ball. How much did the ball cost?

6. STORE-BOUGHT LOSS

A man went into a store and bought $70 worth of goods with a counterfeit $100 bill. The clerk gave him $30 change in good money. How much did the store lose?

7. FROM THE 1824 *OLD FARMER'S ALMANAC:*

Tho' highly I'm priz'd,
Yet I own a mean birth,
For at my beginning
I was formed from the earth.

So strange my appearance,
You'll believe me a noddy;
Tho' my mouth's very large,
I've neither head nor body.

I have breath without life
And my nature is so frail;
I inhale at my mouth
And exhale at my tail.

I'm esteem'd by the rich;
By the poor I'm admir'd,
Who are fond of the air
Which I have once expir'd.

Let me live with whom I will,
My food is still the same.
Tell me, for you know me,
What is my real name?

Do you have a favorite puzzler for "Maddening Mind-Manglers" that you'd like to share? Send it to us at Mind-Manglers, The Old Farmer's Almanac, P.O. Box 520, Dublin, NH 03444, or via Almanac.com/Contact, Subject: Mind-Manglers.

ANSWERS

1. icicle (only one not also a verb).
2. dessert (only one with just one pronunciation and spelling).
3. pickleball (only one played with a solid paddle). **4.** 27 (only one not a prime number). **5.** 10 cents. **6.** $200 ($70 in goods, $30 in good cash, left with $100 in worthless cash). **7.** In the early days of the Almanac, answers to one year's puzzles were published in the following year's edition. Readers would mail their answers to the editor, who would list the initials and hometowns of the correct guessers as part of the next Anecdotes & Pleasantries section. It was the fashion in those days for the answers to such cryptic rhyming riddles to themselves be presented in the same form, giving the editor just enough information to be able to understand that the solver did indeed have the correct answer. Readers could submit their response as a simple word or two, or they could go for greater glory by submitting a rhyming answer in hope of seeing it published. In the *1825 Old Farmer's Almanac,* the editor printed the initials of eight readers who had submitted simple correct answers to our #7. He also published two correct rhyming answers that can serve here as further clues for our riddle: **a.** *Priz'd I am by young and old, / In some the ruling passion. / Preceding both in hot or cold / Ere dandies came in fashion.* **b.** *Priz'd as you be, / I hate to see / Pug sucking thee / Eternally.* The answer? A tobacco pipe.

ESSAY AND RECIPE CONTEST RULES

Cash prizes (first, $300; second, $200; third, $100) will be awarded for the best essays in 200 or fewer words on the subject "The Best Money I Ever Spent" and the best "Favorite Holiday Dish" recipes. Entries must be yours, original, and unpublished. Amateur cooks only, please. One recipe per person. All entries become the property of Yankee Publishing, which reserves all rights to the material. The deadline for entries is January 31, 2024. Enter at Almanac.com/EssayContest or at Almanac.com/RecipeContest or label "Essay Contest" or "Recipe Contest" and mail to The Old Farmer's Almanac, P.O. Box 520, Dublin, NH 03444. Include your name, mailing address, and email address. Winners will appear in *The 2025 Old Farmer's Almanac* and on Almanac.com. ∎

ANECDOTES & PLEASANTRIES

A sampling from the thousands of letters, clippings, articles, and emails sent to us during the past year by our Almanac family in the United States and Canada.

ILLUSTRATIONS BY TIM ROBINSON

MIRTHFUL MAGIC, OR HOW TO TURN A DULL PARTY INTO A MERRY ONE

When young people, and often old ones also, first arrive at a party, they are apt to feel a little stiff and awkward, and to stand about in corners, as if oppressed with the responsibility of their best gloves and clothes, and the giver of the entertainment seeks in vain to enliven and stir them up. For her aid we propose to give a few simple recipes which will answer the purpose, and give them a good laugh, after which they will be ready for the harder games which will follow. First she may ask them to join in the game of "Satisfaction."

Every person in the room is invited to stand up, and all join hands in a ring, in the center of which the leader stands, holding a cane in her hand, with which she points to each one in turn, and asks this question, after requesting silence and careful attention, "Are you satisfied?" Each replies in turn as he or she pleases, many probably saying "No," and others "Yes." The leader then says, "All who are satisfied may sit down. The others may stand up until they are satisfied."

–*G. B. Bartlett,* Harper's Young People— An Illustrated Weekly, *July 6, 1880*

THE EASTERNMOST POINT IN THE U.S. IS IN MAINE. *WRONG!*

How far apart are the western- and easternmost points in the United States? Would you say 3,000 miles? 5,000? *How about 63 miles?*

That's right. It turns out that Alaska is home to both the westernmost place—Amatignak Island, at 51°16'7"N latitude, 179°8'55"W longitude—and easternmost point—Semisopochnoi Island, at 51°57'42"N, 179°46'23"E.

How can this be? It's all about the longitude meridian at 180° E/W that separates the Eastern and Western Hemispheres. Whereas Amatignak is 51 minutes, 5 seconds to the east of it—or very, very far west in the Western Hemisphere— Semisopochnoi is only 13 minutes, 37 seconds to the west of it—or very, very far east in the Eastern Hemisphere. Across the water, though, they are separated by only about 63 miles.

–A. Y., Fairbanks, Alaska

BIG TECH GOES INTO THE GARDEN

Apparently failing a basic spelling lesson, one popular social networking app flagged a garden club for its continued use of the word "hoe," which it said violated community standards. Even after the parties agreed that this word did not represent a person, this dastardly group later had its Comments function disabled because it was possibly inciting violence or hate—all due to pest postings that included such evil bug directives as "kill them all" and "drown them in soapy water."

–B. R., East Greenbush, New York

Breaking Bovine Bulletins

• Cattle cooped up in barns were fitted with virtual reality headsets that simulated the experience of being outside in beautiful green pastures. In one study, the mellowed-out moo-ers on VR produced 23% more milk. *–G. H., Saskatoon, Saskatchewan*

• In search of cost savings, scientists replaced normal cattle feed with hemp left over from industrial processing. Guess what? The hemped-up bovines acted sillier, yawned and drooled more, and engaged in "excessive tongue play." The question, though, was whether drinking milk from these cows would get you stoned. The answer was yes, so that was that—unfortunately for the cows.

–N. M., Stevens Point, Wisconsin

(continued)

WHEN THAT SHADOW THE GROUNDHOG SEES IS, UH, REALLY, *REALLY* DARK

R.I.P. Fred la Marmotte, age 9, former furry prognosticator at Val d'Espoir, Quebec, who was found deceased hours before scheduled to make a recent observation. Apparently he had chucked his last wood some months before, which was no doubt a relief to any onlookers fearing that he had taken a sneak peek the day before and died of fright right then and there. But what about the prediction? *Pas de problème!* A youngster in the crowd wearing a groundhog hat was handed a stuffed marmot, which then somehow made the call. *Miracle des miracles!*

–P. W., Lévis, Quebec

How to Hypnotize Your Foot

1. Sit in a chair.

2. Looking down at your feet, say, "Toes goes. Toes goes. Toes goes."

3. Lift your right foot off the floor and make clockwise circles with it.

4. Quickly say again, "Toes goes. Toes goes. Toes goes."

5. As your foot is still circling, draw the number 6 in the air with your right hand.

6. You have now hypnotized your foot into changing direction. *–T. T., Salt Lake City, Utah*

HANDY TIPS TO MAKE YOU A BETTER PERSON— OR SOMETHING LIKE THAT

• You—yes, *you!*—need a better password. Even if you have one of 6 or fewer characters consisting of numbers, upper- and lowercase letters, *and* symbols, a hacker using sheer, brute-force computer power can figure it out instantly; if it's 9 characters, in 2 days. The good news is that if it's 12 characters, it's safe for 3,000 years.

–S. C., Lloydminster, Alberta

• Can't tell after a power outage whether your freezer has partially or totally thawed while "dark"? Keep a cup of frozen water in it with a quarter on top. If it has sunk all the way to the bottom of your refrozen cup, you've had a total thaw. *–T. S., Barre, Vermont*

• For better sleep, say the experts, put your Christmas tree in your bedroom, as it will bring both the calming effects of nature and the comforting fuzzy-wuzzies of nostalgia to your dreamland vibe. Furthermore, say we, it will serve as a random alarm when the cat knocks it over on you.

–A. K., Columbus, Ohio

Scientific Studies of the Year

DISCO BALL SCALLOPS: Marine scientists in the UK wanted to find an easier way to catch crabs, so they tried outfitting pots with colored lights to attract them. To their surprise, the pots filled with scallops, not crabs. Subsequently, researchers set out 1,886 test traps, half with colored lights and half without, to see if the illuminated pots did indeed attract scallops. Did they ever! Scallops showed up by the hundreds (518) in the lit pots and virtually not at all (2) in the unlit ones, which makes scallops the ultimate marine party animal.

–P. R., Truro, Nova Scotia

BIRD FEEDER PECKING ORDER: Somehow analyzing almost 100,000 reports from citizen scientists, ornithologists created a power ranking of the Top 100 seedy characters at parks and home feeders. Ranked as the #1 most aggressive gobbler was the wild turkey. Among more common backyard diners, the "top dog" bird was #5, the American crow, which was roughly followed by a bunch of woodpeckers and then jays (aka a "descent" of the former and "party" of the latter). The weakest, meekest, and most bullied wannabe diners bringing up the tail end of the list were sparrows, finches, hummingbirds, and, at #100, the brown creeper. (Just for the record, the Almanac's #1-ranked bird feeder boss is the squirrel.) *–A. B., Palo Alto, California*

NESSIE AND CLIMATE CHANGE: Experts are now saying that climate change and rising temperatures may create changes in the diet–whatever it might be–of Scotland's Loch Ness Monster that could cause it to leave the lake in search of food. You have been warned.

–L. D., Shoreham, New York

LUCKIEST AND UNLUCKIEST STATES: After looking at data about Powerball winners, emergency room admissions, federally declared disasters, and fatal traffic accidents, researchers determined that the five luckiest states are, in order, Minnesota, Rhode Island, Wisconsin, Maryland, and Delaware. The unluckiest state was found to be Arkansas, with Oklahoma, Louisiana, Texas, and Florida not far behind–or ahead, as the case may be.

–D. A., Eden Prairie, Minnesota

MOST POPULAR PIE IN AMERICA: Apple, right? Nuts to you! Pecan pie takes the cake (best liked in 15 states), with apple pie right behind (14). Key lime was next (4), with coconut cream and pumpkin (3 each) also on the menu.

–G. P., Fayetteville, Arkansas

Send your contribution for *The 2025 Old Farmer's Almanac* by January 31, 2024, to "A & P," The Old Farmer's Almanac, P.O. Box 520, Dublin, NH 03444, or via Almanac.com/Contact.

256

A Reference Compendium

REFERENCE

CALENDAR

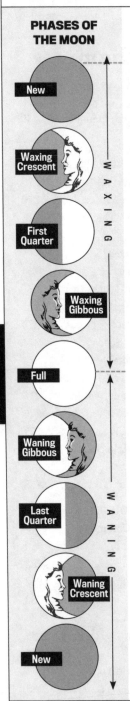

PHASES OF THE MOON

New

Waxing Crescent

First Quarter

Waxing Gibbous

Full

Waning Gibbous

Last Quarter

Waning Crescent

New

WAXING

WANING

REFERENCE

WHEN WILL THE MOON RISE?

Use the following saying to remember the time of moonrise on a day when a Moon phase occurs. Keep in mind that the phase it-self may happen earlier or later that day, depending on location.

The new Moon always rises near sunrise;

The first quarter, near noon;

The full Moon always rises near sunset;

The last quarter, near midnight.

Moonrise occurs about 50 minutes later each day.

FULL MOON NAMES

NAME	MONTH	VARIATIONS
Full Wolf Moon	JANUARY	Full Greetings Moon
Full Snow Moon	FEBRUARY	Full Hungry Moon
Full Worm Moon	MARCH	Full Eagle Moon Full Sore Eye Moon Full Sugar Moon Full Wind Strong Moon
Full Pink Moon	APRIL	Full Budding Moon Moon When the Geese Lay Eggs
Full Flower Moon	MAY	Full Frog Moon Full Planting Moon
Full Strawberry Moon	JUNE	Full Hoer Moon Full Hot Moon
Full Buck Moon	JULY	Full Raspberry Moon Full Salmon Moon
Full Sturgeon Moon	AUGUST	Full Black Cherries Moon Full Flying Up Moon
Full Harvest Moon*	SEPTEMBER	Full Corn Moon Full Yellow Leaf Moon
Full Hunter's Moon	OCTOBER	Full Falling Leaves Moon Full Migrating Moon
Full Beaver Moon	NOVEMBER	Full Frost Moon
Full Cold Moon	DECEMBER	Full Long Night Moon

*The Harvest Moon is always the full Moon closest to the autumnal equinox. If the Harvest Moon occurs in October, the September full Moon is usually called the Corn Moon.

THE ORIGIN OF FULL MOON NAMES

Historically, some Native Americans who lived in the area that is now the United States kept track of the seasons by giving a distinctive name to each recurring full Moon. (This name was applied to the entire lunar month in which it occurred.) The names were used by various tribes and/or by colonial Americans, who also brought their own traditions.

Meanings of Full Moon Names

JANUARY'S full Moon was called the **Wolf Moon** because wolves were more often heard at this time.

FEBRUARY'S full Moon was called the **Snow Moon** because it was a time of heavy snow. It was also called the **Hungry Moon** because hunting was difficult and hunger often resulted.

MARCH'S full Moon was called the **Worm Moon** because, as the weather warmed, wormlike insect larvae emerged from winter homes such as the bark of trees.

APRIL'S full Moon was called the **Pink Moon** because it heralded the appearance of the moss pink, or wild ground phlox—one of the first spring flowers.

MAY'S full Moon was called the **Flower Moon** because blossoms were abundant everywhere at this time.

JUNE'S full Moon was called the **Strawberry Moon** because it appeared when the strawberry harvest took place.

JULY'S full Moon was called the **Buck Moon;** it arrived when a male deer's antlers were in full growth mode.

AUGUST'S full Moon was called the **Sturgeon Moon** because this large fish, which is found in the Great Lakes and Lake Champlain, was caught easily at this time.

SEPTEMBER'S full Moon was called the **Corn Moon** because this was the time to harvest corn.

The **Harvest Moon** is the full Moon that occurs closest to the autumnal equinox. It can occur in either September or October. Around this time, the Moon rises only about 30 minutes later each night, providing extra light after sunset for harvesting.

OCTOBER'S full Moon was called the **Hunter's Moon** because this was the time to hunt in preparation for winter.

NOVEMBER'S full Moon was called the **Beaver Moon** because it was the time when beavers finished preparations for winter and retreated to their lodges.

DECEMBER'S full Moon was called the **Cold Moon.** It was also called the **Long Night Moon** because nights at this time of year were the longest.

REFERENCE

THE ORIGIN OF MONTH NAMES

JANUARY. For the Roman god Janus, protector of gates and doorways. Janus is depicted with two faces, one looking into the past, the other into the future.

FEBRUARY. From the Latin *februa*, "to cleanse." The Roman Februalia was a festival of purification and atonement that took place during this time of year.

MARCH. For the Roman god of war, Mars. This was the time of year to resume military campaigns that had been interrupted by winter.

APRIL. From the Latin *aperio*, "to open (bud)," because plants begin to grow now.

MAY. For the Roman goddess Maia, who oversaw the growth of plants. Also from the Latin *maiores*, "elders," who were celebrated now.

JUNE. For the Roman goddess Juno, patroness of marriage and the well-being of women. Also from the Latin *juvenis*, "young people."

JULY. To honor Roman dictator Julius Caesar (100 B.C.–44 B.C.). In 46 B.C., with the help of Sosigenes, he developed the Julian calendar.

AUGUST. To honor the first Roman emperor (and grandnephew of Julius Caesar), Augustus Caesar (63 B.C.–A.D. 14).

SEPTEMBER. From the Latin *septem*, "seven," because this was the seventh month of the early Roman calendar.

OCTOBER. From the Latin *octo*, "eight," because this was the eighth month of the early Roman calendar.

NOVEMBER. From the Latin *novem*, "nine," because this was the ninth month of the early Roman calendar.

DECEMBER. From the Latin *decem*, "ten," because this was the tenth month of the early Roman calendar.

Easter Dates (2024–27)

Christian churches that follow the Gregorian calendar celebrate Easter on the first Sunday after the paschal full Moon on or just after the vernal equinox.

YEAR	EASTER
2024	March 31
2025	April 20
2026	April 5
2027	March 28

The Julian calendar is used by some churches, including many Eastern Orthodox. The dates below are Julian calendar dates for Easter converted to Gregorian dates.

YEAR	EASTER
2024	May 5
2025	April 20
2026	April 12
2027	May 2

FRIGGATRISKAIDEKAPHOBIA TRIVIA

Here are a few facts about Friday the 13th:

In the 14 possible configurations for the annual calendar (see any perpetual calendar), the occurrence of Friday the 13th is this:

6 of 14 years have one Friday the 13th.
6 of 14 years have two Fridays the 13th.
2 of 14 years have three Fridays the 13th.

No year is without one Friday the 13th, and no year has more than three.

Months that have a Friday the 13th begin on a Sunday.

2024 has a Friday the 13th in September and December.

THE ORIGIN OF DAY NAMES

The days of the week were named by ancient Romans with the Latin words for the Sun, the Moon, and the five known planets. These names have survived in European languages, but English names also reflect Anglo-Saxon and Norse influences.

ENGLISH	LATIN	FRENCH	ITALIAN	SPANISH	ANGLO-SAXON AND NORSE
SUNDAY	dies Solis (Sol's day)	dimanche	domenica	domingo	Sunnandaeg (Sun's day)
		from the Latin for "Lord's day"			
MONDAY	dies Lunae (Luna's day)	lundi	lunedì	lunes	Monandaeg (Moon's day)
TUESDAY	dies Martis (Mars's day)	mardi	martedì	martes	Tiwesdaeg (Tiw's day)
WEDNESDAY	dies Mercurii (Mercury's day)	mercredi	mercoledì	miércoles	Wodnesdaeg (Woden's day)
THURSDAY	dies Jovis (Jupiter's day)	jeudi	giovedì	jueves	Thursdaeg (Thor's day)
FRIDAY	dies Veneris (Venus's day)	vendredi	venerdì	viernes	Frigedaeg (Frigga's day)
SATURDAY	dies Saturni (Saturn's day)	samedi	sabato	sábado	Saeterndaeg (Saturn's day)
		from the Latin for "Sabbath"			

How to Find the Day of the Week for Any Given Date

To compute the day of the week for any given date as far back as the mid–18th century, proceed as follows:

Add the last two digits of the year to one-quarter of the last two digits (discard any remainder), the day of the month, and the month key from the key box below. Divide the sum by 7; the remainder is the day of the week (1 is Sunday, 2 is Monday, and so on). If there is no remainder, the day is Saturday. If you're searching for a weekday prior to 1900, add 2 to the sum before dividing; prior to 1800, add 4. The formula doesn't work for days prior to 1753. From 2000 through 2099, subtract 1 from the sum before dividing.

Example:

THE DAYTON FLOOD WAS ON MARCH 25, 1913.

Last two digits of year: 13
One-quarter of these two digits: 3
Given day of month: 25
Key number for March: 4
　　　　　　　　　　　　　Sum: 45

45 ÷ 7 = 6, with a remainder of 3. The flood took place on Tuesday, the third day of the week.

KEY	
JANUARY	1
LEAP YEAR	0
FEBRUARY	4
LEAP YEAR	3
MARCH	4
APRIL	0
MAY	2
JUNE	5
JULY	0
AUGUST	3
SEPTEMBER	6
OCTOBER	1
NOVEMBER	4
DECEMBER	6

GLOSSARY OF TIME

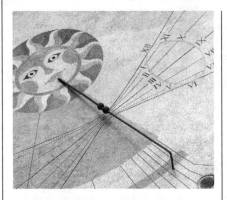

ATOMIC TIME (TA) SCALE: A time scale based on atomic or molecular resonance phenomena. Elapsed time is measured by counting cycles of a frequency locked to an atomic or molecular transition.

DATE: A unique instant defined in a specified time scale. NOTE: The date can be conventionally expressed in years, months, days, hours, minutes and seconds, and fractions thereof.

GREENWICH MEAN TIME (GMT): A 24-hour system based on mean solar time plus 12 hours at Greenwich, England. Greenwich Mean Time can be considered approximately equivalent to Coordinated Universal Time (UTC), which is broadcast from all standard time-and-frequency radio stations. However, GMT is now obsolete and has been replaced by UTC.

INTERNATIONAL ATOMIC TIME (TAI): An atomic time scale based on data from a worldwide set of atomic clocks. It is the internationally agreed-upon time reference conforming to the definition of the second, the fundamental unit of atomic time in the International System of Units (SI).

LEAP SECOND: A second used to adjust UTC to be within 0.9 sec of UT1 (a time scale based on Earth's varying rotation rate). An inserted "positive" second or omitted "negative" second may be applied at the end of June or December of each year.

MEAN SOLAR TIME: Apparent solar time corrected for the effects of orbital eccentricity and the tilt of Earth's axis relative to the ecliptic plane; in other words, corrected by the equation of time, which is defined as the hour angle of the true Sun minus the hour angle of the mean Sun.

SECOND: The basic unit of time or time interval in the International System of Units (SI), which is equal to 9,192,631,770 periods of radiation corresponding to the transition between the two hyperfine levels of the ground state of cesium-133 as defined at the 1967 Conférence Générale des Poids et Mesures.

SIDEREAL TIME: The measure of time defined by the apparent diurnal motion of the vernal equinox; hence, a measure of the rotation of Earth with respect to the reference frame that is related to the stars rather than the Sun. A mean solar day is about 4 minutes longer than a sidereal day.

–(U.S.) National Institute of Standards and Technology (NIST)

A Table Foretelling the Weather Through All the Lunations of Each Year, or Forever

This table is the result of many years of actual observation and shows what sort of weather will probably follow the Moon's entrance into any of its quarters. For example, the table shows that the week following January 3, 2024, will be fair and frosty, because the Moon enters the last quarter on that day at 10:30 P.M. EST. (See the **Left-Hand Calendar Pages, 120-146,** for Moon phases.)

EDITOR'S NOTE: Although the data in this table is taken into consideration in the year-long process of compiling the annual long-range weather forecasts for *The Old Farmer's Almanac*, we rely far more on our projections of solar activity.

TIME OF CHANGE	SUMMER	WINTER
Midnight to 2 A.M.	Fair	Hard frost, unless wind is south or west
2 A.M. to 4 A.M.	Cold, with frequent showers	Snow and stormy
4 A.M. to 6 A.M.	Rain	Rain
6 A.M. to 8 A.M.	Wind and rain	Stormy
8 A.M. to 10 A.M.	Changeable	Cold rain if wind is west; snow, if east
10 A.M. to noon	Frequent showers	Cold with high winds
Noon to 2 P.M.	Very rainy	Snow or rain
2 P.M. to 4 P.M.	Changeable	Fair and mild
4 P.M. to 6 P.M.	Fair	Fair
6 P.M. to 10 P.M.	Fair if wind is northwest; rain if wind is south or southwest	Fair and frosty if wind is north or northeast; rain or snow if wind is south or southwest
10 P.M. to midnight	Fair	Fair and frosty

This table was created more than 180 years ago by Dr. Herschell for the Boston Courier; *it first appeared in* The Old Farmer's Almanac *in 1834.*

SAFE ICE THICKNESS*

ICE THICKNESS	PERMISSIBLE LOAD	ICE THICKNESS	PERMISSIBLE LOAD
4 inches	Single person on foot	8-10 inches	Passenger car, small SUV
5 inches	Small group skating	10-12 inches	Light truck, compact SUV
5-7 inches	Snowmobile, small ATV	12-15 inches	Medium truck, mid-size SUV
7-8 inches	Multi-rider ATV, UTV	16 inches	Heavy truck, full-size SUV

Ice is never 100 percent safe. It forms on lakes and ponds unevenly, so while it may be 4 inches thick in one area, it could be much thinner a few feet away. Avoid ice that is cracked or near inlets or moving water.

*Solid, clear, blue/black pond and lake ice

The strength value of river ice is 15 percent less. Slush ice has only half the strength of blue ice.

REFERENCE

WEATHER

HEAT INDEX °F (°C)

TEMP. °F (°C)	RELATIVE HUMIDITY (%)								
	40	45	50	55	60	65	70	75	80
100 (38)	109 (43)	114 (46)	118 (48)	124 (51)	129 (54)	136 (58)			
98 (37)	105 (41)	109 (43)	113 (45)	117 (47)	123 (51)	128 (53)	134 (57)		
96 (36)	101 (38)	104 (40)	108 (42)	112 (44)	116 (47)	121 (49)	126 (52)	132 (56)	
94 (34)	97 (36)	100 (38)	103 (39)	106 (41)	110 (43)	114 (46)	119 (48)	124 (51)	129 (54)
92 (33)	94 (34)	96 (36)	99 (37)	101 (38)	105 (41)	108 (42)	112 (44)	116 (47)	121 (49)
90 (32)	91 (33)	93 (34)	95 (35)	97 (36)	100 (38)	103 (39)	105 (41)	109 (43)	113 (45)
88 (31)	88 (31)	89 (32)	91 (33)	93 (34)	95 (35)	98 (37)	100 (38)	103 (39)	106 (41)
86 (30)	85 (29)	87 (31)	88 (31)	89 (32)	91 (33)	93 (34)	95 (35)	97 (36)	100 (38)
84 (29)	83 (28)	84 (29)	85 (29)	86 (30)	88 (31)	89 (32)	90 (32)	92 (33)	94 (34)
82 (28)	81 (27)	82 (28)	83 (28)	84 (29)	84 (29)	85 (29)	86 (30)	88 (31)	89 (32)
80 (27)	80 (27)	80 (27)	81 (27)	81 (27)	82 (28)	82 (28)	83 (28)	84 (29)	84 (29)

RISK LEVEL FOR HEAT DISORDERS: CAUTION — EXTREME CAUTION — DANGER

EXAMPLE: *When the temperature is 88°F (31°C) and the relative humidity is 60 percent, the heat index, or how hot it feels, is 95°F (35°C).*

THE UV INDEX FOR MEASURING ULTRAVIOLET RADIATION RISK

The U.S. National Weather Service's daily forecasts of ultraviolet levels use these numbers for various exposure levels:

UV INDEX NUMBER	EXPOSURE LEVEL	ACTIONS TO TAKE
0, 1, 2	Low	Wear UV-blocking sunglasses on bright days. In winter, reflection off snow can nearly double UV strength. If you burn easily, cover up and apply SPF 30+ sunscreen.
3, 4, 5	Moderate	Apply SPF 30+ sunscreen; wear a hat and sunglasses. Stay in shade when sun is strongest.
6, 7	High	Apply SPF 30+ sunscreen; wear a hat, sunglasses, and protective clothing; limit midday exposure.
8, 9, 10	Very High	Apply SPF 30+ sunscreen; wear a hat, sunglasses, and protective clothing; limit midday exposure. Seek shade. Unprotected skin will be damaged and can burn quickly.
11 or higher	Extreme	Apply SPF 30+ sunscreen; wear a hat, sunglasses, and protective clothing; avoid midday exposure; seek shade. Unprotected skin can burn in minutes.

REFERENCE

85	90	95	100
135 (57)			
126 (52)	131 (55)		
117 (47)	122 (50)	127 (53)	132 (56)
110 (43)	113 (45)	117 (47)	121 (49)
102 (39)	105 (41)	108 (42)	112 (44)
96 (36)	98 (37)	100 (38)	103 (39)
90 (32)	91 (33)	93 (34)	95 (35)
85 (29)	86 (30)	86 (30)	87 (31)

What Are Cooling/Heating Degree Days?

In an attempt to measure the need for air-conditioning, each degree of a day's mean temperature that is above a base temperature, such as 65°F (U.S.) or 18°C (Canada), is considered one cooling degree day. If the daily mean temperature is 75°F, for example, that's 10 cooling degree days.

Similarly, to measure the need for heating fuel consumption, each degree of a day's mean temperature that is below 65°F (18°C) is considered one heating degree. For example, a day with a high of 60°F and low of 40°F results in a mean of 50°, or 15 degrees less than 65°. Hence, that day had 15 heating degree days.

HOW TO MEASURE HAIL

The **TORRO HAILSTORM INTENSITY SCALE** was introduced by Jonathan Webb of Oxford, England, in 1986 as a means of categorizing hailstorms. The name derives from the private and mostly British research body named the TORnado and storm Research Organisation.

INTENSITY/DESCRIPTION OF HAIL DAMAGE

H0 True hail of pea size causes no damage

H1 Leaves and flower petals are punctured and torn

H2 Leaves are stripped from trees and plants

H3 Panes of glass are broken; auto bodies are dented

H4 Some house windows are broken; small tree branches are broken off; birds are killed

H5 Many windows are smashed; small animals are injured; large tree branches are broken off

H6 Shingle roofs are breached; metal roofs are scored; wooden window frames are broken away

H7 Roofs are shattered to expose rafters; autos are seriously damaged

H8 Shingle and tile roofs are destroyed; small tree trunks are split; people are seriously injured

H9 Concrete roofs are broken; large tree trunks are split and knocked down; people are at risk of fatal injuries

H10 Brick houses are damaged; people are at risk of fatal injuries

HOW TO MEASURE WIND SPEED

The **BEAUFORT WIND FORCE SCALE** is a common way of estimating wind speed. It was developed in 1805 by Admiral Sir Francis Beaufort of the British Navy to measure wind at sea. We can also use it to measure wind on land.

Admiral Beaufort arranged the numbers 0 to 12 to indicate the strength of the wind from calm, force 0, to hurricane, force 12. Here's a scale adapted to land.

"Used Mostly at Sea but of Help to All Who Are Interested in the Weather"

BEAUFORT FORCE	DESCRIPTION	WHEN YOU SEE OR FEEL THIS EFFECT	WIND SPEED (mph)	WIND SPEED (km/h)
0	CALM	Smoke goes straight up	less than 1	less than 2
1	LIGHT AIR	Wind direction is shown by smoke drift but not by wind vane	1–3	2–5
2	LIGHT BREEZE	Wind is felt on the face; leaves rustle; wind vanes move	4–7	6–11
3	GENTLE BREEZE	Leaves and small twigs move steadily; wind extends small flags straight out	8–12	12–19
4	MODERATE BREEZE	Wind raises dust and loose paper; small branches move	13–18	20–29
5	FRESH BREEZE	Small trees sway; waves form on lakes	19–24	30–39
6	STRONG BREEZE	Large branches move; wires whistle; umbrellas are difficult to use	25–31	40–50
7	NEAR GALE	Whole trees are in motion; walking against the wind is difficult	32–38	51–61
8	GALE	Twigs break from trees; walking against the wind is very difficult	39–46	62–74
9	STRONG GALE	Buildings suffer minimal damage; roof shingles are removed	47–54	75–87
10	STORM	Trees are uprooted	55–63	88–101
11	VIOLENT STORM	Widespread damage	64–72	102–116
12	HURRICANE	Widespread destruction	73+	117+

RETIRED ATLANTIC HURRICANE NAMES

These storms have been some of the most destructive and costly.

NAME	YEAR	NAME	YEAR	NAME	YEAR	NAME	YEAR
Gustav	2008	Ingrid	2013	Irma	2017	Eta	2020
Ike	2008	Erika	2015	Maria	2017	Iota	2020
Igor	2010	Joaquin	2015	Nate	2017	Laura	2020
Tomas	2010	Matthew	2016	Florence	2018	Ida	2021
Irene	2011	Otto	2016	Michael	2018	Fiona	2022
Sandy	2012	Harvey	2017	Dorian	2019	Ian	2022

ATLANTIC TROPICAL (AND SUBTROPICAL) STORM NAMES FOR 2024		
Alberto	Helene	Oscar
Beryl	Isaac	Patty
Chris	Joyce	Rafael
Debby	Kirk	Sara
Ernesto	Leslie	Tony
Francine	Milton	Valerie
Gordon	Nadine	William

EASTERN NORTH-PACIFIC TROPICAL (AND SUBTROPICAL) STORM NAMES FOR 2024		
Aletta	Ileana	Rosa
Bud	John	Sergio
Carlotta	Kristy	Tara
Daniel	Lane	Vicente
Emilia	Miriam	Willa
Fabio	Norman	Xavier
Gilma	Olivia	Yolanda
Hector	Paul	Zeke

The lists above are used in rotation and recycled every 6 years, e.g., the 2024 list will be used again in 2030.

How to Measure Hurricane Strength

The SAFFIR-SIMPSON HURRICANE WIND SCALE assigns a rating from 1 to 5 based on a hurricane's intensity. It is used to give an estimate of the potential property damage from a hurricane landfall. Wind speed is the determining factor in the scale, as storm surge values are highly dependent on the slope of the continental shelf in the landfall region. Wind speeds are measured at a height of 33 feet (10 meters) using a 1-minute average.

CATEGORY ONE. Average wind: 74–95 mph. Significant damage to mobile homes. Some damage to roofing and siding of well-built frame homes. Large tree branches snap and shallow-rooted trees may topple. Power outages may last a few to several days.

CATEGORY TWO. Average wind: 96–110 mph. Mobile homes may be destroyed. Major roof and siding damage to frame homes. Many shallow-rooted trees snap or topple, blocking roads. Widespread power outages could last from several days to weeks. Potable water may be scarce.

CATEGORY THREE. Average wind: 111–129 mph. Most mobile homes destroyed. Frame homes may sustain major roof damage. Many trees snap or topple, blocking numerous roads. Electricity and water may be unavailable for several days to weeks.

CATEGORY FOUR. Average wind: 130–156 mph. Mobile homes destroyed. Frame homes severely damaged or destroyed. Windborne debris may penetrate protected windows. Most trees snap or topple. Residential areas isolated by fallen trees and power poles. Most of the area uninhabitable for weeks to months.

CATEGORY FIVE. Average wind: 157+ mph. Most homes destroyed. Nearly all windows blown out of high-rises. Most of the area uninhabitable for weeks to months.

REFERENCE

HOW TO MEASURE A TORNADO

The original **FUJITA SCALE** (or F Scale) was developed by Dr. Theodore Fujita to classify tornadoes based on wind damage. All tornadoes, and other severe local windstorms, were assigned a number according to the most intense damage caused by the storm. An enhanced F (EF) scale was implemented in the United States on February 1, 2007. The EF scale uses 3-second gust estimates based on a more detailed system for assessing damage, taking into account different building materials.

F SCALE		EF SCALE (U.S.)
F0 · 40-72 mph (64-116 km/h)	LIGHT DAMAGE	EF0 · 65-85 mph (105-137 km/h)
F1 · 73-112 mph (117-180 km/h)	MODERATE DAMAGE	EF1 · 86-110 mph (138-178 km/h)
F2 · 113-157 mph (181-253 km/h)	CONSIDERABLE DAMAGE	EF2 · 111-135 mph (179-218 km/h)
F3 · 158-207 mph (254-332 km/h)	SEVERE DAMAGE	EF3 · 136-165 mph (219-266 km/h)
F4 · 208-260 mph (333-419 km/h)	DEVASTATING DAMAGE	EF4 · 166-200 mph (267-322 km/h)
F5 · 261-318 mph (420-512 km/h)	INCREDIBLE DAMAGE	EF5 · over 200 mph (over 322 km/h)

Wind/Barometer Table

BAROMETER (REDUCED TO SEA LEVEL)	WIND DIRECTION	CHARACTER OF WEATHER INDICATED
30.00 to 30.20, and steady	WESTERLY	Fair, with slight changes in temperature, for one to two days
30.00 to 30.20, and rising rapidly	WESTERLY	Fair, followed within two days by warmer and rain
30.00 to 30.20, and falling rapidly	SOUTH TO EAST	Warmer, and rain within 24 hours
30.20 or above, and falling rapidly	SOUTH TO EAST	Warmer, and rain within 36 hours
30.20 or above, and falling rapidly	WEST TO NORTH	Cold and clear, quickly followed by warmer and rain
30.20 or above, and steady	VARIABLE	No early change
30.00 or below, and falling slowly	SOUTH TO EAST	Rain within 18 hours that will continue a day or two
30.00 or below, and falling rapidly	SOUTHEAST TO NORTHEAST	Rain, with high wind, followed within two days by clearing, colder
30.00 or below, and rising	SOUTH TO WEST	Clearing and colder within 12 hours
29.80 or below, and falling rapidly	SOUTH TO EAST	Severe storm of wind and rain imminent; in winter, snow or cold wave within 24 hours
29.80 or below, and falling rapidly	EAST TO NORTH	Severe northeast gales and heavy rain or snow, followed in winter by cold wave
29.80 or below, and rising rapidly	GOING TO WEST	Clearing and colder

NOTE: *A barometer should be adjusted to show equivalent sea-level pressure for the altitude at which it is to be used. A change of 100 feet in elevation will cause a decrease of ¹/₁₀ inch in the reading.*

WINDCHILL TABLE

As wind speed increases, your body loses heat more rapidly, making the air feel colder than it really is. The combination of cold temperature and high wind can create a cooling effect so severe that exposed flesh can freeze.

		TEMPERATURE (°F)													
Calm	35	30	25	20	15	10	5	0	-5	-10	-15	-20	-25	-30	-35
5	31	25	19	13	7	1	–5	–11	–16	–22	–28	–34	–40	–46	–52
10	27	21	15	9	3	–4	–10	–16	–22	–28	–35	–41	–47	–53	–59
15	25	19	13	6	0	–7	–13	–19	–26	–32	–39	–45	–51	–58	–64
20	24	17	11	4	–2	–9	–15	–22	–29	–35	–42	–48	–55	–61	–68
25	23	16	9	3	–4	–11	–17	–24	–31	–37	–44	–51	–58	–64	–71
30	22	15	8	1	–5	–12	–19	–26	–33	–39	–46	–53	–60	–67	–73
35	21	14	7	0	–7	–14	–21	–27	–34	–41	–48	–55	–62	–69	–76
40	20	13	6	–1	–8	–15	–22	–29	–36	–43	–50	–57	–64	–71	–78
45	19	12	5	–2	–9	–16	–23	–30	–37	–44	–51	–58	–65	–72	–79
50	19	12	4	–3	–10	–17	–24	–31	–38	–45	–52	–60	–67	–74	–81
55	18	11	4	–3	–11	–18	–25	–32	–39	–46	–54	–61	–68	–75	–82
60	17	10	3	–4	–11	–19	–26	–33	–40	–48	–55	–62	–69	–76	–84

WIND SPEED (mph)

FROSTBITE OCCURS IN ▢ 30 MINUTES ▨ 10 MINUTES ▨ 5 MINUTES

EXAMPLE: *When the temperature is 15°F and the wind speed is 30 miles per hour, the windchill, or how cold it feels, is –5°F. See a Celsius version of this table via Almanac.com/2024.*
–courtesy of National Weather Service

HOW TO MEASURE EARTHQUAKES

In 1979, seismologists developed a measurement of earthquake size called **MOMENT MAGNITUDE**. It is more accurate than the previously used Richter scale, which is precise only for earthquakes of a certain size and at a certain distance from a seismometer. All earthquakes can now be compared on the same magnitude scale.

MAGNITUDE	DESCRIPTION	EFFECT
LESS THAN 3	MICRO	GENERALLY NOT FELT
3–3.9	MINOR	OFTEN FELT, LITTLE DAMAGE
4–4.9	LIGHT	SHAKING, SOME DAMAGE
5–5.9	MODERATE	SLIGHT TO MAJOR DAMAGE
6–6.9	STRONG	DESTRUCTIVE
7–7.9	MAJOR	SERIOUS DAMAGE
8 OR MORE	GREAT	SEVERE DAMAGE

A GARDENER'S WORST PHOBIAS

NAME OF FEAR	OBJECT FEARED
Alliumphobia	Garlic
Anthophobia	Flowers
Apiphobia	Bees
Arachnophobia	Spiders
Botanophobia	Plants
Bufonophobia	Toads
Dendrophobia	Trees
Entomophobia	Insects
Lachanophobia	Vegetables
Mottephobia	Moths
Myrmecophobia	Ants
Ophidiophobia	Snakes
Ornithophobia	Birds
Ranidaphobia	Frogs
Rupophobia	Dirt
Scoleciphobia	Worms
Spheksophobia	Wasps

PLANTS FOR LAWNS

Choose varieties that suit your soil and your climate. All of these can withstand mowing and considerable foot traffic.

Ajuga or bugleweed (*Ajuga reptans*)
Corsican mint (*Mentha requienii*)
Dwarf cinquefoil (*Potentilla tabernaemontani*)
English pennyroyal (*Mentha pulegium*)
Green Irish moss (*Sagina subulata*)
Pearly everlasting (*Anaphalis margaritacea*)
Roman chamomile (*Chamaemelum nobile*)
Rupturewort (*Herniaria glabra*)
Speedwell (*Veronica officinalis*)
Stonecrop (*Sedum ternatum*)
Sweet violets (*Viola odorata* or *V. tricolor*)
Thyme (*Thymus serpyllum*)
White clover (*Trifolium repens*)
Wild strawberries (*Fragaria virginiana*)
Wintergreen or partridgeberry (*Mitchella repens*)

Lawn-Growing Tips

• Test your soil: The pH balance should be 6.2 to 6.7; less than 6.0 puts your lawn at risk for fungal diseases. If the pH is too low, correct it with liming, best done in the fall.

• The best time to apply fertilizer is just before a light rain.

• If you put lime and fertilizer on your lawn, spread half of it as you walk north to south, the other half as you walk east to west to cut down on missed areas.

• Any feeding of lawns in the fall should be done with a low-nitrogen, slow-acting fertilizer.

• In areas of your lawn where tree roots compete with the grass, apply some extra fertilizer to benefit both.

• Moss and sorrel in lawns usually means poor soil, poor aeration or drainage, or excessive acidity.

• Control weeds by promoting healthy lawn growth with natural fertilizers in spring and early fall.

• Raise the level of your lawn-mower blades during the hot summer days. Taller grass resists drought better than short.

• You can reduce mowing time by redesigning your lawn, reducing sharp corners and adding sweeping curves.

• During a drought, let the grass grow longer between mowings and reduce fertilizer.

• Water your lawn early in the morning or in the evening.

Flowers and Herbs That Attract Butterflies

Allium........................ *Allium*
Aster.......... *Aster, Symphyotrichum*
Bee balm .... *Monarda*
Butterfly bush.............. *Buddleia*
Catmint .... *Nepeta*
Clove pink .... *Dianthus*
Coreopsis.................. *Coreopsis*
Cornflower .... *Centaurea*
Creeping thyme ..... *Thymus serpyllum*
Daylily.................. *Hemerocallis*
Dill .... *Anethum graveolens*
False indigo................ *Baptisia*
Fleabane.................... *Erigeron*
Floss flower................ *Ageratum*
Globe thistle .... *Echinops*
Goldenrod .... *Solidago*
Helen's flower .... *Helenium*
Hollyhock.................... *Alcea*
Honeysuckle .... *Lonicera*
Lavender .... *Lavandula*
Lilac .... *Syringa*
Lupine...................... *Lupinus*

Lychnis..................... *Lychnis*
Mallow .... *Malva*
Mealycup sage .... *Salvia farinacea*
Milkweed.................. *Asclepias*
Mint........................ *Mentha*
Oregano .... *Origanum vulgare*
Pansy .... *Viola*
Parsley .... *Petroselinum crispum*
Phlox........................ *Phlox*
Privet .... *Ligustrum*
Purple coneflower . *Echinacea purpurea*
Rock cress................... *Arabis*
Sea holly................... *Eryngium*
Shasta daisy .... *Leucanthemum*
Snapdragon............. *Antirrhinum*
Stonecrop ...... *Hylotelephium, Sedum*
Sweet alyssum ....*Lobularia*
Sweet marjoram .. *Origanum majorana*
Sweet rocket............... *Hesperis*
Verbena .... *Verbena*
Zinnia...................... *Zinnia*

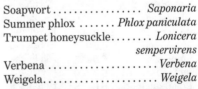

FLOWERS* THAT ATTRACT HUMMINGBIRDS

Beard tongue .... *Penstemon*
Bee balm .... *Monarda*
Butterfly bush.............. *Buddleia*
Catmint .... *Nepeta*
Clove pink .... *Dianthus*
Columbine .... *Aquilegia*
Coral bells .... *Heuchera*
Daylily................. *Hemerocallis*
Desert candle .... *Yucca*
Flag iris .... *Iris*
Flowering tobacco ..... *Nicotiana alata*
Foxglove.................... *Digitalis*
Larkspur .... *Delphinium*
Lily .... *Lilium*
Lupine..................... *Lupinus*
Petunia..................... *Petunia*
Pincushion flower .... *Scabiosa*
Red-hot poker............. *Kniphofia*
Scarlet sage.......... *Salvia splendens*

Soapwort .... *Saponaria*
Summer phlox .... *Phlox paniculata*
Trumpet honeysuckle........ *Lonicera sempervirens*
Verbena .... *Verbena*
Weigela..................... *Weigela*

*NOTE: *Choose varieties in red and orange shades, if available.*

pH PREFERENCES OF TREES, SHRUBS, FLOWERS, AND VEGETABLES

An accurate soil test will indicate your soil pH and will specify the amount of lime or sulfur that is needed to bring it up or down to the appropriate level. A pH of 6.5 is just about right for most home gardens, since most plants thrive in the 6.0 to 7.0 (slightly acidic to neutral) range. Some plants (azaleas, blueberries) prefer more strongly acidic soil in the 4.0 to 6.0 range, while a few (asparagus, plums) do best in soil that is neutral to slightly alkaline. Acidic, or sour, soil (below 7.0) is counteracted by applying finely ground limestone, and alkaline, or sweet, soil (above 7.0) is treated with ground sulfur.

COMMON NAME	OPTIMUM pH RANGE	COMMON NAME	OPTIMUM pH RANGE	COMMON NAME	OPTIMUM pH RANGE
TREES AND SHRUBS		Bee balm	6.0–7.5	Snapdragon	5.5–7.0
Apple	5.0–6.5	Begonia	5.5–7.0	Sunflower	6.0–7.5
Azalea	4.5–6.0	Black-eyed Susan	5.5–7.0	Tulip	6.0–7.0
Beautybush	6.0–7.5	Bleeding heart	6.0–7.5	Zinnia	5.5–7.0
Birch	5.0–6.5	Canna	6.0–8.0		
Blackberry	5.0–6.0	Carnation	6.0–7.0	**VEGETABLES**	
Blueberry	4.0–5.0	Chrysanthemum	6.0–7.5	Asparagus	6.0–8.0
Boxwood	6.0–7.5	Clematis	5.5–7.0	Bean	6.0–7.5
Cherry, sour	6.0–7.0	Coleus	6.0–7.0	Beet	6.0–7.5
Crab apple	6.0–7.5	Coneflower, purple	5.0–7.5	Broccoli	6.0–7.0
Dogwood	5.0–7.0	Cosmos	5.0–8.0	Brussels sprout	6.0–7.5
Fir, balsam	5.0–6.0	Crocus	6.0–8.0	Cabbage	6.0–7.5
Hemlock	5.0–6.0	Daffodil	6.0–6.5	Carrot	5.5–7.0
Hydrangea, blue-flowered	4.5–5.5	Dahlia	6.0–7.5	Cauliflower	5.5–7.5
Hydrangea, pink-flowered	6.0–7.0	Daisy, Shasta	6.0–8.0	Celery	5.8–7.0
		Daylily	6.0–8.0	Chive	6.0–7.0
Juniper	5.0–6.0	Delphinium	6.0–7.5	Collard	6.5–7.5
Laurel, mountain	4.5–6.0	Foxglove	6.0–7.5	Corn	5.5–7.0
Lemon	6.0–7.5	Geranium	5.5–6.5	Cucumber	5.5–7.0
Lilac	6.0–7.0	Gladiolus	5.0–7.0	Eggplant	6.0–7.0
Maple, sugar	6.0–7.5	Hibiscus	6.0–8.0	Garlic	5.5–8.0
Oak, white	5.0–6.5	Hollyhock	6.0–8.0	Kale	6.0–7.5
Orange	6.0–7.5	Hyacinth	6.5–7.5	Leek	6.0–8.0
Peach	6.0–7.0	Iris, blue flag	5.0–7.5	Lettuce	6.0–7.0
Pear	6.0–7.5	Lily-of-the-valley	4.5–6.0	Okra	6.0–7.0
Pecan	6.4–8.0	Lupine	5.0–6.5	Onion	6.0–7.0
Plum	6.0–8.0	Marigold	5.5–7.5	Pea	6.0–7.5
Raspberry, red	5.5–7.0	Morning glory	6.0–7.5	Pepper, sweet	5.5–7.0
Rhododendron	4.5–6.0	Narcissus, trumpet	5.5–6.5	Potato	4.8–6.5
Willow	6.0–8.0	Nasturtium	5.5–7.5	Pumpkin	5.5–7.5
		Pansy	5.5–6.5	Radish	6.0–7.0
FLOWERS		Peony	6.0–7.5	Spinach	6.0–7.5
Alyssum	6.0–7.5	Petunia	6.0–7.5	Squash, crookneck	6.0–7.5
Aster, New England	6.0–8.0	Phlox, summer	6.0–8.0	Squash, Hubbard	5.5–7.0
Baby's breath	6.0–7.0	Poppy, oriental	6.0–7.5	Swiss chard	6.0–7.0
Bachelor's button	6.0–7.5	Rose, hybrid tea	5.5–7.0	Tomato	5.5–7.5
		Rose, rugosa	6.0–7.0	Watermelon	5.5–6.5

REFERENCE

How to Rotate Crops

Crop rotation is the practice of planting annual vegetables with their botanical families. Each vegetable family rotates together; it is not necessary to grow every family or every plant in each family. The benefits of rotating crops include fewer pests and soil-borne diseases, improved soil nutrition, and better soil structure. Failure to rotate vegetable crops eventually results in plants that fail to thrive and decreased harvest.

Here's how crop rotation works: In a single-crop plot, legumes (pea family) are planted in year 1, nightshade plants (tomatoes, etc.) in year 2, and gourds in year 3. In year 4, the cycle begins again. Alternatively, these three crops could be planted in three separate plots in year 1 and moved to the next plot in ensuing years. Additional families can be added. A simple plot plan keeps track of what goes where.

PLANT FAMILIES AND MEMBERS

Plants in the same family are genetically related and thus share similar characteristics (e.g., leaf appearance, tendrils for climbing).

CARROT, aka PARSLEY (Apiaceae, aka Umbelliferae): caraway, carrot*, celeriac, celery, chervil, coriander, dill, fennel, lovage, parsley, parsnip

GOOSEFOOT, aka CHARD (Chenopodiaceae): beet*, orache, quinoa, spinach, Swiss chard

GOURD, aka SQUASH (Cucurbitaceae): cucumber, gourd, melon, pumpkin, squash (summer and winter), watermelon

GRASS (Poaceae, aka Gramineae): sweet corn

MALLOW (Malvaceae): okra

MINT (Lamiaceae, aka Labiatae): basil, Chinese artichoke, oregano, rosemary, sage, summer savory, sweet marjoram

MORNING GLORY (Convolvulaceae): sweet potato

MUSTARD (Brassicaceae, aka Cruciferae): arugula, bok choy, broccoli, brussels sprouts, cabbage, cauliflower, collard, kale, kohlrabi, komatsuna, mizuna, mustard greens, radish*, rutabaga, turnip

NIGHTSHADE (Solanaceae): eggplant, pepper, potato, tomatillo, tomato

ONION (Amaryllidaceae*): chives, garlic, leek, onion, shallot

PEA (Fabaceae, aka Leguminosae): bush, kidney, lima, pole, and soy beans; lentil; pea; peanut

SUNFLOWER (Asteraceae, aka Compositae): artichoke (globe and Jerusalem), calendula, chamomile, endive, escarole, lettuce, radicchio, salsify, sunflower, tarragon

These can be planted among any family.

REFERENCE

SOWING VEGETABLE SEEDS

SOW OR PLANT IN COOL WEATHER	Beets, broccoli, brussels sprouts, cabbage, lettuce, onions, parsley, peas, radishes, spinach, Swiss chard, turnips
SOW OR PLANT IN WARM WEATHER	Beans, carrots, corn, cucumbers, eggplant, melons, okra, peppers, squashes, tomatoes
SOW OR PLANT FOR ONE CROP PER SEASON	Corn, eggplant, leeks, melons, peppers, potatoes, spinach (New Zealand), squashes, tomatoes
RESOW FOR ADDITIONAL CROPS	Beans, beets, cabbage, carrots, kohlrabi, lettuce, radishes, rutabagas, spinach, turnips

A Beginner's Vegetable Garden

The vegetables suggested below are common, easy-to-grow crops. Make 11 rows, 10 feet long, with at least 18 inches between them. Ideally, the rows should run north and south to take full advantage of the sun. This garden, planted as suggested, can feed a family of four for one summer, with a little extra for canning and freezing or giving away.

ROW
1. Zucchini (4 plants)
2. Tomatoes (5 plants, staked)
3. Peppers (6 plants)
4. Cabbage

ROW
5. Bush beans
6. Lettuce
7. Beets
8. Carrots
9. Swiss chard
10. Radishes
11. Marigolds (to discourage rabbits!)

SOIL FIXES

If you have **sandy** soil, amend with compost; humus; aged manure; sawdust with extra nitrogen; heavy, clay-rich soil.

If your soil contains a lot of **silt**, amend with coarse sand (not beach sand) or gravel and compost, or aged horse manure mixed with fresh straw.

If your soil is dense with **clay**, amend with coarse sand (not beach sand) and compost.

TO IMPROVE YOUR SOIL, ADD THE PROPER AMENDMENT(S) . . .

bark, ground: made from various tree barks; improves soil structure

compost: an excellent conditioner

leaf mold: decomposed leaves, which add nutrients and structure to soil

lime: raises the pH of acidic soil and helps to loosen clay soil.

manure: best if composted; never add fresh ("hot") manure; is a good conditioner

coarse sand (not beach sand): improves drainage in clay soil

topsoil: usually used with another amendment; replaces existing soil

IN THE GARDEN

IMPORTANT TIMES TO . . .

	. . . FERTILIZE:	. . . WATER:
BEANS	After heavy bloom and set of pods	When flowers form and during pod-forming and picking
BEETS	At time of planting	Before soil gets bone-dry
BROCCOLI	3 weeks after transplanting	Continuously for 4 weeks after transplanting
BRUSSELS SPROUTS	3 weeks after transplanting	Continuously for 4 weeks after transplanting
CABBAGE	2 weeks after transplanting	Frequently in dry weather
CARROTS	5 to 6 weeks after sowing	Before soil gets bone-dry
CAULIFLOWER	3 to 4 weeks after transplanting	Frequently
CELERY	At time of transplanting, and after 2 months	Frequently
CORN	When 8 to 10 inches tall, and when first silk appears	When tassels form and when cobs swell
CUCUMBERS	1 week after bloom, and every 3 weeks thereafter	Frequently
LETTUCE	3 weeks after transplanting	Frequently
MELONS	1 week after bloom, and again 3 weeks later	Once a week
ONION SETS	At time of planting, and then every 2 weeks until bulbing begins	In early stage to get plants going
PARSNIPS	1 year before planting	Before soil gets bone-dry
PEAS	After heavy bloom and set of pods	When flowers form and during pod-forming and picking
PEPPERS	At time of planting, and after first fruit-set	Need a steady supply
POTATO TUBERS	At bloom time or time of second hilling	When the size of marbles
PUMPKINS	Just before vines start to run, when plants are about 1 foot tall	1 inch of water per week; water deeply, especially during fruit set
RADISHES	Before spring planting	Need plentiful, consistent moisture
SPINACH	When plants are one-third grown	Frequently
SQUASHES, SUMMER & WINTER	When first blooms appear	Frequently
TOMATOES	When fruit are 1 inch in diameter, and then every 2 weeks	For 3 to 4 weeks after transplanting and when flowers and fruit form

IN THE GARDEN

HOW TO GROW HERBS

HERB	START SEEDS INDOORS (WEEKS BEFORE LAST SPRING FROST)	START SEEDS OUTDOORS (WEEKS BEFORE/AFTER LAST SPRING FROST)	HEIGHT/ SPREAD (INCHES)	SOIL	LIGHT**
BASIL*	6–8	Anytime after	12–24/12	Rich, moist	○
BORAGE*	Not recommended	Anytime after	12–36/12	Rich, well-draining, dry	○
CHERVIL	Not recommended	3–4 before	12–24/8	Rich, moist	◑
CHIVES	8–10	3–4 before	12–18/18	Rich, moist	○
CILANTRO/ CORIANDER	Not recommended	Anytime after	12–36/6	Light	○◑
DILL	Not recommended	4–5 before	36–48/12	Rich	○
FENNEL	4–6	Anytime after	48–80/18	Rich	○
LAVENDER, ENGLISH*	8–12	1–2 before	18–36/24	Moderately fertile, well-draining	○
LAVENDER, FRENCH	Not recommended	Not recommended	18–36/24	Moderately fertile, well-draining	○
LEMON BALM*	6–10	2–3 before	12–24/18	Rich, well-draining	○◑
LOVAGE*	6–8	2–3 before	36–72/36	Fertile, sandy	○◑
MINT	Not recommended	Not recommended	12–24/18	Rich, moist	◑
OREGANO*	6–10	Anytime after	12–24/18	Poor	○
PARSLEY*	10–12	3–4 before	18–24/6–8	Medium-rich	◑
ROSEMARY*	8–10	Anytime after	48–72/48	Not too acidic	○
SAGE	6–10	1–2 before	12–48/30	Well-draining	○
SORREL	6–10	2–3 after	20–48/12–14	Rich, organic	○
SUMMER SAVORY	4–6	Anytime after	4–15/6	Medium-rich	○
SWEET CICELY	6–8	2–3 after	36–72/36	Moderately fertile, well-draining	○◑
TARRAGON, FRENCH	Not recommended	Not recommended	24–36/12	Well-draining	○◑
THYME, COMMON*	6–10	2–3 before	2–12/7–12	Fertile, well-draining	○◑

*Recommend minimum soil temperature of 70°F to germinate

** ○ FULL SUN ◑ PARTIAL SHADE

GROWTH TYPE
Annual
Annual, biennial
Annual, biennial
Perennial
Annual
Annual
Annual
Perennial
Tender perennial
Perennial
Perennial
Perennial
Tender perennial
Biennial
Tender perennial
Perennial
Perennial
Annual
Perennial
Perennial
Perennial

DRYING HERBS

Before drying, remove any dead or diseased leaves or stems. Wash under cool water, shake off excess water, and put on a towel to dry completely. Air-drying preserves an herb's essential oils; use for sturdy herbs. A microwave dries herbs more quickly, so mold is less likely to develop; use for moist, tender herbs.

HANGING METHOD: Gather four to six stems of fresh herbs in a bunch and tie with string, leaving a loop for hanging. Or, use a rubber band with a paper clip attached to it. Hang the herbs in a warm, well-ventilated area, out of direct sunlight, until dry. For herbs that have full seed heads, such as dill or coriander, use a paper bag. Punch holes in the bag for ventilation, label it, and put the herb bunch into the bag before you tie a string around the top of the bag. The average drying time is 1 to 3 weeks.

MICROWAVE METHOD: This is better for small quantities, such as a cup or two at a time. Arrange a single layer of herbs between two paper towels and put them in the microwave for 1 to 2 minutes on high power. Let the leaves cool. If they are not dry, reheat for 30 seconds and check again. Repeat as needed. Let cool. Do not overcook, or the herbs will lose their flavor.

STORING HERBS AND SPICES

FRESH HERBS: Dill and parsley will keep for about 2 weeks with stems immersed in a glass of water tented with a plastic bag. Most other fresh herbs (and greens) will keep for short periods unwashed and refrigerated in tightly sealed plastic bags with just enough moisture to prevent wilting. For longer storage, use moisture- and gas-permeable paper and cellophane. Plastic cuts off oxygen to the plants and promotes spoilage.

SPICES AND DRIED HERBS: Store in a cool, dry place.

COOKING WITH HERBS

A **BOUQUET GARNI** is usually made with bay leaves, thyme, and parsley tied with string or wrapped in cheesecloth. Use to flavor casseroles and soups. Remove after cooking.

FINES HERBES use equal amounts of fresh parsley, tarragon, chives, and chervil chopped fine. Commonly used in French cooking, they make a fine omelet or add zest to soups and sauces. Add to salads and butter sauces or sprinkle on noodles, soups, and stews.

HOW TO GROW BULBS

COMMON NAME	LATIN NAME	HARDINESS ZONE	SOIL	LIGHT*	SPACING (INCHES)
SPRING-PLANTED BULBS					
ALLIUM	*Allium*	3–10	Well-draining/moist	○	12
BEGONIA, TUBEROUS	*Begonia*	10–11	Well-draining/moist	◐ ●	12–15
BLAZING STAR/ GAYFEATHER	*Liatris*	7–10	Well-draining	○	6
CALADIUM	*Caladium*	10–11	Well-draining/moist	◐ ●	8–12
CALLA LILY	*Zantedeschia*	8–10	Well-draining/moist	○◐	8–24
CANNA	*Canna*	8–11	Well-draining/moist	○	12–24
CYCLAMEN	*Cyclamen*	7–9	Well-draining/moist	◐	4
DAHLIA	*Dahlia*	9–11	Well-draining/fertile	○	12–36
DAYLILY	*Hemerocallis*	3–10	Adaptable to most soils	○◐	12–24
FREESIA	*Freesia*	9–11	Well-draining/moist/sandy	○◐	2–4
GARDEN GLOXINIA	*Incarvillea*	4–8	Well-draining/moist	○	12
GLADIOLUS	*Gladiolus*	4–11	Well-draining/fertile	○◐	4–9
IRIS	*Iris*	3–10	Well-draining/sandy	○	3–6
LILY, ASIATIC/ORIENTAL	*Lilium*	3–8	Well-draining	○◐	8–12
PEACOCK FLOWER	*Tigridia*	8–10	Well-draining	○	5–6
SHAMROCK/SORREL	*Oxalis*	5–9	Well-draining	○◐	4–6
WINDFLOWER	*Anemone*	3–9	Well-draining/moist	○◐	3–6
FALL-PLANTED BULBS					
BLUEBELL	*Hyacinthoides*	4–9	Well-draining/fertile	○◐	4
CHRISTMAS ROSE/ HELLEBORE	*Helleborus*	4–8	Neutral–alkaline	○◐	18
CROCUS	*Crocus*	3–8	Well-draining/moist/fertile	○◐	4
DAFFODIL	*Narcissus*	3–10	Well-draining/moist/fertile	○◐	6
FRITILLARY	*Fritillaria*	3–9	Well-draining/sandy	○◐	3
GLORY OF THE SNOW	*Chionodoxa*	3–9	Well-draining/moist	○◐	3
GRAPE HYACINTH	*Muscari*	4–10	Well-draining/moist/fertile	○◐	3–4
IRIS, BEARDED	*Iris*	3–9	Well-draining	○◐	4
IRIS, SIBERIAN	*Iris*	4–9	Well-draining	○◐	4
ORNAMENTAL ONION	*Allium*	3–10	Well-draining/moist/fertile	○	12
SNOWDROP	*Galanthus*	3–9	Well-draining/moist/fertile	○◐	3
SNOWFLAKE	*Leucojum*	5–9	Well-draining/moist/sandy	○◐	4
SPRING STARFLOWER	*Ipheion uniflorum*	6–9	Well-draining loam	○◐	3–6
STAR OF BETHLEHEM	*Ornithogalum*	5–10	Well-draining/moist	○◐	2–5
STRIPED SQUILL	*Puschkinia scilloides*	3–9	Well-draining	○◐	6
TULIP	*Tulipa*	4–8	Well-draining/fertile	○◐	3–6
WINTER ACONITE	*Eranthis*	4–9	Well-draining/moist/fertile	○◐	3

REFERENCE

DEPTH (INCHES)	BLOOMING SEASON	HEIGHT (INCHES)	NOTES
3–4	Spring to summer	6–60	Usually pest-free; a great cut flower
1–2	Summer to fall	8–18	North of Zone 10, lift in fall
4	Summer to fall	8–20	An excellent flower for drying; north of Zone 7, plant in spring, lift in fall
2	Summer	8–24	North of Zone 10, plant in spring, lift in fall
1–4	Summer	24–36	Fragrant; north of Zone 8, plant in spring, lift in fall
Level	Summer	18–60	North of Zone 8, plant in spring, lift in fall
1–2	Spring to fall	3–12	Naturalizes well in warm areas; north of Zone 7, lift in fall
4–6	Late summer	12–60	North of Zone 9, lift in fall
2	Summer	12–36	Mulch in winter in Zones 3 to 6
2	Summer	12–24	Fragrant; can be grown outdoors in warm climates
3–4	Summer	6–20	Does well in woodland settings
3–6	Early summer to early fall	12–80	North of Zone 10, lift in fall
4	Spring to late summer	3–72	Divide and replant rhizomes every 2 to 5 years
4–6	Early summer	36	Fragrant; self-sows; requires excellent drainage
4	Summer	18–24	North of Zone 8, lift in fall
2	Summer	2–12	Plant in confined area to control
2	Early summer	3–18	North of Zone 6, lift in fall
3–4	Spring	8–20	Excellent for borders, rock gardens, and naturalizing
1–2	Spring	12	Hardy, but requires shelter from strong, cold winds
3	Early spring	5	Naturalizes well in grass
6	Early spring	14–24	Plant under shrubs or in a border
3	Midspring	6–30	Different species can be planted in rock gardens, woodland gardens, or borders
3	Spring	4–10	Self-sows easily; plant in rock gardens, raised beds, or under shrubs
2–3	Late winter to spring	6–12	Use as a border plant or in wildflower and rock gardens; self-sows easily
4	Early spring to early summer	3–48	Naturalizes well; a good cut flower
4	Early spring to midsummer	18–48	An excellent cut flower
3–4	Late spring to early summer	6–60	Usually pest-free; a great cut flower
3	Spring	6–12	Best when clustered and planted in an area that will not dry out in summer
4	Spring	6–18	Naturalizes well
3	Spring	4–6	Fragrant; naturalizes easily
4	Spring to summer	6–24	North of Zone 5, plant in spring, lift in fall
3	Spring	4–6	Naturalizes easily; makes an attractive edging
4–6	Early to late spring	8–30	Excellent for borders, rock gardens, and naturalizing
2–3	Late winter to spring	2–4	Self-sows and naturalizes easily

REFERENCE

Substitutions for Common Ingredients

ITEM	QUANTITY	SUBSTITUTION
BAKING POWDER	1 teaspoon	¼ teaspoon baking soda plus ¼ teaspoon cornstarch plus ½ teaspoon cream of tartar
BUTTERMILK	1 cup	1 tablespoon lemon juice or vinegar plus milk to equal 1 cup; or 1 cup plain yogurt
CHOCOLATE, UNSWEETENED	1 ounce	3 tablespoons cocoa plus 1 tablespoon unsalted butter, shortening, or vegetable oil
CRACKER CRUMBS	¾ cup	1 cup dry bread crumbs; or 1 tablespoon quick-cooking oats (for thickening)
CREAM, HEAVY	1 cup	¾ cup milk plus ⅓ cup melted unsalted butter (this will not whip)
CREAM, LIGHT	1 cup	⅞ cup milk plus 3 tablespoons melted, unsalted butter
CREAM, SOUR	1 cup	⅞ cup buttermilk or plain yogurt plus 3 tablespoons melted, unsalted butter
CREAM, WHIPPING	1 cup	⅔ cup well-chilled evaporated milk, whipped; or 1 cup nonfat dry milk powder whipped with 1 cup ice water
EGG	1 whole	2 yolks plus 1 tablespoon cold water; or 3 tablespoons vegetable oil plus 1 tablespoon water (for baking); or 2 to 3 tablespoons mayonnaise (for cakes)
EGG WHITE	1 white	2 teaspoons meringue powder plus 3 tablespoons water, combined
FLOUR, ALL-PURPOSE	1 cup	1 cup plus 3 tablespoons cake flour (not advised for cookies or quick breads); or 1 cup self-rising flour (omit baking powder and salt from recipe)
FLOUR, CAKE	1 cup	1 cup minus 3 tablespoons sifted all-purpose flour plus 3 tablespoons cornstarch
FLOUR, SELF-RISING	1 cup	1 cup all-purpose flour plus 1½ teaspoons baking powder plus ¼ teaspoon salt
HERBS, DRIED	1 teaspoon	1 tablespoon fresh, minced and packed
HONEY	1 cup	1¼ cups sugar plus ½ cup liquid called for in recipe (such as water or oil); or 1 cup pure maple syrup
KETCHUP	1 cup	1 cup tomato sauce plus ¼ cup sugar plus 3 tablespoons apple-cider vinegar plus ½ teaspoon salt plus pinch of ground cloves combined; or 1 cup chili sauce
LEMON JUICE	1 teaspoon	½ teaspoon vinegar
MAYONNAISE	1 cup	1 cup sour cream or plain yogurt; or 1 cup cottage cheese (puréed)
MILK, SKIM	1 cup	⅓ cup instant nonfat dry milk plus ¾ cup water

REFERENCE

ITEM	QUANTITY	SUBSTITUTION
MILK, TO SOUR	1 cup	1 tablespoon vinegar or lemon juice plus milk to equal 1 cup. Stir and let stand 5 minutes.
MILK, WHOLE	1 cup	½ cup evaporated whole milk plus ½ cup water; or ¾ cup 2 percent milk plus ¼ cup half-and-half
MOLASSES	1 cup	1 cup honey or dark corn syrup
MUSTARD, DRY	1 teaspoon	1 tablespoon prepared mustard less 1 teaspoon liquid from recipe
OAT BRAN	1 cup	1 cup wheat bran or rice bran or wheat germ
OATS, OLD-FASHIONED	1 cup	1 cup steel-cut Irish or Scotch oats
QUINOA	1 cup	1 cup millet or couscous (whole wheat cooks faster) or bulgur
SUGAR, DARK-BROWN	1 cup	1 cup light-brown sugar, packed; or 1 cup granulated sugar plus 2 to 3 tablespoons molasses
SUGAR, GRANULATED	1 cup	1 cup firmly packed brown sugar; or 1¾ cups confectioners' sugar (makes baked goods less crisp); or 1 cup superfine sugar
SUGAR, LIGHT-BROWN	1 cup	1 cup granulated sugar plus 1 to 2 tablespoons molasses; or ½ cup dark-brown sugar plus ½ cup granulated sugar
SWEETENED CONDENSED MILK	1 can (14 oz.)	1 cup evaporated milk plus 1¼ cups granulated sugar. Combine and heat until sugar dissolves.
VANILLA BEAN	1-inch bean	1 teaspoon vanilla extract
VINEGAR, APPLE-CIDER	—	malt, white-wine, or rice vinegar
VINEGAR, BALSAMIC	1 tablespoon	1 tablespoon red- or white-wine vinegar plus ½ teaspoon sugar
VINEGAR, RED-WINE	—	white-wine, sherry, champagne, or balsamic vinegar
VINEGAR, RICE	—	apple-cider, champagne, or white-wine vinegar
VINEGAR, WHITE-WINE	—	apple-cider, champagne, fruit (raspberry), rice, or red-wine vinegar
YEAST	1 cake (⅗ oz.)	1 package (¼ ounce) or 1 scant tablespoon active dried yeast
YOGURT, PLAIN	1 cup	1 cup sour cream (thicker; less tart) or buttermilk (thinner; use in baking, dressings, sauces)

REFERENCE

Types of Fat

One way to minimize your total blood cholesterol is to manage the amount and types of fat in your diet. Aim for monounsaturated and polyunsaturated fats; avoid saturated and trans fats.

MONOUNSATURATED FAT lowers LDL (bad cholesterol) and may raise HDL (good cholesterol) or leave it unchanged; found in almonds, avocados, canola oil, cashews, olive oil, peanut oil, and peanuts.

POLYUNSATURATED FAT lowers LDL and may lower HDL; includes omega-3 and omega-6 fatty acids; found in corn oil, cottonseed oil, fish such as salmon and tuna, safflower oil, sesame seeds, soybeans, and sunflower oil.

SATURATED FAT raises both LDL and HDL; found in chocolate, cocoa butter, coconut oil, dairy products (milk, butter, cheese, ice cream), egg yolks, palm oil, and red meat.

TRANS FAT raises LDL and lowers HDL; a type of fat common in many processed foods, such as most margarines (especially stick), vegetable shortening, partially hydrogenated vegetable oil, many commercial fried foods (doughnuts, french fries), and commercial baked goods (cookies, crackers, cakes).

FREEZER STORAGE TIME
(freezer temperature 0°F or colder)

PRODUCT	MONTHS IN FREEZER
FRESH MEAT	
Beef	6 to 12
Lamb	6 to 9
Veal	6 to 9
Pork	4 to 6
Ground beef, veal, lamb, pork	3 to 4
Frankfurters	1 to 2
Sausage, fresh pork	1 to 2
Cold cuts	Not recommended
FRESH POULTRY	
Chicken, turkey (whole)	12
Chicken, turkey (pieces)	6 to 9
Cornish game hen, game birds	6 to 9
Giblets	3 to 4
COOKED POULTRY	
Breaded, fried	4
Pieces, plain	4
Pieces covered with broth, gravy	6
FRESH FISH AND SEAFOOD	
Clams, mussels, oysters, scallops, shrimp	3 to 6
Fatty fish (bluefish, mackerel, perch, salmon)	2 to 3
Lean fish (flounder, haddock, sole)	6
FRESH FRUIT (PREPARED FOR FREEZING)	
All except those listed next	10 to 12

PRODUCT	MONTHS IN FREEZER
Avocados, bananas, plantains	3
Lemons, limes, oranges	4 to 6
FRESH VEGETABLES (PREPARED FOR FREEZING)	
Beans, beets, bok choy, broccoli, brussels sprouts, cabbage, carrots, cauliflower, celery, corn, greens, kohlrabi, leeks, mushrooms, okra, onions, peas, peppers, soybeans, spinach, summer squashes	10 to 12
Asparagus, rutabagas, turnips	8 to 10
Artichokes, eggplant	6 to 8
Tomatoes (overripe or sliced)	2
Bamboo shoots, cucumbers, endive, lettuce, radishes, watercress	Not recommended
CHEESE (except those listed below)	6
Cottage cheese, cream cheese, feta, goat, fresh mozzarella, Neufchâtel, Parmesan, processed cheese (opened)	Not recommended
DAIRY PRODUCTS	
Margarine (not diet)	12
Butter	6 to 9
Cream, half-and-half	4
Milk	3
Ice cream	1 to 2

REFERENCE

WHEN TO REPLACE/CLEAN/RENEW COMMON HOUSEHOLD ITEMS

How long do commonly used food products stay viable or safe after opening or using? What are the recommended time frames for replacing or cleaning things—inside and outside the home? Here are some guidelines for items found around the house.

ITEM	STATUS	STORAGE	DURATION	TIPS
Baking soda	Open	Pantry, cupboard	6 months	Put a little in bowl, add lemon juice or vinegar. If it fizzes, it's still suitable for baking.
Butter	Open	Counter	1 to 2 days	Can turn rancid; refrigeration will extend life.
	Open	Refrigerator	1 to 2 months	
Jelly/jam	Open	Refrigerator	6 to 12 months	Replace if smell or color changes; mold may occur.
Mayonnaise	Open	Refrigerator	2 months	Throw away if discoloration or odor occurs.
Nut oils	Open	Pantry, cupboard	3 to 8 months	Store in a cool, dry place; refrigeration may extend life.
Olive/ vegetable oil	Open	Pantry, cupboard	3 to 5 months	Store in a cool, dry place; refrigeration may extend life.
Peanut butter	Open	Pantry, cupboard	2 to 3 months	Replace if rancid taste or smell occurs.
	Open	Refrigerator	6 to 9 months	
Red/white wine	Open	Refrigerator	2 to 5 days	Use a stopper for a tight seal.

ITEM	USE	STORAGE	REPLACE	TIPS
20-lb. propane tank	As needed	Outside	10 to 12 years	Can not be refilled past date on tank; recertified tanks good for additional 5 years.
Bleach	As needed	Laundry area	6 to 12 months	Will begin to break down after 6 months.
Fire extinguisher	As needed	Kitchen, other	12 years	Check gauge monthly to ensure factory-recommended pressure level.
Gasoline for equipment	As needed	Shed, detached garage	3 to 6 months	Store in tightly closed container, away from heat sources and light.
Smoke alarms	Ongoing	Bedrooms, hallways	10 years	Test monthly to ensure proper function.
Sponges	Daily	Kitchen	1 to 2 weeks	To clean between replacements, soak in 1:10 bleach/warm water solution for 1 minute, microwave damp (if nonmetallic) for 1 minute, or run through dishwasher cycle.
Toothbrushes	Daily	Bathroom	3 to 4 months	Replace more often if bristles fray or when user(s) have been sick.

ITEM	USE	LOCATION	CLEAN	TIPS
Bird feeders	Daily	Outdoors	Twice a month	To avoid bacteria buildup, wash with soap and boiling water or diluted bleach solution; rinse and dry completely.
Chimney	Heating season	Furnace, fireplace	Once a year	Professional inspection will show if chimney sweep or maintenance is needed.
Dryer vent hose	Daily, weekly	Dryer to outdoor vent	Once a year	Clean lint trap after each use; if clothes do not dry properly, check/clean vent hose.
Gutters	During storms	Roofline	Twice a year	Leaves will be more prevalent during fall, so clean out more often.

PLASTICS

In your quest to go green, use this guide to use and sort plastic. The number, usually found with a triangle symbol on a container, indicates the type of resin used to produce the plastic. Visit **EARTH911.COM** for recycling information in your state.

PETE

NUMBER 1 · *PETE or PET (polyethylene terephthalate)*
IS USED IN . . . . microwavable food trays; salad dressing, soft drink, water, and juice bottles
STATUS . . . . hard to clean; absorbs bacteria and flavors; avoid reusing
IS RECYCLED TO MAKE. . . carpet, furniture, new containers, Polar fleece

HDPE

NUMBER 2 · *HDPE (high-density polyethylene)*
IS USED IN . . . . household cleaner and shampoo bottles, milk jugs, cutting boards
STATUS . . . . transmits no known chemicals into food
IS RECYCLED TO MAKE. . . detergent bottles, fencing, floor tiles, pens

V

NUMBER 3 · *V or PVC (vinyl)*
IS USED IN . . . . clear food packaging, window frames, blister packs for medicine and retail packaging
STATUS . . . . is believed to contain phalates that interfere with hormonal development; avoid reusing
IS RECYCLED TO MAKE. . . cables, mud flaps, paneling, roadway gutters

LDPE

NUMBER 4 · *LDPE (low-density polyethylene)*
IS USED IN . . . . bread and shopping bags, carpet, clothing, furniture
STATUS . . . . transmits no known chemicals into food
IS RECYCLED TO MAKE. . . envelopes, floor tiles, lumber, trash-can liners

PP

NUMBER 5 · *PP (polypropylene)*
IS USED IN . . . . food storage containers, medicine and syrup bottles, drinking straws, yogurt tubs
STATUS . . . . transmits no known chemicals into food
IS RECYCLED TO MAKE. . . battery cables, brooms, ice scrapers, rakes

PS

NUMBER 6 · *PS (polystyrene)*
IS USED IN . . . . disposable cups and plates, egg cartons, take-out containers
STATUS . . . . is believed to leach styrene, a possible human carcinogen, into food; avoid reusing
IS RECYCLED TO MAKE. . . foam packaging, insulation, light switchplates, rulers

OTHER

NUMBER 7 · *Other (miscellaneous)*
IS USED IN . . . . 3- and 5-gallon water jugs, nylon, some food containers
STATUS . . . . contains bisphenol A, which has been linked to heart disease and obesity; avoid reusing
IS RECYCLED TO MAKE. . . . custom-made products

Metric Conversion

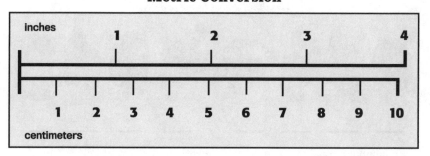

U.S. MEASURE	X THIS = NUMBER	METRIC EQUIVALENT	METRIC MEASURE	X THIS = NUMBER	U.S. EQUIVALENT
inch	2.54	centimeter		0.39	inch
foot	30.48	centimeter		0.033	foot
yard	0.91	meter		1.09	yard
mile	1.61	kilometer		0.62	mile
square inch	6.45	square centimeter		0.15	square inch
square foot	0.09	square meter		10.76	square foot
square yard	0.8	square meter		1.2	square yard
square mile	2.59	square kilometer		0.39	square mile
acre	0.4	hectare		2.47	acre
ounce	28.0	gram		0.035	ounce
pound	0.45	kilogram		2.2	pound
short ton (2,000 pounds)	0.91	metric ton		1.10	short ton
ounce	30.0	milliliter		0.034	ounce
pint	0.47	liter		2.1	pint
quart	0.95	liter		1.06	quart
gallon	3.8	liter		0.26	gallon

If you know the U.S. measurement and want to convert it to metric, multiply it by the number in the left shaded column (example: 1 inch equals 2.54 centimeters). If you know the metric measurement, multiply it by the number in the right shaded column (example: 2 meters equals 2.18 yards).

REFERENCE

SIGN LANGUAGE: WHAT'S THE TITLE?

Use the alphabet below to decode.

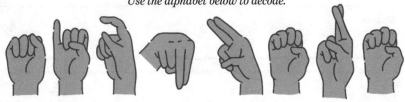

Sign language is a way to communicate without using your voice. It involves using your hands, body posture, and facial expressions. Although sign language is used mostly by people who are deaf or can't hear well, it can be used by anyone. There are even animals that use sign language. A gorilla named Koko learned more than 1,000 signs! In North America, we use American Sign Language, but there are different versions across the world.

Using the alphabet below, spell your name.

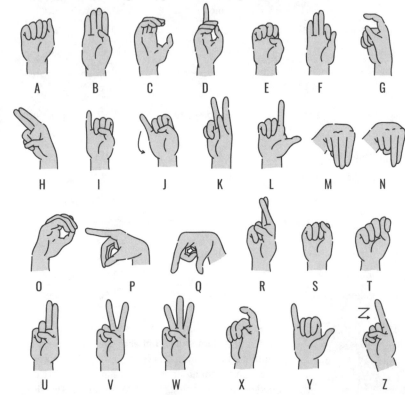

REFERENCE

Here are some common signs and phrases to get you started...

HELLO: Open your hand with all of your fingers pointing up and your thumb crossed in front of your palm. Touch the side of your forehead, then quickly move your hand away from your head.

GOOD-BYE: Open your palm, fold down your fingers, then open your palm again. Repeat once or twice.

YES: Make an "S" sign and bend your wrist forward like you are nodding "yes."

NO: Open and close your index and middle finger over your thumb twice.

FAMILY: Make an "F" sign with each hand, palms facing out, with thumbs touching. Move your hands away from each other, making a circle in front of you. End with the backs of your hands facing out.

SORRY: Make an "S" sign and rub your chest in a circular motion toward your shoulder.

I LOVE YOU: With your palm facing out, hold up your thumb, index finger, and pinky.

LOVE: Make a fist with each hand and cross your arms over your chest.

PLEASE: Open your hand and rub your chest in a circular motion.

THANK YOU: Open your hand and touch your chin with your fingertips. Move the hand away from you.

REFERENCE

Where Do You Fit in Your Family Tree?

Technically it's known as consanguinity; that is, the quality or state of being related by blood or descended from a common ancestor. These relationships are shown below for the genealogy of six generations of one family. *–family tree information courtesy of Frederick H. Rohles*

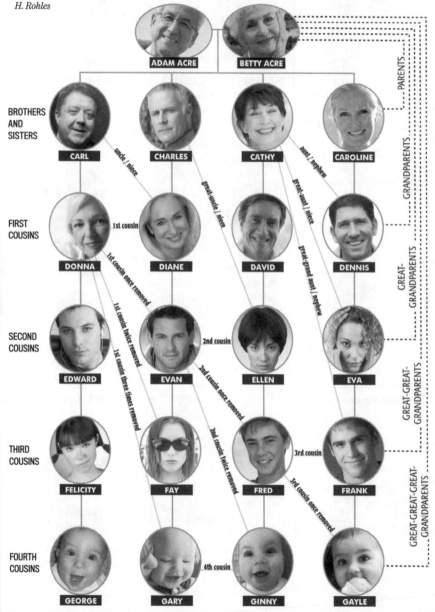